Yonsei Korean Studies Series No. 1

Koryŏsa chŏryo Ib

Essentials of Koryŏ History

Translated by

Sem Vermeersch

Yonsei University Press

Koryŏsa chŏryo Ib

Essentials of Koryŏ History

Translated by Sem Vermeersch

Published and Printed in the Republic of Korea by Yonsei University Press.
50 Yonsei-ro, Seodaemun-gu, Seoul, 03722, Republic of Korea

Tel: 82-2-2123-3378~80
Fax: 82-2-2123-8673
E-mail: ysup@yonsei.ac.kr
http://press.yonsei.ac.kr

ISBN 978-89-6850-913-1(93910)

₩ 25,000

Preface

Yonsei University has long been a center for the study of Korea. Through the establishment of its Kukhak yŏn'guwŏn (Institute of Korean Studies) in 1977, it further systematized and optimized the existing research capacity that centered on Korea's role in East Asian history, literature, religion, and philosophy. The Institute of Korean Studies inherited and continues the academic achievements of the Tongbanghak yŏn'guso (Institute of East Asian Studies) in researching Korean culture and history from the perspective of its interrelatedness with East Asian culture. The Institute has also reproduced and published a number of classics including the *Siyong hyangak po* 時用鄉樂譜, *Wŏrin Sŏkpo* 月印釋譜, *Soaron* 小兒論, *Tongmun yuhae* 同文類解, *P'alsea* 八歲兒, *Samyŏk ch'onghae* 三譯總解, *Han-Han ch'ŏngmungam* 韓漢淸文鑑, and *Koryŏsa* 高麗史. Moreover, besides publishing the *Koryŏsa* (History of Koryŏ) in 1953, on two occasions—in 1961 and 1996—it published an index to the *Koryŏsa*, thereby contributing to a broad understanding of traditional Korean literature, thought, and society.

In tune with the Institute's efforts to promote Korean Studies through the *Koryŏsa*, it is also striving to internationalize Korean Studies by preparing an English translation of the *Koryŏsa chŏryo* 高麗史節要 (Essentials of Koryŏ History), which can be regarded as an abbreviation of the *Koryŏsa*. With increasing internationalization and globalization, there is also an increased need for mutual understanding and cultural exchange. In response to Korea's socio-economic development, internationally interest in Korean studies has increased. The establishment of university centers and departments dedicated to the study of Korea in the US and Europe has led to the introduction of more courses and programs on Korea. In many cases, in-depth research on pre-modern Korean society is being carried out at major US universities in particular, but although knowledge of the Korean language is a prerequisite for such research, Korea can and should play an active role too in the internationalization of Korean studies through the translation into English of its classics. Thus, the translation of a key work such as the *Essentials of Koryŏ History* can contribute greatly to research on not only Korean history but also literature, philosophy, and society.

This English translation of the *Essentials of Koryŏ History* is the outcome of a special project under Yonsei University's "Globalization of Korean Studies" program (Sep. 2005–Feb. 2007), directed by Professor Do Hyeonchul. The first instalment, Edward J. Shultz and Hugh H.W. Kang's translation of the sections dealing with Ŭijong's reign and the Military Period (*kwŏn* 11-17), appeared in December 2014; the second instalment, Sem Vermeersch's translation of the first five chapters (*kwŏn*), appeared in 2021, followed shortly after in 2022 by Edward J. Shultz's translation of the chapters on the Mongol period (*kwŏn* 18-23). This part contains chapters 6 to 10; hence the period from the founding of Koryŏ (918) up to 1313 is now complete. I hope that publication of this book may provide an opportunity for understanding Korea's traditional culture, and contribute to the development of Korean Studies as a well-established global discipline.

Finally I would like to thank Professor Do Hyeonchul for making publication of this book possible by initiating the research project and providing the institutional support. Also, I would like to thank the editorial team of Yonsei University Press under the directorship of Nam Hye Hyun for taking care of publication of the Institute's books in spite of the difficult situation the publishing world is facing.

Kim Hyunjoo
Director, Institute of Korean Studies
Yonsei University
August 2025

Contents

Introduction

This is the second part of my translation of the first ten fascicles of the *Koryŏsa chŏryo* (Essentials of Koryŏ history). The first part, covering the period 918 to 1083, or the first five fascicles, was published by Yonsei University Press in 2021.[1] The five following fascicles that are translated here cover the years 1084 to 1146. This concludes my contribution to the full, unabridged translation of this important work. The period 1147 to 1313, covered in fascicles 11 to 23, has been translated by Edward Shultz in two parts,[2] while the final volume (from 1314 to 1392, fascicles 24 to 35) is now being translated.

Although I have included an introduction to the *Koryŏsa choryŏ* in part Ia, I decided to add a new introduction here. While it reprises much of the same information, it also adds a few new insights. The translation of this text has been a learning experience, and as I progressed slowly and painfully through the chronology of events, I continuously had to revise my translation of certain terms. Some of the idiosyncrasies of the original text only became clear towards the end of the translation project; many still remain outside my grasp. My changing understanding of the original text and what it is trying to convey prompted me to change the way I handled some terms or

---

1 Sem Vermeersch, trans., *Koryŏsa chŏryo Ia—Essentials of Koryŏ History* (Seoul: Yonsei University Press, 2021).

2 Edward J. Shultz and Hugh H. W. Kang, trans., *Koryŏsa chŏryo II—Essentials of Koryŏ History* (Paju: Jimoondang, 2014); Edward J. Shultz, trans., *Koryŏsa chŏryo IIb—Essentials of Koryŏ History* (Seoul: Yonsei University Press, 2022).

expressions; unfortunately, this means that there are slight inconsistencies across the volumes. Even among the two parts I translated, all the more so among those by the other translators. In the end, the differences are perhaps minimal, and most readers might not notice them; yet once you realize a term can (or should) be translated differently, it is better to change. Hence in this introduction I want to explain why such changes were made.

But first I should briefly highlight what this work means for Korean history. Perhaps more than for any other period in world history, we are uniquely dependent on it for almost all our information on the "middle period" of Korean history, the Koryŏ dynasty (918–1392). This is both a blessing and a curse: it is a blessing in that it has preserved a detailed chronology of events, giving us more information than we have for most other regions of the world in this time frame, but a curse in that it gives us a very redacted, sanitized version of events, heavily colored by the biases and agendas of the compilers. The degree of "tampering" with the original documents by the compilers is also a matter of intense debate among scholars; and since views on the historiography of Koryŏ are constantly evolving, I think it is worth reprising this story here.

Together with the *Koryŏsa* (History of Koryŏ), completed a year earlier in 1451, the *Koryŏsa chŏryo* forms the culmination of a series of historiographical disputes that were waged right from the start of the founding of the Chosŏn dynasty in 1392. None less than the "ideological architect" of the Chosŏn dynasty, Chŏng Tojŏn 鄭道傳 (1342–1398), was the first to compile a history of Koryŏ: His *Koryŏ kuksa* 高麗國史 (History of the Koryŏ state) was completed in 1395, but proved controversial. Although praised by T'aejo (r. 1392–1398),[3] King T'aejong (r. 1400–1418) was very critical of it,[4] and pushed for a new version; Chŏng's *Koryŏ kuksa* has hence not been preserved. Therefore, we are unfortunately not certain what was controversial, but according to Pyŏn T'aesŏp's research it omitted many facts, altered the phrasing, disparaged certain people, and also changed

3 *T'aejo sillok* 7.2b [1395/1/25].

4 See e.g. *T'aejong sillok* 27.32a [1414/5/10].

terminology that was no longer deemed conform to a Confucian world view that put China at the center.[5]

Later attempts at compiling a history of Koryŏ were also shot down either by kings or officials.[6] According to Ro Myoungho [No Myŏngho], one of the key controversies was whether to preserve the original phrasing of the Koryŏ veritable annals (*sillok*) as it was (*chiksŏ* 直書) or to change it to conform to the new world view (*kaesŏ* 改書). In principle the former option had to be followed because of the historiographical principle of reproducing sources verbatim (*suribujak* 術而不作). However, doing so would risk offending the Ming, because Koryŏ tended to use terminology that was the prerogative of the Chinese emperor, the "Son of Heaven." For example, Koryŏ sources used the expression "Great pardon of Under Heaven" (*taesa ch'ŏnha* 大赦天下). Since "Under Heaven" was the preserve of the emperor, officials advocated changing it to "Great pardon within the borders" *(taesa kyŏngnae* 大赦境內). King Sejong (r. 1428–1450), however, argued strongly for not changing the wording, hence preferred omitting the "Under Heaven" and simply retaining "great pardon"[7]—although the wording was not changed, this still constituted a creative redaction of the text.

Chŏng Tojŏn's *Koryŏ kuksa* would thus have been an example of a history altering the wording of the sources; a further elaboration of this work by Pyŏn Kyeryang 卞季良 (1369–1430) and others at the beginning of Sejong's reign allegedly went even further in changing the source texts, and was

---

5 Pyŏn T'aesŏp, Koryŏsa *ŭi yŏn'gu* (Seoul: Samyŏngsa, 1982), 9.

6 See Graeme Reynolds, "Culling Archival Collections in the Koryŏ–Chosŏn Transition," *Journal of Korean Studies* 24, no. 2 (2019): 225–253.

7 No Myŏngho, "Sogae," https://db.history.go.kr/introduction/goryeo/intro_kj.html (Accessed Dec. 9, 2024); see also No Myŏngho, "Koryŏsa ŭi 'ch'amŭi chi sa' wa 'taesa ch'ŏnha' ŭi 'isil chiksŏ:' Haeksim i sakche toen Koryŏ ŭi hwangje chedo" [The "straight copying of facts" regarding the "overstepping the limits [of a kingdom]" and the "great pardon of the Under-Heaven" in the *Koryŏsa*: Deleting the core of the Koryŏ imperial system], *Han'guksaron* 60 (2014): 1–56. For a good discussion of Sejong's arguments, see Graeme Reynolds, "The Histories of Koryŏ: Their Production, Circulation, and Reception from the Chosŏn Period to the Present" (PhD Diss., Harvard University, 2021), 156–158. Reynolds shows that this was a compromise decision, in that Sejong originally wanted to retain the "Under Heaven."

hence also not preserved. After this, Yun Hoe 尹淮 (1380–1436) compiled the *Sugyo Koryŏsa* 讎校高麗史 ([Newly] collated version of the History of Koryŏ), presented to Sejong in 1424, in which he, albeit reluctantly, seems to have followed Sejong's instruction to quote sources verbatim.[8] Though this text too has not been transmitted—probably due to the protest of officials like Pyŏn—Ro Myoungho argues that in the end it formed the basis of the *Koryŏsa chŏryo*. Indeed, whenever the king proclaims a pardon, the term used is simply *sa* or *taesa*, without any further additions.

Yet Sejong seems to have felt that the *Sugyo Koryŏsa* was still not satisfactory, because in court discussions he kept insisting that it was not comprehensive enough and had omitted too many important facts. In 1442 the fifth iteration of this historiographic project was finalized,[9] a work now known as the *Koryŏsa chŏnmun* 高麗史全文 (Complete text of Koryŏ history). While this seemed to be satisfactory, once again Sejong found fault with it—notably accusing one of the compilers, Kwŏn Che 權踶 (1387–1445), of giving in to requests to tamper with entries related to people's ancestors.[10] Sejong sternly admonished his officials, and ordered them to make a list of all mistakes and omissions, and in early 1449 ordered them to redo everything. This time it was decided to opt for the thematic system (*kijŏn* 紀傳, lit. annals–biography), consisting of annals, treatises, and biographies. This had the advantage that the contentious reigns of Kings U (1374–1388) and Ch'ang (1388–1389), regarded as offspring of the monk Sin Ton (d. 1371) rather than of King Kongmin (r. 1351–1374), could be relegated to the biographies section.

Sejong passed away before the *Koryŏsa* could be completed, so it was

8 See Yun Hoe, "Chin Sugyo Koryŏsa sŏ" 進讎校高麗史序, in *Tongmun sŏn* 93. This introduction is the only part of the work that has been transmitted.

9 Since none of these early versions have been preserved, and the sources are not clear on the exact titles and interrelatedness of these versions, any count is tentative. I here follow Pyŏn T'aesŏp's interpretation: 1. *Koryŏ kuksa*, by Chŏng Tojŏn (1395); 2. Emendated version by Ha Yun, *Ch'anjŏng Koryŏ kuksa* 竄定高麗國史 (1414-1416); 3. Further emendated version by Ryu Kwan and Pyŏn Kyeryang, the *Kaesu Koryŏ kuksa* 改修高麗國史 (1418-1421); and 4. The *Koryŏsa sugyŏ* 高麗史讐校 by Ryu Kwan and Yun Hoe (1423-1424). Pyŏn T'aesŏp, Koryŏsa *ŭi yŏn'gu*, 8-14.

10 Reynolds, "The Histories of Koryŏ," 165.

presented to his successor Munjong (r. 1450–1452) in the eighth month of 1451.[11] A cynic might point out that it was the absence of Sejong's meddling that finally allowed this project to be completed; however, undoubtedly Sejong's interventions also managed to salvage many details from oblivion. Barely six months later, in the second month of 1452, the same Kim Chongsŏ 金宗瑞 (1382–1453) who presented the *Koryŏsa*, now presented the *Koryŏsa chŏryo* to the throne.[12] Although he writes in the memorandum of presentation that Sejong had ordered to "first write a comprehensive history and next a chronological history,"[13] there appears to be no entry in the *Sejong sillok* to confirm that this was in fact what Sejong had planned.[14]

Given the similarity of the compilers (nineteen of the thirty-five compilers of the *Koryŏsa* are also listed as compilers of the *Koryŏsa chŏryo*), the close proximity in time, and the fact that Kim Chongsŏ himself claims that the *Koryŏsa chŏryo* is simply a reordering and editing of the *Koryŏsa* in chronological, shorter format, one could easily suppose that it is indeed derivative of the *Koryŏsa*. A rough comparison of the contents would confirm that. However, a more detailed comparison shows that the *Koryŏsa chŏryo* actually contains facts that are not found in the *Koryŏsa*, and some descriptions of the same events sometimes differ markedly in tone if not in wording.

Hence it is eminently possible that, as Ro Myoungho argues, the *Koryŏsa chŏryo* is actually a redaction of the *Sugyo Koryŏsa*. Whether or not this is the case, the fact remains that the *Koryŏsa chŏryo* is very much an independent work. And though it should be read in conjunction with the *Koryŏsa*,[15] which contains much additional information (notably in its

---

11 *Munjong sillok* 9.17b [1451/8/25].

12 *Munjong sillok* 12.16b [1452/2/20].

13 Vermeersch, *Koryŏsa chŏryo Ia*, 3.

14 An entry in the *Sejong sillok* however shows that officials convinced Sejong that first you need to write a comprehensive, viz. annals-biography style (*kijŏn ch'e*) history before you can write a purely chronology history (*p'yŏnnyŏn ch'e*). Since Sejong accepted this advice, this could be seen as the "order" issued by Sejong. *Sejong sillok* 123.15b [1449/2/5]. I would like to thank Graeme Reynolds for pointing me to this passage.

15 An English translation of the Annals section of the *Koryŏsa* is currently underway. For the first instalment see Howard Kahm, John B. Duncan, Lee Junghoon, Park Jongki, and

treatises), to grasp the basic flow of Koryŏ history it is much better to start with the *Essentials*. Even though the Annals section of the *Koryŏsa* contains a succinct political history, many key facts are missing. Thus, to understand for example Yun Kwan's ill-fated campaign against the Jurchen in 1108, one would have to read the annals part together with his biography. The *Essentials* on the other hand contains a detailed overview of all events as they unfolded chronologically.

Unfortunately, a systematic study of all the differences between the two works is beyond the scope of this translation. Only occasionally have I verified certain facts in the *Koryŏsa*, and here and there noted down differences. For a more systematic comparison, the reader can refer to the modern edition of the *Koryŏsa chŏryo* compiled under the editorial guidance of Ro Myoungho.[16] Besides comparing critically all remaining editions of this work, it also notes where material has been added that is not found in the *Koryŏsa*.

Despite the incisive research carried out over the past few decades on how the *Koryŏsa* and *Koryŏsa chŏryo* were compiled, we still do not know how faithfully they reflect the original historical notes carried over from the Koryŏ dynasty, the Koryŏ *sillok*. We now know that at the very least some of their original phrasing was changed so as to conform to the perspective of a kingdom rather than an empire; we also know that there were attempts by officials to tamper with the records of how they or their ancestors appeared, some of which were thwarted. Finally, we also know thanks to discussions at the court of T'aejo of Chosŏn, that there were attempts at manipulating these *sillok*; at the very least it appears that records from late Koryŏ were culled according to the wishes of T'aejo.[17]

Unfortunately, what remained of the Koryŏ *sillok* disappeared at the beginning of the Imjin Wars (1592–1598),[18] so that this question will likely

---

Edward J. Shultz eds., *Koryŏsa: The History of Koryŏ, the Annals of the Kings, 918–1095* (Honolulu: University of Hawai'i Press, 2024).

16 No Myŏngho oe kyogam, *Kyogam Koryŏsa chŏryo* (Seoul: Chimmundang, 2016).

17 Reynolds, "Culling Archival Collections."

18 *Sŏnjo sujŏng sillok* 26.7a [1592/4/14, 28th entry]. I am grateful to Graeme Reynolds for

never be resolved. As pointed out in the introduction to part Ia, the Koryŏ *sillok* themselves may have varied in quality; those of the first century or so had to be recompiled after their destruction in 1010, and we know very little about either who compiled them or how detailed they were. One of the most obvious omissions is likely to have been Buddhist events: though we know that Buddhism was an essential part of the Koryŏ state, in the *Koryŏsa chŏryo* Buddhist events or facts are only included when the king participated; no information is given on Buddhist administration or the connections between kings and monks, or between officials and monks. In short, the whole context necessary to understand how Buddhism operated is missing, and almost certainly the *sillok* would have contained such information.

Cross-referencing with other sources—notably epigraphic sources—would allow to fill in some of these blanks, but in the end this is too far beyond the remit of this translation, which simply aims to introduce the text with minimal annotation. Since this part starts right after the reign of King Munjong, the bureaucratic structure has reached its mature form, and we see only very minor changes during this period. As before, the key offices in the Royal Secretariat-Chancellery and the Department of Ministries have been noted in tables in Appendix, while all other important offices can be verified in the Glossary. These are—apart from a few cases, which have been pointed out in notes—consistent with the terms found in part Ia, and also largely consistent with translations in the other volumes. Again, I have primarily based my translations first on Charles Hucker's invaluable *Dictionary of Official Terms*;[19] second on a master list of translations compiled by Edward Shultz; and finally, for those terms not satisfactorily addressed in either work, I have coined my own translations based on Korean reference works or studies.

---

pointing me to this passage. It refers to the "Historical drafts of the previous dynasty" (前朝史草). An interlinear note clarifies that these were the drafts made for compiling the *Koryŏsa* (修高麗史時所草)—hence it is not clear whether this were the original *sillok* from Koryŏ or draft notes copied from them to compile the Koryŏ histories.

19 Charles O. Hucker, *A Dictionary of Official Titles in Imperial China* (Stanford: Stanford University Press, 1985).

While in many respects the Koryŏ bureaucracy is closely modelled on the Tang model, it also took over some Song innovations, and of course interpreted all those in its own way. While the Tang holdover of the Royal Secretariat-Chancellery was mentioned in part Ia, here I want to briefly mention the Security Council as an example of Song influence. As could be seen in part Ia, King Sŏngjong adopted it in 991 on the recommendation of Han Ŏngong. Having returned from a mission to Song in the fourth month of that year, in the tenth month Han recommended to the king that the "Security Council (Ch'umirwŏn 樞密院) of the Song dynasty corresponds exactly to the offices of those officials who are on permanent call (*sukchik* 宿直 or *chiksuk* 直宿) in our court." After this, it is said that the king established the Security Council (Chungch'uwŏn 中樞院).[20]

As can be seen, this office actually goes under different names: whereas it was known as Shumiyuan (K. Ch'umirwŏn) in China, in Korea it was immediately renamed Chungch'uwŏn, a name that is not used in China. In 1095 it was again renamed Ch'umirwŏn, while in late Koryŏ it was also known as Milchiksa 密直司. Also, though most scholars still emphasize the fact that it was an innovation taken over from the Song, in fact its origins go back to the Tang. It was founded in 765 as a palace secretariat, "to coordinate and supervise the Emperor's paperwork." Still according to Hucker, it was staffed by eunuchs, and "gradually grew in importance until from the 870s [the] eunuchs … dominated and manipulated the palace and central government."[21] Hence, after the fall of the Tang it was reformed as the Bureau of Military Affairs (using Hucker's translation), and became "the paramount central government agency in control of the state's military forces." However, in Koryŏ it clearly did not have a pronounced military role: it is almost never mentioned when military decisions are made.

Also, Han Ŏngong suggests that it corresponds nicely to "offices of those officials who are on permanent call in our court." (卽我朝宿直員吏之職) "*Sukchik*" literally means "on duty and sleep," hence refers to those officials

20 Vermeersch, *Koryŏsa chŏryo Ia*, 154.

21 Hucker, *Dictionary of Official Titles*, 435, entries no. 5450–1.

and clerks who are always on call. In fact, as can be seen in Table 3 (see Appendix), the lower-ranking officials of this office were mainly in charge of handling edicts or important communications to and from the throne, and hence had to be on call at all times. As always, the laconic, lapidary statements from the sources cannot be taken at face value; it is very hard to imagine that Sŏngjong was not aware of all the major government institutions of China even before Han Ŏngong's mission, so this was likely simply used as a precedent to create an institution that was from the beginning quite different from the Song model, and likely intentionally so.

According to the terse description of the Security Council in the *Koryŏsa* treatise on the bureaucracy, it "manages the administration of outgoing and incoming [correspondence to the throne], defense of the sleeping quarters [of the king], and the military apparatus."[22] As seen, while it was definitely not a central bureau to coordinate military affairs, it did have some authority regarding military armament and cooperated with other military institutions such as the Capital Military Command (Tobyŏngmasa 都兵馬使).[23] Overall, its areas of responsibility seem to have covered local tribute to the court, storing government documents, management of investiture and ennoblement, pardons for criminals, military registers, inspection of royal palace guards, and managing of various ritual events.[24]

Most importantly, however, it was an institution on a par with the Royal Secretariat-Chancellery, and hence could help to balance power within the central administration. Together the two institutions were often known as the "Two Administrations" (Yangbu 兩府), and their highest functionaries effectively constituted a state council. The seven highest ranking positions of the Security Council were referred to as *ch'usin* 樞臣 or *ch'umil* 樞密, i.e. the state councilors of the Security Council. They were on a par with the five highest offices of the Royal Secretariat-Chancellery, which were known as

22 *Koryŏsa* 76.10a4 (Paekkwan 1, Milchiksa).

23 See Pak Yong'un, "Koryŏ ŭi Chungch'uwŏn yŏn'gu," *Han'guksa yŏn'gu* 12 (1976), 115–120 for a full discussion of what the term *kungi* 軍機 may have entailed in this context.

24 Pyŏn T'aesŏp, "Chungang ŭi t'ongch'i kigu," in *Han'guksa* 13 (Kwach'ŏn: Kuksa p'yŏnchan wiwŏnhoe, 1993), 55.

the *chaesin* 宰臣; together the councilors were hence referred to as *chaech'u* 宰樞. In the translation I refer to them collectively as state councilors, without breaking down specifically for either the Security Council or the Royal Secretariat-Chancellery.

The dual nature of the Security Council is shown in the fact that there are two "senior 3" level echelons, as Table 3 makes clear. Though nominally of the same rank, only those on the level of vice-commissioner were considered councilors, from the administrator of memorials downwards staff were considered rank and file, or part of the Munmu yangban 文武兩班.[25] It were these lower echelons who were tasked with the transmission of memorials, edicts, and other important letters. Hence, these two levels appear to show the hybrid nature of the Koryŏ Security Council: the lower echelons are closer to the Tang concept of this office, while the upper echelons somewhat resemble the functioning of the Song Bureau of Military Affairs.

This digression into the details of just one government agency, albeit one of the most important, is likely very off-putting for most readers. However, the vast majority of entries in the *Essentials* concerns such details of official appointments. Understanding how and why certain appointments were made, to what people, and to what purpose, is one of the keys to understanding this text. Hence to adequately understand the text, a full exposition of the Koryŏ bureaucratic system would be necessary, but unfortunately this would require another book. It is hoped however that by calling attention to this problem, and by devising a vocabulary that at least reflects the different office levels, this translation may provide readers with the necessary tools to embark on such a project.

Hence this translation has tried to be more precise in rendering the different posts into English. One of the most common constructions for administrative positions is the 知 … 事 construction. As Hucker explains, this simply means "managing the affairs of…," hence "administrator of [a particular office]."[26] Originally it was used as a kind of additional responsibility, a "specially

---

25 Ibid., 51.

26 Hucker, *Dictionary of Official Titles*, 155, entry no. 934.

authorized appointment of someone with nominally different status to serve in a normally more prestigious post as administrator of an agency."[27] Hence I assumed it to have this quality of an additional (to one's main office) and temporary caretaking quality, and in part Ia often translated it as "intendant" or "in charge of…." Yet, although Hucker notes that "not later than Sung times, some titles of this sort became regularized," in Koryŏ they seem to have been "regularized" from the beginning, and hence simply denote a specific office. In particular, one of the most often encountered offices is that of administrator of the Security Council (知中樞院事) (See Table 3).

A similar case is the 判 … 事 construction; here too Hucker notes the irregular aspect of this title, "signifying that an official holding a regular post was assigned on a temporary or otherwise irregular basis to take charge of an agency … as a special duty assignment."[28] But in this case as well the Koryŏ situation is quite different, as this construction clearly denotes a regular office. In the case of the six ministries, I have translated it simply as minister. Thus, 判工部事 simply means "minister of works." (see Table 2) In the case of the Security Council, since it is a higher position than the 知中樞院事, I have translated it as "superintendent of the Security Council."[29] Another example is the "superintendent of the Finance Commission" (判三司事).

So what terms did Koryŏ use for irregular appointments? One of the most often encountered ones are *su* 守 "probationary" and *kŏmgyo* 檢校 "acting."[30] However, in almost all cases these are used either for soon to be retired officials or for royal relatives. Hence, they mostly seem to have been honorary appointments. Sometimes the term *kwŏn* 權 "provisional" is used in the sense that someone is assigned to office despite lacking the

27 Ibid.

28 Ibid., 364, entry no. 4436.

29 It should be noted however that I could not find a single instance of an incumbent of this office.

30 See Hucker, *Dictionary of Official Titles*, 431, entry no. 5355 (*shou*) and 146, entry no. 804 (*chien-chiao*). Whereas the former seems to have, amongst others, the meaning of "being on probation" for appointees in their first year in office, the latter was predominantly used from Song times to denote honorary offices, i.e. without real responsibility. In Koryŏ both seem to have had this meaning.

requisite rank, or that the appointment was otherwise irregular (see e.g. the fourth month of 1092).[31] The term *kyŏm* 兼 "concurrent" is perhaps the most straightforward, denoting that someone combines more than one office, yet is not often used.[32] Finally, another tricky term that is used is *tong* 同 "associate." In part Ia, following Hucker I interpreted this as "jointly," in the sense of "indicating that an official already serving in one post had been assigned, additionally, to take part in the work of another post."[33] In Koryŏ, while it occasionally seems to be used in this sense, mostly it seems to mean "associate" in the sense of someone being assigned to the same post already occupied by someone else (see e.g. the 同知院使 or "associate administrator of the Security Council," Table 3). Finally and anticlimactically, when an official occupies several positions, these are often simply listed consecutively without any special terminology added.[34]

This extended discussion of (some of) the nuts and bolts of this translation should not mask the fact that it is still unsatisfactory. When Prof. Do Hyeonchul, then director of the Institute of Korean Studies at Yonsei University, contacted me late in 2014 to undertake the translation of the first 10 chapters, I promised to finish this in five years. This proved overly optimistic, but now finally I am able to pay off this debt. Though still leaving a lot to be desired, at least I hope that this translation has struck a balance between readability and relative accuracy, so that at long last the story of Koryŏ's history is made available to a readership outside the Korean peninsula. Finally, I would be remiss if I failed to mention my indebtedness to the pioneering work of Korean translators of this text; notably the version made available through the website of the National Institute of Korean History was extremely helpful.[35] I would also like to thank Prof. Do for

31 Ibid., 198, entry no. 1704. Here Hucker's description of the term's usage matches its Koryŏ usage.

32 Ibid. 145, entry no. 785.

33 Ibid., 553, entry no. 7464.

34 Occasionally one can also find the term *sŏp* 攝, also denoting "acting" but usually with the implication that the person in this position is underqualified. Ibid., 416, no. 5127.

35 https://db.history.go.kr/goryeo/itemLevelKrList.do?itemId=kj (Accessed December 10, 2024). For the list of editors and translators, see the introductory notes to the translation:

entrusting me with this task, Timothy Atkinson for reading through the whole draft translation and catching numerous errors, and Dr. Graeme Reynolds for his invaluable feedback on the intricacies of state historiography in the fifteenth century.

Conventions

As mentioned above, like part Ia this part also includes a separate glossary of important terms, mainly offices and titles. However, I have omitted the run-of-the-mill terms of the Chinese-style bureaucracy, such as Director of the Chancellery or Vice-minister at one of the ministries in the Department of Ministries. Instead, these terms can be found in Tables 1 to 3, which make it easier to grasp the relative position of these posts within a particular office.

As much as possible I have tried to translate terms. This is the case for offices and titles as described above, but also for the generic part in proper nouns: thus rather than writing Hoegyŏng-jŏn 會慶殿, I have rendered it Hoegyŏng Hall. Likewise -chŏng 亭 is translated "pavilion," -chin 鎭 "garrison," -kang 江 "river," and -yŏk 驛 "station." As for the main administrative divisions, -to 道 is rendered as province, -mok 牧 as shepherdship (rather than "department" as in Part Ia), -no 路 as "circuit," and -kye 界 as "border circuit." The most commonly used divisions, however, are -chu 州 "greater prefecture," -kun 郡 "prefecture," -pu 府 "district," -hyŏn 縣 "county," and *sokhyŏn* 屬縣 "subordinate county." For some cases however where it was difficult to find a suitable equivalent I have left the original term untranslated, notably for *pugok* 部曲 and *so* 所, places reserved for special classes of disenfranchised people.[36] Also -wŏn 院, -sa 寺 are left as such: the former is used for either monastic or palace compounds,

https://db.history.go.kr/introduction/goryeo/intro_kj.html (accessed December 10, 2024). The source text I used is a reprint of the 1453 edition (Hosa bunkō, Nagoya) published by Asea munhwasa in 1972.

36 The best introduction in English to the problem of Koryŏ local administration is Yokeun Jeong, "The Management of Koryŏ: Local Administration (Kunhyŏn) and its Operation," *Korean Studies* 41 (2017): 99–127.

while the latter denotes Buddhist monasteries. Weights and measures have also been left untranslated, since any Western equivalent is tenuous at best; the reader is referred to a separate glossary of weights and measures in appendix.

I have tried to keep explanatory footnotes to a minimum; most allusions to classics are very briefly explained because without such context it would be difficult to understand what is being argued.[37] Place names are also given the closest modern equivalent at first mention, in notes.[38] For the rest, the footnotes are fairly haphazard, since I inserted them where I felt a historical place name of particular office needed some explanation, or where a problem needed to be flagged. Most offices and titles are however left without further explanation in English translation, since they can be checked in the tables or glossary, in Hucker's dictionary, or in Vol. II.

Given the laconic terseness of the original, I have in some cases tried to infer the general tone or intention of certain passages and added text in square brackets to indicate my interpolation. Also, to break the sheer repetitiveness of the original I have not always translated a word consistently with the same equivalent in English. Dialogues for example are invariably introduced by the verb "*wal* 曰" but rather than simply translating "the king said…" "the council said…," depending on the context I have rendered it as "argued" "rebuked," etc. Another example: every time the Censorate critiques a decision by the king or an official makes a policy proposal, when the king agrees it is simply noted "*chong chi* 從之" or "[the king] agreed with this." Depending on the context however, I have translated "the king put this into effect" or "the king agreed with this proposal" or other expressions This will hopefully aid readability; after all, the originally intended readers of this text were far more knowledgeable about the courtly procedures, and

---

37 Mostly I used the site ctext.org to access Chinese classics. This includes the translations made by James Legge for the *Sacred Books of the East* series. Hence, I have not provided specific references to each classic but simply noted the title of the classic and the section under which a quotation can be found.

38 To identify modern equivalents I have relied mostly on the following dictionary: Han'guk yŏksa chimyŏng sajŏn p'yŏnch'an wiwŏnhoe, author, *Han'guk yŏksa chimyŏng sajŏn* (Seoul: Yŏgang ch'ulp'ansa, 2008).

could fill in this information for themselves. This is not the case for modern readers, however.

Different from part Ia, I have tried to consistently add Chinese characters at the first mention of a new person or office; here and there characters have also been inserted when it was felt they are needed to aid understanding. Regarding the romanization of names, for Korean names the McCune-Reischauer system is used; Chinese names follow the Pinyin system (without tone markers). How to treat Khitan and Jurchen names was a headache; because we do not know how they should be Romanized following the Khitan or Jurchen language, I have chosen to Romanize both the Khitan (Liao) and the Jurchen names in Pinyin. In part Ia I Romanized Jurchen names according to the Korean pronunciation, since there Jurchen peoples are invariably treated as subordinate to Koryŏ, either as "barbarian" others or (quasi) vassals, but mostly within the orbit of Koryŏ. Here though we see the full emancipation of the Jurchen, culminating in the founding of the Jin Empire. Since Anglophone scholarship mostly Romanizes Jin names according to modern Chinese pronunciation, I have followed this convention in this part.

Sem Vermeersch
Seoul, Dec. 21, 2024

6. Sŏnjong, Hŏnjong, Sukchong

Sŏnjong, Great King Mindful of Filial Piety

His given name was Un 運, and his courtesy name Kyech'ŏn 繼天; his original given name was Chŭng 蒸, and he was also called Ki 祁. He was a brother of Sunjong, and he was born on *kyŏngja* day [the 10th] of the ninth month of the third *sach'uk* year of Munjong [1049]. He displayed his intelligence from a young age and was filial and respectful, observant of propriety and frugal as an adult. His knowledge was vast and diverse; he had widely perused the classics and histories, and he excelled at composition. He was on the throne for eleven years and lived to the age of forty-six.

Sŏnjong First year [1084]

Seventh year of the Yuanfeng era of Song, tenth year of the Dakang era of Liao

Spring, third month. The Eastern Jurchen General Fennalao 分那老 and others, twenty people, came to present horses.

Summer, fourth month. Liao dispatched as imperial sacrificial envoy 勅祭使 the Surveillance Commissioner[1] for the Jurisdiction of Yizhou

1 *Guanchashi* 觀察使: "in Liao, coordinating agents overseeing groups of prefectures." Hucker no. 3269.

益州[2] 管內觀察使, Yelü Xin 耶律信, and as mourning envoy 慰問使 the Surveillance Commissioner for the Jurisdiction of Guangzhou 廣州[3] Yelü Yan 耶律彦 to offer sacrifices for Munjong and Sunjong.

Fifth month. Ko Minik 高旻翼 and fifteen others passed the composition test of the civil service examination, and four passed the classics examination.

Sixth month. The Eastern Jurchen raided the agricultural estate of Mosan Ferry 母山津 in Hŭnghae Prefecture 興海郡.[4] The local camp soldiers attacked and defeated them, capturing five people.

The Japanese merchant Sint'ong 信通 from Sakuzen prefecture 筑前 came to present 250 *kŭn* of mercury.

The royal prince named Wang Uk 王昱 was born.[5]

Autumn, eighth month. The king decreed that Director of the Chancellery Pak Sŏnggŏl 朴成傑, who had served Hyŏnjong during his journey south, had established a deed of merit, and should be given an emolument equal to the emolument certificate (*nokkwŏn* 錄券) of Samhan Supreme Merit Subject 三韓後壁上功臣 [whose portrait is drawn] on the back wall [of the Ancestral Shrine][6] Yang Kyu 楊規.

Song dispatched as sacrificial offerings envoy 祭奠使 the Senior Policy Critic Yang Jinglüe 楊景略 and as deputy envoy the Foreign Relations Commissioner 禮賓使 Wang Shunfeng 王舜封; as condolence envoy 弔慰使 the Junior Policy Critic Qian Xie 錢勰 and deputy envoy the Vice Commissioner of the Palace Audience Gate of the West 西上閤門副使 Song Qiu 宋球. Yang Jinglüe and the other members of the embassy gathered monks to organize a Buddhist mass in the spirit halls (*hondang* 魂堂) for Munjong and Sunjong and then offered sacrifices.

The king's birthday was officially called the Ch'ŏnwŏn Festival 天元節.

---

2 *Liaoshi* 38 (Zhonghua shuju ed., 2016), 533. Belonged to Longzhou, itself subordinate to the Eastern Capital. Probably located north of modern Changchun.

3 Located near modern Yilan country, Heilongjiang Province. *Liaoshi* 38, 529.

4 Now part of Yŏngil-gun in North Kyŏngsang Province.

5 He would later succeed his father as King Hŏnjong (1094–1095).

6 Inferred meaning. This exact phrasing occurs only four times in the *Koryŏsa chŏryo*, two times in connection with Yang Kyu, who died in the first Khitan invasion of 1010-1011.

Ninth month. The king held a banquet for the Song envoys in Hoegyŏng Hall 會慶殿.

Winter, eleventh month. The king ordered the Directorate for Military Uniforms 征袍都監 to take more than 1,000 bolts of ordinary cloth from Kŏnmyŏng Depot 乾明庫 and cut them into uniforms for the officers and soldiers serving in encampments and along the border.

Sonjong Second year [1085]

Eighth year of the Yuanfeng era of Song, first year of the Da'an era of Liao

Spring, second month. Liao announced that it had changed the era name.

The king for the first time ordered a procession by carriage. At the time someone carrying the *Humane Kings* and *Prajñāpāramitā Sūtras* lead the way.

Tsushima dispatched an envoy to present tangerines.

The king went to Kwibŏp-sa 歸法寺. From this time onwards he frequently travelled to temples and cloisters.

Third month. The king wanted to go to the spirit hall to perform sacrifices. An official criticized the fact that there was no "wailing seat" [for the officials]. The king said: "Ritual should accord with the circumstances." Then he reduced the number [of officials] who accompanied him and went.

The historian comments: The principle of acting as a minister is to correct what is wrong and to follow what is good [in the sovereign]. Before ending the mourning, the king was already holding a banquet with music for the Song envoys, yet the officials said nothing about this. As for being turned back from the spirit hall, the ministers meet the king morning and evening, yet this is all they can choose for criticism? How is this possible?

Mizhou 密州[7] in Song reported that the emperor [Shenzong, r. 1067–1085]

---

7 Prefecture located in the area of modern Zhucheng city on the southern side of the

had died.

Summer, fourth month. The monk Wang Hu 王煦 had escaped to Song.[8] Initially, Wang Hu wanted to go to Song in search of the dharma, but King Munjong did not allow him to go. When Sŏnjong ascended the throne, he again sent numerous requests, so the king deliberated with his ministers but they were unanimous in their opposition. Wang Hu then took two of his disciples and stole on the ship of the merchant Lin Ning 林寧 and went to Song. The king dispatched Assistant Director of Foreign Relations 禮賓丞 Chŏng Kŭn 鄭僅 and others to enquire whether he had arrived safely.

Kim Chun 金晙 and twenty-one others passed the composition test of the civil service examination, three passed the classics examination, and two passed by royal grace.

Because of the drought, the king ordered his officials to lecture on the *Clouds and Rain Sūtra*[9] at the Imhae Cloister 臨海院 for seven days, and release those on the prison rolls for light offenses or crime by association.

Sixth month. The king received the bodhisattva precepts in Kŏndŏk Hall 乾德殿.

Autumn, seventh month. The king gave a banquet for men and women over the age of eighty on the polo court, and bestowed clothes, belts, and presents commensurate with rank.

Eighth month. The king dispatched Vice-minister of Taxation Kim Sanggi 金上琦 and Executive at the Ministry of Rites Ch'oe Samun 崔思文 to Song to offer condolences [on the death of Emperor Shenzong]. Vice-minister of Works Im Kae 林槩 and Executive at the Minister of War Yi Chain 李資仁 were also dispatched to offer congratulations [on the accession of the new

---

Shandong peninsula, west of Qingdao.

8 This is the personal name of the monk Ŭich'ŏn (1055-1101), also known under his posthumous title Taegak kuksa. He was the fourth son of King Munjong, and brother to Sŏnjong.

9 *Unu kyŏng* 雲雨經: This is likely an abbreviated form of the *Tae ullyun ch'ŏng'u kyŏng* 大雲輪請雨經, "Scripture of the Great Cloud Wheel to Request Rain." It was translated by the esoteric monk Amoghavajra (705–774) and can be found in the Taishō edition of the Tripitaka (henceforth T.) volume 19, nos. 989 and 990. Additional scriptures with similar titles can be found under T.991-993.19.

emperor, Zhezong, r. 1085–1100].

The spirit portrait of Munjong was enshrined in Kyŏngnyŏng Hall 慶靈殿,[10] and the king personally went to offer sacrifices.

The king went to Sŏnjŏng Hall 宣政殿 to personally adjudicate the capital punishment cases reported by the Ministry of Punishments. He changed the court dinner to simple dishes and did away with the music [for the day].

Ninth month. The king personally offered sacrifices in the spirit hall for Sunjong.

Liao dispatched Vice Censor-in-chief 御史中丞 Li Ke 李可 to offer congratulations on the king's birthday, but he did not arrive on time.

Winter, tenth month. Munjong's [spirit tablet] was enshrined in the Ancestral Shrine.

The king organized a Hundred Seat Assembly[11] in the Hoegyŏng Hall for three days and provided food for 30,000 monks.

Eleventh month. Sunjong's [spirit tablet] was enshrined in the Ancestral Shrine.

Liao dispatched the Surveillance Commissioner for the Jurisdiction of Gaozhou 高州[12] Yelü Sheng 耶律盛 as the end-of-mourning envoy 落起復使.

Liao dispatched Military Governor of the Baojing Army 保靜軍 節度使, Xiao Zhang 蕭璋, and the Chief Minister of the Court of Imperial Entertainment 崇祿卿, Wen Jiao 溫嶠, to invest the king as Specially Promoted Acting Grand Preceptor, cum Royal Secretary, Supreme Pillar of State with a Stipend Village of Ten Thousand Households, one thousand of which were effective. The emperor also bestowed crown, chariot, mace, seal, robes, belt, colored silk,

---

10 The Hall of Spectacular Numina: A shrine where portraits of deceased kings were venerated.

11 Paekchwa toryang 百座道場: A ritual prescribed by the *Humane Kings Sūtra* (*Inwang kyŏng*) with the goal of protecting the country by averting looming calamities. It exists in different versions; the oldest extant translation, from the fifth century, can be found under T.245.8, while an esoteric version translated by Amoghavajra can be found under T.246.8.

12 Probably located near modern-day Chifeng in Inner Mongolia. It was subordinate to the Central Capital of Liao, and was, according to the *Liaoshi*, used to settle Koryŏ prisoners of war. It also had nominal jurisdiction over what is termed Sanhan county, i.e. the three Han states. See *Liaoshi* 39 (Zhonghua shuju ed., 2016), 547.

and other presents. The king received the investiture in the suburbs south of the capital.

Sŏnjong Third year [1086]

First year of the Yuanyou era of Emperor Zhezong of Song, second year of the Da'an era of Liao

Spring, first month. The king bestowed palace titles down from matron (*sanggung* 尙宮) on Lady Wang, wife of the royal in-law, Executive at the Ministry of Rites Yi Ye 李預, and others, and made them palace officials for the Queen Dowager 王太后. He also gave them emoluments according to rank.

Second monk. The king granted an investiture title to the queen dowager and gave a banquet to his officials [to celebrate the event].

The king's younger sister Princess Chŏkkyŏng 積慶宮 married his younger brother, Marquis of Puyŏ Wang Su 王邃. Before this [officials] had remonstrated [the marriage of] the king's younger brothers the Marquis of Kŭmgwan 金官侯 Wang Pi,[13] the Marquis of Pyŏn Han 卞韓侯 Wang Ŭm 王愔, and the Marquis of Chin Han 辰韓侯 Wang Yu 王愉 on account of having the same surname [as the bride], but the king did not listen.

There was a general amnesty.

The king appointed the Duke of Chosŏn 朝鮮公, Wang To 王燾 and the Duke of Kyerim 鷄林公, Wang Hŭi 王熙, as Probationary Grand Guardian 守太保, and the Marquis of Sangan 常安侯, Wang Su 琇, the Marquis of Puyŏ, Wang Su 邃, the Marquis of Kŭmgwan Wang Pi, and the Marquis of Pyŏn Han Wang Ŭm Probationary Minister of Education 守司徒, and the Marquis of Chin Han Wang Yu Probationary Minister of Works 守司空.

Intercalary [second] month. The king dispatched Deputy Director of the Office of Regalia 衛尉小卿 Ch'oe Sayŏl 崔思說 to Liao to congratulate

13 The character for Pi is quite rare so it has been omitted here.

the emperor on the Tianan Festival 天安節 [Festival of Heavenly Peace],[14] Deputy Director of the Office of Royal Clan Affairs 殿中少監 Kwak Sang 郭尙 to offer local products, and Executive at the Ministry of Taxation Kim Sajin 金士珍 to proffer thanks for the birthday wishes to the king.

Third month. Tsushima dispatched an envoy to present local products.

Summer, fourth month. Because of the long drought the markets were moved.

The king personally sacrificed at the Ancestral Shrine and conferred higher posthumous titles [on his forebears]; a partial amnesty was declared.

Yi Chŏnggong 李靖恭 was appointed Director of the Chancellery and Minister of Personnel; Ch'oe Sŏk 崔奭 and Kim Yanggam 金良鑑 were both made Executive Chief of the Chancellery; Yu Hong 柳洪 and Wang Sŏk 王錫 were made Executive Chief of the Royal Secretariat; No Tan 盧旦 was made Vice-director of the Department of Ministries and Assistant Executive in Political Affairs; Ch'oe Saryang 崔思諒 was made Commissioner of the Security Council; and Mun Hwang 文晃 was made Administrator of the Security Council.

Fifth month. Pak Kyŏngbaek 朴景伯 and twenty-nine others passed the composition test of the civil service examination, and three passed the classics examination.

The king dispatched Executive at the Ministry of Rites Ch'oe Hongsa 崔洪嗣 to Liao to give thanks for the end-of-mourning [envoy], Director of the Foreign Relations Office 禮賓卿 Yi Chaji 李資智 to congratulate the emperor on the new year, and Administrator of the Security Council Yi Chawi 李資威 to thank the emperor for the Decree of Investiture. Furthermore, as memorial envoy 告奏使 Junior Assistant Director of the Department of Ministries Han Yŏng 韓瑩 was dispatched. At the time Liao was about to build a log bridge[15] across the Amnok River, and therefore he had to request that this be stopped.

---

14 I.e. the emperor's birthday. Both Koryŏ kings and Song, Liao, and Jin emperors had personalized titles for their birthday.

15 *Kakchang* 榷場: literally a place for a log-bridge; in the wider sense, a tollgate or trading and exchange place.

Sixth month. The monk Wang Hu returned from Song. When he first traveled there, the emperor personally received him in Chuigong Hall 垂拱殿, treating him lavishly as an honored guest. Wang Hu requested to travel to the countryside in search of the dharma, and an imperial decree appointed the Vice-director of the Bureau of Receptions 主客員外郞, Yang Jie 楊傑, as hostel escort [commissioner] 館伴使. They traveled to the Wu region, and in various temples he was received with the decorum of a royal minister. The king sent a memorial requesting his return, and the emperor issued a decree that allowed him to return to the east. When he reached the Yesŏng River 禮成江, the king personally accompanied the Queen Dowager to Pong'ŭn-sa 奉恩寺 to welcome him back. The welcoming reception was so lavish that its likes had not been seen before. Wang Hu presented 1,000 scrolls of Buddhist sutras, classics, and other books. Furthermore, he requested the establishment of a directorate for printing the Buddhist Canon at Hŭngwang-sa 興王寺, and procured as many as 4,000 scrolls of books from Liao, Song, and Japan; these were all printed and published.

A decree stated: "Receiving the decree bequeathed my predecessor I presumptuously occupy this throne. Recently, many anomalous events have occurred, and the drought has turned into a disaster. Thus I put my trust in the efficacy of the numinous protection of Buddhas and spirits and the assistance of my ministers, so that the balance of yin and yang and the harmony between those above and those below be restored. I also reflected on my own mistakes and have on several occasions shown my grace through pardons. Yet still it has not rained, hence this must be the consequence of my lack of virtue. Also, I must consider that the actions of some of my officials may not accord with righteousness, or that the wise talents of the age have not been recruited to office. All you state councilors of the civilian and military ranks,[16] retired worthies, and those with prestige titles of rank 3 and above ought to send me a letter with blunt assessment of my mistakes, what I got right or wrong in administering justice, and also the misdemeanors of

---

16 *Sangch'amgwan* 常參官: officials of rank 5 and above, i.e. those who take part in the regular court audiences.

the people. Furthermore, you should each select one person of outstanding loyalty, one person of outstanding uprightness, and one person of outstanding virtue. Also, present a record of men and women, monks and priests who are zealous or filial, or who are not filial or attentive; of officials who do not follow the path of public service, break the law, or harass the people."

Autumn, seventh month. A decree read: "I have perused the letters sent to me by the officials, and many of them state that 'it has become customary to esteem luxury and indulgence, to the point that there are not enough restrictions.' Have the relevant offices together with the state councilors, academicians, and those in charge of statutory rules examine the canons of previous kings and determine what is appropriate in terms of dress, means of transport, and sumptuary laws, and report to the throne."

King Tŏkchong's queen, Lady Kim, passed away. She was given the posthumous title Kyŏngsŏng 敬成, and her tomb was called Chil-lŭng 質陵.

Eighth month. The king personally comforted the state elders and hosted a banquet for them at the Office for Audience Ceremonies 閣門. The royal carriage then took him to the polo court where he personally feasted elderly men and women and bestowed presents commensurate with rank. Those seriously and terminally ill were separately served wine and food.

Ninth month. The king summoned military officials from the two capitals to examine their archery skills at the Eastern Pavilion 東亭. This continued for several months.

Liao dispatched Acting Director of the Palace Administration 守殿中監 Shi Xunzhi 史洵直 to congratulate the king on his birthday.

Winter, tenth month. The king ordered officials of the central and local administrations to present congratulatory memorials on the queen dowager's birthday. The same was to be done on the first day of the new year, the winter solstice, and the day of the P'algwan Festival 八關會.[17] This henceforth was made into a regular custom.

---

17 Festival of the Eight Commandments: originally this refers to the eight precepts lay Buddhists were to observe on certain days of the month as a kind of purification. In Koryŏ this developed into an eclectic festival that included many elements of native tradition. It was usually held on the fifteenth of the eleventh month.

Eleventh month. The personally held sacrificial prayers for snow.

Twelfth month. The king summoned civil officials of the two capitals to examine their archery skills at the Eastern Pavilion.

Because floods had damaged crops in Ch'ŏngju 淸州 and Chŏnju 全州, the king ordered to provide relief food from the granaries.

Sŏnjong Fourth year [1087]

Second year of the Yuanyou era of Song, third year of the Da'an era of Liao

Spring, first month. The king dispatched as memorial envoy Director of the Palace Library 秘書監 Im Ch'anggae 林昌槩 to Liao.

The Eastern Jurchen General Aluhan 阿盧漢 and others, nineteen people in total, came to present local products.

The king dispatched as confidential envoy 密進使 Reception Official at the Office for Audience Ceremonies 閤門引進使 Kim Hanch'ung 金漢忠 to Liao.

Second month. Im Kae was appointed censor-in-chief 御史大夫.

The Eastern Jurchen General Guaiba 恠八 and others, nineteen people altogether, came to present horses.

Third month. The Western Jurchen chief Suoyindou 所隱豆 and others, thirteen people in all, came to present local products. The king granted them office titles.

The Japanese merchant Chungwŏn Ch'injong 重元親宗 and others, thirty-two people in all, came to present local products.

The Song merchant Xu Jian 徐戩 and others, twenty people in all, came to present printing blocks for the *Avataṃsaka Sūtra* 華嚴經.

The king personally sacrificed to the Supreme Singular [star] 太一 in Mundŏk Hall 文德殿 to pray that the winds and rain would be well attuned.

The king went to Sŏnjŏng Hall to take care of government affairs. Executive Chiefs of the Chancellery Ch'oe Sŏk and Kim Yanggam, and Executive Chief of the Royal Secretariat Yu Hong discussed the achievements and failures of current policies.

Summer, fourth month. The Song merchant Fu Gao 傅高 and others, twenty people in all, came to present local products.

Executive Chief of the Royal Secretariat Wang Sŏk died.

The king visited the three tombs of Hyŏn-nŭng 顯陵, Kyŏng-nŭng 景陵, and Ch'ang-nŭng 昌陵.[18]

Kim Haenggyŏng 金行瓊 was appointed Executive of the Chancellery, Associate Executive of the Royal Secretariat; Ch'oe Saryang was appointed Assistant Executive in Political Affairs and concurrently Commissioner for the Resident Governor of the Western Capital 西京留守使.

Autumn, seventh month. Wŏnp'yŏng 元平 and others, forty people in all, from Tsushima in Japan, came to present local products.

Eighth month. The king went to Sŏnjŏng Hall to adjudicate trials punishable by capital punishment.

On *pyŏng'o* day [the 27th] the king went to the Western Capital.

Ninth month. The king gave a banquet for his close ministers on a pavilioned ship on the Taedong River 大同江.

Liao dispatched Surveillance Commissioner for the Gaozhou jurisdiction Gao Hui 高惠 to congratulate the king on his birthday.

Winter, tenth month. The king went sightseeing to Kwanp'ung Pavilion 觀風亭 and Kuje Palace.[19] After this he went to Yŏngmyŏng-sa 永明寺 to offer incense, and then took the dragon boat to the Taedong River. It was already night when he returned.

The king dispatched as memorial envoy Deputy Director of the Foreign Relations Office 禮賓小卿 Ryu Sin 柳伸 to Liao.

The king went to the two temples of Hongbok 弘福寺 and Inwang 仁王寺, and then visited the Che Pond 梯淵. He took the tower boat 樓船 to organize a wine party and while floating along the Taedong River he watched an archery [contest].

---

18 The tombs of respectively T'aejo, Munjong, and Sejo (the father of T'aejo Wang Kŏn).

19 Kuje-gung 九梯宮: Palace of the Nine Stairways; said to have been the Palace of King Tongmyŏng of Koguryŏ.

A Hundred-seat Assembly was held in the Hoegyŏng Hall of the Supreme Capital,[20] and 30,000 monks were given food on the polo court.

Eleventh month. On *ŭlmyo* [the 7th] the king returned from the Western Capital.

The king dispatched Deputy Director of the Office of Regalia Yu Sŏk 庾哲 to Liao to give thanks for the birthday congratulations; and Deputy Director of the Office of Royal Clan Affairs Kim Tŏkkyun 金德均 to offer tribute.

Twelfth month. The king dispatched Executive at the Ministry of Punishments Ch'oe Chŏ 崔翥 to Liao to offer congratulations on the Tianan Festival.

Ch'oe Sŏk was made Probationary Grand Marshal 守太尉, Minister of Personnel, and Supervising Editor of National History 監修國史; Kim Yanggam was made Probationary Grand Marshal, and Yu Hong Probationary Minister of Works; Ch'oe Saryang was made State Historiographer 修國史; Mun Hwang was made Administrator of the Security Council[21] and Yi Chawi Associate Administrator.

Sŏnjong Fifth year [1088]

Third year of the Yuanyou era of Song, fourth year of the Da'an era of Liao

Spring, first month. Liao dispatched as ad-hoc envoy 橫宣使 Censor-in-chief Yelü Yanshou 耶律延壽 .

Because Liao was debating the construction of a log bridge on the shore of the Amnok River, Vice-commissioner of the Security Council Yi An 李顔 was entrusted as envoy to burn incense for the Tripitaka and dispatched to Kwiju[22] to secretly prepare border affairs.

Third month. Kim Pup'il 金富弼 and twenty-two others passed the

20 Likely referring to Kaesŏng, the term is here probably used to distinguish with the Western Capital, where the king was still staying.

21 Note that he already had been appointed to the exact same position in the fourth month of 1086.

22 Kwiju 龜州: also pronounced Kuju; modern Korean translations render it both ways. Modern Kusŏng in North P'yŏngan Province.

composition test of the civil service examination, and three passed the classics examination; one person was passed by royal grace.

Summer, fourth month. Because the drought was severe, a dharma cart was prepared and the king led all the officials to the southern suburbs to hold a prayer for rain, twice. Blaming himself for [failing in] the six virtues,[23] the king said "Our government is not unified, alas! The people no longer know what to do, alas! The palace buildings are [too] high, alas! The consorts demand luxury, alas! Bribes are flowing, alas! Slander is rampant, alas!" Eight boys and eight girls were chosen to dance and to cry for rain. The king avoided the main hall of the palace and reduced the number of side dishes in his daily meals. Music was suspended and the seats were bared [of cushions] when the king listened to policy meetings. In the streets and markets, people were forbidden from wearing hats or using fans. Furthermore prayers were held in the Ancestral Shrine 宗廟, the [Altar of] Grain and Earth Deities 社稷, and the mountain and river [shrines].

Fifth month. The returning the courtesy envoy 回禮使 from the Eastern Capital of Liao,[24] Acting Junior Policy Advisor Gao Dexin 高德信, arrived.

Mingzhou 明州[25] in Song returned a party of twenty-three people including Yang Pok 楊福 from Naju who had been cast adrift.

A decree read: "I am not pure in matters of virtue, and thus August Heaven has castigated be by not letting it rain for three months. I am trembling in fear; how could I let those wrongly imprisoned linger in jails throughout the country! Release all those sentenced for light crimes and pardon them"

Autumn, seventh month. Mingzhou in Song returned a party of ten including Yonghyŏp 用叶 from T'amna 耽羅,[26] who had been cast adrift.

---

23 *Yuksa* 六事: kindness, frugality, diligence, caution, sincerity, and wisdom. Here however it seems to refer to the following six kinds of failures in moral government, which may, however, be regarded as opposites of the six virtues.

24 Dongjing 東京: one of the five capitals of Liao, which also corresponded to a division of the country into five administrative regions. Located in modern Liaoyang, Liaoning Province, it was closest to Koryŏ and hence often in charge of Koryŏ affairs.

25 Modern Ningbo, Zhejiang Province. This was the main port through which envoys and merchants to and from Koryŏ passed.

26 I.e., modern Cheju island.

Eighth month. Freezing rain damaged the crops.

The historians comment: "According to the *Great Plan* [of the *Book of Documents*], 'foolishness begets constant rain.'[27] Now as the king builds many Buddhist temples the people harbor resentment for the labor. When Heaven and man start interfering with each other, how frightful this is!"

Ninth month. The king dispatched Vice-chamberlain for the Royal Stud 太僕少卿 Kim Sŏnsŏk 金先錫 to Liao to beg them to stop constructing the log bridge.

Winter, tenth month. Liao dispatched Vice-Chamberlain for Ceremonials 大常少卿 Zheng Suo 鄭碩 to offer birthday congratulations to the king.

Eleventh month. Kim Sŏnsŏk returned from Liao with a reply edict saying "You repeatedly sent letters of protest requesting to halt the log bridge [construction]. Truly for such an insignificant reason, how can you waste such cumbersome words? It will be discussed in all serenity in due course. Moreover, it has not even been built, so it is your duty to calmly and peacefully with complete devotion hear my instructions. Release your deep mistrust and absorb my words."

Twelfth month. Yi An was appointed Vice-minister of Punishments and Assistant Executive in Political Affairs.

Sŏnjong Sixth year [1089]

Fourth year of the Yuanyou era of Song, fifth year of the Da'an era of Liao

Spring, first month. Grain was released from Sinhŭng Granary and donated

27 According to Legge's translation, "[There are also the unfavorable verifications], namely, of recklessness, emblemed by constant rain." This passage lists the first of six types of negative "verifications," i.e. the effects of moral behavior on the elements. The drought that plagued the country for months could be blamed on assumption, i.e. excess (僭), hence the king's decision to release prisoners in the fifth month. Here the historians seek to explain the freezing rain by the king's sponsoring of Buddhism, seen as an example of foolishness or recklessness.

to the Buddhist temples of the capital to set up maigre rituals to pray for blessings.

Second month. The king personally sacrificed to Heaven and earth, mountains and rivers on the polo court to pray for blessings.

Summer, fifth month. The bones [of people who died] because of the drought in streets and markets were covered up.

Sixth month. Ch'oe Saje 崔思齊 was made Assistant Executive in Political Affairs; Pak Illyang 朴寅亮 was made Associate Administrator of the Security Council.

Autumn, eighth month. The Eastern Jurchen General "Seeking Refuge in Virtue" 歸德將軍 Xihai 西害 and others, fourteen people in all, came to present horses.

Mingzhou in Song returned twenty-four people including Yi Kŭnbo 李勤甫 who had been cast adrift.

In order to repair the National Academy 國學, the [plaque of] Confucius was moved to Sunch'ŏn Hostel 順天館 with due decorum.

Merchants from Japan came to present local products.

Ninth month. Liao dispatched Surveillance Commissioner for the Yongzhou 永州[28] jurisdiction Yang Lin 楊璘 to congratulate the king on his birthday.

On the occasion of the Ch'ŏnwŏn Festival, the king gave a banquet for the Liao envoy in Kŏndŏk Hall. The king composed a *ci*-poem[29] to congratulate the Liao emperors.

Winter, tenth month. The Song merchants Yang Zhu 楊註, Xu Cheng 徐成 and others, ninety-nine people in all, came to present local products.

[Monks] lectured on the *Humane Kings Sūtra* for three days in Hoegyŏng Hall, and 30,000 monks were provided meals.

A newly cast thirteen-story golden pagoda was placed in Hoegyŏng Hall and a ceremony was held in celebration of this.

---

28 See *Liaoshi* 37 (Zhonghua shuju ed., 2016), 504.

29 *Ci* 詞: lyrical poetry, i.e. literally poetry written to a set melody, hence of irregular length, which sets it apart from the strictly regulated *shi* poetry.

The Song merchants Li Zhu 李珠, Yang Fu 楊甫, Yang Jun 楊俊 and others, 127 people in total, came to present local products.

The queen dowager founded Kukch'ŏng-sa 國淸寺 in the western suburbs of the capital.[30]

Eleventh month. *Chŏngmyo* day, the first day of the month. There was a solar eclipse.

The Eastern Jurchen chief Gushe 古舍 and others, twenty-one people in all, came to present horses.

Sŏnjong Seventh year [1090]

Fifth year of the Yuanyou era of Song, sixth year of the Da'an era of Liao

Spring, first month. Junior Vice-director of the Department of Ministries and Assistant Executive in Political Affairs Ch'oe Saryang requested to retire on account of illness. The king decreed that in retirement he should be given half the amount of his normal salary. An official remonstrated as follows: "Only those officials who retire at the age of seventy are granted half their salary, this is done in order to provide for the state elders. I have never heard of someone being given a stipend after retiring due to illness." The king said: "For several generations [of kings] Ch'oe Saryang served as a key official; his writings, his competence, and his wisdom all surpass the ordinary, so how would I be restrained by mere precedent?" In the end the king did not follow the remonstrance.

The envoy for T'angna[31] reported: "The Star-leader, General 'Seaborne Strike' 游擊將軍 Karyanging 加良仍[32] has died, and his half-brother, the vice-lieutenant aide-de-camp Kobongnyŏng 高福令, has succeeded him.

30 This was to become the headquarters for the Ch'ŏnt'ae School founded by the monk Ŭich'ŏn, her nephew.

31 乇羅 勾當使: T'angna is clearly a variant spelling of T'amna, modern Cheju island. Kudang-sa is a term for a centrally appointed official who mostly was dispatched to places where ferries operated.

32 See the second month of 1068 for his first mention; there however his name is given as Kayaing.

Please send condolence gifts according to precedent." The king agreed.

Suryuk Hall at Poje-sa 普濟寺 burned. Its origins are as follows: A favorite of the king, the manager of affairs at the Bureau of Astrology Ch'oe Sagyŏm 崔士謙, managed to obtain the text of the Water-Land Ritual[33] during a mission to Song, and proposed to the king to build this hall. Yet it burned before work was completed.

The historians comment: "Does not Heaven warn against those who entice the ruler with flattery to earn his favor? Formerly Emperor Wu of Liang built Tongtai-si 同泰寺, but its pagoda was barely finished when calamities arose. Heaven and man react to and influence each other, this is the same now as in the past. Those who are enticed by the Buddhist stories about misfortune and blessing should take heed from this!"

Second month. The Eastern Jurchen Commandant Yesha 也沙 and others, seventeen people altogether, came to present horses. The king bestowed presents according to rank.

Yu Hong was appointed Executive Chief of the Chancellery and Minister of War; Ch'oe Saje was appointed Executive Chief and Jointly Executive of the Royal Secretariat; Yi Chawi was appointed Junior Vice-director of the Department of Ministries, Assistant Executive in Political Affairs, and State Historiographer.

The Eastern Jurchen Commandant Niaoyunai 裹於乃 and others, twenty-two people, came to present horses. Tuda 禿達 and others, thirty-four people, came to court.

Third month. The Song merchant Xu Cheng and others, 150 people, came to preset local products.

On *muja* day [the 23rd] at night lightning struck Sinhŭng Granary 新興倉 with a thundering noise, and all the goods stored in there went up in flames

33 Suryuk-ŭi 水陸儀: A rite designed to placate the spirits of all creatures, whether they have died on land or in the water. It is said to have started with Emperor Wu of Liang, hence the historians' criticism of him.

completely, the sparks filling the air. Both the court and the people were greatly frightened, yet people's houses were spared. The Censorate blamed the astrologers: "In the case of conflagrations, there are bound to be omens, yet you did not say anything." Aide to the Grand Astrologer 太史丞 O Sang 吳相 replied: "Last year a fire star was guarding the Celestial Granary constellation;[34] this was all reported to the Bureau of Astronomy, yet the manager Ch'ae Sagyŏm suppressed this information and did not report it." Thereupon Ch'oe Sagyŏm was dismissed from office together with O Sang and others who were deemed guilty by association.

The Ministry of Rites petitioned: "During the fourth month of the second year of the Qinglong era of Emperor Ming of the Wei (234) there was a fire. The emperor asked [his minister] Gao Tanglong 高堂隆, 'What did I do wrong? And according to the Rites, does it make sense to pray for the aversion of calamities?'

Gao replied: 'Fire or other calamities occur as a warning. All you can do is accord yourself with ritual and cultivate virtue, and then it can be overcome.' Furthermore, according to ancient prophecies, fire occurs as a censure for luxurious buildings. Hence you should halt all corvée labor and implement frugality; also you should order officials to organize Buddhist and Daoist rituals."

The king followed this, and immediately ceased the corvée labor for Hongwŏn-sa and Kukch'ŏng-sa.

Summer, fifth month. Yi Kyŏngp'il 李景泌 and twenty-five others passed the composition test of the civil service examination, two passed the classics examination, and three people were qualified by royal grace.

Sixth month. The Censorate petitioned: "The Recording Officer for the Military Commissioner of Yŏngwŏn[35] 寧遠兵馬錄事, U Yŏyu 禹汝維, raided and harassed border people to grab their possessions and extort bribes. We request that he be tried by the Law Enforcement Office."[36] The king

---

34 Ch'ŏngyun 天囷: Name of a constellation, partially corresponding to the Cetus constellation.

35 Yŏngwŏn: modern Nyŏngwŏn-gun in the northeastern tip of North P'yŏngan Province.

36 Chŏngwi 廷尉: Chamberlain for Law Enforcement, one of the Nine Chamberlains

agreed.

A decree read: "This year there have been numerous fires and other calamities, as the seasonal rains did not arrive on time; I am deeply apprehensive of this. Throughout the country, those punished with light sentences such as banishment for public crimes or beatings for private crimes should all be released. Among those officials dismissed from office for breaking the law, if they have not been adjudicated to have made personal gain or harmed others, they should be given an office according to their original rank. Those officials or civilians who borrowed from Sinhŭng Granary after the *chŏngmyo* year [1087] and have not returned it shall be exempted [from returning the loan]."

Autumn, seventh month. The king dispatched Vice-minister of Taxation Yi Chaŭi 李資義 and Executive at the Ministry of Rites Wi Kyejŏng 魏繼廷 to Song to give thanks for grace bestowed and to offer presents.

Eighth month, *sinhae* day [the 19th]. A rain and hail [thunderstorm] shook the people and horses in the alleys west of the market; [lightning] also struck pine trees near the Kŏn-nŭng Romb and to the northeast of the city walls. The Grand Astrologer 太史 petitioned: "According to the *Ruixiang zhi*,[37] 'when lightning kills people, harms the six types of livestock, and destroys the trees on grave mounds, it means that the ruler is not just in meting out punishment, carrying out capital punishment on the basis of slander. If [those innocently sentenced] are not saved, then we have to worry about insurrection. The way to saving them lies in dismissing the slanderous officials, reining in the conceited and violent, and in scrupulously investigating all documents; only then will the calamities be dispelled.' The king was terrified, and went to report [his intentions] to the [ancestral] tombs, and also ordered propitiating rites to be carried out.

Ninth month. Liao dispatched Surveillance Commissioner for the Lizhou

(*jiuqing*), an office instituted since the Qin Dynasty (Hucker 6767). In Koryŏ this is the only mention of this term.

37 *Tiandi Ruixiang zhi* 天地瑞祥志: A book of astrological portents attributed to the early Tang court astrologer Sa Shouzhen 薩收眞.

利州[38] jurisdiction Zhang Shishuo 張師說 to congratulate the king on his birthday. The king twice invited the envoy for a banquet in Kŏndŏk Hall and allowed the people of the three guard escorts for the embassy to sit inside the hall. Officials petitioned "There is no precedent at all for giving a second banquet for the envoy; as for the three guard escorts sitting inside the hall, this too is unheard of." The king said: "Since the envoy came with the imperially drafted text of the Tianqing-si 天慶寺 stele,[39] I added this extra ritual for the occasion" and ignored their protests.

The Eastern Jurchen General "Embraced by Koryŏ" 懷化將軍 Ayuda 阿於大 and others, fifteen people altogether, came to present horses.

Winter, tenth month. The king took the queen dowager on a trip to Samgak-san 三角山. On the road they saw one person who was 100 years old and three who were in their eighties. The king gave presents to them and inquired after their wellbeing.

Eleventh month. The king returned from Samgak-san and declared an amnesty.

Twelfth month. Liao dispatched as ad-hoc envoy the Surveillance Commissioner for the Yizhou jurisdiction Yelü Licheng 耶律利稱.

Sŏnjong Eighth year [1091]

Sixth year of the Yuanyou era of Song, seventh year of the Da'an era of Liao

Spring, first month. Military Commissioner 兵馬使 for the Northwest Circuit 西北面 and concurrently Military Commissioner for the Central Army Yu Hong requested the construction of a military arsenal in Kwiju to prepare for any eventualities. The king gave permission.

The king gave a banquet for his officials in Kŏndŏk Hall, and gave each of them a horse from the royal stable.

---

38 *Liaoshi* 39, 547. Subordinate to the Central Capital of Liao, which is located near modern Ningcheng, Liaoning Province; located to its south.

39 A temple with this name was founded during the Liao Dynasty in 1093, located in modern Chaoyang.

Second month. The returning the courtesy envoy from the Eastern Capital of Liao, Vice-commissioner of the Foreign Relations Office Wu Yelü 烏耶呂, arrived.

Third month. The Eastern Jurchen General "Keeping the Frontier Tranquil" 寧塞將軍 Jieduohan 皆多漢 and others, forty people, arrived and presented camels and horses.

Summer, fourth month. The retired Executive Chief of the Chancellery, Chŏng Yusan 鄭惟産, died.

Fifth month, *sami* day, the first day of the month. There was a solar eclipse. Venus was visible during the day and after moving across the expanse disappeared after seventy days.

Prayers for rain were held at the Shrine for Earth and Grain Deities, the Ancestral Shrine, and the seven tombs.

Sixth month. The Capital Military Command 都兵馬使 petitioned: "Last year in the seventh month barbarian bandits raided Ch'angju 昌州.[40] The Recording Officer for the Military Commissioner, An Sŏnjun 安先俊, together with others led his troops and set up camp at Tŏngnyŏng Guard Station 德寧戍. He dispatched Junior Colonel 郎將 Ko Maeng 高猛 to pursue the enemy. They attacked them and inflicted heavy casualties; Lieutenant 校尉Sung Kŏm 崇儉, Sub-lieutenant 隊正 Pyŏn Hak 邊鶴 and others then suddenly charged right into the middle of the enemy, greatly encouraging our soldiers who redoubled their vigor and establishing their merit. We request that they be promoted and rewarded to encourage others." The king agreed.

Yi Chaŭi and the rest of the embassy returned from Song China. At the time, the emperor had heard that our country harbored many good books, and he ordered the Hostel Escort Commissioner to make a list of the books required and give them [to the Koreans], telling them "Even if there are insufficient copies, you should make copies and return those."

Autumn, seventh month. No Tan, who retired as Vice-director of the Department of Ministries, died.

40 Ch'angsŏng-gun in North P'yŏngan Province.

Kim Sanggi was appointed Vice-minister at the Ministry of Taxation and Assistant Executive in Letters [at the Department of Royal Secretariat-Chancellery]; Yu Sŏk was Associate Administrator of the Security Council.

Eighth month. The Capital Military Command petitioned: "Not forgetting danger during times of peace is a crucial task of the states. We request that a shooting range be prepared on the unused land near the southern corridor of the Ministry of Taxation. All guard troops and all those learning archery should practice there. Those who hit the bull's eye should be awarded a silver plate." The king agreed.

Executive Chief of the Royal Secretariat Ch'oe Saje died.

A decree read: "Tian Sheng 田盛 from Song is good at drafting letters, and his compatriot Chen Yang 陳養 is good at military arts. We sincerely request that they be given permission to reside here, and that they be granted office rank, so as to encourage others to come here."

Intercalary [eighth] month. The king avoided the main hall and ate simple dishes. Sentences were written down with a red brush.

A Tripitaka Assembly was held in Hoegyŏng Hall. The king offered incense and composed a poem to show his recourse in and admiration of [Buddhism].

Ninth month. The king went to Sangch'un Pavilion 賞春亭 and summoned the Duke of Kyerim Wang Hŭi, the Duke of Puyŏ Wang Su, Executive Chief of the Chancellery Yu Hong, Vice-director of the Department of Ministries So T'aebo 邵台輔, Vice-minister of War Sŏ Chŏng 徐靖, Supreme General Wang Kungmo 王國髦, Intendant of the Chancellery 直門下省 Ko Kyŏng 高景, Hallim Academician Son Kwan 孫冠 and others for drinks, and asked them informally about the border situation.

Liao dispatched Surveillance Commissioner for the jurisdiction of Yongzhou Gao Chong 高崇 to congratulate the king on his birthday.

The Capital Military Command petitioned: "Sang'ŭm County 霜陰縣 within Anbyŏn[41] Protectorate 安邊都護府 is located in the most vulnerable position on the border; we request that a fortress be constructed to defend

41 Anbyŏng-gun in South Hamgyŏng Province.

against external bandit attacks." The king agreed.

Winter, eleventh month. Executive Chief of the Chancellery Yu Hong died. Although he was a military official he was well versed in the Zuo Commentary on the *Spring and Autumn Annals* as well as in various works on military strategy. Every time the country was confronting a crisis, day and night he would deeply ponder ancient stratagems to draw on; more often than not they would provide the solution. He was highly esteemed in contemporary discourse.

Twelfth month. Executive Chief of the Chancellery Yi An died.

Sŏnjong Ninth year [1092]

Seventh year of the Yuanyou era of Song, eighth year of the Da'an era of Liao

Spring, first month. The Eastern Jurchen Aluhan 阿盧漢 and others, twenty people in all, came to present local products.

Second month. The Eastern Jurchen General "Embraced by Koryŏ" Sanbin 三彬 and others came to present horses.

The T'amna Star-leader Ŭiin 懿仁 came to present local products. He was granted the title of General "Settling the Distant" 定遠將軍 and also was given robes and belt.

So T'aebo was appointed Assistant Executive in Political Affairs.

Third month. In the capital, 640 houses were destroyed by fire.

The king was indisposed, and ordered the court physician to present medicines to nourish his constitution. Suddenly he composed a poem that ended as follows: "How would I dare worry about the effect of medicine? Since this fleeting life has a beginning how could it be without an end! All I should wish for is to cultivate good deeds, and ascending to the pure regions pay my respects to the Indian Hero." Those who read this were greatly astonished.

Summer, fourth month. Assistant Executive in Political Affairs So T'aebo was provisionally appointed Administrator of the Military Commission for the Northwestern Region and concurrently Military Commissioner for the Central Army. Assistant Executive in Letters Kim Sanggi was provisionally appointed Administrator of the Military Commission for the Northeastern Region and concurrently appointed as Military Commissioner for the Expedition Corps. Associate Administrator of the Security Council Im Kae was made Military Commissioner for the Northeastern Region and concurrently appointed Military Commissioner for the Expedition Corps.

The king granted the Marquis of Kŭmgwan Wang Pi[42] the title of Acting Grand Marshal, concurrently Royal Secretary; soon after he died. The king said: "Earlier when the Marquis of Changsun 章順侯[43] died without issue, his body was cremated and the bones dispersed according to Buddhist custom. Now Wang Pi also has no heirs, so we should follow the precedent of the Marquis of Changsun's burial. Yet even though the custom of dispersing the cremated remains stems from Buddhism, this is not worth following. Divine an auspicious day and bury him with due honors, so that he can be eternally offered to in spring and autumn." The officials protested to the end, and thus it was not implemented.

The envoy in charge of ritual from the Eastern Capital of Liao, Gao Liangqing 高良慶, arrived.

Kim Sŏng 金誠 and others, thirty-two people altogether, passed composition test of the civil service examination; three passed the classics test, and two were accredited by royal grace.

Sixth month. Sŏ Chŏng was made Assistant Executive in Political Affairs; Yu Sŏk was made Administrator of the Security Council, ad Yi Ye was made Associate Administrator of the Security Council.

A decree read: "Before, I listened to the astrologer Ch'oe Sagyŏm's advice to repair Kyŏngnŭng Tomb, which had become derelict. Recently, I received a letter from Vice-director of the Bureau of Astronomy 司天少監 Hwang Ch'unghyŏn 黃忠現 and others that claims that Ch'oe Sagyŏm actually

42 A younger brother of King Sŏnjong and son of King Munjong; his mother was a daughter of Yi Chayŏn. KRS 90.17a.

43 Also a brother of King Sŏnjong, who had died a few years before in 1086 and was posthumously given the title Marquis of Changsun. KRS 90.17b.

intended to use the repairs to avert calamities [for himself]. This will distress the spirit of the deceased king in his grave; the Ministry of Punishments should interrogate him under torture and banish him to Sŏnsan Island 仙山島."

Autumn, seventh month. Assistant Executive in Political Affairs Ch'oe Saryang died. He was a man of elegant demeanor, reserved and of little words. Yet for important matters of state he drafted the texts, and his skill in this was such that he stood out among his generation.

Eighth month. Yi Chawi was appointed Junior Vice-director of the Department of Ministries, and provisional Administrator of the Chancellery. Concurrently he was also made Commissioner to the Resident Governor of the Western Capital. Originally as a state councilor he had been responsible for the editing the memorial to be presented to the Song court. However, erroneously he used the Liao era name in the letter, so the Song court rejected the letter. As a result, he was dismissed from office. But barely a few months later he approached a court favorite and as a result the king reappointed him like this.

On *mujin* day [the 17th] the king left for the Western Capital.

Ninth month. The queen dowager died. She was buried in Tae-nŭng 戴陵 Tomb and given the posthumous title Inye 仁睿.

Liao dispatched Wang Ding 王鼎 to congratulate the king on his birthday. An official petitioned: "According to the ancient classics, for the son of Heaven and the liege lords the period of mourning is three years; after the burial, the mourning clothes are taken off and the rites are finalized by mourning in mind [rather than through external display]. This is not the same rite as for the scholar-officials. Now the congratulation emissary has already arrived; respectfully we petition that months are substituted by days, and that you take off the mourning clothes after twenty-seven days to receive the imperial edict [of congratulation]." The king agreed.

Winter, tenth month, *pyŏngja* day [the 27th]. The king returned from the Western Capital.

Eleventh month, *kyŏngja* day [the 21st]. Venus was observed on its celestial path during the day.

Twelfth month. The Eastern Jurchen Yuluofo 餘羅弗 and others, twenty people in all, came to present local products.

On the *imsin* day [the 24th] there was an earthquake.

Sŏnjong Tenth year [1093]

Eighth year of the Yuanyou era of Song, ninth year of the Da'an era of Liao

Spring, second month. The Responding to the State Letter Envoy[44] from Mingzhou in Song, Huang Zhong 黃仲, arrived.

Summer, fourth month. Retired Director of the Chancellery Mun Chŏng 文正 died.

A decree read: "Last year the prefectures and garrisons of the Eastern Circuit suffered from bad harvests, and many among the populace suffer from hunger and hardship. When considering the ordinary people, how could I forget about providing relief for them in times of distress? Grains and salt from the Righteous Granaries should be issued to help them."

Liao dispatched the Surveillance Commissioner for the jurisdiction of Gaozhou, Feng Xingzong 馮行宗 to order the king to end his mourning and return to full duties.

Fifth month. So T'aebo was appointed Executive Chief of the Royal Secretariat, and Minister of Punishments; Sŏ Chŏng was made Vice-director of the Department of Ministries, Assistant Executive in Political Affairs, and Administrator of the Finance Commission 判三司事; Kim Sanggi was appointed Vice-minister of Personnel, Assistant Executive in Political Affairs, Minister of Taxation, and State Historiographer; Yu Sŏk was made Vice-minister of Rites and Assistant Executive in Political Affairs.

The king wished to construct a temple and ordered the Grand Astrologer to investigate the land east of the city walls [to find a suitable location], and then personally went to inspect [the site]. Subsequently a great temple was

---

44 Posin-sa 報信使: This is the only occurrence of this particular term, which makes it difficult to construe its intended purpose.

constructed, and the king bestowed the name Hongho-sa 弘護寺 on it.

Sixth month. The kind personally performed a sacrifice[45] in the inner halls of the palace to pray for a good harvest.

So T'aebo petitioned: "Among the officers and soldiers stationed in the border fortresses in the northern circuit many have been drawn from prefectures and districts south of the mountains to supplement [the regular troops]. Since their allocated fields [*chŏngjŏn* 丁田] are [in their hometowns] very far [from where they are stationed], they have insufficient resources to support themselves. Should a military incident occur, they will bear the brunt of the attack. I request that henceforth the ablest among them be selected to serve and protect the embassies sent to Liao, so that they can observe the situation in the border region and can obtain profit from trade; people will certainly compete to be recommended for such a mission." The king followed this advice.

The Capital Military Command petitioned: "The 'Thousand-picul Arbalest' 千鈞弩constructed by Vice-director Pak Wŏnjak 朴元綽 is truly effective, and therefore it was used in firing drills in the suburbs. Now it has fallen in disuse for a long time so we request that it be practiced from this year as before." The king agreed.

The correct rite of greeting was determined between all ranks of officials and clerks and censorial officials.

Autumn, seventh month. The royal inspector for Sŏhae Route[46] petitioned: "A patrol brigade from Yŏnp'yŏng Island 延平島 under the jurisdiction of Ansŏ protectorate[47] 安西都護府 seized one ship: its crew consisted of twelve

45 *Ch'o* 醮: this term was strongly associated with Daoist ritual from the Song period onwards, so it may be surmised that this was a Daoist ritual; however, the character originally has the general meaning of sacrifice, thus in the absence of any contextual evidence I simply translate it throughout as "sacrifice."

46 Sŏhae-do 西海道: although *to* mostly refers to the ten provinces instituted in early Koryŏ or the five as reorganized by Yejong (KRS 56.1a-b), Sŏhae is not among these. As the first treatise on military affairs makes clear, Sŏhae is one of twenty-two routes along postal stations; rather than an administrative unit, it appears to be a logistical device to facilitate transport and communication. KRS 82.9a ff, "ch'amyŏk" 站驛.

47 Centered around modern Haeju, in Hwanghae Province. The island, located south of Haeju, still carries the same name.

people from Song and nineteen Japanese; they had bows and arrows, knives and swords, and armor, as well as mercury, pearls, sulfur, conch shells, and other products. Undoubtedly, they were pirates from the two countries who wanted to invade our border territories with joint forces. We request that officials accept and deal with the weapons and other goods seized and that the pirates be banished to areas outside the passes; we also request that the soldiers who caught the pirates be rewarded." The king followed this request.

The king dispatched Vice-minister of War Hwang Chonggak 黃宗殼 and Executive at the Ministry of Works Ryu Sin to Song to give thanks for the grace bestowed.

A decree ruled: "The prayers for the deceased kings and queens on their memorial days have gradually deteriorated; a granary should be constructed in the Kwang'in Hostel 廣仁館 and named Pongsŏn 奉先 [Revering the former (kings and queens)] Granary. The grains stored there should be used for the ceremonies; officials should be assigned to manage affairs."

Eighth month. A decree ruled: "Of old it has been the custom in our country that on [royal] birthdays, the first day of the year, and the winter solstice only one of the state councilors is assigned to lead the official ranks in their offering of congratulations, the other state councilors do not even join the ranks. Recently I heard that the Song court has ruled that on all festive days the ritual is the same as when the emperor is in audience. Henceforth we should follow the Song custom."

The Capital Military Command petitioned: "According to the books on military arts, 'for rapid deployment of troops, quilted clothes should be worn;' this is what we today call 'stitched clothes.' We request that moth-eaten cloth from the Repository of Clothing Materials 大盈庫 be turned into three- to four-thousand sets [of quilted clothes] by the Directorate for Military Uniforms 征袍都監, and sent to the Eastern and Northern Circuits and the two border circuits to be stored in barrack storages; they should be worn in case of emergency." The king agreed.

All those condemned to the death penalty throughout the country were pardoned, their sentence commuted to banishment to a sea island.

Ninth month. Liao dispatched the Surveillance Commissioner for the Yongzhou jurisdiction Da Guiren 大歸仁 to congratulate the king on his birthday.

Winter, tenth month. The Letter-bearing envoy[48] Wang Kuo 王廓 from Mingzhou in Song came to announce the passing of the emperor and empress.

Twelfth month. Liao dispatched as ad hoc envoy the Surveillance Commissioner for the Anzhou 安州[49] jurisdiction Yelü Gua 耶律括.

Sŏnjong Eleventh year [1094]

First year of the Shaosheng era of Song, tenth year of the Da'an era of Liao

Spring, first month. On *imjin* day [the 20th] a comet appeared around the sun from east to west, with a white halo that pierced the sun. On *musul* day [the 26th] it was also like this.

Second month. Because of the celestial anomalies the kind declared an amnesty.

The king was preparing to inspect the troops but the Censorate protested: "The military represents the metal element, which overcomes wood. Now spring is rising, and its power rests in wood. Thus inspecting the military is going against the live force." The king did not listen.

In the Eastern Circuit, the eight prefectures of Koju 高州, Hwaju 和州, Munju 文州, Yongju 湧州, Chŏngju 定住, Changju 長州, Tŭngju 登州, and Kyoju 交州,[50] and the six garrisons of Sŏndŏk 宣德, Wŏnhŭng 元興,

48 *Chich'ŏpsa* 持牒使: This term occurs here for the first time, and appears only once more in the *Koryŏsa chŏryo*.

49 Anzhou: located between modern Shenyang and Changchun, Changtu county. See *Liaoshi* 38, 538.

50 These prefectures are spread out over a wide area from the northern part of Kangwŏn Province and across most of Hamgyŏng Province. Koju corresponds to modern Kowon; Hwaju to Yŏnghŭng; Munju to Munch'ŏn; Yongju to Tŏgwŏn in Munch'ŏn-gun; Chŏngju to Chŏngp'yŏng; Changju to Changgok county in Chŏngp'yŏng; Tŭngju to Anbyŏn; and Kyoju to Hoeyang. Only Hoeyang is located in Kangwŏn, the others in South Hamgyŏng

Yŏng'in 寧仁, Changp'yŏng 長平, Yŏnghŭng 永興, and Yongjin 龍津, the people suffered from famine due to recent floods and drought. The king dispatched as Granary Inspection Commissioner 監倉使 for the Eastern Circuit the Executive Kim Ŭisŏn 金義璿, and as Granary Inspection Commissioner for Sakpang Province the Audience Usher 閤門祇候 So Ch'ung 蘇忠; as Investigating Censor 監察御史 Im Yŏn 林衍 was sent. They were to comfort the people and provide relief.

Third month. The Eastern Jurchen General Rengyu 仍于 and others came to present nine horses.

Chŏng Kŭkkong 鄭克恭 and twenty-seven others passed the composition test of the civil service examination, four passed the classics test, and four were qualified through royal grace.

Summer, intercalary fourth month. On *imjin* day [the 22nd] the king was indisposed.

Fifth month. On the *imin* day [the 2nd] the king passed away in the Yŏnyŏng Hall 延英殿. His eldest son Wang Uk 王昱 received the king's testamentary injunction [appointing him as successor] and was enthroned in Chunggwang Hall 重光殿. He bestowed as title for the late king Sahyo 思孝 and as temple name Sŏnjong 宣宗. On *kabin* day [the 14th] he was buried in In-nŭng 仁陵 Tomb.

Yi Chehyŏn 李齊賢 commented in his eulogy: "Poems are containers for one's intention; if the mind's intention is expressed in words it becomes poetry. Looking at the king's poem 'Taking Medicine at Mundŏk Hall,' one is reminded of the words 'When I see the sun's shadow … I begrudge a day's passing' by Zhao Meng 趙孟.[51] How so? Zhao Meng was a minister of one of the warring states; but his words were irresponsible and hence he

Province.

51 See Stephen Durrant, Wai-yee Li, and David Schaberg, *Zuo Tradition* 左傳. *Commentary on the "Spring and Autumn Annals"* (Seattle: University of Washington Press, 2016), 1320–1321, Zuo Commentary for the year 541 BCE. Like Sŏnjong, Zhao Meng made frequent allusions to his imminent demise; the implication seems to be that this is tempting fate and hence irresponsible.

became the ridicule of true Confucian gentlemen. How much more so if the king [utters such words]! Since Sŏnjong was clever and loved learning, he did not read books that were not sagely, and so he did not have any crooked intentions. In the songs exchanged between ruler and his ministers there is reverence; instead of frivolous fabrications like the 'Song of the Mighty Wind'[52] how could they not follow this? Before reaching the three-year point, he threw away the ministers, how lamentable!"

Sixth month. The king [Hŏnjong] honored his mother Lady Yi with the title of queen dowager, and [her] hall was designated Chunghwa Hall 中和殿; all the officials offered felicitations.

So T'aebo and Yi Chawi were appointed Executive Chief of the Chancellery; Yu Sŏk was appointed Vice-director of the Department of Ministries; Im Kae was made Assistant Executive in Political Affairs; Yi Chaŭi was appointed intendant of the Security Council; Ch'oe Sach'u 崔思諏 was appointed Associate Administrator of the Security Council and Senior Policy Advisor.

A general amnesty was declared.

The Song Chief Merchant Xu You 徐祐 and others, sixty-nine people, and Kojŏk 高的 from T'angna, 194 people in all, came to offer felicitations on the king's accession and offered local products.

The Duke of Chosŏn, Wang To, and the Duke of Kyerim, Wang Hŭi, were made Acting Grand Preceptor; the Duke of Sang'an, Wang Su, and the Duke of Puyŏ, Wang Su, were made Acting Grand Guardian; the Marquis of Chin Han, Wang Yu, and the Marquis of Hansan, Wang Yun 王昀, together with the Earl of Nangnang, Wang Yŏng 王瑛, were made Probationary Minister of Education.

Autumn, seventh month. The Song Chief Merchant Xu Yi 徐義 and others came to present local products.

Eighth month. A decree read: "Within the jurisdiction of Sŏndŏk Garrison in Chŏngju, locusts have caused disaster; I hereby order the ministers to each

52 Dafengge 大風歌: A dirge attributed to the founder of the Han Dynasty, Gaozu.

present a letter to the throne [offering solutions]."

The Song Chief Merchant Ou Bao 歐保, with Liu Ji 劉及, Yang Bao 楊保, and others, sixty-four people in all, arrived.

Winter, eleventh month. The king gave a banquet for all those aged eighty and over on the Polo Court 毬庭, and bestowed presents according to rank.

Twelfth month. Liao dispatched as Imperial Sacrificial Envoy the Surveillance Commissioner for Yongzhou jurisdiction Xiao Zunlie 蕭遵烈, and as Deputy Envoy Vice-director of the Office of Regalia Liang Zushu 梁祖述. As Condolence Envoy was dispatched the Defense Commissioner of Guangzhou, Xiao Chi 蕭褫; and as Interrupting the Mourning Envoy 起復使[53] the Acting Chief Minister of the Court of Imperial Entertainment 守崇祿卿[54] Guo Renwen 郭人文. The imperial sacrificial envoy went to the spirit chamber to offer sacrifices to Sŏnjong; the condolence envoy transmitted the edict [of condolence] in Kŏndŏk Hall and also bestowed condolence gifts. The ending the mourning envoy also transmitted an edict in Kŏndŏk Hall; this edict ordered the king to lay off the mourning clothes, and made him Cavalry General-in-chief 驃騎大將軍, Acting Grand Marshal and concurrently Royal Secretary, Supreme Pillar of State, King of Koryŏ, with a stipend village of 7,000 households, including 700 households effective.

Hŏnjong, Great King who Died Young

His given name was Uk 昱. He was the oldest son of Sŏnjong, and his mother was Queen Dowager Sasuk 思肅太后, née Yi. He was born on the first year, cyclical name *kapcha*, of Sŏnjong [1084], on *ŭlmi* day [the 27th] of the sixth month. He was bright and intelligent, and from the age of nine

53 *Kibok* 起復 means to resume work while still in mourning: hence this envoy was likely sent to instruct the king to resume his duties despite being in mourning. At least once (see above, eleventh month of 1085) a *nakkibok* 落起復 envoy was sent: this may refer to the end of this period of working during mourning, i.e. the complete end of the mourning period and the resumption of work as normal.

54 Following Hucker (no. 1666) I regard Chongluqing 崇祿卿 as Guangluqing 光祿卿 (no. 3348), an alternative form because of a taboo on the "*guang*" character.

loved calligraphy and painting. Whatever he heard or saw, he would never forget. He was on the throne for one year and lived to the age of fourteen.

Hŏnjong First year [1095]

Second year of the Shaosheng era of Song, first year of the Shoulong era of Liao

Spring, first month. On *musul* day, the first day of the month, there was a northwesterly wind; there was a halo around the sun and comets appeared on its sides. The Grand Astrologer reported: "If there is a northwesterly wind on the first day of the year there is cause for worry; if there are comets around the sun, this means that close ministers would rise up and that among the various lords there would be one who wants to rebel." The king was young and did not know how to control himself or those around him. All he did was call three or four court physicians to discuss with them medical books or practice calligraphy or painting.

Wang Kungmo was provisionally made Minister of War. As the court was weak, power reversed to the military class. Those with knowledge of state lamented this.

Second month. The Eastern Jurchen General "Embraced by Koryŏ" Soluo 所羅 and others, twenty-eight people in total, and the General "Upholding the Country" 奉國將軍 Doumen 豆門 and others, forty-eight people in total, came to present horses. The king went to Sŏnjŏng Hall and allowed them a meeting. He ordered the close minister Ch'oe Hongsa to enquire about the border situation, and also to bestow alcohol and food, clothing and belts, cloth and silk.

The Song merchant Huang Chong 黃冲 and others, thirty-one people, arrived, bringing with them the monk of the Ci'en School 慈恩宗 Huizhen 惠珍. The king ordered close ministers to welcome them and house the monk in Poje-sa. Huizhen frequently requested: "I came here to see the sacred cave of Potalaka Mountain;[55] please allow me to witness it." This was not granted.

---

55 This likely refers to Naksan-sa in Kangnŭng, a place where Avalokiteśvara is said to

Summer, fourth month. Yu Chin 兪進 and twenty-five others passed the composition test of the civil service examination, three passed the classics examination, and three passed by royal grace.

Fifth month. Yu Sŏk was made Administrator of the Finance Commission; Yi Ye was made Assistant Executive in Letters and Vice-minister of War; Yi Chaŭi was appointed Commissioner of the Security Council, while Son Kwan was made Superintendent of the Security Council; Son Kwan was also appointed Hallim Academician and Recipient of Edicts.

The Returning the Courtesy Envoy from the Liao Eastern Capital, Gao Sui 高遂, arrived. Gao Sui privately presented a lot of fine patterned silk and colored silk. The king went to Kŏndŏk Hall and invited him for an audience, bestowing wine and food, as well as clothes.

Sixth month. The king received the bodhisattva precepts[56] in Kŏndŏk Hall.

Autumn, seventh month. The king personally sacrificed at the Ancestral Shrine. Even though he was still in mourning, he held sacrifices at the Round Altar 圜丘, at the Square Pond 方澤, at the Ancestral Shrine, at the Altar for the Earth and Grain Deities 社稷, … of all the sacrifices prescribed by the codes, there was none he did not perform.

Komul 高勿 and others from T'angna, eighty people in all, came to offer local products.

Originally, King Sŏnjong had taken as queen the daughter of Vice-minister Yi Sŏk 李碩, who gave birth to the king [Hŏnjong]. He also betrothed the daughter of Chancellor Yi Chŏng 李頲, Princess Wŏnsin 元信宮主, who gave birth to the Duke of Hansan, Wang Yun. Since the king was young, weak, and sick, he could not handle government affairs. Thus all state affairs were handled by the royal [step] mother. All officials were thus caught in the middle of these two sides. Commissioner of the Security Council Yi Chaŭi

have appeared to the monk Ŭisang and others. Hence it was named after the abode of Avalokiteśvara, Potalaka. The Ci'en School is named after the temple where Xuanzang resided, and is hence another name for the Yogacara or "Consciousness-only" school.

56 The text has *mokch'a* 木叉, a transliteration of *mokṣa* "liberation" but likely an abbreviation for *pratimokṣa*, i.e. the complete set of disciplinary rules to be observed by monks. Since kings mostly received the bodhisattva precepts early in their reign, this is likely meant here as well.

was the older brother of Princess Wŏnsin. He coveted riches and assembled an unreliable lot of speedy and brave men for horse riding and shooting.

He often told them "The present ruler is sick, and we are never sure whether he will make it through the day. Among the royal in-laws there are those who are waiting for their chance [to grab power], so you should protect the Duke of Hansan with all your might; don't let the throne go to anyone else."

Then he gathered troops in the palace to prepare for a coup. Meanwhile the Duke of Kyerim, Wang Hŭi, had secretly followed the situation from his residence, the Myŏngbok Palace. He instructed So T'aebo as follows: "The fate of the country rests in the hands of the state councilors. The situation is urgent, so the public officials need to make plans."

So T'aebo ordered Supreme General Wang Kungmo to lead troops into [the palace] to protect [the king]. He also ordered the strongman Ko Ŭihwa 高義和 to behead Yi Chaŭi and his henchmen, the Audience Usher Chang Chung 張仲 and the Secretarial Clerk at the Security Council Ch'oe Ch'ungbaek 崔忠伯, at the Sŏnjŏng Gate. Separately they also caught and killed Yi Chaŭi's son, the registrar Yi Chak 李綽, and the Generals Sungnyŏl 崇列 and T'aekch'un 澤春, as well as others, seventeen people altogether. Executive Chief of the Chancellery Yi Chawi, Vice-director Kim Ŭiyŏng 金義英, Vice-director of the Bureau of Astronomy Hwang Ch'unghyŏn and others, more than fifty people, were banished to the deep south. Wives and children of the rebellious faction were stripped of their status and made slaves in the prefectures and garrisons of the two border circuits. Yi Chawi was in cahoots with Yi Chaŭi and dominated politics completely, hence his fate. The people ridiculed Sŏnjong for passing the throne to his young son rather than one of his five cherished brothers, which lead to this rebellion.

So T'aebo was provisionally made Minister of Personnel, and Wang Kungmo provisional Minister of War. These were rewards for their merit.

Eighth month. Hwang Chungbo 黃仲寶 was appointed Vice-director of the Department of Ministries.

The king made his uncle, the Duke of Kyerim, Royal Secretary. The officials flocked to his residence to congratulate him.

The Song merchants Chen Yi 陳義, Huang Yi 黃宜, and others, sixty people in all, came to present local products.

Son Kwan was appointed Commissioner of the Security Council, and Ch'oe Sach'u Vice-minister of Personnel and Intendant of the Security Council.

The king ordered the restoration of the Hwangnyong-sa 皇龍寺 pagoda in the Eastern Capital.

Ninth month. So T'aebo was appointed Specially Promoted Probationary Minister of Education, and Minister of Personnel; Kim Sanggi and Yu Sŏk were both appointed as Executive and Jointly Executive Chief of the Royal Secretariat; Im Kae was appointed Probationary Minister of Works, Vice-director of the Department of Ministries and Minister of Taxation; Wang Kungmo was made Junior Vice-director of the Department of Ministries and Assistant Executive in Political Affairs, Minister of War, and Pillar of State; Hwang Chonggak was made Associate Administrator of the Security Council.

Executive at the Ministry of War Kim Tŏkch'ung 金德忠 was exiled to a distant place due to his association with the rebellious party.

A decree read: "Recently, a powerful clique of traitors plotted insurrection, but the affair was uncovered and they were duly executed. This is truly thanks to the good efforts of generals and state councilors. Even though the rebellion has already been eradicated, we should still increase our diligence in cultivating virtue and reflect upon our wrongs. All those who feel wrongly imprisoned should be sentenced leniently; for small crimes such as those that could be indemnified for money, the sentenced should be released."

Wang Kungmo was appointed Intendant for the Capital Military Command; although he could not take care of his duties due to illness, his authority held sway over the court.

A decree read: "Henceforth those following the carriages of the state councilors or security councilors are allowed to unfold parasols; this is to be a permanent rule."

Winter, tenth month, *sagi* day [the 7th]. An edict read: "I inherited the throne from my late father and was enthroned without due qualification; I was too young and immature, and my constitution was sickly. Thus I failed to uphold the authority of the state and thwarted the hopes of the officials and the people alike. A treasonous plot and other nefarious discussions emerged from among powerful groups. Rebellious bandits and treasonous ministers frequently infringed upon the inner palace chambers. This was all brought about by my lack of virtue. Whenever I think of the difficulty of being a ruler, I look at my uncle, the Duke of Kyerim: All the signs point to the fact that he is the person to rule, deserving assistance from both the spirits and the people. I ask that you all accept him as the right successor. I should resign and retire to a lesser palace where I can spend the remainder of my days." Then he ordered the close minister Kim Tŏkkyun to meet the Duke of Kyerim, Wang Hŭi, in his residence. The duke refused two or three times, and only then [agreed to] enter the palace. On *kyŏng'o* day [the 8th] he was enthroned in Chunggwang Hall.

Yi Chehyŏn commented: "When Emperor Yu passed the throne to his son, this was because he considered later generations. Establishing a posthumously born heir and entrusting the court to a leather-clad [person][57] and yet Heaven not moving—this meant that the tasks had been correctly allotted. The three sons of King Hyŏnjong succeeded one another from older to younger brother and then the throne was passed to Sunjong, [son of Munjong]. In mourning, Sunjong was excessively overcome with grief and died young; not having any progeny, the throne passed to Sŏnjong [his younger brother]. When Sŏnjong died the heir apparent succeeded him; this was Hŏnjong. Now the people of the country had become accustomed to this [succession from older to younger brother], so when Sŏnjong enthroned his young son despite having five younger brothers, they regarded something

57 I am not sure what story is alluded to here. Yu the great left his family to work on the great flood control project for thirteen years, so perhaps the "posthumous child" should rather be read as "Abandoned before birth" because for thirteen years Yu did not visit his home even once.

that is right as wrong. How could they be so thoughtless! If you cannot obtain someone like the Duke of Zhou among your relatives or a top-notch minister as your close official to entrust government affairs to and assist you, then peril and chaos will surely ensue. Later generations should take heed lest an unfortunate event befalls [the king] and a child in swaddling clothes is thrown in at the deep end!"

Princess Wŏnsin, née Yi, and her son the Marquis of Hansan and his younger brother were exiled to Kyŏngwŏn Prefecture 慶源郡.[58]

The king dispatched First Office Chief at the Department of Ministries Yun Kwan 尹瓘 and Executive at the Ministry of Punishments Im Ŭi 任懿 to Liao to announce the accession of the new king.

So T'aebo was appointed Probationary Grand Marshal and Director of the Chancellery; Kim Sanggi was appointed Probationary Minister of Education and Executive of the Chancellery, Jointly Executive Chief of the Royal Secretariat and Chief Compiler of Dynastic History; Yu Sŏk was appointed Probationary Minister of Works; Im Kae was made Executive Chief of the Royal Secretariat and Minister of Punishments; Wang Kungmo was appointed Probationary Minister of Education; Son Kwan was appointed Junior Vice-director of the Department of Ministries, Assistant Executive in Political Affairs, and Minister of Taxation; Ch'oe Sach'u was made Probationary Minister of Works, Commissioner of the Security Council, and Hallim Academician Recipient of Edicts; Kim Sŏnsŏk was made Administrator of the Security Council.

The king granted the Duke of Chosŏn Wang To a stipend village of 5,000 households, with an effective enfeoffment of 500 households; the Duke of Puyŏ, Wang Su, was made Probationary Grand Mentor with a stipend village of 3,000 households, with an effective enfeoffment of 300 households; the Marquis of Chin Han, Wang Yu, was made Director of the Department of Ministries; the Earl of Nangnang, Wang Yŏng, was made Commander

---

58 This corresponds to the area of modern Inch'ŏn, and was the home basis of the Kyŏngwŏn (Inju) Yi; thus they were effectively "exiled" to their home prefecture.

Unequalled in Honor and promoted to Marquis of Nangnang; Hwang Chungbo was appointed Vice-director of the Department of Ministries; Yun Singŏl 尹莘傑 was appointed Supreme General of Dragon-Tiger Army 龍虎軍 and Vice-minister of War; Hwang Yuhyŏn 黃俞顯 was appointed Vice-minister of Works; Ch'oe Chŏk 崔迪 was made Supreme General of the Golden Bird Division 金吾衛 and Acting Vice-minister of Punishments. For the rest, those who were promoted to offices above their rank numbered several hundred. Among the artisans, merchants, and official slaves, those who obtained their present office above their rank were also many, yet the officials did not dare to speak out on this.

Assistant Executive in Political Affairs Wang Kungmo died.

Eleventh month. The king went to the Sinbong Tower 神鳳樓 and declared an amnesty. He also gave a banquet for those aged eighty and over, and for those with serious or terminal illness, for the righteous husbands and chaste wives, for filial sons and grandsons, for widows and widowers, and for orphans, and bestowed presents according to rank. As for the descendants of T'aejo's merit subjects and of Sam Han merit subjects, both patrilineal and matrilineal, those without office were allowed to have one person per household enter officialdom. As for the descendants of T'aejo who were on the military roster, they were exempted [from military duty] and those without office were allowed to enter one person into officialdom. Military and civil clerks were granted one rank. Those who had taken the civil service examination or classics examination ten times without passing were allowed to wear official robes. The descendants of the merit subjects of Hyŏnjong's reign, General Ha Kongjin 河拱辰 and Song Kukhwa 宋國華, together with the descendants of the envoys detained in Khitan after they went there in *kyŏngsul* year [1010] were allowed to have one person enter officialdom. Military of various stripes were granted grain and cloth according to rank. All the prefectures and counties were exempted from this year's taxes. Those with overdue corvée or tribute tax were exempted for anything due before *kyeyu* year [1093].

Ch'oe Yugŏ 崔惟擧 was dispatched to Liao to present tribute, Ch'oe

Yonggyu 崔用圭 to congratulate on the new year, and Tong P'aengjae 董彭載 to congratulate on the Heavenly Peace festival [the emperor's birthday].

Liao dispatched Surveillance Commissioner for the Taizhou 泰州[59] jurisdiction Liu Zhi 劉直 to congratulate the previous king on his birthday. The king received him instead of [the previous king] in Kŏndŏk Hall.

Twelfth month. The Liao envoy Liu Zhi on his return was entrusted with a memorial for the emperor. The previous king's memorial read: "Your subject, while suffering from a weak constitution, was erroneously entrusted with a weighty responsibility. As unfortunate events happened one after the other, my illness gradually grew worse. Since I could not take care of government affairs and could not even move my body as I pleased, I provisionally entrusted the affairs of this vassal state to my relative, and a house servant hastened to inform the celestial court of this. How could I have anticipated, however, that now you undeservedly bestowed your benevolence by sending an envoy with a missive that brought us sincere and warm comfort and instruction! Moreover you showed even more generosity by bestowing precious gifts. Unfortunately anemic and vacant I could not get out of bed [to receive the edict and gifts], and had it accepted on my behalf, making me feel even more trembling in awe [of this undeserved grace]. I pledge that even in a hundred rebirths I will endeavor to repay this great favor a little."

The king added his own memorial: "The king of this country, the subject named above, has long been stricken by illness and cannot see or stand by himself. Then suddenly he received this great favor from the emperor, yet in the end could not receive it himself. Your subject then provisionally took charge of this vassal country and received what you bestowed on behalf of the king. The edict received and its additional records, as well as the gifts, have all been passed on already."

Ch'oe Sach'u was appointed Vice-minister of Personnel and Assistant Executive in Political Affairs; Kim Sŏnsŏk was appointed Commissioner of the Security Council; Hwang Chongŭi 黃宗懿 was made Administrator of the Security Council; Hwang Yŏng 黃瑩 was made Vice-minister of

59 South of modern Qiqihar, Heilongjiang Province. *Liaoshi* 37, 503.

Rites, and Associate Administrator of the Security Council. The king made Vice-commissioner for the Hwangju Shepherdship 黃州牧[60] Yi Wi 李瑋 as Second Assistant Office Chief at the Department of Ministries. The king highly esteemed Yi Wi's uprightness and diligence, and his concern for the people. Even though his term had not yet finished, he was thus recalled and given this new office.

Sukchong , Great King Enlightening Filial Piety (1)

His given name was Ong 顒 and his courtesy name Sanggo 常古; his original given name was Hŭi 熙. He was a younger half-brother of Sŏnjong, and was born on *sach'uk* day [the 28th] of the seventh month of the eighth, *kabo*, year of Munjong [1054]. From a young age he showed his intelligence and when he became adult he was filial and respectful, diligent and frugal; he was also brave, upright, and decisive. He widely perused the *Five Classics*, the works of various schools of thought, and the histories. Munjong loved him and frequently said "the one who will later revive this dynasty is you!" In the ninth year of Sŏnjong he was accompanying the king to the Western Capital when a purple vapor rose above his tent; those who witnessed it saw it as a sign of his kinghood. He was on the throne for ten years and lived to the age of fifty-two.

Sukchong First year [1096]

Third year of the Shaosheng era of Song, second year of the Shoulong era of Liao

Spring, first month. The Eastern Jurchen Afuhan 阿夫漢, Gaolankun 高闌昆, Doumen, and others, 179 people in all, came to present local products.

A decree read: "I look up to and model myself on previous kings; I wish to practice frugality and virtue, and will reduce expenses for food and drink and not indulge in any private hobbies. Recently however I heard that across the

---

60 Located in modern Hwangju, Hwanghae Province.

country it has become customary to show of luxury and indulgence without restraint; going to excess in food and drink, the number of cups and dishes is excessive, so that customs have become decadent. This greatly pains me. Henceforth strict limits will be set and the Censorate will inspect their observance."

The king's birthday was called the Festival of Great Primordial (Taewŏnjŏl 大元節).

Second month. The king dispatched U Wŏllyŏng 禹元齡 to Liao to give thanks for the congratulations on the previous king's birthday. The memorial read: "Recalling the birthday of a vassal, you dispatched a Chinese envoy to bestow gracious blessings. Your gracious edict has already been received; in principle it should certainly be received and greeted in person, but weakened by disease [the previous king] could not receive it in person. Your subject has provisionally taken charge of this territory and received great grace instead. The edict and its attachments that we received have already been passed on [to the previous king]."

The previous king stated in his memorial: "Your servant early on contracted a serious disease and there is little hope that it will be cured. The weighty task of governing this vassal country definitely cannot be left vacant for even a moment, and I also do not dare to be remiss in the regular offering of tribute. Thus I took the liberty of recommending my uncle to the court and then entrusted state authority to him. I retired from the world and went to live in a residence separate from the palace. In my weakened and anemic state, all I could do was lie down the whole time by the side of the water. My soul, hovering between life and death, was already among the highest mountain tops; in such grave danger, how could I harbor any hope of getting better? Recently I heard that an official letter arrived, and I was appraised of the emperor's words bestowed on me. Hearing that I have been reprieved of both the special rite of laying off the mourning clothes and the lavish rite of investiture, this accords with what I had wished for. Moreover, I was told in advance of the fact that you exceptionally granted the privilege of promulgating a birthday edict; considering that I am not far away from breathing my last, there is no way to repay this grace even in the slightest. How then can I in such state receive this favor? Prostrating myself, I beg that you refrain from your kind compassion and rescind the edict with your considerate words; refrain from sending an envoy to me and then this disease-ridden body of mine will be eternally released from this burden."

The previous king requested to leave the palace and resided in the Hŭngsŏng Palace 興盛宮. The king granted this.

The Western Jurchen Aluohuo 阿羅火 and others came to court.

Third month. The Censorate made the following request: "The treasonous minister Yi Chaŭi and others privately amassed a vast quantity of grains; this was all extorted from the people. We request that it be all confiscated by the officials." The king agreed.

The king dispatched Ko Minik 高民翼[61] to Liao as Envoy in Charge of Ritual.

Kim Posin 金輔臣 and twenty-nine others passed the composition test of the civil service examination, four passed the classics examination, and four passed by royal grace.

Summer, fourth month. The king went to Sŏnjŏng Hall for an audience which lasted till sunset. The Royal Secretariat petitioned: "Although it is the time of growing and nurturing of the myriad things, since the third month the seasons seem to have gone awry: water froze, and frost damaged the crops. At night there was thunder and lightning. According to the commentary on the "five phases" in the "Great Plan" [chapter of the *Book of Documents*],[62] "Hail is a sign of the yin force threatening the yang." And according to the Jing Fang commentary on the *Book of Changes*,[63] "If death sentences and punishments do not accord with principle, the calamity of frost will appear." Also, it says, "If the ruler is partial in adjudicating those below, there will

61 Note the different spelling from the Ko Minik mentioned in the fifth month of 1084; this is likely one and the same person.

62 It is not clear from which commentarial text this is drawn. There is no statement to this effect in the Great Plan (Hong fan) chapter, which does however discuss the five phases.

63 Kyŏng Pang yŏk 京房易: Jing Fang (77–37 BCE) created a new sequence of hexagrams, hence with new meanings imbued in them.

be a loss of trust, and it will be impossible to avert danger or obtain benefit. Mistakes will be made in emergencies. The punishment [from Heaven] for this is permanent cold." Furthermore, "If troops are raised and people are wantonly killed, this is called 'destroying the law.' The ensuing calamity is frost, which will kill the grains even in summer." At the time when the young ruler was bedridden, he was not muddled in his decisions. The queen mother usurped power, but caving in to temptation she was partial in her ruling. This gave evil people the chance to plan rebellion. As a result many were sentenced and the faction [of traitors] was removed completely. However, without being able to account for the complexity of the situation, undoubtedly many were unjustly implicated. Thus their resentful spirits fill heaven and earth and turn the harmonious energy into natural disasters. Prostrate, we venture that by according with the mandate of Heaven, Your Majesty has succeeded the authority and put the myriad affairs in order. We humbly request that the Censorate and the Ministry of Punishments be ordered to investigate the facts of all doubtful imprisonments and make decisions where sentences are pending. If this is quickly and correctly resolved, there will be no excessive resentment. All those who have made accusations that turn out to be false should themselves be prosecuted. If Heaven's warning is answered in this way, the people's hearts will be gladdened, and the calamities will transform into blessings." The king accepted this advice.

The king went to Hyŏn-nŭng and Kyŏng-nŭng Tombs.

Fifth month. The Envoy in Charge of Ritual from the Eastern Capital of Liao, Vice-commissioner of Foreign Relations Gao Liangding 高良定, arrived.

Sixth month. Kyŏngjong's spirit tablet was moved from the Ancestral Shrine to Yŏng-nŭng 榮陵, [his tomb]; Sŏnjong's spirit tablet was enshrined in the Ancestral Shrine.

The Commissioner for the Local Navy Command of Chinmyŏng 鎭溟[64] and Administrative Assistant to the Defense Commissioner of Munju, Yi

64 Located southeast of modern Wŏnsan, South Hamgyŏng Province.

Sunhye 李順蹊 and others engaged in a battle with pirates and beheaded seventeen of them.

The Eastern Jurchen Yingsun 英孫 and others, seventeen people in all, came to court.

The king took a boat trip on the Eastern Pond and held a drinking party. He summoned the state councilors and close officials for a banquet and composed poetry with them till deep into the night; when it started to thunder and rain, the party was ended.

The king requested that marriage between merit subjects and the royal family be forbidden.[65]

Autumn, seventh month. The king went to Mundŏk Hall and perused the documents and books that had been secretly stored there for generations. He selected those that were complete and distributed them for storage in Mundŏk Hall, Changnyŏng Hall 長齡殿, and the repositories for royal writings. He also bestowed copies on state councilors of the Chancellery and the Security Council, as well as on drafters of edicts and decrees, historians, and literary officials among the palace attendants, according to rank.

Eighth month. The king gave a banquet for the state elders in the Eastern Pavilion 東閣. The elderly were seated to the right and the left in the Tongnak Pavilions 同樂亭. The king introduced the officials and himself urged everyone [to eat]. He then also bestowed robes, gifts, and silk according to rank.

The Eastern Jurchen Wotu 臥突, Yigu 乙古, Mayao 馬要, and others arrived. The king paid them a visit and inquired about affairs in the border lands. He bestowed wine and drinks, and also silk.

The king went to Kwiryŏng Pavilion 龜齡閣 to personally inspect the equestrian and archery skills of military officials of the rank of general and below. These [royal inspections] continued till the eleventh month.

Kim Wije 金謂磾, who had a position equivalent to Assistant at the Office of Regalia, submitted a letter to the throne, in which he requested moving the capital to the Southern Capital, the gist of which is as follows: "According to

65 Kongch'in 功親: It is not clear what this term means, hence this is a tentative translation.

the *Tosŏn ki* 道詵記 [Record of Tosŏn], 'the land of Koryŏ has three capitals: Song'ak is the Middle Capital, Mongmyŏgyang[66] is the Southern Capital, and Pyongyang is the Western Capital. During the eleventh, twelfth, first, and second months [the king should] reside in the Middle Capital; during the third, fourth, fifth, and sixth months, in the Southern Capital; and during the seventh, eighth, ninth, and tenth months, in the Western Capital. If he does so, then the thirty-six countries will flock to the Son of Heaven.' It also says 'more than 160 years after the founding of the country, Mongmyŏgyang should be the capital.' Your subject thinks that now is the time to inspect and temporarily reside in the new capital. Now the country has a Middle Capital and a Western Capital, yet the Southern Capital is still lacking. Prostrating myself, I venture the hope that a capital will be established south of Samgak-san on the plain north of Mongmyŏk, and that you will go there on a tour at the designated time." The astrologer Mun Sang 文象 endorsed these words.

Ninth month. Junior Vice-director of the Department of Ministries and Assistant Executive in Political Affairs Pak Illyang died. Pak Illyang was famed for his beautiful prose. During the Xining era [1068–1077] he was sent as an envoy to Song together with Kim Kŭn 金覲. His epistles, memorials, and encomia were all praised by the Song people, who even published the poems and prose of the two gentlemen in a collection called *Xiaohuaji* 小華集 [Collection from the Little China]. When the Liao wanted to push the boundary south beyond the Amnok River, Pak Illyang composed a memorial to express his feelings: "Generally, of what is Below Heaven, there is nothing that is not the king's land and nobody who is not the king's subject; for this small morsel of land, what need is there to speak of 'my land' or 'my jurisdiction?'" He also wrote, "Just as the 'Return of our former land on the north bank of the Wen River,'[67] if you put at ease and comfort

---

66 Mongmyŏgyang 木覓壤: The term Mongmyŏk occurred earlier as the name of a shrine in Pyongyang (see third year of Hyŏnjong [1012], twelfth month), so this appears to be the name of a deity, possibly the mountain god.

67 A phrase drawn from the *Zuo Commentary*, 8th year of Lord Cheng (583 BCE): see Durrant, Lee, and Schaberg, *Zuo Tradition*, 768–769. Here Lu resisted Jin's demand to return the land north of the Wen River to Qi, its allied state. Clearly Pak Illyang cites this with the understanding that Lu's claims are legitimate.

our cities, like [King Ding of] Changsha who danced clumsily because of his small fief,[68] we will dance for joy at this splendid turn." The Liao emperor upon reading this stopped the deliberations. He was posthumously given the title Munyŏl 文烈.

The T'angna Star-leader dispatched someone to congratulate the king on his accession.

There were lectures on the *Humane Kings Sūtra* at Hoegyŏng Hall for three days, and ten thousand monks were fed.

Winter, tenth month. The king sent an envoy to Director of the Chancellery So T'aebo with an appointment certificate, and at the same time to bestow gold and silver utensils, robes, brocade, cloth and silk, a saddle, music books, and flower wine and then gave a banquet in his house.

The king went to the shooting pavilion near the Eastern Pond and summoned vice-director of the Department of Ministries Hwang Chungbo and others. He gave them bows and arrows and had them practice. Vice censor-in-chief Kim Kyŏngyong 金景庸 was the first to hit the bull's eye. The king gave him five silver plates and a horse from the royal stable. All the others who hit the bull's eye were also given presents.

The Song merchant Hong Fu 洪輔 and others, thirty people in all, came to present local products.

The king dispatched O Yŏnch'ong 吳延寵 to Liao to congratulate the emperor on the Heavenly Peace festival.

Eleventh month. The kind dispatched So Ch'ung to Liao to present tribute and Paek Kasin 白可臣 to give new year's felicitations.

Twelfth month. Liao dispatched Li Weixin 李惟信 to congratulate the previous king on his birthday.

An edict read: "According to the old regulations, all officials and clerks

68 This refers to an anecdote about King Ding 定王 of Changsha, a small fief of the Han dynasty. When Emperor Jing of Han (157–141 BCE) invited his liege barons to court and asked them to dance, King Ding danced clumsily, his sleeves too long so that his hands could not emerge; when asked about this, he replied that his territory was so small that there was barely space to turn around; the king then granted him more land. From the *Taiping yulan* 150, "Huangqin bu di 16" 皇親部第16.

should determine court cases within five days for small affairs, within ten days for medium cases, and within twenty days for heave cases. For crimes punishable by banishment and above, it is thirty days. These deadlines have already been clearly determined, so make sure that all government organs, both in the center and in the provinces, are aware of this fact and that they do implement the rules."

Sukchong Second year [1097]

Fourth year of the Shaosheng era of Song, third year of the Shoulong era of Liao

Spring, first month. Liao dispatched as ad-hoc envoy the Defense Commissioner for the Haizhou 海州[69] jurisdiction Yelü Kuo 耶律括 with the following edict for the previous king: "You have from early on supported the vassal country and respectfully submitted tribute; suffering disease from young age you have requested time for convalescence; officials have investigated the law codes, and as we have bestowed a favor on you every other year, my concern is still called for. It is fitting that you accept my concern. Herewith I bestow on you robes, silk, a saddle, bow and arrows, and other gifts."

Second month. The Eastern Jurchen Wotu 臥突 came to court.

Kukch'ŏng-sa was completed. The king went there in person to hold the ritual of completion, and summoned the retired Director of the Chancellery Yi Chŏnggong and State Councilors of the Chancellery and Security Council for a banquet.

Intercalary [second] month, *kapchin* day [the 19th]. The previous king died in Hŭngsŏng Palace. He was given the posthumous title of Hoesang 懷殤.

The Eastern Jurchen Woying 臥英 and others, seven people altogether, came to court.

Third month, *kyŏngsin* day [the 6th]. [The previous king] was buried in Ŭn-nŭng 隱陵 Tomb. A letter was dispatched to the Eastern Capital of Liao,

69 Corresponding to modern Haicheng city, Liaoning Province. See *Liaoshi* 38, 524.

saying "From the moment he retired [from governing] and resided in his private residence, the previous king's disease grew worse by the day, and on the nineteenth of the intercalary [second] month he passed away. Now the funeral has already been completed. In his testamentary injunction the previous king said: 'the other day I requested to be released from my duties, and fortunately I received an edict that allowed me to retire and convalesce during the time that remained for me. Recently my disease grew worse, and there will be certainly no way to prolong my life. As for my funeral, it should be held as frugally as possible; there should be no report to the suzerain country so as not to trouble them needlessly.' In accordance with the late king's wishes we did not dare to send an envoy to report our bereavement." After Yejong became king, he changed the posthumous title to Kongsang 恭殤 and bestowed the temple name Hŏnjong 獻宗.

Ch'oe Sach'u was appointed Executive Chief of the Royal Secretariat and Minister of Punishments, and concurrently Commissioner to the Resident Governor of the Western Capital; Kim Sŏnsŏk was appointed Vice-director of the Department of Ministries and Minister of Taxation; Hwang Yŏng was made Assistant Executive in Political Affairs; Im Kan 林幹 was made Administrator of the Security Council and Administrator of the Finance Commission.

Summer, fourth month. The king went to Sangch'un Pavilion and there displayed the poem "Rewarding the flowers" written by himself. He made the scholars of various offices present matching poems, and then graded them himself, giving silk as reward, according to rank.

Im Wŏnt'ong 林元通 and thirty-two others passed the composition test of the civil service examination, four passed the classics examination, and four passed by royal grace. Among those who qualified, Kim Puch'ŏl 金富轍 ranked fifth. His older brothers Kim Pup'il, Kim Puil 金富佾, and Kim Pusik 金富軾 had already passed the civil service examination before him. According to the old system, if three sons passed the examination, their mother would be rewarded with an annual gift of thirty *sŏk* of grain from the Great Granary. To this the king added an additional ten *sŏk*, and this would become an established practice.

Fifth month. The custom of greeting for functionaries and clerks of the capital and the provinces was determined.

Sixth month. The king went to Pong'ŭn-sa. Henceforth he visited temples frequently.

Director of the Chancellery Yi Chŏnggong presented the text of the Hŭngwang-sa stele that he had composed. The king bestowed an edict of encouragement and also gifted silk, silver vessels, tea, cloth, a saddle, and other presents.

The Song merchant Shen Huan 愼奐 and others, thirty-six people in total, arrived.

Song returned three of our castaways, including one called Chasin 子信. Originally twenty people had sailed from T'amna but when they drifted into the Country of Naked people[70] they were killed; only these three managed to escape and entrusted themselves to Song, which then returned them.

Autumn, seventh month. Ten Eastern Jurchen pirate ships attacked Chinmyŏng County. The Military Commissioner for the Northeastern Sector, Kim Hanch'ung 金漢忠, dispatched his administrative assistant Kang Chŭng 康拯 to battle with them. He vanquished them and seized three ships, executing forty-eight. The king bestowed on Kim Hanch'ung and Kang Chŭng silver, silk, tea, and medicine.

Eighth month. Kim Sŏnsŏk was appointed Executive Chief of the Royal Secretariat; Im Kan was appointed Commissioner of the Security Council and Vice-director of the Department of Ministries.

The Eastern Jurchen Weiying 未應 and others, twenty-four people in all, came to court.

On the *chŏngmi* day [the 26th] a comet was seen between the Root and Room Stars.[71]

---

70 Naguk 躶國: literally "naked country." Usually appears in works of fiction; perhaps it is a reference to a locality where people stripped to the waist.

71 *Chŏsŏng* 氐星: third of the twenty-eight traditional Chinese constellations (lunar mansions), with Libra as the determinative star; *pangsŏng* 房星: fourth of the twenty-eight traditional Chinese constellations, with Scorpio as the determinative star.

Ninth month. The Eastern Jurchen Shahaoluo 沙好羅 and others, twenty-three people in all, came to court.

A Hundred-Seat Assembly was held in Hoegyŏng Hall, and 10,000 monks were fed.

Winter, tenth month. The Eastern Jurchen Lingbo 令波, Afu 阿夫, and others, fifty people in all, came to court.

The king dispatched An In'gam 安仁鑑 to Liao to congratulate the emperor on the Heavenly Peace Festival and Ryu T'aek 柳澤 to give thanks for the ad-hoc embassy.

Eleventh month. The king dispatched Yu Yu'u 庾惟祐 to Liao to give thanks for the birthday felicitations for the previous king, P'il Kongch'an 畢公贊 to offer tribute, and Pak Yumun 朴有文 to give felicitations for the new year.

Twelfth month. Liao dispatched Military Governor of the Linhai Army 臨海軍[72] Yelü Siqi 耶律思齊 and Chamberlain for the Royal Stud Li Xiang 李湘 to invest the king as Specially Advanced Acting Grand Marshal, and concurrently Royal Secretary, Supreme Pillar of State, King of Koryŏ with a Stipend Village of 1,000 households, 700 of which were effective. The emperor also bestowed a jade tablet, mace, seal, crown, palanquin, robes, a saddle, silk, and other presents. The king accepted the investiture in the southern suburbs.

An edict read: "From old the customs of our country are simple and plain, but from the reign of Munjong onwards cultural products, rites, and music have flourished in this land. I have succeeded to the previous kings, and will endeavor to make the people prosperous. An Office for Casting Coinage should be created so that [coins] can circulate widely among the people."

---

72 Based in Jinzhou 錦州 (modern Jinzhou, Liaoning Province), pertaining to the Central Capital. *Liaoshi* 39, 552.

Sukchong Third year [1098]

First year of the Yuanfu era of Song, fourth year of the Shoulong era of Liao

Spring, first month. An edict read: "This insignificant person has succeeded to the project of my ancestors; barely having had the time to settle into this great plan, the great Liao dispatched an envoy especially to invest and honor me [as king]. It is fitting that the delightful presents received should be distributed, and that a response should be drafted to the emperor's beautiful edict. From the officials who received the edict on the day of investiture to the officials who conducted the ritual when walking up the altar and the officials who received and accompanied the visiting [Liao] envoys, all should be promoted by one rank.[73] As for those who were punished for infractions [against ritual propriety] should be pardoned. Soldiers should be given presents according to rank."

Second month. The Eastern Jurchen Changkun 昌昆 and others came to court.

Third month. The king visited Ch'ang-nŭng and Tae-nŭng Tombs.[74]

The Office of the Heir Apparent was established and officials were assigned to it.

The Eastern Jurchen Yaozhen 要眞 and others came to court.

Summer, fourth month. The Eastern Jurchen Gudou 古豆 and others came to court.

Yi Tŏkku 李德久 and twenty-six others passed the composition test of the civil service examination, three passed the classics examination, and five passed by royal grace.

The king went to Hŭngwang-sa and gave food to 3,000 monks.

Autumn, seventh month. The king dispatched Yun Kwan and Cho Kyu 趙珪 to Song to inform them of his accession and to present local products.

Winter, tenth month. The king led all his officials to conduct the triennial

---

73 Literally the text says that they were "given office/office rank" (賜爵一級) so it might also mean that these were non-ranking officials who were given the lowest office rank (9B).

74 The first was for Sejo, the second for Queen Dowager Inye.

joint sacrifice for all the royal spirit tablets[75] in the Ancestral Shrine. On the way back he went to the Sinbong Gate and declared an amnesty. He also granted all descendants of kings without office one office rank. To the office managers at the ritual and to the guards and clerks of the Ancestral Shrine and the Nine Tombs he also granted one office rank. To all the prefectures, districts, and counties [surrounding the tombs] he halved this year's taxes. Those presented scholars and classics scholars who had fallen into army service were exempted.

The king dispatched Administrator of the Security Council Kim Yong 金庸 and Executive at the Ministry of Ritual Cho Yanghyu 曹揚休 to Liao to give thanks for the investiture.

The Ministry of Punishments reported: "The prisons are empty." The state councilors sent memorials of congratulation.

The king dispatched Kim Yakch'ung 金若冲 to Liao to congratulate the emperor on the Heavenly Peace Festival.

Eleventh month. The Song merchant Hong Bao 洪保 and others, twenty people in total, arrived.

The king dispatched Wang Ha 王嘏 and Yun Kyehyŏng 尹繼衡 to Liao to present tribute and Chang Yŏng 蔣寧 to give felicitations for the new year.

Twelfth month. Liao dispatched Senior Policy Critic Lai Gaofu[76] to congratulate the king on his birthday.

The king invested his son Wang P'il 王佖 as Acting Grand Guardian, Probationary Grand Marshal, concurrently Director of the Department of Ministries, Marquis of Sangdang 上黨侯.

---

75 Hyŏphyang 祫享: A memorial ritual held every three years in which the king gathers the tablets of all deceased kings in the shrine for T'aejo.

76 Although this appears to be a name, 來告符 literally means "coming to announce a sign."

Sukchong Fourth year [1099]

Second year of the Yuanfu era of Song, fifth year of the Shoulong era of Liao

Spring, second month. Kim Sanggi was appointed Probationary Grand Mentor; Hwang Yŏng was appointed Executive at the Royal Secretariat and jointly Executive at the Royal Secretariat-Chancellery; Cho Inch'ung 趙藺忠 was appointed Probationary Minister of Works, Vice-director of the Department of Ministries.

A Song edict allowed [Koryŏ] exam takers to [take part in] the guest examination.[77]

Third month. The Princess of the Yŏndŏk Palace 延德宮主, née Ryu 柳, was invested as royal consort.

Summer, fourth month. The king went to Gossamer Tower 紗樓 and ordered the literary officials to compose prose poems and poems, and granted them silk according to rank.

The ad-hoc envoy dispatched by Liao, the Surveillance Commissioner for the Ningzhou 寧州[78] jurisdiction Xiao Lang 蕭朗, arrived, also bestowing a Buddhist canon.

The king went to Yŏnyŏng Hall to inspect the royal writing stored there.

Fifth month. Retired Director of the Chancellery Yi Chŏnggong died.

Autumn, seventh month. Song returned Cho Sŏm 趙暹 and others, six people in total, from our T'angna who had suffered shipwreck.

Ninth month. The king ordered the state councilors and astrologers to debate the founding of a Southern Capital in Yangju 楊州.[79]

The Envoy in Charge of Ritual, So Sasŏk 邵師奭, went to the Eastern Capital of Liao.

On *chŏngmyo* day [the 28th] the king together with his consort and eldest son went to Samgak-san. In the intercalary [ninth] month they arrived in

---

77 Bingong 賓貢: During the Tang Dynasty, foreigners were allowed to take part in the first stage of the Chinese civil service examination.

78 Located in the area of modern Wafangdian city, on the Liaodong Peninsula, Liaoning Province. *Liaoshi* 38, 537.

79 Corresponding to the area of modern Seoul.

Yangju and inspected the site for establishing the capital.

The king dispatched Mun Kwan 文冠 to Liao to offer congratulations to the emperor on the Heavenly Peace Festival.

Winter, tenth month. On *kyemyo* day [the 5th] the king returned from Samgak-san and declared an amnesty.

The king dispatched Mun Ik 文翼 to Liao to request an edict of investiture for his oldest son, Yi Su 李壽 to give thanks for the felicitations for the king's birthday, Han I 韓彝 to present local products, and Cho Sinjun 趙臣俊 to offer felicitations for the new year.

The Eastern Jurchen Alaohuo 阿老火 and others, twenty-six people in all, came to court.

Eleventh month. The Duke of Puyŏ, Wang Su, was banished to Yangmok Prefecture 若木郡.[80]

Twelfth month. Liao Dispatched Da Shu 大淑 to congratulate the king on his birthday.

The Returning the Courtesy Envoy of the Eastern Capital of Liao, Da Yi 大義, arrived.

Sukchong Fifth year [1100]

Third year of the Yuanfu era of Song, sixth year of the Shoulong era of Liao

Spring, first month. The Eastern Jurchen General Biaoyunai 表於乃 and others, sixty people in all, arrived at court.

The king's oldest son Wang U 王俁, was invested as heir apparent.

Second month. The king went to Sinbong Tower and declared an amnesty. Civil and Military officials of both capitals were promoted by one rank; officials of the Palace of the Heir Apparent were promoted by two ranks. Greater prefectures, prefectures, districts, and counties all had their cloth tax for the year reduced by half.

The king went to Changwŏn Pavilion 長源亭.

---

80 Located in the area of modern Ch'ilgok-kun, west of Taegu.

Third month. Ch'oe Sach'u was appointed Executive Chief of the Chancellery.

Summer, fourth month, *chŏngyu* day, the first day of the month. There was a solar eclipse.

Han Suktan 韓淑旦 and thirty-five others passed the composition test of the civil service examination, three passed the classics examination, and six passed by royal grace.

Mingzhou in Song sent a letter to report that the emperor had died. The king wanted to pray for the deceased emperor in Taean-sa 大安寺, but the remonstrance officials insisted it should not be done, so the king desisted.

Liao dispatched Vice-director of the Palace Library Zhang Chenyan 張臣言 to transmit the edict of investiture for the king's oldest son. He also bestowed robes, bolts of silk, silver, plain silk, and other gifts.

Sixth month. The king dispatched Vice-minister Im Ŭi and Executive Paek Kasin to Song to offer condolences.

Autumn, seventh month. The king dispatched Vice-minister Wang Ha and Executive O Yŏnch'ong to Song to congratulate the [new emperor] on his enthronement.

Ninth month. The king dispatched Office Chief at the Ministry of Rites Yi Chae 李載 to Liao to give thanks for the edict. Originally, the Liao envoy Wang E 王蕚 had seen a small bell at Hŭngwang-sa and expressed his admiration: "How beautiful! We have nothing like this in our country." [Wang] Hu[81] then told Wang E: "I heard that your emperor reveres Buddhism. Please let us present this bell as a present." Wang E expressed his approval, and Wang Hu then requested permission from the king to cast two golden bells to be presented to the Liao emperor. Eventually the Clerk for all Purposes 孔目官 Yi Pok 李復 was sent together with Yi Chae to report their intention. Liao judged that Wang E had overstepped his authority of envoy by asking for a gift and punished him severely, and did not allow for the bells to be presented. When the envoys returned to Koryŏ, the Ministry of Punishments requested that Yi Pok be punished for his crime, and Yi Chae

81 I.e. the monk Ŭich'ŏn (1055–1101); see above.

too for failing to stop him. Both were relieved of their office.

Winter, tenth month. Liao dispatched the Surveillance Commissioner for the Gaozhou jurisdiction, Xiao Haogu 蕭好古, and Director of the Office of Regalia, Gao Shining 高士寧, to invest the heir apparent as Military Governor of the Obedient Righteousness Army; Surveillance and Supervisory Commissioner for Sakchu 朔州,[82] Muju 武州,[83] and other prefectures; Grand Master of Splendid Happiness, Acting Grand Mentor and jointly Commissioner to the Executive of the Royal Secretariat-Chancellery; Roving Prefect of Sakchu Commissioned with Extraordinary Powers for all Military Affairs in Sakchu; Supreme Pillar of State; Duke of the Three Han States, with a stipend village of 3,000 households, 500 households effective.[84] They also bestowed seal and cord, palanquin, robes and belt, bolts of silk, saddle, bow and arrows, and other gifts. The king and the heir apparent went to the southern suburbs to receive the investiture.

The king dispatched Pak Ho 朴浩 to Khitan to congratulate the emperor on the Heavenly Peace Festival.

Eleventh month. The king dispatched Kim Husŏn 金侯善 to Liao to give thanks for the birthday felicitations to the king.

Song merchants, T'angna people, Jurchens, and others came to present local products.

The king dispatched Kim Kwinyŏn 金龜年 to Liao to give thanks for grace bestowed, Hyŏngnyŏn Chŏng 赫連挺[85] to present local products, and Ch'oe Sŏnwi 崔善緯 to give felicitations for the new year.

Twelfth month. Liao dispatched Chamberlain for the Royal Stud Wang Zhizhong 王執中 to congratulate the king on his birthday.

---

82 Modern Sakchu, North P'yŏngan Province.

83 Modern Kwangju, South Chŏlla Province.

84 This is virtually the same title as the one bestowed on the future King Sunjong in 1057. See *Koryŏsa chŏryo* [hereafter KRSC] Ia, 384. Minor corrections have been applied.

85 He is known as the author of the *Kyunyŏ-jŏn*, a biography of the Hwaŏm monk Kyunyŏ (923–973); this is one of the rare occasions that we have writings of an official mentioned in the early volumes of the *Koryŏsa chŏryo*. See Adrian Buzo and Tony Prince, *Kyunyŏ-jŏn: The Life, Times and Songs of a Tenth Century Korean Monk* (Broadway: Wild Peony, 1993).

Sukchong Sixth year [1101]

First year of the Jianzhong era of Huizong of Song, first year of the Qiantong era of Emperor Tianzuo of Liao

Spring, first month. It was decreed that one copy each of the Nine Classics, the philosophers' works, and the histories be deposited at the Censorate, the Departments, and the Security Council.

The heir apparent's birthday was designated as Ch'angnyŏng 昌寧 festival.

The Eastern Jurchen Yuluofo 余羅弗, Shawen 沙溫, and others, seventy-five people in all, came to present local products.

The Envoy in Charge of Ritual from the Eastern Capital of Liao, Vice-commissioner of Foreign Relations 禮賓副使 Gao Keshao 高克少, arrived.

Shao Gui 邵珪, Lu Tingjun 陸廷俊, and Liu Ji 劉伋 from Song submitted themselves. The king summoned them to be tested in Mundŏk Hall and then conferred offices of the eighth rank on them. On Lu Tingjun he conferred the personal name Chŏnggŏl 廷傑.

The wife of the Registrar 主簿 Yi Kyŏngt'aek 李景澤, née Kim, wanted to murder her husband's stepmother. Secretly she made a female slave put poison in her food and presented it to her. The mother knew it and alerted the Censorate. Lady Kim did not confess, so the Censorate requested that she be interrogated with more severe torture. The king said, "It is already clear that she committed the crime so proceed with the sentencing." Since Lady Kim was an affinal relative of a previous king, the death sentence was commuted to banishment to Ansan County 安山縣.[86] Yi Kyŏngt'aek died in prison.

The Ministry of Punishments reported: "Cho Chunmyŏng 趙俊明, who has a position equivalent to registrar, lost his father four years ago, yet he does not look after his mother and does not care for his siblings, who as a result have all lost their residence. We request that he be dealt with according to the law." The king said "In governing I put filial piety and brotherly love in first place. How can there be such a person! Do as you suggest."

Second month. The Eastern Jurchen General "Seeking Refuge in Virtue"

[86] Modern Ansan, Kyŏnggi Province.

Fuma 甫馬 and others, fifty people in all, requested to come to court. This was allowed.

The Eastern Jurchen General Leader, Guaifu 怪夫, and others, thirty people in all, came to court.

The retired Assistant Executive in Political Affairs Sin Su 愼脩 died. He was originally from Song China, and had considerable academic knowledge. He excelled in medicine.

An edict allowed those sentenced because of their association with the traitor Yi Chaŭi to stay in a less remote place of banishment.

It was decreed that officials posted to local offices and their clerks should receive their local salary (*ŭmnok* 邑祿) from land rents allocated for official use.

Third month. It was decreed that since the documents and prints that had been piled up in the Palace Library had become damaged, an airing platform[87] was to be installed in the National Academy, where they were to be transferred to so that they could be widely copied and printed.

To avoid a taboo on the Liao emperor's name, the king changed his given name to Ong 顒, and reported this to the Ancestral Shrine and the Eight Tombs. The officials presented their felicitation letters.

Liao dispatched Acting Junior Policy Advisor Yelü Gu 耶律轂 to announce the demise of the emperor.

Summer, fourth month, *sinmyo* day, the first day of the month. There was a solar eclipse.

The National Academy reported: "On side corridors of the Hall for King Munsŏng [i.e., Confucius] paintings have been made of the sixty-one [known] disciples [of Confucius] and the twenty-one worthies. We request that your majesty take part in the annual sacrifice at the shrine." The king agreed to this.

The Censorate petitioned: "After the Envoy to Announce the Mourning

87 P'o 鋪: to spread, to display [as in a shop]. Either because of water or mold damage, or because they had not been properly stored, books and paper documents had to be spread out regularly in sunlight to dry.

from Liao had transmitted the edict, he went to the banquet still wearing the black shirt and cap, which is against propriety. We request that the reception clerks be punished for this." The king said "This is the fault of the envoy; what could the reception clerks have done about this?" and did not heed this advice. The Censorate also reported "The Master of Divination at the Bureau of Astronomy 司天卜正, Ryu Nokch'un 柳祿春, made a mistake in reporting the time of a solar eclipse, so we request that he be sentenced according to the law." The king agreed.

An edict stipulated that the Disaster Relief Store[88] should assist those people who had fallen into poverty and had no way of sustaining themselves until the time of the ripening of the barley.

The heretic monk Kakchin 覺眞 from P'yŏngju 平州[89] gave false divinations that deceived the people. An edict ordered him to be banished to Kokchu 谷州.[90]

The king dispatched Vice-director of the Palace Treasury 大府小卿 Wang Kongyun 王公胤 and Audience Commissioner No Chakkong 魯作公 to Liao to offer condolences and assist in the funeral.

The Hallim Academy petitioned: "Please have the Department of the Palace Library 秘書省 carve a list of characters rhyming with your majesty's name to be widely promulgated so that the people will know how to avoid using the character for your name." The king followed this advice.

A group of ministers sent the following letter to the throne: "The pine beetles are proliferating yet rituals of suppression have no effect. Respectfully we invoke the words of the Jing Fang commentary on the *Book of Changes*, which says 'Insects manifested by Heaven that eat green do not aid the sagely transformation.' We have no right to needlessly worry Your Highness. We wish that you promote the wise and demote the unworthy so as to respond to Heaven's censure." The king did not reply.

---

88 Chewi-p'o 濟危鋪: this is the first occurrence of this term; it occurs three more times in the *Koryŏsa chŏryo*, but without any details on its functioning.

89 Modern P'yŏngsan, Hwanghae Province.

90 Modern Koksan, Hwanghae Province.

The king ordered Pot'ong-wŏn 普通院 in Imjin County 臨津縣[91] to provide for travelers over the next three months.

The king travelled to Irwŏl-sa 日月寺 for the completion ceremony of a gold-letter *Lotus Sūtra*. Once the ceremony was finished, the king went to a hill behind the temple to have wine and music together with the queen and heir apparent. The Censorate protested "This is the busiest time in the agricultural calendar, yet the drought threatens to wreak havoc. If you enjoy a wine party here, the people will think that Your Majesty has no concern for the people's worries." The king then desisted.

An edict read: "Now is the time for agriculture, but for a long time no rain has fallen from the sky. I fear that the officials and functionaries in the prefectures and districts have not understood my intention. Not relaying or twisting the words of my instructions regarding the exemption form land rent and taxation, they have prevented the people from reaping the benefits. Some feel wrongly imprisoned or have been languishing in prison for a long time without their case having been resolved. The corpses and bones of those who died of hunger have been discarded and not buried. Furthermore, the taxes collected for official and private purposes are onerous, making the people resentful and leading to feelings of disharmony. Officials should spread virtue and benefice and forbid what is against the law. They should investigate all cases of imprisonment, and give proper burial to all human remains, thus responding to Heaven's censure."

The Jurchen carpet maker Gushemao 古舍毛 and others, six people in all, came to submit. The king granted fields and thatched huts and had them entered into the household registers.

Fifth month. An edict read: "Since the Changsaeng Storehouses 長生庫 have already accumulated lots of grain, they are used for loans on which interest can be collected. I have heard that after a number of years the grains go bad and the people are troubled by it. The functionaries in charge [of the storehouse] should trade it for silver or cloth to avoid this waste."[92]

---

91 Modern Changdan-myŏn, near the mouth of the Imjin River.

92 Changsaenggo 長生庫: Originally a Buddhist foundation, here it appears to be operated

The king again ordered his officials to distribute free meals to travelers at the Pot'ong-wŏn in Imjin County, until the Beginning of Autumn (*ipch'u* 立秋).

Im Ŭi and Paek Kasin returned from the Song court. The emperor had granted the book *Divine Medicine to Save the Country* (*Shenyi pujiufang* 神醫普救方), and the king received the imperial edict in Sŏnjŏng Hall. All members of the embassy had greedily engaged in trade for profit, with the exception of Im Ŭi, who remained upright and restrained. The Song people praised him for this.

Sixth month. An edict read: "Gold and silver are natural resources and the most valuable things for the country. Recently treacherous people have counterfeited [silver ingots] by alloying them with copper. Henceforth all silver ingots are to bear a stamp; this should be a permanent practice. Those who break this rule should be severely punished." This marks the beginning of using silver ingots (*ŭnbyŏng* 銀甁) as currency. They were made by shaping one *kŭn* of silver in the likeness of the country's geography. Commonly they were called "broad mouths" (*hwalgu* 闊口).[93]

Because Changyŏn County 長淵縣[94] had suffered from either floods or drought for several years, it was exempted from tax and corvée labor for three years.

Wang Ha and O Yŏnch'ong returned from Song. The emperor had bestowed on the king the *Imperial Readings from the Taiping Era*[95] in 1,000

by the Koryŏ state. It was based on the idea that temple propriety is inalienable once donated, hence it could only be used for loans; it was not to be decreased. Clearly this led to problems when the grain was stored too long, hence the edict to exchange the grain for other products of the same value.

93 Presumably they were shaped as people imagined the Korean peninsula: Remaining examples are in the shape of a gourd; perhaps the larger bottom bulb represented the southern part up to the T'aean promontory, and the smaller top bulb the promontory that is most of current South Hwanghae Province. However, the mouth of these ingots is comparatively small.

94 Modern Changyŏn-gun, Hwanghae Province.

95 *Taiping yulan* 太平御覽: A vast compendium of knowledge created during the Taiping Xingguo era (976–983). It acquired its title because Emperor Taizong (976–997) is said to have read through the whole text. The title is actually mistakenly given as *Daping yulan* 大平御覽.

fascicles. O Yŏnch'ong made the following petition to the king: "When your subject was in Song with the other members of the embassy, the hostel attendant, Drafting Advisor Xie Wenguan 謝文瓘, told us the following: 'I have heard that the king of your country loves culture. Recently cultural products from your country have become popular. Also the memorials and other writings presented by your court are excellent, and highly praised by our court.'" The king said: "For a long time my deceased father, King Munjong, sought to obtain the *Imperial Readings from the Taiping Era* but failed to do so. The *Divine Medicine to Save the Country* is a crucial work for saving the world. Now I have obtained both works; this is thanks to the ability of my envoys." To the envoy and deputy envoy as well as the assisting officials of both the embassy to congratulate the new emperor and of the embassy of condolence the king granted promotion and reward.

Im Kan was appointed Minister of Punishments; Wi Kyejŏng was made intendant for the Hallim Academy; O Sujŭng 吳壽增 was made Administrator of the Finance Commission.

It was forbidden for monks and men on the one hand, and nuns and women on the other, to mingle together in 10,000 Buddha Assemblies (Manbulhoe 萬佛會).

An edict exempted soldiers from the two capital armies from non-urgent corvée labor.

It was forbidden to donate one's house to be turned into a temple.

Autumn, eighth month. An edict read: "Since I became king, I have always tried to tread carefully. To the north we interact with the Great Liao, to the south we serve the Great Song. But in the East the Jurchen are stubbornly throwing their weight around. In the task of militarizing the country, putting the people at ease is the most crucial. Therefore all non-urgent corvée labor should be halted so as to give the people respite."

The Capital Military Command petitioned: "Now the Military Chief Administration Office of the Liao Eastern Capital has sent us a letter requesting that the garrison within the Chŏngju Pass should be removed. Earlier during the Da'an era [1085–1095] Liao wanted to establish an office and a log bridge on the Amnok River. Our court sent envoys to request them to stop construction, and the Liao emperor listened to us. Now it is also fitting that that we abide by their request." The king followed this advice.

Ninth month. The king dispatched Associate Administrator of the Security Council Kwak Sang and Senior Assistant Director of the Department of Ministries Hŏ Kyŏng 許慶 to Liao to congratulate the emperor on his accession.

The Western Jurchen Gushimao 古時毛 came to submit; he was granted fields and a house.

The king went to Ch'ongji-sa 摠持寺 to visit the sickbed of Sŏk Hu.[96] Barely ten days after this he died. Assistant Executive in Letters Yi O 李頫 argued that although Sŏk Hu was a relative of the king, as a monk however it would not be appropriate to wear mourning. However, since his talent and achievements were beyond compare, and because he was famous in both Liao and Song, it would be impossible not to wear mourning. Thereupon the king and his ministers wore black caps and plain robes, and court audiences were suspended for three days. The king also gave a lavish condolence gift.

A Humane Kings Assembly was held in Hoegyŏng Hall, the polo court, and on temples outside the capital, and 30,000 monks were fed.

The Directorate for Constructing the Southern Capital was established, and the king ordered Executive Chief of the Chancellery Ch'oe Sach'u, Censor-in-chief Im Ŭi, Administrator of Memorials Yun Kwan and others to [inspect] the features [of the terrain].

Winter, tenth month. The king went to Kwiryŏng Pavilion on the Eastern Pond and inspected the military officials' archery and horse riding skills.

The Censorate petitioned: "Patrols for catching thieves in Kyŏnggi are looting from the people, causing severe harm. We request that they be stopped." The king agreed.

The T'angna Star-leader, Lieutenant Assisting the Military Kudae 具代, was given the title of General Seaborne Strike.

Ch'oe Sach'u and others reported to the king: "We went to Nowŏn Station

---

96 I.e., Ŭich'ŏn, identified above as Wang Hu.

盧原驛, Haech'on 海村, Yongsan 龍山, and many other places to inspect the terrain but none was suitable for building a capital. Only the area south of Myŏn'ak on Samgak-san[97] has a suitable topography that accords with the old writings. We request that the capital be built on the spot where the mountains back up to the main central trunk in the north and bend towards the south. The king followed this advice.

Eleventh month. Song merchants, people from T'amna, Eastern and Northern Barbarian chiefs, and others came to present local products.

The Capital Military Command petitioned: "Districts and counties under the jurisdiction of the Eastern Capital have suffered from a severe drought and the people are afflicted by this disaster. We request that [grains from] Changsaeng Storehouse and various granaries be released. Grain that has been used outside of its normal purpose [i.e. famine relief] for public or private purposes should be reclaimed during a year of good harvests." The king agreed to this.

Twelfth month. Liao dispatched Surveillance Commissioner for the Gaozhou Jurisdiction Gao Dexin 高德信 to congratulate the king on his birthday. Chief Minister of the Court of Imperial Entertainment Wu Quan 吳佺 came to present the clothing, belt, and other presents bequeathed by Emperor Daozong 道宗.

Wi Kyejŏng was appointed Executive Chief of the Royal Secretariat, jointly Executive Chief of the Royal Secretariat-Chancellery, Pillar of State; Yi O was appointed Assistant Executive in Political Affairs and Pillar of State; O Sujŭng was appointed Vice-director of the Department of Ministries and Concurrently Advisor to the Heir Apparent; Ryu Sin was appointed Vice-minister of Rites and Associate Administrator of the Security Council, Hallim Academician Recipient of Edicts; Kim Kyŏngyong was appointed Vice-minister of War and Associate Administrator of the Security Council; Han Yŏng was made Junior Vice-director of the Department of Ministries.

---

97 三角山面嶽之南: Myŏn'ak appears to function as a place name here. It is however not clear to which localities these names refer to exactly.

Sukchong Seventh year [1102]

First year of the Chongning era of Song, second year of the Qiantong era of Liao

Spring, second month. The Western Jurchen Gaoshe 高舍 and others, eighteen people in all; and Ahaoluo 阿號羅 and others, fifteen people in all, came to present local products.

The Eastern Jurchen Andan 安旦, Fennalao 分那老, and others, eighteen people in all, came to court.

Three times Executive [Chief of the Royal Secretariat] Kim Sŏnsŏk sent a memorial to the throne requesting [permission to retire] on account of old age. The king allowed him to.

Third month. Yi O was appointed Minister of Taxation; Kwak Sang was appointed Vice-director of the Department of Ministries, Assistant Executive in Political Affairs, Concurrently Commissioner for the Resident Governor of the Western Capital.

The Finance Commission petitioned: "Because of a long-lasting drought last year, many people in various prefectures, districts, townships, and boroughs, nineteen administrative divisions within the jurisdiction of the Eastern Capital, are hungry and destitute. We request that, in accordance with the regulations, those who have lost four parts[98] or more will be exempt from land tax; those who have lost six parts or more will be exempt from land tax and local tribute; those who have lost seven parts or more will be exempt from all impositions and corvée. As for those whose [tax] has already been shipped, hear their case to decide how much has to be deducted from next year's taxes." The king followed this.

The Censorate petitioned: "The Presented Scholar from the Four Gates [School],[99] Yi Chero 李齊老, is the son of the blind monk Pŏpchong 法宗. He is not fit for applying to the civil service examinations." The king replied, "Confucius told Zhong Gong 'if the calf of a dappled ox is red and has horns,

---

98 Sabun 四分: presumably four parts out of ten is meant, i.e., forty per cent of their crops were lost.

99 Samun[hak] 四門學: A branch of the National Academy that also accepted outstanding talents from among the people besides the sons of ranked officials.

even if we decide not to use it, would the mountains and rivers discard it?'[100] For all examination courses we seek out the wisest people. If Yi Chero has talent in learning, why would we discard him on account of his father? He should be allowed to take the examination."

The Department of the Royal Secretariat-Chancellery petitioned: "For the newly constructed Southern Capital, the amount of land that has to be measured out is necessarily vast, and many people will have to be expropriated. We request that in accordance with the explanations in the *Kyŏngwiryŏng* 京緯令,[101] we sometimes follow the mountains to determine the space, and sometimes accord with the water to express the shape. First, following the mountains' forms at the center we should expand east to Taebong 大峯, south as far as Sari 沙里, west until Kibong 岐峯, and north up to Myŏn'ak as the outer border." The king agreed.

Summer, fourth month. The king ordered the Store to Save from Crisis to give food to hungry people until the Beginning of Autumn.

Kang Ch'ŏk 康滌 and thirty-two others passed the composition test of the civil service examination, three passed the classics examination, and five passed by royal grace. The king also summoned the presented scholar from Song, Chang Ch'im 章忱, to the test. He bestowed on him a special grade[102] and just as all successful candidates he received a red plaque and a saddle.

The Eastern Jurchen chief Yingge 盈歌 dispatched an envoy to court.

Fifth month. Yu Noksung 庾祿崇 was appointed Commissioner of the Security Council and Concurrently Advisor to the Heir Apparent.

Because of the damage caused by pine insects, the king personally led his officials to make sacrifices to the Supreme Emperor in the palace; he was

100 *Analects* 6.4. The implication seems to be that though the calf is adequate to be used (presumably for sacrifice), humans prefer not to because it is the offspring of a less than perfect animal; Confucius counters this by saying that nature would accept it as it is, rather than judging from whence it came.

101 A manual of geomancy that was used for those taking the examination in geomancy. KRS 73.8a.

102 *Pyŏltu ŭlkwa* 別頭乙科: *Pyŏltu* appears to be a term applied to Chinese examination passers, *ŭlkwa* is the second rank in the palace examination.

paired with T'aejo for three nights.[103]

Sixth month. The king ordered the councilors of state to divide themselves over three places to make sacrifices to the mountains of the five directions 五方山 and the Sea Spirit Lord 海神君 to pray for the pine insects to disappear. The king declared an amnesty.

The king ruled that 500 soldiers should nab the pine insects on Song'ak Mountain.

Intercalary [sixth] month. State Councilor So T'aebo and others petitioned: "To cultivate scholars in the national schools, expenses are enormous, a true blight for the people. Moreover, the Chinese laws and customs are difficult to implement in our country, so we request that [this program] be stopped." The king did not reply.

The historians comment: "Schools are institutions for fostering morality and for cultivating the next generations for the country. Therefore, from antiquity till now, from the palace and the capital to commoners' villages, there was nowhere without a school. Even among uncouth barbarians there are no instances of abolishing schools. Searching through the classics and various documents, there are no prior cases of abolishing schools because of their excessive expenditure. Now So T'aebo requesting to abolish schools are words that even an ordinary fellow from a poor village would not dare to utter. Sukchong selected him and appointed him to an office that should be used to discuss the Way and manage the country [on the basis of the Way]. As for him requesting to retire three times, and the king refusing on account of his being a 'consummate Confucian,' what does this mean?[104] It is not that Sukchong was unaware of the man's nature, but he was beholden to So T'aebo for helping him to the throne, and these private feelings of indebtedness

103 This probably means that a statue of the Supreme Emperor (Sangje) was placed next to that of T'aejo during the sacrificial rites.

104 Details of his request for retirement and the king's reasons for refusing can be found in the biography of So T'aebu, but not in the *Koryŏsa chŏryo*; see *Koryŏsa* [hereafter KRS] 95, So T'aebu. Sukchong mentioned in particular his experience and his talents as reasons for refusing his request to retire.

muddled his objectivity when it came to the process of selecting state councilors. The people at the time praised Sukchong as a man of letters. But this 'love of letters' was limited to playing to one's heart's content with beautiful phrasing and composing poems with officials. When it comes to the way of exhausting principle and rectifying the mind so as to govern the county and save the people, [or 'letters' in the true sense of the word], he was ignorant and far removed from it."

The king went to Kwiryŏng Pavilion on the Eastern Pond to inspect cavalry skills and present rewards.

Autumn, seventh month. The Directorate-General of National Affairs[105] petitioned: "Those who passed the 'Three Rites Course'[106] and the 'Three Biographies Course'[107] should be allowed to enter office so as to encourage future generations." The king followed this.

On *kyŏngsul* day [the 27th] the king departed for the Western Capital. The Ministry of Rites petitioned: "Respectfully, we would like to invoke the *Book of Documents* where it says that the reason for a king's tour of inspection is that if the liege lords monopolize government in their domain, the authority and blessings all rest with them; in such a case, it may be feared that they block missives from the king, or do not pass on blessings to those below. Therefore the king has to inspect personally and eradicated any practices that harm the people. [However] it would be fitting to order the resident governor of the Western Capital and the royal inspectors that have been sent ahead to first visit the people to inquire about their woes, reduce their burdens and offer them support. Also, as for the previously bestowed pardons or other forms of grace, the officials should first check which of them have not been completely implemented, and have them put into effect." The king agreed

---

105 Singmok togam 式目都監: An office formed under Munjong that was especially concerned with standards and procedures.

106 Samnyeŏp 三禮業: One of the "Various" exam courses (*chapkwa*), considered lower than the civil service examination. The name refers to the three rites text one had to study: *Li jing*, *Zhou li*, and *Yi li*.

107 Samjŏnŏp 三傳業: one of the "Various" exam courses in which candidates had to study the three commentaries on the Spring and Autumn Annals.

with this course of action.

Eighth month. The king reached the Taedong River and gave a banquet on the dragon boat for the heir apparent, the accompanying ministers, and the civil and military officials of the Western Capital. The king watched water plays and various performances until the evening.

The king visited the Portrait Hall of T'aejo.

The king gave a small banquet at Mihwa Pavilion 美花亭, composed one short poem, and ordered the Confucian officials of the two capitals to present matching versions.

The king went to Hŭngbok-sa 興福寺 and Yŏngmyŏng-sa and after that to the Kuje Palace. He composed a poem and ordered Confucian officials to present matching versions. He then went to the dragon boat and hosted a banquet for the officials.

The Resident Governor of the Western Capital, Assistant Executive in Political Affairs Kwak Sang, together with others invited the king for a dinner in Changnak Hall 長樂殿.

Ninth month. The king decreed: "For a long time I have not inspected the country. Now I came to the Western Capital and hope to be lenient in sentencing and punishing. Since my carriage brought me here, the minor crimes reported by the envoys sent in advance among my cortege together with the resident governor of the Western Capital will all be pardoned."

A decree read: "The four classes of people all specialize in their vocation, this is truly the foundation of the country. Now I heard that it is customary in the Western Capital not to support merchants, and thus they lose profit. Let the officials of the Resident Governor dispatch two Special Commissioners for Market Inspection[108] to daily inspect markets and shops so that merchants and sellers would all obtain profit from their transactions."

The Hall of the Ten Kings at Hŭngbok-sa was completed and the king ordered the heir apparent to offer incense. The king and his consorts personally attended the completion ceremony.

---

108 Hwach'ŏn pyŏlgam 貨泉別監: more literally, a special directorate or special commissioner for coinage (currency).

The king went to Changgyŏng-sa 長慶寺 to inspect cavalry and shooting practice.

The king went to Sinho-sa 神護寺 to hold a Buddhist Canon Ceremony for its completion. From the palace to the temple the narrow road was lit by thousands of lanterns.

Winter, tenth month. The Ministry of Rites petitioned: "The edification in rites and righteousness of our country started with Kija, yet a shrine to him still does not exist and he is not mentioned in the sacrificial manuals. We beg that people be sent out to find his tomb and built a shrine next to it so that he can be sacrificed to." The king agreed.

The king went to Changgyŏng-sa to inspect officers' cavalry division. He arranged a wine party and ordered the state councilors and those officials from the royal cortege to practice target shooting. Those who hit the bull's eye were granted a horse from the royal stable and silk according to rank.

The king went to Changnak Hall to give a banquet to the senior civil and military officials of the two capitals, and bestowed presents according to rank.

The king summoned men and women aged eighty and over for a banquet in the palace. He ordered the heir apparent to personally encourage them to drink and eat, and to bestow presents according to rank.

The king dispatched An Chagong 安子恭 to Liao to give felicitations for the Heavenly Florescence Festival (Tianxingjie 天興節).

Eleventh month. On *chŏnghae* day [the 6th] the king returned from the Western Capital.

The king decreed that all the famous mountains and great streams he passed on his journey should be granted a virtuous epithet, and that all the officials and functionaries of the prefectures and counties he passed through had committed minor misdemeanors should be dealt with leniently, and that the land rents of those localities for this year should be reduced. The officials and functionaries who had accompanied him were granted one [additional] office rank.

The Eastern Jurchen Shuangkun 霜昆 and others, thirty people in all, came to present horses.

The king dispatched Yang Sinbu 楊信孚 to Liao to give thanks for the birthday wishes, Kwak Chunmok 郭峻穆 to present local products, and Kim T'aeksŏn 金澤先 to give new year felicitations.

Yun Kwan was appointed Vice-commissioner of the Security Council.

The king went to Kŏndŏk Hall and invited the newly qualified candidates, bestowing robes, wine, and food.

The Eastern Jurchen Yingge 盈歌 sent an envoy to request silver craftsmen. The request was granted.

Twelfth month. A decree read: "To make the people prosperous and benefit the country, nothing is more important than currency. Both the Western and the Northern Dynasty[109] have been using it for a long time. Our Eastern Country is the only one that has not yet been circulating it. Now for the first time I have ordered the method of casting metal [coins] be implemented, and so far 15,000 strings of cash have been cast and distributed to the state councilors, civil and military officials, and soldiers as the first step [in circulating money]."

Liao dispatched as ad-hoc envoy the Surveillance Commissioner for the Guizhou 歸州[110] Jurisdiction, Xiao Ke 蕭軻. Also it sent the Drafting Advisor Meng Chu 孟初 to congratulate the king on his birthday.

The fact that cash had been used for the first time was reported by the king to the Ancestral Shrine and the Eight Tombs, and the officials presented memorials of felicitation.

The king ruled that a Left and Right Liquor Commission[111] be set up. Also, on both sides of the road shops of all kinds, both rudimentary and refined, should be opened so as to fully realize the profits of money.

The Eastern Jurchen chief Guluogu 古羅骨 and others, thirty people in all, came to present horses.

---

109 I.e., respectively the Song and the Liao.

110 In the area of modern Gaizhou city, Liaodong Peninsula, Liaoning. *Liaoshi* 38, 537.

111 Chwa-u chumu 左右酒務: likely to collect taxes on the selling or consumption of alcohol.

7. Sukchong (II), Yejong

Sukchong Eighth year [1103]

Second year of the Chongning era of Song, third year of the Qiantong era of Liao

Spring, first month. The Eastern Jurchen Gaoluogu 高羅骨 and others, thirty people in all, arrived at court.

The Western Jurchen Wangjian 亡間 and others, twenty-four people, came to court.

Director of the Chancellery So T'aebo thrice requested permission to retire on account of old age. A compassionately formulated edict did not grant permission, but instead bestowed table and walking stick, and ordered him to oversee affairs [at court].

Second month. The Eastern Jurchen General Doumenxiao 豆門小 and others, thirty people, came to offer local products; General Gaofulao 高夫老 and others, thirty people, came to present horses; and Doumen Huiba 豆門恢八, and others, ninety people, came to court.

So T'aebo was appointed Probationary Grand Mentor, Minister of Taxation, Administrator of the Western Capital Residential Governor; O Sujŭng was appointed Assistant Executive in Political Affairs; and Kim Kyŏngyong was appointed Administrator of the Security Council.

The Military Instructor[1] Zhang Zongmin 張宗閔 and others from Mingzhou, together with the Chief Merchant[2] Yang Shao 楊炤 and others, thirty-eight people in all, arrived at court.

Yu Noksung was appointed Vice-director of the Department of Ministers and Assistant Executive in Political Affairs; Yun Kwan was appointed Vice-minister of Personnel and jointly Administrator of the Security Council; Wang Ha was made Vice-commissioner of the Security Council.

Summer, sixth month. Executive at the Ministry of Taxation Liu Kui 劉逵 and Reviewing Policy Advisor Wu Shi 吳拭 arrived—they were dispatched by Song to bestow on the king robes, belt, silk, gold and jade objects, bow and arrows, a saddle, and other presents. Song also dispatched four medical officials: Mou Jie 牟介, Lü Bing 呂昞, Chen Eryou 陳爾猷, and Fan Zhicai 范之才. They came in response to a memorial requesting them.

Liao dispatched Bian Tangying 邊唐英 to report the investiture reception.[3]

Ryu Sin was appointed Vice-director [of the Department of Ministries] and Assistant Executive in Letters; Ch'oe Hongsa was appointed Commissioner of the Security Council; and Yun Kwan was appointed Administrator of the Security Council.

Autumn, seventh month. The Eastern Jurchen chief Kundou 昆豆 dispatched someone to present local products.

The Eastern Jurchen Grand Preceptor Yingge[4] dispatched an envoy to court. There was a physician from our country who resided among the Wanyan clan[5] and was good at curing illness. At the time one of Yingge's

---

1 *Kyoryŏnsa* (Ch. *jiaolianshi*) 敎練使: a military office in the Tang dynasty, responsible for training soldiers. It is however also possible that this refers to a kind of diplomatic office.

2 *Kangsu* 綱首: Here I interpret this term as similar to the *togang* 都綱, the term which I have so far rendered as "chief merchant."

3 Literal translation. Normally Koryŏ as vassal state would not be able to invest anyone in its suzerain, Liao. Perhaps it might be interpreted as "Liao dispatched Bian Tangying to thank [Koryŏ] for receiving investiture."

4 Yingge 盈歌 ruled over the Wanyan tribe, which would unify all Jurchen tribes, from 1094 to 1103. According to the *Jinshi*, the title Grand Preceptor (Ch. *taishi*) was an appellation by the Liao for the military governors (Ch. *jiedushi*) they appointed among the Jurchen, then subordinate to Liao. *Jinshi* 1, *shiji* 1. http://chinesenotes.com/jinshi/jinshi001.html

5 Wanyan bu 完顔部: The family who would found the Jin Dynasty. This passage clearly

relatives was ill and he told the physician "If you can cure this person's disease, then I will send someone to return you to your native country." The person was effectively cured, and true to his word Yingge dispatched someone to take him to the border. When the physician arrived [at the Koryŏ court], he told the king: "As for the Jurchen tribes who reside along the Black Water 黑水,[6] they are getting stronger by the day, and their military is becoming increasingly sophisticated." The king then for the first time exchanged envoys, and exchanges continued from this onwards without interruption.[7] Yingge then destroyed Xiaohai village 蕭海里 and reported this victory to us; we then again sent people to congratulate them. Yingge then sent his younger clan brother Xiege 斜葛 to reciprocate the embassy, and the king received him lavishly.

Eighth month. The censors reported that they had annotated the books on punishment.

Grand Generals Ko Mungae 高文盖, Chang Hongjŏm 張洪占, and Yi Kungje 李弓濟, and General Kim Chajin 金子珍 and others secretly plotted rebellion. When the affair was discovered the king ordered the Censorate to apprehend them and banish them to the southern border.

Ninth month. The king summoned palace attendants and close court officials to Chunggwang Hall. He ordered them to compose poetry on a set theme, and bestowed wine.

The king dispatched Yi Kyeŭng 李繼應 and Pak Kyŏngjak 朴景綽 to Liao to offer congratulations on the conferral of a higher honorific title.

Ch'oe Sach'u was appointed Director of the Chancellery; Im Kan was appointed Executive Chief of the Chancellery; Yi O was appointed Executive Chief of the Royal Secretariat.

Food was given to 10,000 monks.

---

marks the emancipation of the Jurchen from any Koryŏ tutelage. In this volume I will thus transcribe Jurchen terms in Pinyin; this is also how most of the Anglophone literature on the Jurchen has transcribed their names and terms, and will make cross-referencing easier.

6 I.e. the Amur or Heilongjiang River.

7 Almost exactly the same account can be found in the *Jinshi* 135, *liezhuan* 73. http://chinesenotes.com/jinshi/jinshi135.html .

Winter, tenth month. As it was the Tianning Festival 天寧節 [Heavenly Repose Festival] of the Song Emperor, the king ordered the heir apparent to set up a maigre ritual at Pong'ŭn-sa. The medical official Mou Jie and others went to attend.

The Returning the Courtesy Envoy from the Eastern Capital of Liao, Vice-commissioner of Foreign Affairs Gao Weiyu 高維玉 and others arrived.

The king dispatched Song Im 宋琳 to Liao to congratulate the emperor on the Heavenly Florescence Festival and Kim Kukchin 金國珍 to express gratitude for the ad-hoc embassy.

The king issued an edict that summoned the hermit Ŭn Wŏnch'ung 殷元忠 from Mt. Mudŭng 無等山.

The king went to the Eastern Pond to inspect archery. Those that hit the target were given presents commensurate to rank.

Eleventh month. The king dispatched Ch'oe Kyebang 崔繼芳 to Liao the give thanks for the birthday felicitations, Cho Kyŏng 趙卿 to present local products, and Sim Hu 沈侯 to give new year felicitations.

On *sach'uk* day [the 13th] an earthquake struck the capital.

The Eastern Jurchen Grand Preceptor Yingge dispatched Gusa 古洒, Shuaifu 率夫, Alao 阿老 and others to present local products.

Twelfth month. Liao dispatched Wu Xingqing 烏興慶 to congratulate the king on his birthday.

On *muo* day [the 13th] an earthquake struck the capital.

The Northern Jurchen Congkun 從昆, Alao, and others, forty-seven people in all, came to present local products.

Sukchong Ninth year [1104]

Third year of the Chongning era of Song, fourth year of the Qiantong era of Liao

Spring, first month. One-thousand seven-hundred and fifty-three Eastern Jurchens came to submit.

The Eastern Jurchen chief Wuluoshou 烏羅首 had a conflict with Funailao

夫乃老 of another tribe, and sent the *gongxiong* Zhizhu[8] to raise an army and attack him. Their cavalry was stationed near Chŏngju outside the pass. The king appointed Executive Chief of the Chancellery Im Kan as Intendant for the Military Commissioner of the Expedition Corps of the Northeastern Sector 判東北面行營兵馬事. The king went to Sŏnjŏng Hall and personally gave him the hatchet and axe to send him off prepared. Furthermore Intendant of the Chancellery Yi Wi 李瑋 was made Military Commissioner of the Expedition Corps for the Northwestern Sector, Director of the Office of Regalia Kim Tŏkchin 金德珍 was made Military Commissioner of the Expedition Corps for the Northeastern Sector.

The Western Jurchen Congkun and others, thirty people in total, came to present local products.

Second month. Im Kan fought with the Jurchen outside the walls of Chŏngju and was defeated. Initially Palace Attendant Im Ŏn 林彥 had advocated the use of military means, but Auxiliarry at the Office of Historiography Yi Yŏng 李永 said "Weapons of war cause destruction, and battle is a dangerous affair; one cannot rashly raise troops. Im Ŏn desires using the military to cause a rift at a time when nothing has happened [yet], this is seriously misguided." The king did not listen. Also, Im Kan was keen to establish merit, and drawing on troops that had not been properly trained led to a sudden defeat in battle, in which the greater half [of our troops] were killed. Only Administrative Aide at the Security Council Ch'ŏk Chun'gyŏng 拓俊京, by requesting weapons and an armor-clad horse from Im Kan and entering the enemy lines, managed to kill one of its leaders, and take with him two people who had been taken hostage. Then with Lieutenants Chunmin 俊旻 and Tŏngnin 德麟 they shot and killed one bandit each. The bandits then retreated slightly to regroup, and then went in pursuit with 100 cavalry. Ch'ŏk Chun'gyŏng together with the *taesang* Injŏm 仁占 shot and killed two of the bandit officers, and the enemy did not dare to advance any further; our army then retreated into the city. Because of his merit Ch'ŏk

---

8 公兄之助: Here I interpret *gongxiong* as a title or office, and Zhizhu as a name.

Chun'gyŏng was promoted to Administrative Supervisor[9] of the Thousand Bull Division 千牛衛. Officials strongly censored Im Kan and the Military Commissioner, Vice-director of the Department of Ministries Hwang Yuhyŏn 黃兪顯, the Vice-commissioners, Grand General Song Ch'ung 宋忠, Executive at the Ministry of Taxation Wang Kongyun 王公胤, and Right Transmitter Cho Kyu 趙珪 for their responsibility in the defeat. They were all dismissed from office.

The Western Jurchen Juluofo 居羅佛, Mapu 麻浦, and others, forty-nine people in all, came to present local products.

Commissioner of the Security Council Yun Kwan was appointed Supreme Commander of the Expedition Corps for the Northeastern Sector. The king went to Chunggwang Hall to personally give him hatchet and axe and send him off. In a battle with the Jurchen Yun Kwan killed more than thirty. More than half of our soldiers were either killed or injured, or disappeared.

Third month. A Humane Kings Assembly was held in Hoegyŏng Hall, and 10,000 monks were fed on the polo court.

The king summoned the Chŏnju Shepherdship Commissioner O Yŏnch'ong and made him Senior Transmitter of Edicts at the Security Council, Executive at the Ministry of Punishment, and Administrator of the Security Council. The background to this is as follows: As the king felt that O Yŏnch'ŏng had the talent to become state councilor, he had great plans for him. Thus he wanted to test him by putting him in charge of the people [of Chŏnju]. Effectively it was reported that his record was "most excellent" and hence he was called back [to the center].

Song Wi 宋瑋 and twenty-six others passed the composition test of the civil service examination, two passed the classics examination, and five passed by royal grace.

Summer, fourth month. Liao dispatched Military Governor of the Anyuan Army Yelü Jiamo 耶律嘉謨 and Surveillance Commissioner for the Lizhou

---

9 *Noksa ch'amgunsa* 錄事參軍事: See no. Hucker 3860. Since this term does not otherwise occur in any of the Koryŏ histories, it is perhaps a mistake or alternate version of *sarokch'amgunsa* 司錄參軍事, a regional post of rank 6 or 7.

jurisdiction Xia Zimu 夏資睦 to invest the king as Loyal and Diligent Merit Subject Upholding the Country, Commander Unequalled in Honor, Probationary Grand Marshal, Concurrently Royal Secretary, Supreme Pillar of State, King of Koryŏ. His stipend village was 7,000 households, 700 effective. The emperor also granted a palanquin, robes, silk, saddle, bow and arrows, and other gifts. The king received the investiture on an altar in the suburbs. The assorted officials offered memorials of felicitation.

Surveillance Commissioner for the Taizhou Jurisdiction Yelü Shifu 耶律師傅 and Chief Minister of the Court for State Ceremonial Zhang Zhi 張織 came to invest the heir apparent as Military Governor of the Obedient Righteousness Army; Surveillance and Supervisory Commissioner for Sakchu, Muju, and other prefectures; Specially Promoted Acting Grand Marshal, concurrently Commissioner to the Director [of the Royal Secretariat-Chancellery]; Roving Prefect of Sakchu Commissioned with Extraordinary Powers for all Military Affairs in Sakchu; Supreme Pillar of State; Duke of the Three Han States, with a stipend village of 3,000 households, 500 households effective. The king also bestowed palanquin, robes, silk, saddle, bow and arrows, and other gifts.

Fifth month. So T'aebo, who had retired as Director of the Chancellery, was appointed Probationary Grand Mentor and was granted the title of Merit Subject Assistant in Planning.

[Construction of] the palace of the Southern Capital was completed.

Sixth month. The Eastern Jurchen themselves destroyed their fortifications and *gongxiong* Zhizhu and others, sixty-eight people in all, came to knock on the gates to request peace.

Autumn, seventh month. Vice-director of the Department of Ministries and Assistant Executive in Letters Ryu Sin died. Although Ryu Sin was of average appearance, he was courageous and magnanimous. In his youth he passed the examination, achieving a high ranking. He was famous for his integrity. Once when he was shepherd of Ch'ŏngju, the people esteemed him as if he was a god. When the country wanted to move the capital to the Southern Capital, all state councilors and officials supported the plan, only Ryu Sin and Senior Policy Advisor Yu Noksung were against. In all deliberations regarding the country's affairs he put loyalty and righteousness first. At the time he was often the subject of [praising] comments.

Yi O was appointed Executive Chief of the Royal Secretariat, and Yun Kwan Assistant Executive in Political Affairs.

Commissioner of the Security Council Ch'oe Hongsa and Director of the Palace Library Chŏng Mun 鄭文 were dispatched to Song to give thanks for grace bestowed.

On *musul* day [the 27th] the king went to the Southern Capital. On *sinch'uk* day [the 30th] when the royal cortege was in Pongsŏng County 峯城縣[10] the king distributed official money to the various officials and soldiers in accordance with rank. At the time money had already been in circulation for three years, yet the people were poor so it could not be widely used. The king then ordered prefectures and counties to use grains to open bars and restaurants and allow the people to trade so that they would come to appreciate the benefits of money.

Eighth month. On *sinhae* day [the 10th] the king reached the Southern Capital, and went visiting various parks and pavilions, all in accordance with what the astronomers had advised him to do. Although this was not in accordance with propriety, there was none among the officials who said anything.

The Song Chief Merchant Zhou Song 周頌 and others came to present local products.

The king gave a banquet for the officials in the Yŏnhŭng Hall 延興殿 and bestowed presents in accordance with rank.

Ch'oe Hongsa was made Assistant Executive in Political Affairs; Im Ŭi was appointed Associate Administrator of the Security Commission; O Yŏnch'ong was made Vice-commissioner of the Security Commission and Hallim Academician; Yuk Cho 陸肇 was appointed Junior Vice-director of the Department of Ministries.

Ninth month. The king went to Changwŏn Pavilion.

---

10 Located in the area of modern P'aju.

The Posŭng Army[11] was formed and the king inspected its drills.

Winter, tenth month. On *sinhae* day [the 11th] the king returned to the palace.

The Eastern Capital of Liao sent an envoy to reciprocate the tribute.

The king dispatched Chi Ch'ongyŏn 智寵延 to Liao to give felicitations on the Tianxing Festival, Mun Kwan to give thanks for the investiture, Ch'oe Chun 崔濬 to give thanks for the birthday wishes, Kim Han'gong 金漢公 to present local products, and Ch'oe Tŏkkae 崔德愷 to give felicitations for the new year.

Eleventh month. Kim Sŏnsŏk, who retired as Executive Chief of the Royal Secretariat, died. He was upright and tenacious and a talented administrator. Yet he was not interested in economic affairs and when he reached the age of seventy he was still attached to his office and did not retire. People ridiculed him for this.

The king dispatched Confidential Envoy Kim Ko 金沽 to Liao.

Twelfth month. Wi Kyejŏng was appointed Executive Chief of the Chancellery.

Liao dispatched Ma Zhiwen 馬直溫 to offer felicitations on the king's birthday.

Yun Kwan petitioned: "The reason why your subject was defeated by the Jurchen is that they had cavalry whereas we only have foot soldiers. Hence we are no match for them." Thereupon he proposed to establish a new Special Army Corps (Pyŏlmuban 別武班): Among civil and military officials, those with prestige titles, clerks, and even traders and servants, and among the various prefectures, districts, and counties, all those who possessed a horse would be drafted into the Cavalry Corps. Those without a horse would be put into either the Sinbo 神步 (Divine Infantry), Tot'ang 跳蕩 (Assault Raider), Kyŏnggung 梗弓 (Strong Bow), Chŏngno 精努 (Elite Arbalest), or Palhwa 發火 (Firing) Corpses. Men above the age of twenty who had not yet taken the examination would all be drafted into the Sinbo Army. The civil and military officials and soldiers of all garrisons

---

11 Posŭng-gun 保勝軍: The "Victory Assured" Army.

and districts would train regularly in every season. Also, monks should be selected for the Dragon-subduing Army 降魔軍. Thus he planned to start a new campaign.

Sukchong Tenth year [1105]

Fourth year of the Chongning era of Song, fifth year of the Qiantong era of Liao

Spring, second month. Executive of the Chancellery Ch'oe Sach'u retired. He earnestly requested retirement on account of his age. Wi Kyejŏng spoke: "With Sir Ch'oe in office, we looked up to him as to a mountain or the Big Dipper. All the important affairs of the country and military decisions flowed from his mouth. If he now takes leave, where should we turn to?" Later during an informal banquet in Such'un Palace 壽春宮, Ch'oe Sach'u rose and offered a toast to the king. The king, holding his hand, said "Sir, if you insist on retiring, then who can I share the task of governing with?" He replied: "To retire is an act of propriety. Your subject is old and has nothing more to offer. My only wish is to spend the remainder of my years in leisure." The king then gave permission.

Summer, sixth month. Wi Kyejŏng was made Grand Mentor to the Heir Apparent; Ch'oe Hongsa Executive Chief of the Royal Secretariat and jointly Executive of the Royal Secretariat, concurrently Grand Guardian to the Heir Apparent; Yun Kwan Junior Guardian to the Heir Apparent and Minister of War; Yi O Probationary Minister of Education and Junior Preceptor to the Heir Apparent; Chŏng Mun Vice-minister of War, Assistant Executive in Letters, concurrently Advisor to the Heir Apparent; Im Ŭi Commissioner of the Security Council and Vice-minister of Personnel; Wang Ha Administrator of the Security Council and Vice-minister of War; O Yŏnch'ong Associate Administrator of the Security Council; and Yi Wi Censor-in-Chief.

Autumn, eighth month. On *ŭlhae* day [the 11th] the king went to the Western Capital.

The king visited T'aejo's likeness in the Kamjin [Experiencing the True

Likeness] Hall, 感眞殿 then visited the Osŏng [Five Stars] Hall 五星殿.

The king dispatched commissioners to make sacrifices at the Shrine for Holy Emperor Tongmyŏng 東明聖帝, and offered clothes and silk.

The king decreed that the prefect of Hapchu 陜州,[12] Ko Minik, since he had extorted the people, should be thrown in jail and interrogated under torture.

The king inspected archery practice at the Ch'anghwa Gate 昌化門. The Heir Apparent hit the target and all the officials offered their congratulations.

Ninth month. The king went to the gate of the Yŏngjak-wŏn 營作院 and inspected mounted archery practice.

On *pyŏngjin* day [the 22nd] the king felt indisposed; on the *chŏngsa* day [the 23rd] he set out from the Western Capital.

In winter, the tenth month, *ŭlch'uk* day [the 1st] day, the king's disease became serious so they stayed at Kŭmgyŏ Station 金郊驛. On *pyŏng'in* day [the 2nd], at night they set out from Kŭmgyo but when they arrived outside the Changp'yŏng Gate 長平門 the king died in his palanquin; at daybreak they reached Sŏhwa Gate 西華門 and changed into mourning dress. The heir apparent and ministers wailed and stamped in grief, and the deceased king was brought into Yŏnyŏng Hall and then moved to Sŏndŏk Hall 宣德殿 where the coffin lay in state. That day the heir apparent, Wang U, received the king's posthumous edict and took the throne in Chunggwang Hall. The deceased king was given the posthumous title Myŏnghyo 明孝 [Bright and Filial] and the temple name Sukchong. On *kapsin* day [the 20th] he was buried in Yŏng-nŭng 英陵.

Yi Chehyŏn commented: "Emperor Gaozu of Han understood people's talents, and used to say 'Emperor Hui is gentle and humane but King Zhao, [Liu] Ruyi, is just as I.'[13] Several times he wished to change the heir

---

12 Modern Hapch'ŏn, South Kyŏngsang Province.

13 The former refers to his son Liu Ying, styled Emperor Xiaohui, the result of his union with Empress Gao of the Lü clan, and the latter to his son Liu Ruyi, styled King Yin of Zhao, the result of his union with a concubine of the Qi Clan. He thought that Liu Ying was too weak to become emperor, but finally was persuaded to go with him; he became Emperor Hui of

apparent but did not foresee that the King of Dai would eventually become son of heaven and enfeoffed him to a border commandery. However, due to this lack of affection he avoided the disasters of the Lü Clan.[14] Emperor Taizong of Tang was wise, yet he failed to determine the succession. In the end ignorant boys were put on the throne, and they were manipulated by evil women; hence his grandsons almost all perished. How lamentable! The two Han dynasties together lasted four hundred years, yet those ruling the Under-Heaen were all scions of Emperor Wen. The Tang dynasty lasted three hundred years, but from Emperors Zhongzong and Ruizong to Zhaozong and Emperor Ai, all were scions of the great emperor (i.e., Taizong). Seen from this perspective, this is all Heaven's work, not that of man. For our dynasty, though Munjong had nineteen sons, the expectation of reviving the dynasty rested on Sukchong's youthful shoulders. As a vassal Sukchong restored the great unity; with wisdom he overcame disturbance, and through benevolence he achieved peace. His sons and grandsons likewise were wise, and his wisdom was thus passed on through the generations for four hundred years to the present. How could this not be Heaven's work! Even so, as the *[Zuo] Commentary* puts it: 'No one knows the sons better than their father.'[15] This surely applies to Munjong!"

[King Yejong] dispatched Drafting Advisor at the Royal Secretariat Kim Yŏn 金緣[16] to Liao to announce the passing of King Sukchong. When Kim Yŏn arrived, Liao prepared a banquet and was also about to provide musical entertainment, but he protested "When I left, all the ministers of my country were in mourning. Now that I am in the suzerain's county, although I am greatly honored by the benevolence you show by bestowing

the Han (r. 195–188 BCE).

14 Liu Heng was a son of Gaozu and Empress Gao of the Bo Clan; he later became known as Emperor Wen (r. 180-157 BC). The disasters of the Lü refers to Empress dowager Gao, who reigned in the stead of her son Emperor Hui.

15 *Chŏn* 傳: while often used as a short form of the *Zuozhuan*, I could not find this quotation in this work nor in any other one.

16 The son of Kim Sanggi, and a scion of the Silla royal house through his ancestor Kim Chuwŏn. He later changed his name to Kim Injon. KRS 96.3a-b.

this banquet, my feelings as a retainer will not be able to endure listening to music." His sincere words moved the Liao emperor; respecting his sincerity he acquiesced to this request. Furthermore, during an audience with the emperor of Liao, he requested that bright robes and dancing be forbidden. Academician Meng Chu 孟初 told him: "The court dress code should be followed insofar as wearing auspicious colors is concerned; however, it is possible to do away with the dances." Upon his return Kim Yŏn was promoted to the office of policy critic.

The king decreed: "All those from *t'ongp'an*[17] and above in the three capitals and eight shepherdships,[18] as well as those among prefects and county magistrates who passed the examination, should additionally administer educational matters."

It was henceforth forbidden for either scholars or civilians to interact with palace eunuchs for personal favors.

To honor his mother Lady Ryu 柳氏, the king made her queen dowager, with her court named the Ch'ŏnhwa [Heavenly Peace] Hall 天和殿, her palace Sungmyŏng [Venerating Brightness] 崇明府, and her birthday the Chiwŏn [Utmost Primordial] Festival 至元節.

Executive at the Ministry of War Ch'oe Wi 崔緯 was sent to Liao to offer congratulations on the Tianxing [Heavenly Florescence] Festival 天興節.

Eleventh month. Wi Kyejŏng was appointed Director of the Chancellery; Ch'oe Hongsa and Yi O were both made Executive of the Chancellery, and jointly Executive Chief of the Chancellery;[19] Yun Kwan was made Executive

17 *T'ongp'an* 通判: a local office title of someone working for the protectorate or shepherdship.

18 *Mok* 牧: previously translated as "department" after the French system of regional administration, to avoid confusion with many other "departments" at the central level here I opt for the more conventional "shepherdship," a literal translation of this term. According to the treatise on the bureaucracy in *Koryŏsa*, this title was introduced only in 1116 to replace that of *p'ansa* (administrator). KRS 77.42a.

19 *Munha sirang tong p'yŏngjangsa* 門下侍郎同平章事: It is the first time that this term is used; it should probably read *Munha sirang tong Chungsŏ p'yŏngjangsa*, since the positions of executive of the Chancellery and of the Royal Secretariat were often combined in one person. See Pyŏn T'aesŏp, "Chungang ŭi Chŏngch'i chojik," in *Han'guksa* 13 (Kwach'ŏn: Kuksa p'yŏnch'an wiwŏnhoe, 1993), 33.

of the Royal Secretariat and jointly Executive Chief of the Royal Secretariat; Im Ŭi was made Assistant Executive in Political Affairs; Wang Ha was appointed Commissioner of the Security Council; and O Yŏnch'ong was made Administrator of the Security Council and Censor-in-Chief.

The king decreed: "Instruct the relevant officials to give special titles and emoluments to those among the officers and clerks who established merit while protecting me when I was heir apparent and during the enthronement."

The king went to Sinbong Gate 神鳳門 and declared an amnesty.

A royal edict read: "I have heard that the grain and silver goods used by the people for trading are of very poor quality; therefore, from the time of former kings there were strict laws banning such practices. However, recently it appears that they are no longer being applied. Hence treacherous types are not afraid of the law, but are focused on profit alone. They add sand or earth to rice and blend silver with copper or iron to cheat ignorant folks. This is a very serious violation of the laws of nature and the super-natural; this is the reason for people's poverty and it should be punished by law. However, Yao and Shun merely had to draw the cap and gown [of officials] for the people to fear the law, so that punishment was not necessary and every household was worthy of reward for virtuous behavior. I truly admire this, and it is my hope that soldiers, citizens, artisans, traders, and people of all walks of life whether in the capital or the provinces will change their ways of thinking, revert to the good and keep criminal behavior far away; then as a matter of course punishments will be few and virtuous instruction will abound. Material prosperity and long life, together with an era of peace, how then would these be hard to achieve! But if there are those who fail to grasp this and continue to break the law, they will be punished without fail and without the chance of pardon."

The Censorate petitioned: "Since the prisons are now empty, we request that the two characters 'prison empty' be written on a board to be hung on the street south of the Court of Justice 法司 to display the beauty of a resplendent court that does not seek recourse in punitive justice." The state councilors sent in congratulatory memorials. At the time a grand pardon had released all convicts, hence the Censorate's request and the congratulations by state councilors. Those in the know laughed at this.

Twelfth month. Assistant Executive in Letters Chŏng Mun died. He was the son of Chŏng Paegŏl 鄭倍傑. He was respectful and modest of character, frugal and not given to much talk. He was not interested in trade for profit, and his house was old and decrepit, barely keeping out wind and rain. As an official he was diligent and cautious, and served for more than ten years in the Ministry of Punishment. Yet he never intervened rashly in the punishment procedures. Once he accompanied the king to the Western Capital and requested the establishment of a shrine for Kija. When he went as an envoy to Song he distributed the gold and silk he received among his retinue, and used the rest to buy books; he did not request anything else to take back. The people of Song praised him.

On *mujin* day [the 5th] Venus was observed during the day.

Junior Policy Advisor Ryu Chayu 柳子維 was appointed Military Commissioner for Raising Troops in the Eastern Border Circuit.

The king summoned the councilors of state to Kŏnmyŏng Hall 乾明殿 to discuss the situation in the Eastern Border Circuit.

O Yŏnch'ong was appointed Military Commissioner for the Expedition Corps of the Eastern Border Circuit; Kim Kigam 金奇鑑 was made Administrator to the Military Commissioner; Im Sinhaeng 任申幸 was made Vice- Military Commissioner.

Taenyŏng Palace 大寧宮 caught fire.

A royal instruction read: "My ancestors built this country by managing the chaos of the founding period. Successive worthies occupied the throne until it was passed to this insignificant person. Now those who are uncorrupted among the officials of provinces, districts, prefectures, and other regional offices and treat the people with compassion barely reach one or two out of every ten. The seeking of profit or reputation harms the great essence. Favoring bribes and fostering their private wealth they harm the ordinary people, who flee the land one after the other so that nine out of every ten houses are empty. I am greatly pained by this. Illustrious officials should be dispatched to inspect the local administrations and report on the achievements and mistakes of prefects and magistrates.

Yejong, Great King of Letters and Filial Piety (1)

His given name was U 佑 and his courtesy name Semin 世民. He was son and heir apparent to Sukchong and his mother was Queen Dowager Myŏngŭi 明懿太后, née Ryu. He was born in *kimi*, the thirty-third year of Munjong's reign [1079] on the *chŏngch'uk* day of the first month. He was of restrained disposition and well-balanced. He was on the throne for seventeen years and lived to the age of forty-five.

Yejong first year [1106]

Fifth year of the Chongning era of Song, sixth year of the Qiantong era of Liao

Spring, first month. The state councilors requested that the king take meat and side dishes, but he refused. After petitioning four times he finally relented.

Chŏngyu day [the 4th]. A comet was observed in the southwest. It was ten feet long, and disappeared after more than a month.

The Ministry of Rites requested that the presentation of a congratulatory memorial for Konsŏng Hall[20] by the two border circuits, three capitals, three protectorates, and eight shepherdships on new year's day, the winter solstice and the Chiwŏn Festival become a regular practice. The king agreed.

The king's birthday was called the Hamnyŏng [Peace for All] Festival 咸寧節.

Liao dispatched as sacrificial offerings envoy Yelü Yan 耶律演 and Zuo Qigong 左企弓.

Military Commissioner for the Eastern Border Circuit O Yŏnch'ong

20 Konsŏng-jŏn 坤成殿: Judging by the name, most likely the palace of the queen or another important female relative of the king.

requested: "Among those drafted into the Divine Cavalry Army, some are only sons and have parents of seventy or more; please exempt them from the draft; if 3-4 people from the same household serve in the army, please reduce by one person; and please exempt sons of councilors of state who did not volunteer to join the army." The king agreed.

Liao dispatched as mourning envoy Yelü Zhong 耶律忠 and Liu Qichang 劉企常, and also dispatched Liu Dingchen 劉鼎臣 to order the king to resume duties after mourning.

The Eastern Jurchen Gongya 公牙 and others, ten people in total, came to court. The king received them in Sŏnjŏng Hall and bestowed wine, food, and presents according to precedent. Earlier, when Im Kan went on a military campaign, the [Jurchen] chief Yangai 延盖 ordered Zhixun 之訓 and others to attack them; our troops were defeated. Thereupon Zhixun ordered Gongya to come to court. The king wanted to personally receive him with full ritual in the main hall. [Censor] of Miscellaneous Affairs Ch'oe Wi objected: "From old when the caitiffs come to court they have never been received in the main hall. Please accord with the old customs and receive them at your official residence." The king agreed.

The king went to the Sinbong Gate to inspect the Divine Cavalry Army.

Second month. The ad-hoc envoy from Liao arrived.

The king appointed his younger brothers Wang Po 王俌 as Acting Grand Marshal, Probationary Minister of Education, concurrent Director of the Department of Ministries, Marquis of Taebang; Wang Hyo 王俘 as Acting Grand Protector, Probationary Minister of Education, Concurrent Director of the Department of Ministries, Marquis of Taewŏn; Wang Sŏ 王偦 as Acting Director of the Department of Ministries, Probationary Minister of Works, Marquis of Chean; and Wang Kyo 王僑 as Acting Director of the Department of Ministries, Probationary Minister of Works, Marquis of T'ongŭi.

The state councilors repeatedly urged the king to take a queen, but on the grounds that his mourning had no yet been finished, the king did not allow this.

The Western Jurchen Wangjian 亡間 and others arrived.

The astrological officials petitioned: "Mt. Songak is the mountain protecting the capital, but because over the years rain has washed away sand and earth, the bare rock is exposed, and wild plants are no longer growing abundantly. We should plant new trees." The king agreed.

The Northern Jurchen Shaba 沙八 and others came to court. The Capital Military Command petitioned: "The bandit leader Gaoshou 高守 whom we defeated in the past is none other than Shaba's father. He is bound to harbor resentment. We request that the be lodged in Sinhŭng Hostel 新興館 and have it guarded by brave officers and soldiers." The king agreed.

The Northern Jurchen chief Gaoluan 高亂, Ayuda 阿於大 and others, forty-two people in total, came to court. The Foreign Relations Office petitioned: "Gaoluan and the others wish to hand in the certificates of appointment they received from Liao and receive our titles." The king ordered that this should be granted, and they were given the rank of *chungyun* 中尹.

Third month. The king ordered the Eastern and Western Directorate to Save from Crises provide relief to the poor and sick.

Liao returned twelve of our soldiers including Chongji 宗志; during the *kapsin* year [1104] war they had been defeated by the Eastern Barbarians and fled to Liao.

The Royal Inspector for Sŏhae petitioned: "Many people in Hyŏpkye County, Kokchu, have become vagrants, and hence there is a shortfall in taxes. We request a three-year reduction in taxation." The king agreed.

The king ordered ten scholar-ministers including Kim Yŏn, Ch'oe Sŏn 崔璿, Yi Chae, Yi Tŏg'u 李德羽, and Pak Sŭngjung 朴昇中, to gather with the astrologers in the Changnyŏng Hall 長寧殿 to gather and compare books on geography from various schools: They should collate them and delete the superfluous and confused passages, and compile a new work under the title *Secret Record of Haedong* (*Haedong pirok* 海東秘錄).

The Eastern Jurchen Zhixun, leading 2,000 cavalry troops, came and set up camp outside the [border] pass to state his allegiance. He stated "As for the battles of the past, I assume that the new king does not know about them. When Gongya came to court to convey his intention [to surrender], you rewarded him lavishly before sending him back. The grace of your highness is lavish indeed; I request permission to diligently serve this dynasty for generations." The king then summoned back to the palace the Military Commissioner for Recruiting Troops in the Eastern Border Circuit, Kim Tŏkchin, and Vice-commissioner Im Sinhaeng.

The soldier of the Xijia army 奚家軍[21] of the Northern Dynasty, Naige 乃哥, came to pledge submission, bringing along with him the barbarian bandit Shuangqiu 霜丘 and his son Azhu 阿主 as well as one suit of armor.

Summer, fourth month. The Northern Jurchen chief Ayuda and others, thirty-eight people in all, came to court.

Hwangbo Hŏ 皇甫許 and thirty-three others passed the composition test of the civil service examination.

The king went to Myot'ong-sa 妙通寺. Henceforth he frequently visited temples.

A royal decree read: "Recently people from An'ak 安岳, Changyŏn 長淵 and other counties in Yuju 儒州[22] in Sŏhae Route turned to vagrancy, so for the first time I dispatched deputy magistrates[23] to appease them, and after that people slowly returned and production resumed gradually. Now people in Ubong 牛峯, T'osan 兎山[24] and other counties, twenty-four altogether, are also gradually abandoning their land, so following the precedent of Yuju deputy magistrates should be installed to appease them."

Fifth month. The king went to Kach'ang Tower 嘉昌樓 to compose poems. He ordered ten of his close officials including Hŏ Kyŏng 許慶 and Ryu Injŏ 柳仁著 to match his poems and bestowed silk according to rank. Then he had a silver bowl placed in front of the tower as target and ordered attending officers and ministers to hold a competition; those who could hit it would receive it as prize.

---

21 The Xi or Kumo Xi 庫莫奚 were related to the Khitan, both believed to be descended from the Xianbei people.

22 Corresponds to modern Munhwa county in Sinch'ŏn-kun, Hwanghae Province.

23 *Kammu* 監務: refers to magistrates of lesser counties (*sohyŏn*). According to the *Koryŏsa*, they were first dispatched only two years later, in 1108, when forty-one deputy magistrates were appointed. KRS 12.30a [1108/7/*sinyu* (13th)]

24 Both located near modern Kŭmch'ŏn-kun, Hwanghae Province.

Sixth month. The king took a daughter of Sŏnjong, the Yŏnhwa Princess 延和宮主, as consort.

The king received the bodhisattva precepts in Kŏndŏk Hall.

The king personally held an assembly on the *Kŭmgangmyŏng Sūtra*[25] *in Kŏndŏk Hall.*

A royal decree read: "From this month there has been a severe drought, which has been caused by lack of virtue. Day and night I exerted myself to the utmost to reflect on my own actions and to atone for my misdeeds. I prayed to Buddha and prayed to spirits, but even though I did not fail to do my utmost, so far I failed to receive any response. After I ascended the throne, in both politics and edification there were many shortcomings, so could this perhaps be a reprimand from Heaven? Close ministers at the Chancellery and Security Council, together with remonstrance officials from the Censorate and Royal Secretariat, as well as the drafters of royal edicts from various offices should all submit a letter with straight talk on current mistakes."

The king pardoned all those sentenced to banishment or lighter sentences.

The king went to Changnyŏng Hall, and ordered the monk Tamchin 曇眞 to pray for rain. At the time the country was holding many sutra processions in the streets. People of the five wards of the capital copied this, and held reading processions in their own quarters. It happened to rain during such a reading procession in a quarter west of the palace, prompting the king to bestow grain and silk. He urged further such processions, but no rain fell.

Autumn, seventh month. The king personally sacrificed to the Supreme Emperor of Heaven 昊天上帝 in Hoegyŏng Hall, and also enshrined T'aejo's tablet [there] to pray for rain.

A royal edict read: "I have perused the letters sent by the Chancellery and Security Council, the remonstrance officers, the drafters of royal edicts, and the editor-collators of Changnyŏng Hall. They discuss my personal comportment and [need for] self-reflection, and urge me to accept the

---

25 More commonly abbreviated as *Kŭmgang-gyŏng*, the *Diamond Sūtra*, one of the most widely used texts in East Asian Buddhism.

injunctions of my ancestors; this I have firmly committed to mind and will endeavor to implement.

Regarding the need to attune to Heaven by adjusting the sacrifices to the seasonal commands, and the repair of the Ancestral Shrine and Altar of Earth and Grain Deities, provision of ritual utensils and clothing for them, etc. I have ordered relevant officials to report on this in detail and then implement it.

Regarding the corvée labor for Ch'ŏnsu-sa 天壽寺, this is something started by my late father, who unfortunately passed away shortly afterwards. This proved to be a hot topic for discussion, with many arguing for the construction to be stopped. I also realize that it is unacceptable, yet I do not dare to interfere with a project passed down by my late father; this is my shortcoming.

Regarding the use of money: this is something that the emperors and kings of old used to make the people prosperous and at ease; my late father had no intention of amassing wealth. Moreover, I learned that the Great Liao has also recently started to use money. When establishing a new law, all kinds of opinions spout forth. Therefore, it is said: 'One cannot let the people share in the thoughts about the beginning of an affair.'[26] Surprisingly, many ministers quote T'aejo's injunction against using the customs of Tang and the Khitan barbarians to advocate abolishing the use of money. However, what the injunction wants to forbid is lavish and decadent customs. If we reject the civilization and laws of China, then what can we use? That T'aejo's injunction is not about forbidding the use of money should be clear. However, what should be banned today is the commodity tax at passes and fords.

Regarding the lack of clear distinction between high and low when it comes to clothing regulations, this is due to the fact that the issue has never been settled since ancient times. Recently regulations have been issued

26 From the *Shang jun shu* [Book of Lord Shang], chapter 1, "Reform of the Law." This legalist text advocates decisive action on the part of a ruler, even if it goes against popular opinion.

that distinguish between high and low; however, because the ruler and his minister are unable to practice frugality in leading the masses, high and low have become indistinguishable. Therefore, it is said 'The people do not follow what [those above] order them to do, but follow [what those above them] like.' Also, it is said 'What those above practice, those below will practice even harder.' If the ruler and minister personally practice frugality and do not syphon off people's profits, then the people will observe this and be moved to adopt the distinction between high and low.

Regarding the fact that civil and military officials receive a stipend without merit, which leads to repeated calamities such as drought and locusts: Promoting the wise and keeping out the unworthy, these are the essentials of government. However, the bureaucracy is extremely complex, so I cannot know about all aspects of it in depth. If there are wise and worthy people below, the councilors of state should recommend them; if there are treacherous people who bribe themselves into positions, the censorial agencies should remove them. As for those banished because of their involvement in the Ŭlhae Revolt [1095], their sentence should be commuted to banishment to a closer place, and they can be employed. As for those who were guilty by association and enslaved, they should be released; if they do not belong to the class of base people they should be comforted and given relief goods.

Regarding the illicit sexual relations carried on by monks: They are enlisted as households in *hyang* forever; even in the event of an amnesty they are not forgiven, how can the law be so harsh? Now the relevant officials should investigate and have them fulfill military service [instead]. As for the torture carried out by law courts across the land, even when the evidence is clear, three rounds of torture has become the norm. As a result, some whose crime was light have died. Even if they have killed an innocent person, would it not be better to not follow the law literally [rather than killing the suspect under torture]? Henceforth let the law courts learn about my compassion. Those who have already confessed to their crime, regardless of whether it is light or heavy, should not be tortured." That day it rained a little.

The Capital Military Command petitioned: "Recently in the fights with Eastern Tribes because the orders were not strict, generals do not dare to fight with all their might and soldiers run away, leading to a string of defeats. Only if leadership and commands are strict will the mind of the rank and file be unified. Allow us to compare this with the commands issued between the *sinhae* [1011] and *muo* [1018] years under King Hyŏnjong: 'At the first intensive drill, those who do not take part regardless of their position shall be beaten fifteen times with the stick. Those who do not show up a second time, or who break ranks during advances or retreats, or who confuse the troops with superstitious talks and divination, or who misuse or lose their weapons, or those of the rank of sub-lieutenant or below who receive an order but do not transmit it, or who transmit the order but do not implement it, or those who soldiers who save a superior but fail to avert [his death], or who leak plans to the enemy, or who do not notify that an enemy has entered the corps—all shall be given twenty strokes of the stick.

Those who miss the time for conscription; those who plan to escape or do not fight in the face of the enemy, or who move around recklessly at the time of battle; those officers or soldiers who do not follow orders from superiors; those who throw weapons to the enemy; those soldiers who do not save their superiors, leading to their defeat or death; those who seeing that the situation is critical yet do not save someone from a different division; those who snatch bow or sword from others or fight with others over enemy heads; those generals or officers who do not fight in the face of battle, or hide among the troops or speak of submitting to the enemy; those who are in a formation yet fail to break the enemy assault—all of them shall be beheaded.

Those who run over to the enemy, their property shall be confiscated and their wife and children shall be enslaved. If the enemy has surrendered but this is not reported and the enemy is killed, those people shall also be executed.'

We request to apply these rules to encourage our soldiers. However, if the enemy submits and one fails to report this and kills the enemy, in this case execution is not appropriate; please replace with twenty strokes of the cane." This was implemented. At the time there were plans for an eastern expedition, hence the king requested this explanation of the art of war.

Eighth month. The king dispatched commissioners to all provinces to give instruction on army formations.

Ninth month. The king personally hosted a banquet in the palace courtyard for those over eighty, as well as righteous husbands, chaste wives, filial sons and grandsons, widows and widowers, orphans and those living alone, and those with serious illness; he bestowed presents according to rank.

An Assembly of the Hundred Seats was held in Hoegyŏng Hall, and 10,000 monks were fed in the palace courtyard, and 20,000 more in the prefectures.

Executive of the Chancellery Yun Kwan was made supervisor for the construction of Ch'ŏnsu-sa and was bestowed a belt with rhinoceros horn. Other officials involved were given silk according to rank.

The king ordered the courtier[27] Chŏng Kŭkkong together with Vice-director of the Bureau of Astronomy Ch'oe Chahyŏn 崔資顯, Grand Astrologers Ŭm Tŏkchŏn 陰德全 and O Chiro 吳知老, Registrar-equivalent Kim Wije 金謂磾 and others to go to the Western Capital and inspect the ancient ruins of the Dragon Embankment.[28] Initially a soothsayer had made a prognostication in which he urged the king to go to the Dragon Embankment in the Western Capital and construct a palace to be used during tours of inspection. The king asked the Chancellery and Security Council, as well as the collator-editors of Changnyŏng Hall to deliberate on this and they all approved. Only O Yŏnch'ong, in charge of the Security Council, demurred: "Recently the construction of the palace in the Southern Capital has only just been completed, and the people are exhausted and the treasury depleted. You

27 Naein 內人: apparently someone who worked for the king personally rather than a member of the regular officialdom; nevertheless, Chŏng had passed the examination in 1094 in first place, so he was likely a scholar-advisor rather than an attendant.

28 Yong'ŏn 龍堰: there is insufficient information as to what type of place this might be, but given the occurrence of dragons in the legends of Wang Kŏn's ancestors it is likely connected to one of them.

cannot draft tired people to raise a new palace; if you want to inspect [the Western Capital] the old palace is fine." The king did not respond.

Winter, tenth month. The king dispatched Executive Kim Powi 金寶威 and Junior Colonel Yi Suk 李璹 to Liao to give thanks for the commemorative sacrifices, and Deputy Director of the Foreign Relations Office Ch'oe Su 崔洙 to congratulate the emperor on the Heavenly Efflorescence Festival.

Eleventh month. The Western Jurchen Yuhouda 於厚大 and others came to court.

Yun Kwan and O Yŏnch'ong inspected the Divine Cavalry Corps and the Divine Infantry Corps outside the Sungin Gate.

The king dispatched Kim Ŭibang 金義方 to Liao to give thanks for the ad-hoc envoy.

Kwak Sang, who had retired as Assistant Executive in Political Affairs, died. He had worked himself up from a lowly clerk and thanks to connections started to serve King Sŏnjong when he was still Marquis of Kugwŏn. After he became king, he did not forget those who were loyal, and appointed him to several offices culminating in that of left transmitter of edicts. His power grew by the day, and he even tampered with royal edicts. Officials tried to impeach him, requesting the king to remove him from office, but this fell on deaf ears. When Sukchong was still crown prince he summoned him and bestowed a belt of rhinoceros horn, but Kwak refused to accept it. When Sŏnjong fell ill, he attended him at his sickbed. When Sukchong arrived at the gate to the king's room to ask about his health, Kwak told him: "The king's sickness is not likely to improve soon; prince, if you do not have a royal summons, I cannot let you straight in." As a result Sukchong had to desist. Later when Sukchong became king, since Kwak had served the previous king single-mindedly, he gave him important offices. At the time, Executive of the Chancellery Yun Kwan requested to introduce money, but Kwak vehemently opposed it because it was not in accord with local customs; he sent ten memorials in protest, but to no avail. Kwak was upright and had no other talents, so he did not engage in any trade or production and as a result his family had nothing to spare.

Director of the Chancellery Wi Kyejŏng thrice sent a memorial requesting retirement on account of old age but the king personally wrote an edict refusing it. When Wi refused to attend court meetings on account of illness, the king sent an envoy to persuade him.

The Western Jurchen Wangjian and others, thirty people in total, came to court.

Twelfth month. On *muo* day, the first day of the month, there was a solar eclipse.

The king went to Mundŏk Hall and ordered Executive of the Chancellery Yun Kwan to lecture on "Against Luxurious Ease" [from the *Book of Documents*] and Executive of the Security Council O Yŏnch'ong on the *Book of Rites*. The king bestowed robes and belts on both officials as reward.

The king went to Chunggwang Hall and ordered soldiers from Supreme Grand General down to practice archery. Those who hit the target were given a horse and silk according to rank.

On *kisa* day [the 12th] a comet was observed.

Kim Kyŏngyong was appointed Vice-director of the Department of Ministries and Assistant Executive in Political Affairs.

The Taenyŏng Palace caught fire.

Director of the Chancellery Wi Kyejŏng entered the Chancellery to attend to affairs. The censor protested: "Wi Kyejŏng has been ill for more than a year and cannot attend to affairs; several times we have reported this to your majesty but without avail; instead you generously gave him 200 days leave. That period has now been used up and he had to resume office yet for several weeks he still did not show up—until suddenly he was propped up by someone and entered the Chancellery; This is not the way of a great minister, please relieve him of his office." The king did not allow this.

The historian Kim Puil commented: "Wi Kyejŏng was famous among his contemporaries for his composition skills; he was upright and straightforward, and served successive kings. Once King Sŏnjong gave a party on the eve of the Lantern Festival. Wi was then transmitter of edicts at the Security Council. The inebriated king ordered him to dance, but Wi declined, saying: 'There are trained entertainers here, so you do not need your minister to dance.' The king did not force him. When he was vice censor-in-chief, Sŏnjong had a favorite concubine called Manch'un 萬春 for whom he built an imposing and beautiful residence. Wi reprimanded the king saying: 'Manch'un has bewitched your highness and has tricked you into using corvée labor to construct a private mansion. I request that it be demolished.' But the king did not reply to his letter. Sŏnjong once sent Yi Chaŭi as envoy to Song, with Wi Kyejŏng as deputy envoy. While Yi Chaŭi procured many precious things, Wi did not seek anything. Even when he entered the Chancellery he did not change his plain and frugal ways. Whereas everybody loved Buddhism and those in high position constructed monasteries or had Buddhist sutras copied, only Wi did not follow this custom. Therefore, the country's people greatly looked up to him and wished for him to be given important positions and see him take charge. However, when he became state councilor unexpectedly he remained silent and never raised any clear proposals. Thus, we know his authority was insufficient; moreover, he was old and sick. He then requested retirement, but the king was loath to let him go and twice sent a personally written edict retaining his services. Moreover, he sent an envoy to talk him out of retirement. Therefore, he went to court but after a few days requested leave. The censors did not know about the situation and hence impeached him. What a mistake!"

Yejong second year [1107]

First year of the Daguan era of Song, seventh year of the Qiantong era of Liao

Spring, first month. Liao dispatched Gao Cunshou 高存壽 to congratulate the king on his birthday and also to bestow a copy of the Buddhist canon.

Director of the Chancellery Wi Kyejŏng again sent three memorials requesting retirement. The king twice refused but then allowed it.

The king issued an edict: "Establishing schools to nurture the worthies, this has been the basis of practicing politics since the Three Dynasties [of Xia, Shang, and Zhou]. But the officials have been debating this [for a while] without reaching a decision; this should be swiftly implemented." The king was keen to develop letters and academic study, hence this decree. Among the great officials not a single one accepted this order. At the time people expressed their regret over this.

Im Kae, who had retired as Executive Chief of the Chancellery, died. Im Kae was uncorrupted and upright, and had the air of a great official. Once he was in charge of the administration of the Great Granary. Someone named Han Sun 韓順 lived next to the granary, and stole grain from it, cheating and manipulating the officials. His house was full of riches, and there were even officials associating with him. Im Kae uncovered his deceit and put him on trial. At court his actions gave rise to much debate.

The monk Tamjin was made royal preceptor. Originally when the king wanted to invest him as royal preceptor, he ordered Junior Policy Critic Kim Yŏn to deliver the letter of investiture. Kim Yŏn refused, saying: "My job is in the remonstrance court, and as such I already advised your majesty that he should not be invested as royal preceptor, but evidently this advice was not retained. Now if I accept this order and deliver the letter I would be deceiving your majesty." The king tried to force him by ordering three times, but he remained steadfast in his refusal. Then the king changed his order and had the Palace Attendant Yu Taesu deliver the letter.

The king bestowed upon Wi Kyejŏng two silver containers, one containing tea and the other medicine.

Second month. The king sent royal commissioners of pacification to each province so as to inspect the state of people's hardships and to determine the achievements and misdemeanors of local magistrates and prefects, and report them to the throne.

Third month. A royal decree read: "At the time when the myriad things come to life, not taking the life of young mammals or birds is truly a firm rule of the classics on rites and part and parcel of the humane government of previous kings. Now as for the magistrates across the provinces, although they talk about sharing the burdens, in fact few follow the regulations. Some claim that they are providing meat [for the palace] but seek out reward; some treat envoys lavishly to put them in a good mood, but to do so they hunt in the fields regardless of the season; sometimes farmers want to clear fields but the fire spreads and harms many creatures. This all goes against the principle of fostering life by according with the season, and upsets the balance between heaven and earth. Henceforth all this is forbidden; those who break the law shall be punished."

The king personally sacrificed to heaven and earth and the spirits of heaven and earth within the country's borders in the courtyard of the palace.

Summer, fourth month. The king held his first audience in Kŏndŏk Hall. For the first time since the start of national mourning the officials could wear their red belts again.

Wi Kyejŏng twice sent a memorial to decline his emolument. A decree read: "You sir are of broad learning and have merit in literary composition; you are a master among the crafters of letters, and without regard for yourself served as an upright minister, famous among his generation. Because of illness you had to leave office, and I deeply regretted your departure. Moreover, you now decline your salary, this is not the way that I cherish the wise and esteem the old. Order the Finance Commission to give two shares of his salary."

Queen Dowager Sasuk 思肅王后, née Yi, was co-enshrined with King Sŏnjong in the Ancestral Shrine. Earlier, when Sŏnjong was still Duke of Kugwŏn, he married the daughter of Yi Ye, but she died soon after; this was Wise Consort Chŏngsin 貞信賢妃. He married again, this time the daughter of Master of Sacrificial Wines Yi Sŏk. When she gave birth to Hŏnjong she was invested as queen; when Hŏnjong was enthroned he made her Queen Dowager. At her demise she was given the title of Sasuk. Then there was debate on enshrining her with King Sŏnjong, but the king wanted to enshrine consort Chŏngsin. The remonstrance officials protested: "Consort Chŏngsin was the wife of Duke Kugwŏn for a very short time only, but Queen Sasuk, from the time that she married the duke to his enthronement, assisted greatly;

when the crown prince was enthroned, for three years she was in charge of governing. When Hŏnjong ceded the throne to Sukchong, she retired to the old palace and never was remiss in her virtue. Please enshrine her." The king then decreed: "The distinction between descent from the main wife and from secondary wives is essential,[29] and should be maintained. Please consult the classics of rites again and report back." The remonstrance officials again replied: "According to the stipulations of the *Spring and Autumn Annals*, if after his enthronement a king reigns for less than a year, he cannot be enshrined in the main halls of the ancestral shrine. If this is the case for the king, how much more for a queen or consort? Please elevate Queen Sasuk to be enshrined." The king complied.[30]

Sixth month. The king dispatched Office Chief at the Office of Merit Evaluation Pak Kyŏngbaek 朴景佰 to Liao to congratulate the emperor on the Tianxing Festival, Assistant Office Chief at the Ministry of Punishment Yi Soyŏng 李韶永 to give thanks for the congratulations given for the king's birthday, Royal Recorder Pak Sŭngjung to give congratulations for the new year, and Attendant Censor Ha Ŏnsŏk 河彦碩 to present tribute.

Autumn, ninth month. Executive of the Chancellery Ch'oe Hongsa and others petitioned: "According to the grand astrologer, it has been 200 years since Song'ak became the royal capital, so in order to extend the dynasty, divination showed that it is necessary to build a new palace on the ruins of the Dragon Embankment in the Western Capital where the king should move to hold audiences." Executive of the Security Council O Yŏnch'ong sent a memorial to counter this: "There are three reasons why the proposal by Ch'oe Hongsa and others to build a palace at Dragon Embankment is not right: Munjong, even though he was bright and intelligent, was once enticed by prognostication theory to build the Chwau Palace 左右宮 in the Western Capital, but came to regret it and thought it would have no effect. In the end

29 The reasoning here seems to be that since Chŏngsin was the first spouse, she was the legitimate wife (*chŏk* 嫡).

30 King Yejong's support of Consort Chŏngsin seems to be due to the fact that his spouse, Princess Yŏnhwa, was a daughter of consort Chŏngsin. KRS 95.14a-b, biography of Yi Ye (sub Yi Chayŏn).

he did not go there on his inspection tours, so funds and manpower were used in vain; this is the first reason. Construction of the Southern Capital has recently been completed, yet for the seven or eight years since, there have been no auspicious responses; this is the second reason. The old palace of the Western Capital and the Dragon Embankment where a new palace is being proposed are not far apart; so it is not guaranteed that the auspiciousness of the site is any different. Moreover, discarding the old palace of our ancestors without a proven formula [for selecting the new site], and to that end destroy people's houses and disturb the people for the new palace, this is another reason for making this proposal unacceptable. Respectfully I express my hope that you will make a wise decision and not doubt what this old minister has submitted; please use the old palace when you visit the Western Capital, and do not follow baseless theories to raise a labor force and incur the people's resentment." In the end the king followed the words of Ch'oe Hongsa and others, and at the time public opinion greatly lamented this.

Winter, tenth month. A Hundred Seat Assembly was held in Hoegyŏng Hall; 10,000 monks were given a vegetarian feast in the palace courtyard, and 20,000 more across the country.

On *im'in* day,[31] in order to prepare for an attack on the Jurchen, the king went to the southern gate of Sunch'ŏn Hostel 順天館[32] to inspect the troops. He bestowed silver, cloth, wine, and food. The Jurchen are a collection of tribes descending from the Malgal; they live scattered among mountains and marshes and have never united. Those living on the border near Chŏngju and Sakchu,[33] even though some have attached themselves to us, they alternate between allegiance and rebellion. Yingge and Wuyashu 烏雅束[34]

---

31 According to the *Koryŏsa* (KRS 12.30a-b), this happened in the intercalary tenth month rather than the tenth month; since there is no *im'in* day in the tenth month, the correct date should likely the 20th day of the tenth intercalary month.

32 This is where envoys from Song China were usually lodged.

33 Sakchu being in the west close to the mouth of the Amnok river, and Chŏngju in the east, near modern Hamhŭng; it was later renamed Chŏngp'yŏng, still the name of a locality in North Korea.

34 Yingge was leader of the Wanyan clan from 1094 to 1103; he was succeeded by his nephew Wuyashu who ruled from 1103 to 1113. Wuyashu in turn was succeeded by his younger brother Aguda, the founder of the Jin Dynasty. The Wanyan clan managed to unify

were successive chiefs who managed to win the hearts of the multitude and their authority gradually expanded. Above the border of Iwi, an unbroken range of mountains rises from the eastern sea shore, extending to the most northern border;[35] they are steep and rough, and neither people nor horses can traverse them. There is only one path through them, which is commonly known as the bottleneck,[36] because at the entrance and exit it is only as big as the entrance to a cave. If this path is blocked, the Jurchen's path is blocked. Hence those wanting to strike them were always clamoring for sending out an army to pacify them. In the seventh year of Sukchong [1102] the Jurchen set up camp outside the pass near Chŏngju. In the eighth year of Sukchong their chiefs Xu Zhen 許貞 and Luofu 羅弗 were captured and imprisoned in Kwangju. Under torture they confessed their schemes against us. They were detained and not sent back. At that time border general Yi Ilsuk 李日肅 and others proposed: "The Jurchen are weak and do not deserve our fear; if we do not attack them now they will be a nuisance later." The following year Im Kan was dispatched with an army to strike them furtively, but he was defeated. On the back of this defeat the Jurchen took advantage by raiding the fortress at Sŏndŏk Pass 宣德關, killing and looting indiscriminately. Now Yun Kwan was dispatched to subjugate them instead of Im Kan, but he too met with defeat. Since no more military power could be raised, he personally asked for peace, concluded an alliance, and returned. Sukchong was enraged and swore to all the gods of heaven and earth that with their aid he would sweep the enemy from the border. After this troops were trained and grain stocked in preparation for a new attack. After the king [Yejong] came to the

---

all different Jurchen tribes. See Hoyt Cleveland Tilman, "An Overview of Chin History and Institutions," in Tilman and West, eds., *China under Jurchen Rule* (Albany: State University of New York Press, 1995) 26-27. See also Herbert Franke, "The Chin Dynasty," in Herbert Franke and Denis Twitchett, eds., *Cambridge History of China*, Vol. 6: Alien Regimes and Border States, 907-1368 (Cambridge: Cambridge University Press, 1994), 220-1.

35 Iwi 伊位 appears to be a designation for the region north of Chŏngju, while the northern border probably refers to the border with Liao in the northwest, along the lower reaches of the Amnok. In other words, the mountains stretch all the way from east to almost the western shore.

36 Probably referring to Hwangch'o pass.

throne, due to mourning he could not raise an army. At that time a border general reported "The Jurchen are making strong incursions into border fortresses. Their chieftain has put a pheasant tail in a gourd and uses this to go around to all the tribes to discuss something, but it is difficult to gauge their intentions." When the king heard this he went to Chunggwang Hall and took an oath sworn by King Sukchong out of a Buddhist retable where it had been stored. He showed it to the officials of the Chancellery and Security Council, who shed tears when they read it. They said: "The bequeathed will of your late father is truly urgent. How can we forget his will?" Then they presented the king with a memorial requesting the continuation of Sukchong's fight against the Jurchen.

The king was still indecisive, so he ordered Ch'oe Hongsa to make a divination at the Ancestral Shrine. The result was the line "already saved" from the hexagram "the abysmal" [*kam* 坎, hexagram no. 29 in the *Book of Changes*], and hence the decision was taken to send out an army. Yun Kwan was put in command, with O Yŏnch'ong second in command. Yun Kwan immediately told the king: "In the past I received the secret order from your august father. Now again I receive an important order, so how would I dare not to unite the three armies to crush the enemy fortresses at the border so as to wipe out this humiliation?" O Yŏnch'ong seemed to have some doubts and spoke softly to Yun Kwan, who then angrily added: "Now if it were not for Sir O and I, who would dare to risk 10,000 deaths to wipe out the shame? The plan has already been decided, what doubt could there be?" O Yŏnch'ong remained silent. Only Kim Yŏn signaled his opposition to sending out an army.

Eleventh month. On *imja* day, the first day of the month and the day of the winter solstice, there was a solar eclipse.

On *kyŏng'o* day [the 19th] the king went to the Western Capital. At the time, an astrologer told the king that he should go to the Western Capital to send off the generals, hence this journey. On *ŭlhae* day [the 24th] the king arrived.

Twelfth month. The king went to the Wibong tower and bestowed on Yun

Kwan and O Yŏnch'ong halberds and sent them off to battle.

On *ŭlyu* day [the 4th] Yun and O arrived at the eastern border and set up camp in Changch'un Station 長春驛. The troops numbered 170,000, [though] 200,000 had been raised. They were split up, with Administrative Assistants to the Military Commissioner Ch'oe Hongjŏng 崔弘正 and Hwang Kunsang 黃君裳 sent into Chŏngju and Changju 長州 [respectively]. The Jurchen were being deceived by being told that Koryŏ would be releasing Xu Zhen and Luofu; they were also told to come listen to a royal order. The Jurchen chiefs believed this and Guluo 古羅 and others, more than 400 people came. They were made drunk with wine and then assassinated. However, about fifty to sixty strong and clever ones among them were suspicious and waited outside the gates of the pass, unwilling to enter. Thus Administrative Assistant to the Military Commissioner Kim Pup'il and Recording Officer Ch'ŏk Chun'gyŏng were ordered to split up and lay an ambush. Furthermore, Ch'oe Hongjŏng was ordered to confront them with crack cavalry, so they were almost all captured and killed.

Ŭlmi day [the 14th]. Yun Kwan himself, leading 53,000 troops, left the Taehwa Gate of Chŏngju. Meanwhile Military Commissioner for the Central Army Kim Hanch'ung 金漢忠, at the head of 36,700 troops left the Allyuk military camp 安陸戍, Military Commissioner for the Left Army, Mun Kwan, leading 33,900 men, left the Honghwa Gate of Chŏngju, and Military Commissioner for the Right Army Kim Tŏkchin led 43,800 soldiers from Sŏndŏk Garrison. Between the Anhae 安海戍 and Kŏbang 拒防戍 military camps, Special Commissioner for the Navy Yang Yusong 梁惟竦, Commissioner for the Wŏnhŭng Local Navy Command 元興都部署[37] Chŏng Sungyong 鄭崇用, Vice-commissioner for the Chinmyŏng Local Navy Command 鎮溟都部署[38] Kyŏn Ŭngdo 甄應陶 and others led 2,600 marines to Torin-p'o 道鱗浦.[39] Yun Kwan passed Tae Naep'aji 大乃巴只

---

37 Wŏnhŭng was located in the area of Yewŏn-hyŏn, Chŏngp'yŏng-kun, South Hamgyŏng Province.

38 Chinmyŏng garrison was located south of modern Wonsan, South Hamgyŏng Province.

39 Also referred to as Toryŏn-p'o; believed to be near the coast east of Hamju, South Hamgyŏng Province. None of the smaller geographic units can be identified, though all

village and marched for half a day. When the Jurchen saw the size of the army they all fled, leaving only the cattle on the fields. Reaching Munnaeni 文乃泥 village, the enemy entered Tong'ŭm Fortress 冬音城 and held it. Yun Kwan sent Controller of the Seal for to the Military Commissioner Im Ŏn and Ch'oe Hongjŏng to lead crack troops to crush them.

On *pyŏngsin* day [the 15th], the Left Army arrived at the bottom of the fortress. Seeing that the Jurchen had gathered there, they sent the translator Taeŏn 戴彦 to tell them to submit. The Jurchen replied: "We want to decide who will win or lose in a battle; how can you talk about submitting." They then withdrew into the castle and resisted. Arrows and stones fell down like rain, and our troops could not advance. Therefore Yun Kwan told Ch'ŏk Chun'gyŏng: "If the sun goes down, the situation will be grave. You and General Yi Kwanjin 李冠珍 should lead an attack." Ch'ŏk replied: "Once when I was working in Changju, I committed an error worthy of punishment, but you, sir, considering me a prize soldier, requested the court to forgive me. Today is the time to kill this body of mine and repay your trust." Then he reached the base of the fortress, donned his armor, grabbed his shield and charged into enemy lines, killing several of their leaders. Thereupon Yun Kwan's army joined forces with the Left Army to attack with all their might, inflicting a heavy defeat. Ch'ŏk Chun'gyŏng was rewarded with thirty bolts of silk. Then [Yun Kwan] also ordered Ch'oe Hongjŏng, Kim Pup'il and Recorder Yi Chunyang 李俊陽 to attack the region of Iwi; although the bandits resisted for a long time they were eventually overcome and 1200 were decapitated. The Central Army destroyed thirty-five villages including Kosahan 高史漢, and decapitated 380 enemy troops and took 230 prisoners. The Right Army destroyed thirty-two villages including Kwangt'an 廣灘, took the heads of 290 enemy troops and captured 300. The Left Army destroyed thirty-one villages including Simgon 深昆, and executed 950. Yun Kwan destroyed thirty-seven villages starting with Great Naepaji, decapitated 2,120 and took 500 prisoners. He dispatched Recorder Yu Hyŏngyak 俞瑩若 to report this victory to the king. The king was overjoyed and granted Yu

seem to have been near Chŏngju (modern Chŏngp'yŏng-ŭp).

an office rank of the seventh grade. Then he ordered Left-vice-recipient of Edicts and Office Chief at the Ministry of War Sim Hu and Palace Attendant and Executive at the Ministry of Punishment Han Kyoyŏ 韓皦如 to deliver an edict of encouragement and comfort. Upon Yun Kwan and O Yŏnch'ong and the various generals he also bestowed presents commensurate with rank. Yun Kwan then divided his generals and sent them on a mission to determine the border line. He also dispatched the astrologer Ch'oe Chaho 崔資顥 to an area below Mongnagol Pass 蒙羅骨嶺 to observe the terrain and construct a wall with a corridor on top of 950 *kan* [for a prefecture] to be named Yŏngju 英州. Below Mt. Hwagot 火串山 he was to construct a wall of 992 *kan*, to be called Ungju 雄州; and at Orimgŭm village 吳林金村 construct a wall of 774 *kan* to be called Pokchu 福州. At Kunghani village 弓漢伊村 the wall was to be 670 *kan* and the new locality would be Kilchu 吉州. Finally he ordered the construction of two temples within the walls of Yŏngju: Hoguk Inwang-sa 護國仁王寺 (State-protecting Humane King Temple) and Chindong Poje-sa 鎭東普濟寺 (Universal Salvation Temple to Suppress the East).[40]

The Eastern Jurchen Niaoyinai 裊乙乃 and others, 3,230 people in all, came to attach themselves to Koryŏ.

Yejong third year [1108]

Second year of the Daguan era of Song, eighth year of the Qiantong era of Liao

Spring, first month. Liao dispatched Chief Minister at the Court of Imperial Entertainment Cao Yongyi 曹勇義 to congratulate the king on his birthday.

Ŭlmi day [the 14th]. Yun Kwan and O Yŏnch'ong, leading 8,000 crack troops left Kahan village and entered the narrow road [through the]

---

40 As will become clear below, this constituted the core of the famous "nine fortresses" constructed by Yun Kwan. Their location has become a matter of intense dispute, with theories ranging from the Hamhŭng plain to the mouth of the Tuman River. Given the time frame of events, the former theory appears more likely. If "Bottleneck Pass" refers to the Hwangch'o Pass as surmised, then some of the fortresses would also have been located in the mountainous interior.

Bottleneck [Pass]. The bandits had set up an ambush inside the forest and when Yun Kwan's army arrived they suddenly attacked. The whole army collapsed; only a dozen or so remained, but Yun Kwan and his soldiers were surrounded several times over, and O Yŏnch'ong was hit by a stray arrow. The situation was extremely grave. Then Ch'ŏk Chun'gyŏng led a dozen or so brave soldiers to relieve them. His younger brother Ch'ŏk Chunsin 拓俊臣 stopped him, saying: "The enemy lines are solid and cannot be broken through; you are just running to your death, there is nothing to be gained." Chun'gyŏng replied: "You return and take care of our old father; my body is dedicated to the country, so righteousness does not allow me to stop now." Letting out a great roar he suddenly stormed into the enemy lines and killed more than ten. Ch'oe Hongjŏng, Yi Kwanjin and others then led troops out of the valley to come and relieve them, and the bandits lifted the siege and fled. He then pursued them and killed thirty-six. Yun Kwan and the rest, because the day was coming to an end, decided to return to Yŏngju Fortress. Weeping, Yun Kwan took Ch'ŏk Chun'gyŏng's hand and said: "From today on I will regard you as my own son, and you should regard me as your father." [Ch'ŏk Chun'gyŏng] then received an edict appointing him audience usher.

The king took the daughter of Reviewing Policy Advisor Yi Chagyŏm 李資謙 as consort. The younger sister of Yi Chagyŏm had been consort to Sunjong, but when Sunjong died she had an affair with a palace slave. When the affair came to light, Yi Chagyŏm as the audience usher was punished by association and dismissed. Now for the first time since then his eminence and high office were restored.

Kyeyu day [the 22nd]. The Jurchen chiefs Gongxiong 公兄, Alaohuan 阿老喚 and others, 403 people in all, came to our encampment to submit.

Pyŏngja day [the 25th]. More than 1,460 Jurchen men and women came to submit to the Left Army. On *chŏngch'uk* day [the 26th], 20,000 enemy infantry and cavalry came and set up camp south of the walls of Yŏngju. With loud shouting they tried to provoke us into battle. Yun Kwan and Im Ŏn conferred: "They are many but we are few; in such a situation we cannot fight them. Rather, we should hold firm and defend the city." But Ch'ŏk Chun'gyŏng said "If we do not go out and engage the enemy in battle, their force will increase by the day, while our food will be depleted. If there is no relief force forthcoming, then what shall we do? Did not you witness the victory a few days ago? Today as well I will fight with my life. Please, let your lords go up the ramparts and watch me." He then led a group of death-defying soldiers on a sortie from the fortress and gave battle. He killed nineteen and the defeated enemy fled north. Ch'ŏk Chun'gyŏng then returned in triumph to the sound of drums and flutes. Yun Kwan and the others descended from the ramparts to welcome him and holding hands they exchanged bows.

Yun Kwan and O Yŏnch'ong then led all the officers to the Superior Area Command[41] in the middle fortress. Specially detached transmitter of edicts Wang Chaji 王字之 was on his way to the Area Command from Konghŏm Fortress 公嶮城 with troops when they encountered troops of the caitiff leader Shixian 史現; they gave battle but were losing, with Wang even losing his horse. Ch'ŏk Chun'gyŏng then immediately took crack troops to come to his rescue; he defeated the enemy and seized an armored horse from the enemy and returned it [to Wang].

The king made his mother née Ryu queen dowager, gave a banquet for all his ministers, and declared an amnesty.

Second month. Executive at the Ministry of Taxation Wang Yu 王維 went to Song as memorial envoy.

Imjin day [the 11th]. Several tens of thousands of Jurchen soldiers besieged Ungju. Ch'oe Hongjŏng drilled and cajoled his soldiers so that they were all full of fighting spirit. He then opened the four gates simultaneously and they stormed out to attack the enemy, inflicting a heavy defeat. They caught and beheaded eighty soldiers. They also recovered more than fifty army carriages, 200 medium-sized carriages, and forty horses. In addition, they obtained countless military equipment.

---

41 Taedodokpu 大都督府

At the time Ch'ŏk Chun'gyŏng was in the city,[42] and the prefect told him: "We have defended the city for a long time and the military provisions are almost depleted. Outside relief did not arrive; sir, if you do not leave the city to gather troops and save us, I'm afraid that the troops within the city will have nothing to eat." Ch'ŏk Chun'gyŏng then changed into the uniform a soldier had discarded, and at night used a rope to climb down the walls. He returned to Chŏngju, gathered soldiers, and then took the route via T'ongt'ae Garrison 通泰鎮; between Yadŭngp'o 也等浦 and Kilchu they encountered the enemy and inflicted a heavy defeat. The people within the walls all cried.

Vice Minister Ryu T'aek 柳澤 was appointed Commissioner for the Superior Area Command of Hamju; he was assisted by a vice-commissioner, administrative assistant, manager of records, chief secretary, court of justice, master of medicine, and other staff. Furthermore the four prefectures of Yŏngju, Pokchu, Kilchu, and Ungju were established, and at Konghŏm Garrison a defense commissioner and vice commissioner, administrative assistant positions were posted, while Hamju and Konghŏm Garrisons were fortified.

Liao dispatched Chief Minister at the Court of Imperial Entertainment Zhang Shan 張掞 to order the king to end mourning and restore normal clothing; they also dispatched Military Governor of the Qing'an Army Xiao Liang 蕭良 and Surveillance Commissioner for the Yizhou jurisdiction Li Renqia 李仁洽 to invest the king as Acting Grand Marshal, concurrently Royal Secretary, and granted a stipend village; they also bestowed a crown, palanquin, robes, belt, silk, saddle and other presents. The king received the investiture in the southern suburbs.

Yun Kwan, on account of the pacification of the Jurchen and the construction of the six fortresses, submitted a memorial of congratulations. [The king] made Chief Controller of the Seal,[43] Left Vice Transmitter of Edicts, Office Chief at the Ministry of Rites Im Ŏn compose a record in

---

42 Presumably Ungju.

43 *Togŏmhal* 都鈐割: usually a title for a military aide, usually a concurrent title for a civil official dispatched to assist a military official in the field. Hucker no. 898. This is the only occurrence of this term.

praise of his merit.[44] It was hung in the South Office of Yŏngju. Also, a stele was established in Konghŏm Garrison marking the furthest reach of the border.

Third month. The king dispatched Recorder at the Office of Regalia, Palace Attendant Kang Yŏngjun 康永俊 to bestow upon Yun Kwan and O Yŏnch'ong sheep and wine, and on the soldiers a silver vessel and forty silver ingots.

The Jurchen set up camp outside the Yŏngju walls. The official army left the fortress to fight them and defeated the enemy, killing twenty and obtaining weapons as well as eight horses.

Yun Kwan presented [to the king] 346 prisoners of war, 96 horses, and more than 300 heads of cattle.

Fortifications were constructed for Ŭiju, T'ongt'ae [Garrison] and P'yŏngyung 平戎 [encampment]. Together with Hamju, Yŏngju, Ungju, Kilchu, and Pokchu Prefectures, and Konghŏm Garrison, these constituted the Nine Fortresses of the northern border.[45] They were all populated by people moved here from the southern border circuit. Vice Military Commissioner Pak Kyŏngjak on account of illness remained in Chŏngju, but he sent Yun Kwan the following letter: "Military merit has already been manifested so it is appropriate that soldiers are brought in to consolidate peace. However, pushing ever deeper into barbarian territory to establish successive fortifications, although it may be easily achieved now, I am afraid that in the future they will be difficult to defend." However, Yun Kwan did not have any use for such words. Yun Kwan and other officials ordered their armies to take apart wood and tiles from fortresses inside [the border] so as to construct the nine fortresses. Military Commissioner Kim Hanch'ung was adamantly opposed. He said "If the outside fortresses are not yet completed and there is a military emergency that requires support [from inside], how

---

44 See KRS 58, s.v. Sŏnhwa-jin, for the text of this record.

45 Pukkye kusŏng: These famous fortifications have been the object of a long-standing academic dispute: their exact locations remain to be determined. The reasons behind their rapid abandonment has probably engendered even more debate; it is clear from what follows that they were already controversial at the time.

will the people be protected if the fortresses inside are not complete? Even though you command me as my superior general, I cannot obey this." Eventually he was proven right.

Summer, fourth month. Yun Kwan was made Merit Subject Promoting Loyalty–Assisting Principle–Settling Conflict–Expanding Territory–Protecting the Country, Director of the Chancellery in charge of the Ministry of Personnel and Important Affairs of State and Military. O Yŏnch'ong was made Merit Subject Assisting in Planning–Equalizing Virtue–Establishing the Distant, Vice Director of the Department of Ministers and Assistant Executive in Political Affairs. The king dispatched his Palace attendant the Office Chief[46] Han Kyoyŏ with an edict and appointment certificates, purple embroidered saddles, and two horses from the royal stable to Ungju to bestow these upon the two officials.

The king visited Yŏng-nŭng Tomb.[47]

The Jurchen built a wooden palisade surrounding Ungju.

Yun Kwan and O Yŏnch'ong returned to the capital in triumph. The king ordered the military to receive them with drums and wind music. He also dispatched the Marquis of Taebang, Wang Po, and the Marquis of Chean, Wang Sŏ, to hold a banquet in the eastern suburbs. The king himself went to Mundŏk Hall where he invited Yun Kwan and O Yŏnch'ong together with the state councilors into the hall and personally asked about the situation on the border.

The king visited Ch'ang-nŭng Tomb[48] and composed a poem on the theme of the pacification of the Jurchen; he showed it to the Confucian scholars among his retinue and ordered them to compose matching poems.

The king personally conducted sacrifices at the Ancestral Shrine and

---

46 *Naesi nangjung* 內侍郎中: this appears to be two separate titles. *Nangjung* or "office chief" is normally a position of rank senior 5 in the Department of Ministries; hence, though we cannot exclude the possibility that it is a separate position, since the next time Han Kyoyŏ is mentioned he had been promoted to *sirang* ("executive," senior 4) at the Ministry of Punishment (while still identified as palace attendant), this is likely to be a combined function, where an official was dispatched to attend to the king personally.

47 The tomb of King Sukchong.

48 This is the tomb of Wang Yung, T'aejo's father.

declared an amnesty.

The king dispatched Vice Military Supreme Leader[49] O Yŏnch'ong and gave him weapons to save Ungju.

Fifth month. The Jurchen had been besieging Ungju Fortress for twenty-seven days. Controller of the Seal for the Military Commissioner Im Ŏn, Chief Military Inspector Ch'oe Hongjŏng and others commanded the generals to divide their troops and firmly stand their ground. But as they had been fighting for many days, both people and horses were exhausted and on the verge of collapse. O Yŏnch'ong ordered Mun Kwan, Kim Chun 金晙, Wang Chaji and others to take 10,000 crack troops and divide them across four routes of attack, both on water and on land. Arriving below Oŭmji 烏音志 and Sao 沙烏 passes, they saw that the Jurchen front guard occupied the top of the passes. Our troops fought their way uphill and made a sudden attack [on the front guard]. They killed 191, and the enemy fled north. They regrouped and wanted to set up the battle lines on the plains. Taking avail of their momentum, the official army fought them with all their might and defeated them. They then burnt the palisades and retreated, executing 291.[50] When O Yŏnch'ong entered the fortress, [he saw that] the officers and soldiers within the city had not waited for the relief force but had dashed out to fight; many had been killed or wounded. He punished [the officers] according to rank.

Sixth month. No Hyŏnyong 盧顯庸 and thirty-three others passed the composition test of the civil service examination, three passed the classics examination, and three passed by royal grace.

The king went to Poje-sa to pray for deliverance from the northern bandits.

Autumn, seventh month. The king ordered the supreme commander of the field army, Director of the Chancellery Yun Kwan, to resume the campaign against the Jurchen.

Forty-one magistracies were created for counties, including T'osan.

---

49 Pyŏngma puwŏnsu 兵馬副元帥: the only occurrence of this combination.

50 It is not clear whether it was the retreating Jurchen who executed 291 or whether this was done by the Koryŏ troops.

Administrative Assistant to the Field Army [supreme commander], Censor Sin Hyŏn 申顯 and others with a naval force attacked enemy ships and executed twenty of them.

The king dispatched Vice-minister of Punishment Kim Sang'u 金商祐 and Executive at the Ministry of Rites Han Kyoyŏ to Song to present local products.

The king dispatched an envoy to the eastern border circuit to organize Buddhist rituals at Chinjŏng-sa and Pisamun-sa[51] to subdue the border bandits.

Eighth month. O Yŏnch'ong returned to the capital. The king invited him to Mundŏk Hall and personally asked him about the situation at the border. He held a dinner to comfort him.

Administrative Assistant to the Military Commissioner of the Field Army Wang Chaji and Ch'ŏk Chun'gyŏng battled the Jurchen in Hamju and Yŏngju and executed thirty-three of theirs.

Recruitment envoys were sent separately to nine provinces [to] select strong men for service.

Yun Kwan presented the severed ears of thirty-one enemy soldiers.

Administrative Assistant to the Military Commissioner Yu Ik 庾翼, General Song Ch'ung, and Pak Hoejŏl 朴懷節 of the Divine Cavalry were killed in battle by the Jurchen at Kilchu. Yu Ik was posthumously appointed Executive at the Ministry of War and Administrator of the Censorate, while Song Ch'ung was posthumously appointed Supreme General and Vice-minister of War.

The Western Jurchen chief Nuhao 奴好 and others, twenty-five people in all, came to court.

Ninth month. The king conferred on Yun Kwan the title of nobility Dynasty-founding Earl of Yŏngp'yŏng County with a stipend village of 2,500 households, 300 of which were effective. On O Yŏnch'ong the king

51 Chinjŏng-sa 鎭靜寺 means "Temple to Suppress and Pacify" while Pisamun-sa 毘沙門寺 means "Temple of Vaiśravaṇa," i.e. one of the four heavenly kings, the one who protects the north.

bestowed the title Merit Subject Chasing Away the Bandits–Safeguarding the Country.

The king inspected archery at Changnyŏng Hall. Those who hit the target were granted horses and colored silk.

Wang Chaji and Ch'ŏk Chun'gyŏng again attacked the Jurchen at Saji Pass 沙至嶺 and killed twenty-seven; three were caught alive.

Kapsul day [the 27th]. The king went to the Southern Capital.

Winter, ninth month. The king dispatched Yi Tŏg'u to Liao to congratulate [the emperor] on the Tianxing Festival.

Eleventh month. The king dispatched Hwang Wŏndo 黃元道 to Liao to give thanks for [the order to] stop mourning and resume normal dress.

The king, on the return journey [from the Southern Capital] had drinks with the state councilors who accompanied him. While deliberating the situation on the border, when the topic turned to the death in battle of Yu Ik and others, the king wept, dampening the hem of his sleeves. The assembled ministers wished him a long life and tried to comfort him.

The king dispatched Ch'oe Chi 崔贄 to Liao to give thanks for the birthday wishes to the king.

On *ŭlmyo* day [the 9th] the king returned to the capital.

The king dispatched Sŏ U 徐祐 to Liao to present tribute.

Twelfth month. Liao dispatched as ad-hoc envoy Acting Minister of Education Yelü Ning 耶律寧.

Yejong fourth year [1109]

Third year of the Daguan era of Song, ninth year of the Qiantong era of Liao

Spring, first month. Liao dispatched Da Yongxin 大永信 to congratulate the king on his birthday.

Recording Officers for the Military Commission of the Eastern Border Circuit Field Army Wang Sagŭn 王思謹, Ha Kyŏngt'aek 河景澤 and others fought with the Jurchen in Hamju and died.

The king went to Changnyŏng Hall and invited fifty tribal leaders from outside the pass at P'yŏngno 平虜關,[52] and bestowed wine, food, and presents.

Because people from the postal stations and roads in the Western Capital [region] were suffering from starvation, relief food was issued from the granaries.

The king invested the Marquis of Taebang, Wang Po, and gave a banquet for all princes, state councilors, and personal staff that lasted till dawn. Censor-in-chief Ch'oe Kyebang was so inebriated that he got up and danced. At the time people criticized him for this.

Second month. The king went to the gate of Kŏndŏk Hall and ordered the generals Kim Hyŏn 金顯, Im Chwa 林佐 and others to line up the two armies in formation for inspection. He then bestowed wine and silver ingots.

The king invested the Marquis of Taewŏn, Wang Hyo, and gave a banquet for state councilors and personal staff that lasted till dawn. Later the king gave a banquet in the Chunggwang Hall; inebriated, he ordered those around him to dance. Executive Kim Kyŏngyong and others got up to dance, but Transmitter of Edicts Im Ŏn feigned drunkenness and retired, saying "The eastern border is not yet pacified, so how can you dare to dance?"

The king invited Wang Yuch'ung 王惟忠, the general who had helped to expand the Eastern Border Circuit. The king bestowed upon the higher officers under his command wine and silver ingots. To commemorate Pak Hoejŏl's death in battle, he bestowed upon his widow and sons silver ingots and both patterned and plain silk.

Junior Policy Critic Yi Chae submitted the following petition: "Now the country and military are suffering numerous hardships and the people have no peace. Yet frequently you have banqueting sessions with ministers. Moreover, the Eastern Tribes continue their attacks and their military encampments have not been removed. They feign suing for peace, and the country believes them; thus you are planning to send envoys to Liao

---

52 In the vicinity of modern Hŭich'ŏn-si, Chagang Province. Also the location of P'yŏngno Garrison.

to announce the return of the nine fortresses. This is highly inappropriate! Please consider this carefully."

The king went to Sŏnjŏng Hall where he invited tribal leaders: from across the border at Yŏnju 延州[53] he met Shoufushou 守弗首 and others, seventeen people; from across the border at Ch'ŏngsae 清塞[54] Guifu 歸夫 and others, eighteen people; from across the border at P'yŏngno Yaofu 要弗 and others, twenty-eight people. The king bestowed wine and food, and also gave presents.

The king went outside Sinbong Gate to inspect the Divine Cavalry Corps.

The king went to Chunggwang Hall and invited the Eastern Tribal Chief Guoxia 果下 and others, sixty-three people in all, bestowing wine, food, and presents.

The king dispatched Yi Yŏrim 李汝霖 to Liao to petition the newly constructed nine fortresses on the eastern border.

The king made an official record of Yang Kyu's merit, and bestowed on his great-grandson Yang Chebo 楊齊寶 a silver ewer.

The king organized a Hundred Seat Assembly in the Hoegyŏng Hall and ordered the capital and provinces to provide vegetarian food to 30,000 monks.

Second month. The king went to Chunggwang Hall to inspect the Divine Cavalry Corps.

Recording Officer for the Military Commissioner of the Field Army Chang Munwi 張文緯 and others fought with the Jurchen at Sungnyŏng Garrison 崇寧鎮 and killed thirty-eight.

The king went to Sinbong Gate to inspect a crack arbalest platoon.

Administrative Assistants for the Military Commissioner of the Field Army Hŏ Chae 許載, Kim Ŭiwŏn 金義元 and others fought with the Jurchen across the border at Kilchu and killed thirty, also obtaining their armor, cattle, and horses.

Summer, fourth month. Vice Military Supreme Leader for the Eastern

53 Located in the area of modern Unsan, North P'yŏngan Province.

54 Located probably near Hŭich'ŏn-si, North P'yŏngan Province.

Border Circuit O Yŏnch'ong took his leave from the palace [to return to the border]; the king went to Kyŏngnyŏng Hall and personally handed him weapons.

The retired Assistant Executive in Political Affairs Mun Kwan died. Mun Kwan was upright and frugal, and he was famed for his literary skills.

The Eastern Jurchen again sent Shixian to knock on the border gates and negotiate peace.

Fifth month. Because of Ch'ŏk Chun'gyŏng's frequent merit in battle, the king summoned his father, Acting Supreme General Ch'ŏk Wigong 拓謂恭, to the palace. He held an informal meeting and bestowed wine, food, a slab of silver, and ten *sŏk* of rice.

A decree read: "People in the capital are contracting an infectious disease and many have died. We should establish a Directorate to Save People 救濟都監 so as to treat them. Furthermore the corpses and bones should not be left exposed [on the roads]."

The Jurchen attacked Sŏndŏk Garrison, killed people and looted.

Because of the Jurchen raids on the border the king went to Pŏbwang-sa 法王寺 to offer incense, and sent out close ministers to pray in various spirit shrines.

The king was planning to declare an amnesty and summoned the councilors of state to deliberate. Ch'oe Hongjŏng thought that this should not be carried out, but the king said: "Recently my advisors keep firmly requesting to raise troops to punish the enemy. Yet now the bandits have not been exterminated, rather they keep frequently invading our border and raiding people's homes. Both officers and soldiers are tired of the constant fighting: that is the urgent political matter we are facing today. I want to declare an amnesty to bring some respite to people's minds, yet you alone refuse, for what reason?" The king then declared an amnesty.

The king ordered Director of the Chancellery Yun Kwan to go the [ancestral] shrine and altar [for the earth and grain deities] and the nine tombs to pray for a military victory.

The king sent out close ministers to provide relief to hungry people in the northeastern and southwestern provinces.

The Jurchen surrounded Kilchu Fortress; about ten leagues from the fortress they constructed small castles and established six [rows of] palisades. For several months on end they launched attacks on the fortress, which was about to fall. Vice Military Commissioner Yi Kwanjin and others thoroughly prepared his soldiers and in one night they constructed a second wall. Thus defending and fighting for a long time took its toll, resources were depleted and the wounded and dead were many. O Yŏnch'ong led a relief force but the Jurchen blocked the road and ambushed them. Our army suffered a crushing defeat, those killed or taken prisoners were beyond count. O Yŏnch'ong prepared a letter requesting to be punished.

The Supreme Military Leader for the Eastern Border Circuit Yun Kwan was sent out the northwestern circuit.

The king gathered all his officials in Sŏnjŏng Hall to discuss whether the nine fortresses should be returned. In previous debates everyone had argued that since beyond Kunghan-ri[55] of the Jurchen mountains were lined up like a wall, with only one small road leading through them, if a gate and wall were erected, this road would be blocked and hence the calamity [of the Jurchen] would be cut off for good. In fact, however, they manage to attack by land and by sea, there is nowhere they do not pass through, so it is very different from what was originally reported. After the Jurchen lost their lair,[56] they swore they would take revenge, and from near and far they gathered chiefs and attacked continuously over the years. With their crafty plans and weapons there was nowhere they could not hit.

Even though our castles were steep and strong and could not be taken, our troops suffered heavy losses in defending them and fighting the enemy. Also, the newly expanded territory was too large, and the distance between the

55 Kunghan-li 弓漢里, also -ch'on 村: is not clear what this term designates; it probably does not refer to a certain village but to the Jurchen tribe who inhabited the East Coast area where Yun Kwan expanded Koryŏ territory into. Perhaps it corresponds to the Kallajŏn mentioned in the *Jinshu* as the area where the fortresses were built: 築九城於曷懶甸. *Jinshi* 1, Shiji 1. http://chinesenotes.com/jinshi/jinshi001.html

56 Kulhyŏl 窟穴: literally "cave," but likely a derogatory term similar to the English lair. It could also refer to significant location or holy site in the mountains.

fortresses too big. The enemy lay in ambush in deep and inhospitable valleys, and raided everyone who passed through. For the country, raising troops was fraught with many difficulties, with many grumbling and resisting throughout the country. Added to this were famine and pestilence, and resentment and complaints surged. Amidst the resentment against the Jurchen, they sent an envoy to request peace and the return of their former territory.

The ministers debated extensively but could not reach an agreement, so the king was at a loss as to what to do. Then [Senior] Policy Critic Kim Yŏn spoke: "When the ruler of men seizes territory, he does so in order to nurture the people. Thus rather than fighting over the fortresses and killing people, it is better to return the territory and give the people some rest. If we do not return it now, then a rift will arise with the Khitan." The king then asked "why would that be the case?" Kim Yŏn replied "When our country first built the fortresses we sent an envoy to the Khitan with a memorial that claimed that Kunghan-ri of the Jurchen was our ancient territory, and that its residents were also people who belonged to us. Furthermore the memorial said that due to the recent incessant attacks on the border, we reclaimed the land and built the fortresses. In spite of these words, many of the chiefs of Kunghan-ri receive office titles from the Khitan, and therefore the Khitan will believe that we lied and will definitely rebuke us. If we have to defend in the east against the Jurchen and in the north against the Khitan, then I fear that the Nine Fortresses will be anything but a blessing for the Sam Han." The king agreed with him.

General Yang Sŏn 良善 led troops to the eastern border circuit, and the king gave him two silver ingots.

The king dispatched Left Transmitter of Edicts Sim Hu to convey the king's instructions to soldiers and officers in the eastern border circuit and to distribute forty silver ingots.

Sixth month. Yun Kwan and O Yŏnch'ong gathered troops in Chŏngju so as to break the siege of Kilchu. When the army reached Nabokki 那卜其村 Village, Manager of Records in Hamju Yu Wŏnsŏ 兪元胥 came with an urgent report that the Jurchen officials[57] Niaofu 裊弗 and Shixian had knocked on the castle gates [of Hamju?] and told him: 'We arrived yesterday at Ajigo village 阿之古村; the Grand Preceptor Wuyashu now wants to negotiate peace, and therefore had us deliver this message to the Military Commissioner. However, because of the military conflict we do not dare enter the border. Please send someone to our camp so that we can relay in detail what the Grand Preceptor told us.' After Yun Kwan had listened to this he returned to the fortress [of Chŏngju?]. The next day he sent Recorder to the Military Commissioner[58] Yi Kwanjung 李管仲 to the enemy camp to tell the Jurchen general Wushe 吳舍 the following: "Negotiating peace is not something a military commissioner can do by himself. You should send the officials to our court to report." Wushe was greatly pleased.

A decree read: "Recently there has been no peace at the Eastern Border, and soldiers and horses are exhausted. This is all caused by the fact that the geomantic force has been depleted. We should use the secret arts of Yin-Yang divination to resolve this. Both the Bureau of Astronomy and the Bureau of Astrology should present a letter on this."

A decree read: "Recently the border troubles are oppressing both army and people, who are in dire straits. Together the ruler and ministers have made a sincere vow before Heaven to implement the founding king's deathbed instructions, so all officials should be ordered to debate on this matter." Moreover the king ordered his close ministers to offer prayers at the mountains of Chinbong-san 進奉山 and Kuryong-san 九龍山.

Executives Ch'oe Hongsa and Kim Kyŏngyong, Assistant Executive in Political Affairs Im Ŭi, and Commissioner of the Security Council Yi Wi gathered in Sŏnjŏng Hall and faced off during a heated debate over Yun Kwan, O Yŏnch'ong, and Im Ŏn's guilt in losing the war.

Niaofu, Shixian and their party returned to Hamju and announced: "We would like to go to your court, yet in the midst of conflict we are afraid

---

57 *Gongxiong* 公兄: Likely a term for "brothers" or trusted allies of the Khitan leader. In Chosŏn a term for important officials at the county level, mostly *samgonghyŏng* 三公兄.

58 *Pyŏngma kisa* 兵馬記事: only occurrence of this term; probably the same as *pyŏngma noksa* 兵馬錄事, recording officer for the military commissioner.

of entering the pass [to cross into Koryŏ]. We request the exchange of hostages." Yun Kwan and the others chose Yi Kwanjung, I Hyŏn 異賢 and others as hostage, and Niaofu and his party then went to court. The king went to Sŏnjŏng Hall and at its southern gate met Niaofu and his party of six, and asked about their reason for coming to court. Niaofu and the others said: "Formerly, our Grand Preceptor Yingge used to say, 'My ancestor came from [your] great country, and up until his children and grandchildren their intention is to return allegiance [to this country].' Now the Grand Preceptor is Wuyashu, and he too regards [your] great country as the country of his parents. Recently the people from Kunghan-ri of themselves disturbed the peace, this was not at the behest of the Grand Preceptor. Your dynasty invoked their transgression of the border as reason for punishing them. Yet you allowed the resumption of good relations, and trusting you we never broke off the presentation of tribute. We could thus scarcely believe that last year you would raise a large army and invade, killing our elderly and children, and erect nine fortresses; this left our poor people bereft and with nowhere to turn to. Therefore the Grand Preceptor sent us to ask for our old territory back. Prostrate, we hope that you show mercy on us and return the nine fortresses so that the people there may live in peace. Then, we swear to heaven, we will from generation to generation forever send tribute and would not dare to throw as much as a tile over the border." The king comforted them and bestowed wine and food.

Autumn, seventh month. The king gathered state councilors, censorial officers, drafters of edicts and proclamations from various offices, officials attending the king, those of the rank of administrative assistant and above at the Capital Military Command, and those of rank three and above among civil and military officials in the Sŏnjŏng Hall to discuss the return of the nine fortresses. All were in favor of their return. The king then went to the gate of the Sŏnjŏng Hall where he called for Niaofu and the rest and told them about the decision to return the nine fortresses. Niaofu was moved to tears and bowed in gratitude.

The king put Executive Chief of the Royal Secretariat Im Ŭi provisionally in charge of military affairs in the northeast sector and concurrently made him Military Commissioner of the Field Army. Junior Policy Critic Kim Yŏn was appointed second in command. The king bestowed the [ceremonial] weapons of war and sent them off.

Special Commissioner for the Field Army Command and Transmitter of Edicts Ch'oe Hongjŏng, Military Commissioner and Vice-minister of Personnel Mun Kwan and others instructed the Jurchen chief Juweiyi 居尉伊 and others as follows: "If you want us to return the nine fortresses you should make an oath to heaven that you will honor the agreements as before." The chiefs then constructed a platform outside the gate of Hamju and swore the following: "Henceforth without evil intentions we will establish tribute relations throughout the generations. May this earth perish if we fail to hold the oath." Having thus sworn they returned. Ch'oe Hongjŏng and the others then started with the withdrawal of the fortresses from Kilchu onwards, gathering weapons and provisions and transporting them to the interior. The Jurchen gladly assisted by using their cattle and horses to transport the old and young back; not one amongst them was hurt. Im Ŭi and his army were delayed, and without doing a single thing at the border they returned.

Yun Kwan and O Yŏnch'ong returned [to the capital]. The king dispatched Transmitter of Edicts Sim Hu to receive their [ceremonial] weapons of war on the central avenue [of Kaesŏng]. They were not allowed to report on their mission and had to return to their private residences. The Royal Secretariat requested that Yun Kwan and O Yŏnch'ong be tried for the crime of losing the war.

The king ordered Ch'oe Minyong 崔敏庸 and others from the Grand Academy,[59] seventy people in total, and Han Chasun 韓子純 and others from the Military Academy, eight people in total, to divide into seven studios, to wit: The Yŏt'aek 麗澤 [Mutual Adornment] studio for the *Book of Changes*; the Taebing 待聘 [Waiting for a Summons] studio for the *Book of Documents*; the Kyŏngdŏk 經德 [Virtue of the Canon] studio for the

59 Taehak 大學: It is not clear in how far this was a specific institution or just a generic name for the academies of learning.

Mao Edition of the Book of Poetry; the Kuin 求仁 [Pursuing Humaneness] studio for the *Rites of Zhou*; the Pog'ŭng 服膺 [Applying the Teachings] studio for the Rites of Dai [the Elder]; the Yangjŏng 養正 [Cultivating the Correct] studio for the *Spring and Autumn Annals*; and the Kang'ye 講藝 [Instructions on (Military) Arts] for the Military Academy.

Eighth month. The Divine Cavalry Corps returned from the eastern border circuit. The king went to the West Tower of Chunggwang Hall to comfort them, saying "Defeat in the eastern expedition was on account of excesses by the officers and generals. How could I forget the sacrifices you made?"

As it was the Mid-autumn Festival, the king took his literary officials to watch the moon from the official residence in Chunggwang Hall, and personally composed an ode on the moon.

The Jurchen Shixian and others came to present local products.

Ninth month. A Hundred Seat Assembly was organized in Hoegyŏng Hall. The king gave an order that throughout the country 30,000 monks ought to be given a vegetarian banquet.

Winter, tenth month. The king's son Wang Ku 王構 was born; later his name was changed to Wang Hae 王楷.[60]

Yi Wi was appointed assistant executive in political affairs.

Winter, eleventh month. The king held audience in Kŏndŏk Hall. Policy Critics Yi Chae and Kim Yŏn, Censor-in-chief Ch'oe Kyebang and others requested that Yun Kwan and O Yŏnch'ong be tried for the crime of losing the war, but the king did not allow this, and retired to his private quarters. Yi Chae and the others prostrated themselves in front of the gate [of the king's quarters] and strongly implored till noon. The king then ordered Transmitter of Edicts Sim Hu to placate and convince them.

The Eastern Jurchen chief Wulao 吳老 and others came to court.

The king went to Sŏnjŏng Hall and received tribal leaders Changduo 長多, Laju 老居 and others from beyond the P'yŏngno and Ch'ŏngsae passes, forty-five people in all, as well as Shixian and others, seven people, and bestowed wine, food, and presents according to precedent.

---

60 I.e. the future King Injong (r. 1122–1146).

State Councilor Ch'oe Hongsa and others together with the offices of remonstrance again request that Yun Kwan and others be put on trial.

Twelfth month. The Song Military Instructor,[61] General Military Commissioner for Mingzhou Ren Guo 任郭 and others, arrived.

The king dispatched close officials to provide relief to hungry people throughout the routes, including Hŭnghwa, Unjung, Sŏhae, the Southern Capital, Kwangju, and Ch'unch'ŏngju.

The king gave a banquet for princes and state councilors in Chunggwang Hall that lasted until daybreak.

The king dispatched Office Chief at the Slave Agency Yi Kukkyŏng 李國瓊 to Liao to report on the return of the nine fortresses to the Jurchen.

Yejong fifth year [1110]

Fourth year of the Daguan era of Song, tenth year of the Qiantong era of Liao

Spring, first month. The tribal chief Mangjian and others, twenty-eight people in all, from outside the pass at Changju came to court

Liao dispatched Director of the Office of Regalia Li Fengzhen 李逢辰 to congratulate the king on his birthday.

The king went to Sŏnjŏng Hall and at its south gate received seventy-four tribal leaders from the northern border region and bestowed presents according to rank. Then he went to the south gate of Chunggwang Hall to receive nineteen people and bestowed wine, food, and presents according to precedent.

The king went to the south tower of Chunggwang Hall to inspect the Divine Cavalry Corps practicing polo. He bestowed presents according to rank.

Second month. The Jurchen chief Wanshui 萬水 and others, thirteen people, came to court.

61 *Jiaolianshi* 教練使 is probably here used as a diplomatic function but it is not clear what purpose such an envoy would have fulfilled.

Im Ŭi was made Executive Chief of the Chancellery and then retired; P'il Kwangch'an 畢光贊 was appointed junior vice-director of the Department of Ministries, and Yi O was provisionally put in charge of the Ministry of Personnel.

Summer, fourth month. The Bureau of Astronomy petitioned: "This year there were epidemics that ravaged the country, leaving the streets littered with corpses. We request that relevant offices gather and bury them." This was followed.

The king granted Yi Chŏngsŭng 李正升 and twenty-eight others [exam passers] by royal grace; also three passed the classics examination, and three passed the composition test of the civil service examination.

The southern corridor building of the Bureau of Medicine caught fire. The king personally went to the eastern gate of the Bureau of Royal Carriages to save it.

Fifth month. The king went to Kŏndŏk Hall for the audience. State Councilors Ch'oe Hongsa and Kim Kyŏngyong together with the remonstrance offices presented a memorial discussing the crimes of Yun Kwan and O Yŏnch'ong in losing the war. The king did not listen to it and went into his private quarters. Ch'oe Hongsa and the others kept imploring at the gates until late afternoon but to no avail. The state councilors and remonstrance officials then returned to their private residences and did not leave them. As the departments were thus empty, the king summoned Executive Yi O and Drafting Advisor Yi Tŏg'u and others to take care of business in the departments. Ch'oe Hongsa and the others did not leave their houses for several weeks. The king then sent his close officials to persuade him and then he returned. The remonstrance officials also started to take care of business again. People at the time ridiculed this situation.

On *ŭlmyo* day [the 17th] a comet was visible; it remained so for nine days.

Sixth month. The king went to Kŏndŏk Hall and summoned the two female musicians who were returned by Mingzhou for a meeting.

An edict read: "By mistake I somehow came to rule the Sam Han with this deficient body of mine. Overwhelmed by myriad affairs, I cannot pay attention to all of them. Punishments fail to be completely impartial, and the seasons are out of whack. For the past three or four years there have been crop failures and the people suffer from hunger and disease. From before sunrise to after sunset I worry and toil without even a moment's respite. Moreover, there has not been a day without a celestial abnormality. Since the beginning of the summer months there has been a chilly wind, and hailstones have fallen. This must be the result of my feeble virtue. My feelings of dread keep worsening, so I express here my intention to spread my humble feelings of respect: above I will respond the Heaven's censure, and below I will comfort the people's minds. This will call forth a harmonious spirit that will protect peace." An amnesty was declared.

Song dispatched Vice-minister of War Wang Xiang 王襄 and Drafter in the Secretariat Zhang Bangchang 張邦昌 carrying an imperial edict. They also brought robes, belt, silk, golden and jade vessels, bow and arrows, and a horse saddle. After the king had received these, Wang Xiang said: "The emperor[62] perceives everything clearly from 10,000 leagues away. He appreciates the king's loyalty and sincerity and wants to show his respect. We are aware that the king has already received investiture from the Northern Dynasty, and that the two dynasties [i.e. Liao and Koryŏ] have carried on friendly relations for a hundred years with the righteousness of brothers. Therefore the emperor does not want to invest you again, but merely entrusted us with an edict in which the character for "provisional" (Ch. *quan* 權) has been removed; he thus cherishes you, king, by extending the rites of a true king. Moreover the emperor has drafted this edict in his own hand; surely the Northern Dynasty cannot match such ritual. Now that we witness how the king received the edict with utmost reverence, when we return and report this to the emperor he will surely be very pleased and increase his munificence. We request that you, king, reply to the emperor's grace with even greater show of devotion and respect."

Autumn seventh month. Wang Xiang and the rest of his embassy returned. The king entrusted them with a memorial that expressed the king's gratitude:

---

62 I.e. Emperor Huizong of Song (r. 1100–1125).

"This small country borders the Great Liao, from whom we received royal investiture and the calendar for a long time. Therefore, we have not dared to receive an official edict [of investiture] from the emperor [of Song], however much this shames us. Now we have received your edict, in which, due to the Liao's investiture, you have finally removed the character for 'provisional' to display [my] correct name. Moreover, you have personally written the edict in your own hand. Such a glorious honor has not been seen even in antiquity. We are ashamed at this undeserved honor, and will endeavor to show our utmost sincerity."

Executive Chief of the Chancellery Yi O died. Yi O was quiet and unassuming by nature, and had few desires. He did not pursue business interests and was an ardent believer in Buddhism. He called himself Layman Kŭmgang 金剛居士.

Intercalary eighth month. On *kyemyo* day [the 7th] the king took the queen dowager on a trip to the Southern Capital. On the way they also visited Changŭi-sa 藏義寺 and Sŭngga Cave 僧伽窟 on Mt. Samgak.

Ninth month. The king gave a banquet for all princes and state councilors in the Ch'ŏnsu Hall 天授殿 which lasted till daybreak. The king gave food and presents to all. The king composed a poem and ordered the Confucian officials to present a matching poem. He then bestowed presents commensurate to rank. A performer reenacted the life of the meritorious subject of yesteryear, Ha Kongjin 河拱辰, and this made the king commemorate his merit. He appointed the great-great grandson, Registrar at the Office of Regalia Ha Chun 河濬 as audience usher, and then also composed a poem especially for him.

The king went to Nammyŏng Gate 南明門 to inspect the soldiers and officers of the Divine Cavalry, Divine Infantry, Elite Arbalest, and Assault Raider Corpses. He then ordered the Divine Cavalry Corps to hold a polo game. He then bestowed presents commensurate to rank.

The king went to the Pungnyŏng Gate 北寧門 to inspect archery practice by civil and military officials. Those who hit the target were granted presents.

Winter, tenth month. On *kapchin* day [the 9th] Venus appeared across the sky by day.

The Western Jurchen Guji 古伋, Guoxia and others, ninety-eight people in total, came to present horses.

The king personally held a banquet for those over the age of eighty as well as filial [sons and grandsons], righteous [husbands], chaste [wives], widows and widowers, orphans and those living alone, and those with serious illness outside Nammyŏng Gate; he bestowed presents commensurate to rank. For one filial son in particular he set a precedent by especially writing a poem for him; he showed it to those around.

Eleventh month. On *ŭlch'uk* day, the first day of the month, the king returned from the Southern Capital, and declared an amnesty.

The Eastern Jurchen Shixian and others, twelve people in total, came to court. The king went to Sŏnjŏng Hall where he invited them and bestowed presents commensurate to rank.

Twelfth month. The king went to the Southern Tower at Chunggwang Hall and invited a party of more than forty Western Jurchen, including chiefs and bestowed drinks and food.

Yun Kwan was accorded the title of Probationary Grand Guardian, Director of the Chancellery, Minister of War; Kim Kyŏngyong was named Executive Chief of the Chancellery, Minister of Punishment; O Yŏnch'ong was made Executive Chief of the Royal Secretariat, Administrator of the Finance Commission; Yi Wi was appointed Executive of the Royal Secretariat, Minister of Taxation, concurrently Commissioner to the Resident Governor of the Western Capital; Hŏ Kyŏng was appointed Vice-minister of Punishment, Commissioner of the Security Council; Yi Chagyŏm was made Director of the Office of Royal Clan Affairs, Associate Admistrator of the Security Council. Prior to this, due to the insistence by assorted officials that Yun Kwan and O Yŏnch'ong be terminated from office, the king had abrogated their titles of merit subject. Now he restored their functions. Yun Kwan and the others sent in a petition in which they refused these appointments, but the king issued a proclamation that rejected this.

Yejong sixth year [1111]

First year of the Zhenghe era of Song, first year of the Tianqing era of Liao

Spring, first month. An amnesty was declared. The king bestowed food and drinks on elderly, widows and widowers, orphans and those living alone, chaste [wives] and righteous [husbands], and filial [sons and grandsons] throughout the country, and also bestowed presents commensurate with rank. Furthermore, he bestowed titles of nobility on the descendants of T'aejo's merit subjects.

Liao dispatched Surveillance Commissioner for the Taizhou jurisdiction Da Zhongxuan 大仲宣 to congratulate the king on his birthday.

The king went to Sŏnjŏng Hall and invited thirty Jurchen village heads from the northern border circuit for a meeting.

Hŏ Kyŏng was appointed Vice-minister of Personnel and Assistant Executive in Political Affairs; Yi Chagyŏm was appointed Censor-in-chief; and Kim Yŏn was made Director of the Palace Library and Vice-commissioner of the Security Council.

Assistant Executive in Political Affairs Mun Kwan retired.

The king gave a banquet for elderly commoners and for chaste [wives] and righteous [husbands], and filial sons and daughters on the palace courtyard; for the state elders, the retired vice-ministers Im Sŏnggae 林成槩, Ryu T'aek and others he gave a banquet in the Office for Audience Ceremonies. The king personally urged them to eat, something that moved many of those watching to tears. Im Sŏnggae carried with him a petition of remonstrance that he presented; it contained five articles, each related to important matters of state. The king wanted to invite the retired Executive Kim Sanggi, who was 81, for a meal in the inner quarters to his special esteem, but Kim Sanggi refused on account of his age and illness. The king then especially commissioned a palanquin to carry him into the inner quarters and absolved him of the need to make obeisance to the king, but Kim Sanggi adamantly refused to go.

Summer, fifth month. Director of the Chancellery Yun Kwan died. He was originally from P'ap'yŏng County 坡平縣. He passed the civil service examination at young age and loved learning to the point that he always had a book in his hands. Even as commander in the field, the five classics never left his side. He loved the worthy and delighted in the good, and was the best of his generation. He was given the posthumous epithet Munsuk 文肅 [Literary refinement].

Autumn, seventh month. The king dispatched vice-commissioner at the Security Council Kim Yŏn and Director of Royal Workshops Im Yumun 林有文 to Song. Embassy Secretary, Intendant of the Hallim Academy Kim Puch'ŏl presented a memorial requesting to attend the Grand Academy[63] so as to attend lectures. The emperor replied with a decree that expressed appreciation for his intention of visiting such an important place to listen to disquisitions on the classics; it also praised his beautiful prose. On the embassy's return Kim Puch'ŏl was selected as investigating censor.

Eighth month. Recording Officer for the Left-Right Division Ho Chongdan 胡宗旦 was provisionally made Intendant of the Hallim Academy. Ho Chongdan was originally from Fuzhou in Song. Once he had been a student of the Superior College at the National University [of Song China]. He was intelligent and widely learned, both skilled in writing and in various arts. When traveling in the region of the Zhejiang Provinces he took a commercial vessel and crossed the sea [to Korea]. The king greatly cherished him and treated him generously. He was thus swiftly promoted to important positions. However, he used mantic arts[64] for this, so it is not surprising that the king was smitten with him.

The grand astrologer petitioned: "The geomantic position of Ch'ŏnsu-sa—built under the previous king—is inauspicious, so we request that it be destroyed. The Medicine Master Cloister[65] should be moved." The king personally went to appraise the territory.

Ninth month. The king organized a banquet for the double ninth festival.

---

63 Pyŏg'ong 璧雍: a name for one of the academies in the Zhou era.

64 Apsŭng sul 壓勝術: dictionaries describe this as the use of written or spoken spells to ward off danger or evil.

65 Yaksa-wŏn 藥師院: Cloister of Bhaiṣajyaguru, the Buddha of the eastern paradise, associated with healing arts and hence always depicted with a medicine bowl.

The king composed a poem and had his attendant ministers present matching poems.

The king ordered his attendants and close officials to practice archery; those who hit the target were given presents commensurate with rank. The king also held a banquet.

Winter, tenth month. The king dispatched Executive at the Ministry of Punishment Yi Chadŏk 李資德 to Liao to congratulate the emperor on the Tianxing Festival.

A Hundred Seat Assembly was held in Hoegyŏng Hall, and food was given to 10,000 monks in the palace courtyard. A further 20,000 monks were fed in the prefectures.

Eleventh month. Officials requested that the construction of Ch'ŏnsu-sa be halted. The king went to the Medicine Master Cloister to again appraise the temple's foundations.

The king dispatched envoys to Liao to give thanks for the birthday wishes; he also sent Director of the Office of Royal Clan Affairs Kim Chin 金縝 to present local products and Deputy Director of the Foreign Relations Office Mun Kong'ŏn 文公彥 to give new year's greetings.

Twelfth month. Hŏ Kyŏng was appointed Executive of the Royal Secretariat, jointly executive chief [of the same institution].

Liao dispatched as ad-hoc envoy the Acting Minister of Works Xiao Zunli 蕭遵禮.

The military commissioner for the northeast sector executed a soldier from Sŏndŏk Garrison, Chŏng Chin 鄭珍, and one Paek Pok 白卜 from Chŏngju, together with the Jurchen Gufu 骨夫. Earlier Chŏng Chin and Paek Pok had committed crimes and sought refuge with the Jurchen, plotting with them to raid the border area. Chŏng Chin's mother was in Wŏnhŭng Garrison, so one night Chŏng Chin, Paek Pok, and Gufu sneaked into the garrison to take away his mother. The military commissioner sent soldiers to either apprehend or kill them. They also retrieved weapons. The king bestowed titles and prizes commensurate with rank.

Yejong seventh year [1112]

Second year of the Zhenghe era of Song, second year of the Tianqing era of Liao

Spring, first month. Liao dispatched the Surveillance Commissioner for the Yongzhou Jurisdiction Liu Gongyun 劉公允 to congratulate the king on his birthday.

Second month. A remonstrance official sent a petition asking to stop construction of Ch'ŏnsu-sa, and the king accepted this.

Kim Kyŏngyong was appointed Acting Grand Guardian, in charge of affairs at the Ministry of Personnel; O Yŏnch'ong was appointed Acting Minister of Education, in charge of affairs at the Ministry of War; Hŏ Kyŏng was appointed Honorary Minister of Education, in charge of affairs at the Ministry of Rites; Ryu Injŏ and Yi Chagyŏm were made Assistant Executive in Political Affairs; and Ch'oe Kyebang and Ko Yŏngsin 高令臣 were additionally appointed to supervise the Security Council.

Third month. Executive Chief of the Chancellery Ch'oe Hongsa three times sent a memorial requesting [retirement on account of] old age, and this was granted.

Chŏng Chiwŏn 鄭之元 and twenty-four others passed the composition test of the civil service examination, and three passed the classics examination. Chŏng Chiwŏn is none other than Chŏng Chisang 知常.

Summer, fourth month. The king went to the Gossamer Tower in the inner quarters of the palace and composed a poem on peonies. He ordered the Confucian ministers to submit corresponding poems, and rewarded them with silk commensurate to rank. King Hyŏnjong had once personally planted peonies in front of the tower, and from Tŏkchong to Sukchong all made poems in praise of the flowers, and ordered attending ministers to compose corresponding poems.

The king held a banquet in Sangch'un Pavilion.

Fifth month. The king gathered all officials of rank three and above and enquired on the correct policy to control the border.

Sixth month. Kim Yŏn returned from Song. When he reached Kyŏngwŏn Prefecture he rushed off for his father's funeral and did not report on his mission. At the time people ridiculed his lack of propriety.

The Duke of Puyŏ Wang Su was moved to Kŏje County 巨濟縣;[66] his son was banished to Chillye County 進禮縣.[67] Since Wang Su had committed another crime in Kyŏngsan District 京山府,[68] he was transferred. When he reached Hyŏnp'ung County 玄風縣[69] he died.

Assistant Executive in Political Affairs Mun Kwan died. Mun Kwan was generous of spirit and upright as an official. He did not engage in profitable activities, and fought the Jurchen on several occasions, thus establishing his merit.

Autumn, seventh month. On *kisa* day [the 14th] the Queen Dowager Lady Ryu was in Purŭn-sa 佛恩寺 when her illness suddenly grew worse. The king sped there and requested that she be brought into the inner palace, but when the procession reached Sinbak-sa 信朴寺 she died. The king gave her the posthumous title Myŏngŭi Wangt'aehu 明懿王太后.

Eighth month, *pyŏngsin* day [the 12th]. The queen dowager was buried in Sung-nŭng 崇陵. The king saw off [the funerary cortege] in the palace courtyard.

The historian Kim Puŭi comments: "The designation 'queen dowager' 太后 is what a son calls his mother while she is alive. According to the *History of the Tang*, while alive she follows the son, but after entering the shrine she follows the husband. In that case, in death she ought to be called queen consort 王后. Now that his mother has died yet giving her the posthumous title of queen dowager is against propriety. This is a mistake by the ritual officials.

The king dispatched Director of the Office of Royal Clan Affairs Yi Tŏg'u to Liao to announce the bereavement.

The abbot of Songni-sa, the *sŭngt'ong* T'aeng 竀, was exiled to Kŏje

---

66 Modern Kŏje-do island.

67 In the area of modern Kŭmsan, South Ch'ungch'ŏng Province.

68 Modern Sŏngju, North Kyŏngsang Province.

69 Modern Hyŏnp'ung-myŏn, Talsŏng-gun, North Kyŏngsang Province.

County. Also exiled to distant places were the Junior Assistant Director of the Department of Ministries Kim Insŏk 金仁碩, the Departmental Commissioner of Chŏnju Yi Yŏrim, Vice-director of the Office of Royal Clan Affairs Ha Ŏnsŏk, Vice-minister of Punishments Im Sinhaeng, Chief Minister[70] Yi Chungp'yŏng 李仲平, Executive at the Ministry of Punishment Yi Ilsuk, Generals Kim T'aeksin 金澤臣 and Song Yŏnghan 宋英漢, Sub-colonel Kim Yusŏng 金有成, Magistrate for Namwŏn District Yi Su 李綏, Commissioner for Yŏngsak Garrison Yi Iryŏn 李日衍, the monk Chasang 資尙 from Sunggyo-sa 崇教寺, as well as the sons of Kim Insŏk, Yi Yŏrim, Im Sinhaeng, and Ha Ŏnsŏk. Chasang was executed on the way to exile. The monk T'aeng was a son of King Munjong, and as the abbot of Songni-sa[71] he amassed a huge fortune, which he used for generous gifts to people in return for their loyalty. Someone reported that T'aeng and Kim Insŏk and the others were associating to plan a rebellion, hence these [punitive] measures. Not long afterwards [T'aeng] died.

Ninth month. Kim Kyŏngyong was made Director of the Chancellery; O Yŏnch'ong and Yi Wi were appointed Chief of the Chancellery and jointly Executive of the Royal Secretariat-Chancellery; Ryu Injŏ was made Vice-director of the Department of Ministries and Minister of Punishments; Yi Chagyŏm was appointed Acting Minister of Works, Vice-minister of War, and Administrator of the Finance Commission; Ch'oe Kyebang was made Acting Minster of Works, Commissioner of the Security Council; Ko Yŏngsin was made Vice-minister of Personnel, Administrator of the Security Council; Kim Yŏn was made Senior Policy Advisor, Associate Administrator of the Security Council; and Kang Chŭng 康拯 was appointed Censor-in-chief.

The king dispatched Executive at the Ministry of Rites Kim Chin to Liao to offer felicitations on the Tianxing Festival.

Winter, tenth month. The king dispatched Executive at the Ministry of

70 Taegyŏng 大卿: this is the first occurrence of this term. Since it usually refers to the head of a Ministry or office, it is likely the head of the Ministry of Punishment that is meant here.

71 Songni-sa: presumably this refers to Pŏpchu-sa 法住寺, which is located on Mt. Songni 俗離山.

Works Yi Ch'ongnin 李寵鱗 to give thanks for the ad-hoc envoys; and Executive at the Ministry of Taxation Kang Yŏl 康悅 to give thanks for the birthday wishes.

Eleventh month. Three times the state councilors petitioned that the king resume normal dishes;[72] the king accepted.

The king dispatched Deputy Director of the Foreign Relations Office Ch'oe Hwa 崔俰 to Liao to present local products, and Executive at the Ministry of Punishment Hŏ Chigi 許之奇 to offer congratulations on the new year.

The Liao envoy in charge of ritual from the Eastern Capital charged with returning the courtesy, Xie Shan 謝善, arrived.

Twelfth month. Ch'oe Sach'u was made Probationary Grand Preceptor, Royal Secretary, and then retired; Im Kan was made Chief of the Chancellery, jointly Executive [of the same department], and then retired; Kim Kyŏngyong was made Merit Subject Joining in Strategy and Protecting the Altar.

72 I.e. after the mourning for his mother.

8. Yejong (II)

Yejong eighth year [1113]

Third year of the Zhenghe era of Song, third year of the Tianqing era of Liao

Spring, first month. Liao dispatched Chief Minister of the Court of Imperial Entertainment Zhang Ruhui 張如晦 to congratulate the king on his birthday.

The Liao imperial funerary envoys, Surveillance Commissioner for the Jurisdiction of Yongzhou, Yelü Gu 耶律固 and Vice-chamberlain for Ceremonials, Wang Shen 王侁, and the condolence envoy, Surveillance Commissioner for the Jurisdiction of Taizhou, Xiao Chan 蕭辿, arrived.

The king went to the memorial hall[1] for the queen dowager; the Liao envoy transmitted the decree, and also performed sacrifices.

The officials jointly petitioned: "From the time of the founding fathers of our dynasty, whenever a queen dowager passed away, the neighboring countries never sent envoys for condolence and sacrifice. Today we witnessed such ritual for the first time. Now the evening before it rained and snowed heavily, but today as the ritual was performed the sun shone brightly in the clear sky. When the rites are straightened, people's minds are gladdened. It is fitting that you should order all officials to offer felicitations." The king followed this.

---

1 Ugung 虞宮: place where the spirit tablet is enshrined after the funeral for the rest of the mourning period.

Liao dispatched Chief Minister of the Court of Imperial Entertainment Yang Juzhi 楊擧直 to order the king to [cast off mourning clothes] and resume wearing normal dress.

Second month. Yelü Gu and the other members of the embassy returned. They requested copies of the *Chunqiu shili*, *Jinhua ji*, and *Yingzhou ji*,[2] and the king granted a copy to each

Two gardens were established in the southwest of the palace. At the time palace offices competed in ostentatiousness to flatter the king. They erected towers and pavilions, built soaring walls, and gathered flowers and plants from people's homes and transplanted them there. Still they thought this insufficient, and purchased [plants] from Song merchants, using gold and brocade from the palace coffers indiscriminately. Moreover they constructed many temples in the capital and beyond, exhausting construction materials. This generated a lot of controversy, and the two gardens were finally abolished.

Hŏ Kyŏng was appointed Executive of the Chancellery and jointly the Royal Secretariat -Chancellery, and then made to retire. Ch'oe Chŏng 崔挺 was appointed Minister of Education and Assistant Executive in Political Affairs, and then also made to retire.

The king went to Wangnyun-sa and then returned via the road south of the Ministry of Punishments. When the prisoners perceived the royal carriage they all shouted "Manse"! The king ordered his attending officials to go to the prison and bestow wine upon them and free those convicted for light offenses.

Third month, *imja* day, the first day of the month. The Grand Astrologer reported that due to dense clouds the solar eclipse could not be observed. All the officials sent in memorials of congratulation.

The king held an audience in Kŏndŏk Hall and invited the new examination passers Chŏng Chiwŏn and others. He bestowed wine and food

2 *Chunch'u sŏngnye, Kŭmhwa Yŏngju chip* 春秋釋例金華瀛洲集: The former appears to be a commentary on the *Spring and Autumn annals*, while the identity of the latter collections is not clear. Yŏngju could refer to a mythical island of the immortals, but is also used for Cheju island.

in the Office for Audience Ceremonies and appointed them to their first office.

Yi Chagyŏm was appointed Vice-director of the Department of Ministries and Ryu Chayu 柳子維 was made Junior Vice-director [of the same institution]. Kim Yŏn was made Vice-minister of War and manager of the Security Council.

The king summoned former Executive Kwak Yŏ 郭輿. Kwak habitually came to attend affairs in the palace wearing a black cap and a coat of crane feathers. In discussions he always talked quietly, seeking to find a harmonious response [rather than stick to his own opinion]. People at the time called him a "feathered guest of the golden gate."

Summer, fourth month. The king personally gave a banquet in the palace courtyard for those over eighty, and for the filial sons and grandsons, righteous [husbands] and chaste [wives], the orphaned and lonely, and those suffering from illness. He bestowed presents commensurate with rank, and especially ordered the retired Vice-minister of Ritual, Im Sŏnggae, to be carried in a palanquin into the palace for a banquet in the Office for Audience Ceremonies. The king personally served him food and bestowed robes.

Intercalary [fourth] month. The Jurchen Wuluogu 烏羅骨, Shixian and others came to give thanks for the return of the nine fortresses. They presented horses and gold.

Fifth month. The Song Chief Merchant Chen Shou 陳守 presented a white pheasant.

Assistant Executive in Letters Ryu Injŏ died. His younger sister was married to King Sukchong. His family became rich and prominent, but he consorted with other Confucian young scholars, studying and eventually passing the examination. Even though he then became state councilor and was rich, not once did he become conceited; he always had the demeanor of a Confucian scholar.

Sixth month. Song returned eight castaways from Chindo County 珍島縣[3] including Han Paek 漢白. Originally Han Paek and the others went to

3 Modern Chindo-gun, an island off the coast of South Chŏlla Province.

T'angna island for business, but were blown off course to Mingzhou in Song China. The prefecture of Mingzhou received an imperial edict instructing to bestow rice and silk upon each of them and send them back.

Pak Kyŏngjak was made Master of Sacrificial Wines at the National Academy. At the time, the king wanted to send envoys to the Chinese court, but Pak, who was then Director of the Office of Royal Clan Affairs, sent a memorial of remonstrance that aimed to stop this. His words were so incisive that the king had no choice but to follow him. Following this, he made this appointment, which generated a lot of controversy and regret.

Autumn, seventh month. Ch'oe Kyebang and Ko Yŏngsin were made Assistant Executive in Political Affairs; Cho Chungjang 趙仲璋 was put jointly in charge of the Security Council, and Kim Chun was made Vice-commissioner of the Security Council.

Eighth month. An Office to Determine Details of Ritual Systems was established.[4]

The king went to Changwŏn Pavilion.

Ninth month. The king dispatched Palace Servitor[5] An Chiksung 安稷崇 to Song to transmit a letter from the Foreign Relations Office to Mingzhou which said: "Last year in the sixth month the letter-presenting envoy Kim Yŏn returned to tell us that next year we should also observe a worship ceremony, and instructing the king of the country to send envoys to the imperial court to observe the grand ceremony.[6] We have already readied officials [for this mission], but suddenly my mother the queen died and we

---

4 Yeŭi sangjŏng so 禮儀詳定所: although there is barely any further information on this office, it may have been tasked with compiling detailed ritual manuals that matched theory and practice. Thus it may have prepared the ground for the *Sangjŏng Kogŭm yemun* 詳定古今禮文, a ritual compendium started under Yejong's successor, King Injong.

5 *Sŏdu kongbong-gwan* 西頭供奉官: *sŏdu*, according to Hucker, is an unofficial name for the Clerk's Office (Ch. Kongmu yuan; Hucker no. 2275), while *kongbong-gwan* (Ch. *gongfeng guan*, Hucker no. 3418) in the sense of "to wait upon, serve" is usually added to another title to signify that the bearer was either supernumerary or serving on a rotational basis, usually in service of the emperor. According to the *Koryŏsa*, an official of the Bureau of Royal Stewards (Aekchŏng-guk). KRS 77.16a.

6 It is not clear what event is here being referred to, but probably a memorial service for a deceased emperor.

did not have the opportunity to dispatch officials to attend to this ritual."

Winter, tenth month. The king dispatched Executive at the Ministry of Rites Yi Yŏng 李永 to Liao to offer congratulations on the Tianxing Festival.

The king dispatched Vice-minister of Rites Hong Kwan 洪灌 and Executive at the Ministry of Punishment Kim Ŭiwŏn 金義元 to Liao to give thanks for the condolences and sacrifices.

A Hundred Seat Assembly was organized in Hoegyŏng Hall, and 10,000 monks were given a maigre feast on the polo court, and 20,000 more in the prefectures.

Eleventh month. The king dispatched Vice-director of the Palace Library Han Ch'ung 韓冲 to Liao to give thanks for the [order to] resume normal dress; Executive at the Ministry of Works Yi Muyŏng 李茂榮 to give thanks for the royal birthday felicitations; and Director of the Office of Royal Clan Affairs Ch'oe Hongjae 崔弘宰 to present local products.

Hallim Academicion and Recipient of Edicts Kim Yŏn together with Royal Lecturer Pak Sŭngjung and others composed and submitted a current policy essentials paper in five fascicles. The king bestowed horn-encrusted belts; Editor of History Kim Puch'ŏl and lower-ranking officials were granted presents commensurate to rank.

The king dispatched Executive at the Ministry of Taxation Yi Chagyŏm to Liao to offer new year felicitations.

Twelfth month. Kim Kyŏngyong was appointed Acting Grand Mentor, Minister of Personnel, and Earl of Nangnang; O Yŏnch'ong was made Acting Grand Marshal, Minister of Rites and of War;[7] Ch'oe Kyebang was made Vice-director of the Department of Ministries, Administrator of the Finance Commission; Kim Yŏn was made Vice-minister of Rites and Assistant Executive in Letters, manager of the Hallim Academy; Cho Chungjang was appointed Vice-minister of War, and [manager] of affairs at the Security Council; Ryu Chayu was made junior Vice-director of the Department of Ministries, Minister of War; Kang Chŭng was made Administrator of the

7 Yebyŏngbu 禮兵部: This appears to be a mistake, since it is highly irregular to combine two ministries.

Security Council; Kim Chun was made Senior Policy Advisor and Associate Administrator of the Security Council.

The king dispatched Deputy Director of the Foreign Relations Office Im Kyŏngch'ŏng 林景淸 to Liao to present local products.

Yejong ninth year [1114]

Fourth year of the Zhenghe era of Song, fourth year of the Tianqing era of Liao

Spring, first month. The Western Jurchen general Wuwuhuan 烏無奐 and others, sixty-one people in all, arrived at court.

Director of the Chancellery Kim Kyŏngyong thrice sent a memorial requesting [retirement] on account of old age. The king bestowed upon him staff and table and ordered him to keep attending to his work.

Liao dispatched Director of the Office of Regalia Zhang Ruhui to congratulate the king on his birthday.

The king declared an amnesty.

Second month. The Western Jurchen general Gulao 古老 and others, sixty-six people in all, came to court.

National Academy students Chang Cha 張仔 and others, sixty people in all, came to the palace to deliver a letter requesting the establishment of a National College.[8]

Third month. Yu Chae 劉載 was appointed Vice-director of the Department of Ministries, Academician of Mundŏk Hall.

Director of the Chancellery Kim Kyŏngyong and Assistant Executive in Political Affairs Ko Yŏngsin retired. O Yŏnch'ong was made Minister of Personnel; Kim Yŏn was appointed Vice-minister of Taxation, Assistant Executive in Political Affairs, Minister of Rites, and concurrently Commissioner to the Resident Governor of the Western Capital; Cho Chungjang was made Vice-minister of War, Assistant Executive in Political

---

8 I.e. the Taehak college 大學; how this would differ from the National Academy (Kukchagam 國子監) is not altogether clear.

Affairs, Minister of Punishment; Kang Chŭng was made Vice-director of the Department of Ministries, Commissioner for the Security Council, Administrator of the Finance Commission; Kim Chun was made Vice-minister of Rites and intendant of the Security Council.

Summer, fourth month. Officials petitioned: "The presented scholar from the Western Capital Chŏng Chiwŏn came first in the National Academy test[9] of the *imjin* year (1112); please follow precedent and give him an appointment in the royal capital." The king agreed.

Paek Yu 白臑 and thirty-seven others passed the composition test of the civil service examination and three passed the classics examination. Furthermore the king especially granted the Song presented scholar Lin Wan 林完 a pass in the civil service examination.

The Eastern Jurchen Guluogu 古羅骨, Shixian, and others, twelve people in total, came to present horses.

On *ŭlch'uk* day [the 20th] there was a heavy rain and hail storm that shook the pillars of the eastern gallery of Mundŏk Hall; on *pyŏng'in* day [the 21st] there was more rain and hail. Censor-in-chief Im Yumun and others took responsibility for these abnormalities and resigned. The king ordered them to resume their office.

Kim Yŏn was appointed Vice-minister of Rites and Assistant Executive in Letters, intendant of the Hallim Academy.

Sixth month. An Chiksung returned from Song. The emperor bestowed upon the king new musical instruments and music scores. The accompanying edict read: "Music flows together with Heaven and Earth, but flourishes only after a hundred years; only after merit is established can it be accomplished. The flourishing culture of ancient kings has run dry, and rites and music decayed. From the end of Zhou till now they have never been reestablished. Inheriting the accomplishments of successive generations of sage kings, I forever contemplated making virtue flourish. I continued this great project,

9 Sŏngsi 省試 or rather Namsŏngsi 南省試, is an alternative name for the Kukchagamsi 國子監試, which is the presented scholar (*chinsa*) test, consisting of poetry composition. KRS 74.10a.

and now announce its completion. Such merit was proclaimed in an edict to my officials, instructing them to use my body as measurement. Based on this measurement cauldrons were cast to produce music. Presenting it to heaven and earth and the Ancestral Shrine, the feathered beings[10] responded timely. Now this music, since it derives from the music of old, it is not something that I can discard: these beautiful and correct sounds should be spread. Today I spread this music widely throughout the world so as to harmonize people's minds. What you, sire, protect is outside of [our world], but looking up to righteousness you came to harmonize. Envoys who came here expressed their wish to listen to these new sounds. I praise their sincere minds and therefore made this bestowal [of the instruments and music]. The beautiful and correct sounds of this Dasheng [music], would they be anywhere but here."[11]

Yu Noksung 庾祿崇, who had retired as Assistant Executive in Political Affairs, died. He had advanced thanks to his mastery of Confucian skills, and he was correct and honest by nature. He was an official for more than forty years, but he was always satisfied with being loyal to the public good, and never bowed to the pressure of others. Although he was a state councilor, his clothes and house were the same as before he became an official. He died at the age of eighty.

Autumn, seventh month. Yi Chagyŏm was made Assistant Executive in Political Affairs; Kim Yŏn was made Vice-minister of Punishment and Minister of Rites; Cho Chungjang was provisionally made Administrator of the Security Council and Administrator of the Department of the Palace Library; Im Yumun was made Senior Policy Advisor; and Ch'oe Chi 崔贄 was appointed Censor-in-chief.

Eighth month. The king went to the Sŏnggyun-gwan[12] and offered wine to

---

10 Umul 羽物: likely refers to phoenixes or cranes that auspiciously appeared.

11 Famously the length of Huizong's digits was used to measure the pitch pipes of the Dasheng 大晟 "great brilliance" musical system. See Robert Provine, "Music, Measurements, Pitch Survivals, and Bell Shapes in Korea," *The World of Music* 49, no. 3 (2007): 13–30.

12 Here identified as Kukhak 國學 or national academy.

deceased sages and masters. He ordered Hallim Academician Pak Sŭngjung to lecture and ordered 700 officials and academy students to stand in the courtyard and listen to the lecture. All presented songs and odes; the king composed a poem, showed to those around him, and then ordered that matching poems should be presented.

The king went to Kwiryŏng Pavilion 龜齡閣 on the Eastern pond and reviewed military officials.

Ninth month. A Hundred-seat Assembly was organized in Hoegyŏng Hall, and 10,000 monks were given a maigre feast on the palace courtyard, and 20,000 more in the prefectures.

Winter, tenth month. The king re-enshrined Hyejong's spirit table in the Ancestral Shine's Second Chamber. He removed Kwangjong's spirit tablet to the Kang-nŭng Tomb.

A banquet was held in Kŏndŏk Hall and for the first time [after ending mourning for the king's mother] music was performed.

The king went to the Yŏng-nŭng and Sung-nŭng Tombs.[13]

The king personally held a sacrifice in the Ancestral Shrine and at the same time employed the new music from the Song. An amnesty was declared.

The king dispatched Yang Yŏng 梁永 to give thanks for the birthday wishes to the king.

The raw Jurchen[14] Aguda 阿骨打 of the Wanyan 完顏 clan raised an army and revolted against the Liao. The General Military Command Office of the Eastern Capital [of Liao] received an imperial rescript instructing them to join the attack so as to [take the central capital of Liao] in a pincer movement; it also warned them to urgently strengthen defenses.

Eleventh month. A banquet was held for all princes and state councilors in Hamwŏn Hall 含元殿 so as to inspect the new Song music.

Liao dispatched the ad-hoc envoys Yelü Zi 耶律諮 and Li Suo 李碩.

Buddhist rites were held in Mundŏk Hall.

---

13 The tombs of King Sukchong and the queen dowager respectively.

14 The term Saeng Yŏjin 生女眞, habitually used in Chinese sources from the eleventh century onwards to designate the northernmost Jurchen tribes that were not incorporated into the Liao empire, occurs here for the first time.

Twelfth month. The king invested the Yŏndŏk princess 延德宮主 Lady Yi as queen consort.

The king dispatched Director of the Office of Regalia Yi Su 李壽 to Liao to give thanks for the informal instruction.

The king went to Kŏndŏk Hall to receive tribal chiefs from outside the four passes in the northern border circuit.

The king inspected archery at the Eastern Pond.

The king went to the southern gate of Sŏndŏk Hall to receive the Eastern Jurchen Azhi 阿只 and others.

Yi Chagyŏm was appointed Executive of the Royal Secretariat and jointly Executive Chief of the Royal Secretariat-Chancellery, concurrently Commissioner to the Resident Governor of the Western Capital. The king also bestowed the title of Merit Subject Promoting Loyalty upon O Yŏnch'ong and Merit Subject Assisting Principle on Yi Wi.

Liao dispatched Wang Jing 王儆 with a decree instructing the king to end mourning and resume normal dress.

Yejong tenth year [1115]

Fifth year of the Zhenghe era of Song, fifth year of the Tianqing era of Liao, first year of Taizu of Jin's founding the country

Spring, first month. Liao dispatched Surveillance Commissioner Gao Qingshun 高慶順 to congratulate the king on his birthday.

The raw Jurchen Aguda of the Wanyan clan declared himself emperor and changed his name to Min 旻, and the country name to Jin 金. Their customs were similar to the Xiongnu 凶奴. Their various tribes did not have city walls, they lived dispersed among the mountains and plains. They did not have a script, instead tying knots to seal a verbal agreement. In their lands there were many pigs, sheep, cows, and horses, with many prize horse among them. As a people they are fierce and brave; when young they can draw a bow to shoot birds or rats, and when they grow up there is none who cannot draw a bow. They practice horse riding to prepare for battle, and make excellent soldiers. Each tribe claims it is the leader so that they cannot unite. To the west of its territory is Khitan, and to its south is our border. Hence for a long time they served both the Khitan and us [as vassals]. Whenever they came to our court they brought alluvial gold,[15] sable skins, and good horses as gifts. Our court also treated them lavishly to silver money; this was an annual custom.

One source claims that "in the past, the monk Kŭmjun 今俊 from P'yŏngju in our territory fled to the Jurchen and lived in Azhigu 阿之古 village. He is regarded as the ancestor of the Jin." Another source claims "The son of the monk Kŭmhaeng 今幸 from P'yŏngju, Kŭksu 克守, entered Jurchen territory and lived in Azhigu village. He married a Jurchen woman who gave birth to a son named Grand Preceptor Guyi 古乙. Guyi begot Grand Preceptor Huoluo 活羅. Huoluo begot many sons, the eldest was called Helibo 劾里鉢, and the youngest Yingge. Yingge was the bravest and smartest, and he captured the people's hearts. After Yingge died, Helibo's eldest son Wuyashu succeeded. After Wuyashu died, his younger brother Aguda was established [as leader]."

Second month. The king invested his son Wang Ku 王構 as royal heir apparent, and declared an amnesty.

The retired Royal Secretary Choe Sach'u died. Ch'oe Sach'u was the Grandson of Duke Munhŏn 文憲公, Ch'oe Ch'ung 崔沖. Through diligent study he passed the civil service examination, and King Munjong employed him as a palace attendant, orally transmitting royal decrees to him. From this time onwards he successively served in both central and provincial posts. Everywhere he went he gained both reputation and results. As a councilor of state, when debating important matters he always looked to preserve the essential structure, he did not dare to lightly alter the ancient codes. Among his disciples and their sons, those who came to him he always instructed on the path of serving the ruler. He never talked about private affairs. Even when retired from office, he never stopped worrying for the country: in this

15 *Pugŭm* 麩金: literally "chaff gold," probably referring to gold dust or flakes such as those recovered by panning in rivers.

his mind was the same from beginning to end. The king just happened to be watching the Lantern Festival when he heard the news of his passing. Greatly saddened, he halted the banquet, and also stopped the court audience. His condolence message and gifts were very lavish, and he ordered all officials to attend the funeral.

Third month. O Yŏnch'ong requested permission to retire on account of illness, but the kind did not allow him to do so.

The king gave a banquet for all officials in the Kŏndŏk Hall. He composed a poem on long life (Mannyŏn sa 萬年詞) and showed it to those around him.

Summer, fourth month. Yi Su and the others returned from Liao with an edict that read: "Recently the border officials were negligent in their defenses and some minor bandits have been harassing the people. They shall soon be punished, and for this we are preparing to raise an army. Since your territory borders on that of the bandits, as liege barons and border screen, we instruct you to prepare well your army so as to drive out this violent mob. Since you sent envoys with a letter of gratitude, clearly you are subjects who appreciate following orders, and who will do their utmost in fulfilling their duty of loyalty. We are worried about the ongoing agricultural work of spring, and lest it be harmed, please make the military drills brief; as for how to proceed, separate arrangements will be made."

The king summoned all princes and state councilors to Sangch'un Pavilion. Pouring drinks, they made merry. Looking back at retired Director of the Chancellery Kim Kyŏngyong, the king said "Of all the elder statesmen, only you are left sir." Kim wept and bowed in thanks, saying "This old subject has received extreme favor from the throne, and does not have the wherewithal to repay this debt." The king composed two *ci* poems and ordered his entourage to present matching poems.

Sixth month. Kim Chŏng 金精 and thirty-eight others passed the composition test of the civil service examination.

The hermit Kwak Yŏ requested a farewell feast for the departing Song envoy and vice-envoy at his residence to the west of the palace. The king specially granted wine and fruits, and ordered palace officials to assist. The tent they provided was extremely luxurious, and many people decried this.

Executive Chief of the Royal Secretariat Yi Chagyŏm was made Merit Subject Assisting the Throne, Acting Grand Marshal. His mother, Lady Kim, was made Grand Lady Communicating Righteousness to the Country, and his wife Lady Ch'oe was made Grand Lady of the Chosŏn State. The king dispatched envoys to deliver these three decrees to their residences.

Autumn, seventh month, *mujin* day, the first day of the month. There was a solar eclipse.

The king dispatched Vice-minister of Personnel Wang Chaji 王字之 and Executive at the Ministry of Taxation Mun Kongmi 文公美 to Song to give thanks for the grace bestowed. At the same time they submitted tribute. Also they dispatched the presented scholars Kim Tan 金端, Kyŏn Yuji 甄惟厎, Cho Sŏk 趙奭, Kang Ch'wijŏng 康就正, and Kwŏn Chŏk 權適 to enroll at the Great College [of Song]. The memorial letter stated "Edifying the people's customs starts from the practice of the *Great Learning*. The Xia tradition can be used to convert the barbarians. These are the teachings of former kings. Therefore Huhan sent his son to the Han court,[16] and Turfan requested a letter from the Tang House.[17] Even though all these cases are somewhat different, in terms of their significance they are no different.

Looking back, from early on this derelict country has looked up to Chinese customs. From the Kaibao era (968–977) to the reign of Emperor Shenzong (1067–1085), whenever envoys were sent students also accompanied them so as to broadly observe in the hope that [Koryŏ] would transform into the state of Lu [where Confucius hailed from]. Afterwards somehow this was abandoned and has now been lacking for a long time. What was practiced in the past was transmitted, but being far removed from the original training received, half of the words recorded were lost; scholars had no way to settle disputes. The many forks in the road of learning left the younger

16 Huhanye 呼漢邪 (d. 31 BCE) was a Xiongnu khan who sent his son to the Han capital to form an alliance.

17 It is not clear to which particular event this refers.

generations of students befuddled, and this desolate situation lasted for years. Moreover, regarding the finer points of the statutes of law, or the form of famous cultural products, the bequeathed classics of succeeding generations or different interpretations of the various schools of thought—without a knowledgeable [teacher] to whom questions can be addressed, how could we establish laws in the future? Every time we raise the topic, our thoughts go back to the old practices.

Now, however, we have again encountered a good time, and we can manifest our original intention. Respectfully we send five students that were ordered to follow [the embassy] to enter the imperial dynasty and go to the palace. Now these students are not the most outstanding ones: Their eyes have not seen the rites of a proper school, their ears have not heard the sounds of exquisite odes. Although they may be of the kind of people like the ones in Huxiang[18] with whom it is difficult to have a conversation, [Confucius] still would not deny them instruction, thus the humane spirit of Confucius's school is still preserved.

Prostrate, we hope for your majesty's compassionate mind to pursue the bright models of the past, and exceptionally send them to the National Academy or entrust them with the capital school supervisors, allowing them to receive instruction; then when the students will be enrolled, they will lift their robes in respect of their tutors. If you send us positive news, we may hope to see the transformation of the owl's hoot, moving to a higher tree, it may avoid the foolishness of barbarian sounds.[19] If you allow the Confucian Way to move to the East, we will be like a small candle burning forever under the great brightness [of China]."

Hŏ Kyŏng, who retired as Executive Chief of the Chancellery, died. Hŏ Kyŏng advanced thanks to his learning of letters. He was upright, just, loyal, and frugal. When Sukchong was still heir apparent he was drafted as an official in the prince's palace. After ascending the throne, Sukchong

---

18 From *Analects* 7:29: despite the apparent obtuseness of people from Huxiang 互鄉, Confucius nevertheless instructed his students to teach them.

19 The exact nature of this metaphor is not clear, but it seems to take the owl's hooting as similar to the uncouth sounds of barbarian tongues, and hence in need of reform.

appointed him Transmitter at the Security Council. His gratitude was beyond the pale, and the king successively promoted him until he became state councilor. Although there is nothing in particular that stands out for being praiseworthy, he was constant in his integrity, and people at the time cherished him for this.

Eighth month. Liao was about to attack the Jurchen and dispatched an envoy requesting troops. The king summoned all councilors of state, close officials, intendants of the Capital Military Command, and grand generals of all armies to debate this. All officials agreed [to the troop request], only Vice-director of the Office of Regalia Ch'ŏk Chun'gyŏng, Office Chief at the Ministry of Rites Kim Puil, Assistant Office Chief at the Ministry of Taxation Han Ch'ung, Junior Reparationer Kim Pusik, and Junior Policy Monitor Min Su 閔修 thought that "following the military turmoil of the *chŏnghae* [1106] and *muja* [1107] years, neither soldiers nor people had obtained any respite; now sending troops on behalf of another country is a recipe for disaster. Unfortunately future benefit or profit remains hard to fathom." The king asked again a few times, but in the end no agreement was reached.

The king held a small banquet in Changnyŏng Hall.

The king personally served old and retired Executive O Sujŭng and others in the Office of Audience Ceremonies; then he also held a banquet for elders at the polo court and bestowed presents commensurate to rank.

Military Commissioner for the Northwest Sector Pak Kyŏngjak came to the palace to retire from office; the king changed his name to Pak Kyŏng'in 朴景仁 and bestowed tea and medicine.

Ninth month. The king summoned close officials to inspect their archery, and gave a small banquet in Sangch'un Pavilion.

Taking avail of the moonlight, the king went anonymously to the house of hermit Kwak Yŏ, Ch'ŏngsim [Cleansing the Mind] Terrace 淸心臺 at Sunbok [Pure Blessing] Hall 純福殿. Drinking wine together with close officials they discussed letters till the break of dawn.

The king personally selected military officials at the Eastern Pond and watched water games.

Winter, tenth month. The Ministry of Rites requested that the heir apparent's birthday be called the Yŏngjŏng Festival 永貞節, and that all palace officials offer their congratulations. Also, orders should be given to the two border circuits, three capitals, eight shepherdships, and three protectorates to send letters of congratulation as an annual custom. The king followed this.

A Hundred Seat Assembly was held in Hoegyŏng Hall for three days. A vegetarian banquet was held for 10,000 monks in the courtyard and for 20,000 more in the provinces.

The king personally inspected the Divine Cavalry generals and officers of the six provinces at the Eastern Pond.

The king ordered Executive Kim Yŏn and others to hold a big parade in the eastern suburbs.

The king dispatched Attendant Censor Yun Ŏnsun 尹彦純 to Liao to give congratulations on the Tianxing Festival.

The king personally inspected the generals and officers of the Western Capital at the Eastern Pond.

Eleventh month. The king held a smally banquet in Ŭnggŏn Hall 膺乾殿.

The king dispatched Office Chief Kim In'gwan 金仁琯 to Liao to give thanks for the edict instructing the end of mourning and the resumption of normal dress.

A P'algwan Assembly was held. When the king returned from the polo court, his carriage stopped in front of the Office of Audience Ceremonies. For a long time [the king] carried on duets,[20] and then ordered the entertainers to sing and dance within the royal cortege,[21] which lasted till the third watch.[22] Censor-in-chief Ch'oe Chi and Censor-of-Miscellaneous Affairs Hŏ Chae 許載 remonstrated with the king, which he happily accepted.

The king held a small banquet in the inner quarters of the palace.

---

20 *Ch'anghwa* 唱和: to sing and respond; could also refer to poetry reciting with someone else matching the poem's rhymes.

21 *Changnae* 仗內: literally within the royal regalia, which I take refers to those surrounding the king's palanquin.

22 Nights were divided into five watches; thus the third watch corresponds to midnight.

Liao dispatched Surveillance Commissioner for the Lizhou jurisdiction Yelü Yi 耶律義 and Vice Minister of the Court of Judicial Review Sun Liangmou 孫良謀 with an imperial edict urging the raising of troops; they also bestowed silk and various presents.

The military commissioner for the Northeast Circuit reported that the Eastern Capital of Liao had received an imperial letter of instruction saying "The three embassies dispatched by Koryŏ, to wit [those in response to the embassies for] the anniversary, for the informal mission, and for the resumption of normal dress, could not enter due to troubles at the border, so they have already been ordered to return to their country."

Yelü Yi and others went to the Office of Audience Ceremonies to take leave before returning, but since the deliberations on sending troops continued without reaching a conclusion, they returned without accomplishing the ritual. The next day they took leave.

Twelfth month. The resident governor of the Eastern Capital of Liao dispatched as envoy to return the courtesy Vice Commissioner of the Foreign Relations Office Gao Xiaoshun 高孝順.

Yejong eleventh year [1116]

Sixth year of the Zhenghe era of Song, sixth year of the Tianqing era of Liao, second year of Jin's founding of the country

Spring, first month. Liao dispatched Minister of the Court of Judicial Review Zhang Yanzhong 張言中 to congratulate the king on his birthday.

The king went to his official residence and gave a small banquet for the princes. It ended late at night.

The king went to Ch'ŏnsu-sa to inspect the newly constructed buildings, and gave rewards to the laborers and craftsmen commensurate with rank.

Intercalary [first] month. The king went to Poje-sa to listen to State Preceptor Tamjin's exposition of Sŏn Buddhism. The king personally donated lavishly.

The king dispatched Editor in the Palace Library Chŏng Yangjik 鄭良稷,

[instructing him] to call himself a "clerk[23] for the Anbuk Protectorate" with a letter to the Eastern Capital of Liao to find out the whereabouts of the festival day envoy Yun Ŏnsun, the letter-presenting envoy Sŏ Pang 徐昉, and the New Year's Congratulations envoy Yi Tŏg'yun 李德允.

Second month. The country of Japan presented sweet oranges.[24]

Gao Xu 高諝 from the Eastern Capital of Liao came to submit.

An extraordinary Lantern Festival was held; the king went to Chunggwang Hall and gave a banquet for all the princes, state councilors, and officials serving the king. It lasted till deep into the night.

Ko Yŏngsin, who had retired as Assistant Executive in Political Affairs, died. He was orphaned at a young age, but was diligent in his studies and good at letters. He passed the civil service examination under King Munjong, and served successively in positions in the capital and in the provinces. He held strong opinions and was unyielding in debates. When floods afflicted Kyŏngsang prefectures and routes he was serving as Policy Advisor, and was sent out as a Royal Commissioner of Pacification. He petitioned for a reduction in the tax on public land, giving the people some respite so as to recover. When he was in government all the notables ardently discussed the import of the new laws,[25] but Ko Yŏngsin opined that the laws of the founding fathers were complete, so why should they be changed? Just keeping them as is without omitting, this would suffice. He was upright and guarded himself against corruption, so when he died his family had insufficient resources.

The king went to Kŏndŏk Hall and invited the new examination passer Kim Chŏng and others, giving drink and food at the Office of Audience Ceremonies and also ordering their first appointments.

Third month. The king heard that the two Liao fortresses of Naewŏn 來遠

---

23 *Ajŏn* 衙前: literally "[working] in front of the office," a generic term for low ranking clerical offices.

24 *Kamja* 柑子: citrus sinensis or similar fruits.

25 *Sinpŏp* 新法: this probably refers to the new policies introduced in Song China under Wang Anshi (1021–1086). Although discredited after his death, Emperor Huizong returned to them, which may have provoked the discussions in Koryŏ.

and P'oju 抱州[26] were being besieged by the Jurchen and were running out of food. He sent 1,000 *sŏk* of rice but the commander of Naewŏn Fortress refused to accept it.

Chŏng Yangjik returned from the Eastern Capital of Liao. At the time Parhae people in the Eastern Capital had rebelled and killed the Resident Governor, Xiao Baoxian 蕭保先. Instead they enthroned Palace Servitor[27] Gao Yongchang 高永昌 and proclaimed him emperor. The country was called Dayuan 大元 and the reign title Longji 隆基. Chŏng Yangjik pretended to be an official and presented a memorial stating his loyalty. The products for the governor sent by his country he presented to Gao Yongchang, and was handsomely rewarded. When he returned he remained in hiding and did not report to the throne. When this became known officials petitioned for him to be thrown in jail and sentenced.

The king went to Ch'ŏnsu-sa and organized a maigre ritual for its completion. Colorful tents with all kinds of entertainment were lined up along the streets for three days. The king gave a banquet for the officials outside the temple gates which lasted till daybreak. After the king returned to the palace he declared an amnesty. The supervising officials and clerks, workers, craftsmen, and corvée laborers were rewarded commensurate to rank. When the royal carriage was stationed in the city, the princes and state councilors toasted to the king's long life. The king grasped Kim Kyŏngyong's hand and spoke about the deceased king and dowager queen, his tears streaming down. All around wailed.

The king travelled to the Western Capital, with Yi Wi and Kim Yŏn taking charge of the royal procession, and Yi Chagyŏm and Cho Chungjang in charge of the affairs concerning the resident governor. The provision of goods from localities they passed through was reduced, and the insignia of the cortege were simplified. If there were uncultivated fields along the way the local magistrate would be summoned and punished.

---

26 Strategic fortresses located on the southern side of the Amnok River. As they controlled the main strategic route into the peninsula, they were of crucial importance.

27 See note 5.

Yun Ŏnsun, Sŏ Pang, Yi Tŏg'yun and others returned from the Eastern Capital of Liao, where they had been detained. Gao Yongchang had ordered them to submit a memorial of congratulations [on his enthronement] and Yun and the others had done as they had been told. Upon their return they concealed this situation, and officials requested that they be tried for this transgression.

Prayers for rain were held at shrines along the way [to the Western Capital].

Summer, fourth month. They reached the Western Capital, where a wine party was organized on the Taedong River. The princes, councilors, and court officials who had followed the king, together with the resident governor of Pyongyang and officials assigned to serve in the Western Capital of grade three and above all attended the banquet. There was a cool breeze and warm sun, and the king was in good spirits, singing together with his close officials. At the time there were no pressing affairs and the country was at leisure; the king cherished the letters and loved carousing. Drafter of Royal Edicts and Proclamations Ch'oe Yak 崔瀹 submitted the following memorial: "In the past, King Wenzong of Tang wanted to establish the post of Academician of Poetry. The councilors protested, saying, 'Poets are prone to superficiality; if you take advice from them we fear that this will mess with your august intelligence.' The emperor then desisted. Sovereigns should devote themselves to the classics, and daily debate classics and histories with the best Confucian scholars so that they can extract the principles of government and improve the customs of the people without such thing as leisure; how could there be such a thing as engaging in child's play, or frequently playing around with superficial poet-officials? This harms the purity and uprightness of the royal mind." The king graciously accepted this.

The king paid his respects at the Portrait Hall of T'aejo.

The hermit Kwak Yŏ arrived from the main capital, and the king arranged a spot for him in the flower garden behind Sang'an Hall 常安殿. The king personally served him food and drinks. Then they suddenly perceived some white clouds in the southeast, some of which resembled a pair of cranes cavorting. The king ordered Kwak Yŏ to compose some couplets on this, and the king composed a matching poem.

The king summoned the princes and Kwak Yŏ for a wine party. The king composed three poems and ordered Kwak Yŏ to present matching poems.

The king traveled to Kŭmgang-sa and Hŭngbok-sa; on the way back he passed by Yŏngmyŏng-sa. Boarding the tower boat he held a party for the princes, councilors, and close officials. Again he composed poems and presented these to the officials.

The Jin ruler Aguda sent Azhi to Koryŏ.

The Royal Secretariat-Chancellery petitioned: "Having suffered the invasion by the Jurchen, Liao is now in a very perilous situation and may perish. The calendar that they bestowed upon us should no longer be used. Henceforward, for all communications, public and private, the era names should be removed and instead only the cyclical date should be used." This was accepted.

The king gave a banquet for various officials in Changnak Hall 長樂殿, and again showed them the poems he composed.

The king visited Gwanp'ung Hall, and inspected the site where T'aejo used to reside [during his visits to the Western Capital]. Next he went to Kuje Palace and late in the evening moved to Yŏngmyŏng-sa. He summoned the princes and Kwak Yŏ and they drank wine and exchanged songs.

Liao refugees from Naewŏn and P'oju Fortress came to submit, taking with them several hundred sheep and horses.

More than twenty Liao refugees came to submit; they presented more than 200 sheep.

A decree read: "Inheriting the accumulated merit of my ancestors I have guarded the Three Han. Afraid that I cannot live up to the expectations of people nor of spirits I worry day and night and do not dare to rest for a moment. Now in accordance with what the astrological officials have requested, we are about to move to the Western Capital; by promulgating this new decree we prepare for a renewal together with the myriad things, and announce to the people a return to the efflorescence of the dynastic enterprise of former kings. As the former king [i.e. T'aejo] instructed, by according with Yin and Yang, upholding all the spirits, making punishment and reward objective, making promotion and demotion just, elevating schools, and making the customs beautiful, if all these affairs are upheld then government will be successfully achieved. Thus all you officials ought to be instructed about the implementation. To [distinguish between] noble and base in dress, the Office to Determine Details of Ritual Systems should refer to the system founding fathers as well as later reforms and determine the standards." The official organization of the capital and provinces was also reformed.

The king gave a small banquet in Kŏnwŏn Hall.

The king went to Hongbok-sa 弘福寺 and then moved to the old city gate pavilion of Tangp'o 唐浦, where he made merry with wine. He renamed the pavilion "Tagyŏng" 多景 and personally wrote the letters for the board. He ordered the poetry official to present matching poems.

The royal cortege departed from the Western Capital. On the road an old woman offered wine. The king felt pity for her sincerity and allowed her to offer one drink. He then composed a poem about it.

The king returned to the capital and promulgated an amnesty. He also reduced the taxes of the prefectures and counties he had passed through. At that time the resident governor and the officials prepared regalia and music troupes to welcome the royal cortege in Mach'ŏn Pavilion 馬川亭. The Grand Music and the Wind and Strings ensemble vied in extravagance, even going as far as having amazons play polo. The king ordered them dismissed.

The king obtained a precious jade stone from Mt. Panyong 盤龍山 in the Western Capital. He ordered the jade craftsmen to make ritual implements to give thanks to the gods [for producing the auspicious jade]. The state councilors offered their congratulations.

Fifth month. Executive Chief of the Chancellery O Yŏnch'ong died. He hailed from Haeju and was of humble origins, and spent his childhood in poor and lowly circumstances. He studied hard and excelled at composition, and passed the examination when still young. He was cautious and diligent, and also trustworthy. Throughout his career he remained loyal and frugal, upholding integrity and following the law: he removed the ills of the time, and never let private interests harm public interest. Therefore the kings cherished him.

Pae U 裵祐 and thirty-seven others passed the composition test of the civil service examination.

Sixth month. Wang Chaji and Mun Kongmi returned from Song, and brought with them robes, silver-inlaid utensils and other presents bestowed upon the king. The Song emperor also allowed Koryŏ youth to enter the [Song] academies. The imperial decree read "Succeeding to the good deeds of the Three Great Dynasties [of Chinese antiquity] I am reviving the schools; all around through all the myriad states the sound of edification and education spreads widely, there is nowhere it does not reach. Considering that the flavor of old customs remains among your country, you sent students to experience the upper country so as to completely erase engrained [bad] habits. Soon we will witness the complete transformation of the world to Chinese customs. Also you pursue the old customs of ritual propriety; such eternal speech towards what is good deserves our admiration."

The emperor also bestowed the Dasheng music, and a decree accompanying it read "After the Three Great Dynasties [of antiquity] the rites were derelict and the music bad. Being an admirer of antiquity, I have studied and brought it to light, reviving them within a hundred years and creating the Dasheng music. After a thousand years the former kings have been succeeded to. Comparing the meters and harmonizing the sounds, we managed to establish the correct pitch.[28] This exquisite and correct sound has spread across the country and pacified guests, and gladdened those from afar, even barbarians. Your country is on the other side of the Eastern Sea. Requesting the mandate be passed to your officials, your envoys are in the courtyard. The liege lords of old, if they were educated and virtuous, would be rewarded with music. The bestowal of these instruments is a blessing for you. To reform the customs, nothing is better than this. Go and bestow this mandate and

---

28 *Umul* 羽物: U "feather" can also refer to the brightest of the five tones (五音), hence this interpretation.

rule your country. Even though your country is distant and cut off from us, achieving this grand harmonization, isn't this wonderful!"

Kim Kyŏngyong was made Acting Grand Preceptor; the Marquis of Nangnang, Yi Wi, was made Probationary Grand Guardian, Director of the Chancellery, Minister of Personnel; Yi Chagyŏm was made Executive of the Chancellery, jointly Executive at the Royal Secretariat-Chancellery, Minister of War; Kim Yŏn and Cho Chungjang were made Probationary Minister of Education, Chief of the Royal Secretariat and jointly Executive at the Royal Secretariat-Chancellery; Kang Chŭng was made Probationary Minister of Works and Assistant Executive in Political Affairs; and Kim Chun was made Vice-minister of War and Commissioner of the Security Council.

The king went to Hoegyŏng Hall and summoned the state councilors and his close officials to observe the Dasheng Music.

Autumn, seventh month. The king gave a banquet and [had the officials compete in] archery at the Sangch'un Pavilion.

The king dispatched Yi Charyang 李資諒 and Yi Yŏng to Song to give thanks for the bestowal of the Dasheng music.

Eighth month. The Eastern Jurchen Ayi 阿伊 and others came to court.

The king went to Kyŏngnyŏng Hall.

A decree read: "We cannot be partial or harm the way of letters and of military arts. Recently the border bandits have been gradually boosting their numbers, and the ministers and generals in charge of planning have concluded that the most urgent task is to prepare armor and weapons and train soldiers. However, we cannot merely rely on the military affairs. Formerly Emperor Shun greatly promoted literary virtue and had the 'shield and feather' dance[29] performed on the steps [in front of the throne]. Merely seventy days later the Youmiao 有苗[30] were conquered. I greatly admire this! This is all the more relevant since the Song emperor has especially bestowed upon us the Dasheng music as well as literary and military dances. Thus we

---

29 *Ganyu* 干羽: the shield for the military officials and the feather for the civil officials.

30 One of the so-called Three Miao (Sanmiao 三苗) Tribes of Chinese antiquity, thought to have resided in the south.

should first present this to the Ancestral Shrine and then have a banquet."

Within the forbidden precinct the Ch'ŏngyŏn-gak 淸讌閣[31] was established, and one academician, one auxiliary academician, and one auxiliary to the hall were selected and appointed. In the mornings and evenings they lectured and debated on the classics and other writings.

The Jin general Sahe 撒喝 attacked Naewŏn-sŏng and P'oju and nearly managed to make it fall. Its commander Yelü Ning 耶律寧 wanted to flee together with his retainers. The king dispatched Administrator of Memorials at the Security Council Han Kyoyŏ to reason with him.[32] However, Yelü Ning refused on account of the lack of a royal writ. Han Kyoyŏ urgently reported this back, and the king ordered the security council to prepare a communication[33] to be sent to him. State councilors and remonstrance officials protested against this: "It is difficult to guess why he is asking for a royal writ, so please do not do this." The king then dispatched an envoy to Jin requesting him to say "P'oju is originally our old territory. We wish it to be returned to us." The Jin ruler told the envoy "Then get it yourself."

Ninth month. Yeju 豫州[34] on the Eastern Border Circuit was fortified and a defense commissioner installed.

Winter, tenth month. The king inspected the Dasheng music in Kŏndŏk Hall.

The king personally sacrificed at the Ancestral Shrine and presented the Dasheng Music as well as the ritual implements made with the auspicious jade found in the western suburbs. He also reported on the newly composed song for the nine chambers [of the shrine].

Hallim Academician and Senior Policy Critic Pak Sŭngjung made fun of the king's close ministers working at the Ch'ŏngyŏn-gak. When this reached the king's ears, he immediately demoted Pak to administrative assistant to

---

31 *Kŭmjung* 禁中: I.e. the inner enclosure of the palace. The Ch'ŏngyŏn-gak "Pavilion of the Bright Banquet" was established to store Chinese classics and study them.

32 Presumably trying to persuade him not to submit.

33 *Cha'ja* 劄子: in general this is used for a petition, i.e. a letter addressed to a higher authority, which does not fit with the situation.

34 Modern Yewŏn, Chŏngp'yŏng-gun, South Hamgyŏng Province.

the Director of the Bureau of Construction and Maintenance.

Eleventh month. As the Ch'ŏngyŏn-gak was located within the forbidden precinct, it was difficult for the academicians to do nightwork or to enter and leave. Thus they repaired the southern gallery underneath the Red Tower as a building where the academicians could gather and lecture. The king granted it the [building] title "Chŏngŭi" 精義 [refined meaning], and to the left and right rooms for repose were made. The title was changed to Pomun-gak 寶文閣, and the academicians from Ch'ŏngyŏn-gak were moved here. Additionally, the position of auxiliary awaiting edicts was created. Those selected for the post were granted gold and brocade, and were all the most eminent scholars of their time.

The king held an audience for Hŏ Yun 許允 and others who had passed the civil service examination. He ordered them to shed their ordinary robes [for their first appointments] and bestowed one set of [official robes] upon each of them. Drinks and food were served at the Office for Audience Ceremonies.

The king went to Ch'ŏngyŏn-gak and ordered Hallim Academician and Royal Transmitter Pak Kyŏng'in to lecture on the second canon of the *Book of Documents*.

It snowed heavily. The king summoned Administrator of Memorials Han Kyoyŏ, Pomun-gak Auxiliary Academician Chŏng Kŭkkong 鄭克恭, Vice-transmitter of Edicts of the Right Mun Kongmi, Auxiliary to the Pomun-gak Yun Hae 尹諧 and others to drink wine and compose eulogies on the snow. Since the former Office Chief at the Ministry of Rites Kwak Chunmok 郭俊穆 had formerly assisted and guided King Sukchong, and Intendant-secretary at the Office for Royal Clan Affairs Kim Wŏn'yŏ 金元輿 had long instructed the king when he was still heir apparent, the king summoned them and ordered them to take a seat to the right of the assorted academicians.

The king perused the *P'yŏnnyŏn t'ongjae*[35] and ordered the Pomun-gak Academician Hong Kwan and others to compile an expanded edition of facts since the Samhan period and present it to the throne.

---

[35] *P'yŏnnyŏn t'ongjae* 編年通載: Chronologically arranged history of Korea; an otherwise unknown text.

Twelfth month. The king ordered the Pomun-gak Proofreader Ko Sŏnyu 高先柔 to lecture on the "Three Counsels"[36] of the *Book of Documents*.

The king ordered the palace attendant and Director of the [Bureau of] Beverage Supervision Chi Ch'anghŭp 池昌洽 to lecture on the chapters "Doctrine of the Mean" and "Game of Pitch-pot"[37] from the *Book of Rites*. He explained to the Pomun-gak academicians and others "the game of pitch-pot is an ancient rite. It has been obsolete for a long time. Now the implements bestowed by the Song emperor are extremely complete, so I want to give this a try. You gentlemen should determine the rules for pitch-pot and also prepare a diagram, and present this to me."

The king organized a banquet in the Ch'ŏngyŏn-gak, and told the assembled academicians: "I used to peruse the *Essentials of Government from the Zhenguan era*. In it Taizong [of Tang] says, 'All that is needed for the realm to be peaceful is to make sure that all the people have enough. Even without auspicious sign, it will still be comparable in virtue to the era of Yao and Shun. If the people do not have enough and the barbarians invade the borders, even if there are auspicious plants [growing in the streets] or phoenixes [nesting in the gardens], what different is it from the [tyranny of] Jie and Zhou?'[38] How true this is! All I wish for is this to be implemented." He then ordered Kim Yŏn and Pak Kyŏng'in together with the academicians from the Pomun-gak to annotate the *Essentials of Government* and present the result to the throne.

A great exorcism was held. Before this the eunuchs had divided the exorcisms left and right to [make sure that they] could obtain victory. The king then also ordered the princes to separately manage this. All clowns and various performers, even the *kisaeng* from provincial administrations, there was no one who did not get summoned. From near and far they came to the capital, their pennants and flags filling the streets up to the forbidden

---

36 *Sammo* 三謨: The *Shangshu* (*Shujing*) actually has only two chapters with the title "counsels," the "Counsels of the Great Yu" (大禹謨) and the "Counsels of Gao-Yao" (皐陶謨).

37 *T'uho* 投壺: this usually consists of throwing arrows in a vase with three narrow openings.

38 *Zhenguan zhengyao* 10, "39: Zaixiang."

compound. The same day the remonstrance officials knocked on the door of the Office for Audience Ceremonies and then the king ordered to have the most outrageous and weird expelled. Towards the evening they gathered again. When the king went to watch the music, from all directions people surged forward and vied to show off their performances. More than 400 were additionally expelled.

Thirty-three Khitan, Fifty-two Han'er,[39] 155 Xijia,[40] fifteen "cooked" Jurchen and forty-four Parhae came to submit.

Yejong twelfth year [1117]

Seventh year of the Zhenghe era of Song, seventh year of the Tianqing era of Liao, first year of the Tianfu era of Jin

Spring, first month. Fifty-two Parhae people, eighty-nine Xijia, sixty Han'er, eighteen Khitan, and eight "cooked" Jurchen came to submit from Liao.

The king ordered Han Kyoyŏ to lecture on the hexagram "Heaven" [*kŏn* 乾] from the *Book of Changes* and made Pak Sŭngjung and Kim Puil ask questions on difficult parts. He then personally served wine and food.

Second month. The king summoned state councilors from the Chancellery and Security Council to discuss the appropriate course of action for events on the northern border.

Three Han'er from Liao came to submit.

The king dispatched Executive Chief of the Royal Secretariat Kim Yŏn to take care of affairs at the northern border.

Eighty-one Jurchen came to court.

The king ordered officials to hold army-subduing sacrifices in the eastern and western suburbs.

Kim Chun was appointed Honorary Minister of Works, Assistant Executive in Political Affairs; Yi Kwe was made Commissioner of the Security

39 Han'er 漢兒: Not certain which people this refers to.

40 See chapter 7, note 21. This sudden influx of various new people was undoubtedly due to the collapse of the Liao empire.

Council; Wang Chaji was made Senior Policy Advisor, jointly Intendant of the Security Council; Han Kyoyŏ was appointed Director at the Office of Royal Clan Affairs and Vice-commissioner of the Security Council.

The king went to Changwŏn Pavilion.

Third month. Kang Chŭng was made Executive Chief of the Royal Secretariat and then ordered to retire.

Kim Yŏn sent an urgent dispatch saying that "The Jin troops have attacked and taken Kaizhou 開州[41] of Liao and are assaulting Naewŏn-sŏng. The three garrisons of Taebu 大夫, Kŏlt'a 乞打, and Yubaek 柳白 were taken and their military vessels completely burned. The General Commander Yelü Ning and the Prefect of Naesŏng-sŏng, Chang Xiaosun 常孝孫, led their troops into 140 vessels, and while boarding the vessels at the river ferry port, passed on a missive to our Yŏngdŏk fortress saying that the two fortresses of Naewŏn and P'oju were being returned to us. They then set sail across the sea and escaped. Our troops entered the fortresses and retrieved weapons as well as large quantities of money and grain." The king was overjoyed and renamed P'oju Ŭiju 義州 [and installed] a defense commissioner. The Amnok River was made into the border and defenses installed at border crossings. All the officials submitted memorials of congratulation on the restitution of the two fortresses.

The Jin ruler Aguda dispatched five people including Azhi with the following letter: "Your older brother, the emperor of the great Jurchen Jin nation, sends this letter to his younger brother, the king of the Koryŏ nation. From the time of our forefathers we have been wedged in a corner [between Liao and Koryŏ], addressing Liao as the suzerain and Great Koryŏ as parent country. Humbly we served them, yet the Khitan are without principle: they violated our borders and enslaved our people, on numerous occasions sending unnamed armies. We had no choice but to resist them; thanks to the support of Heaven we managed to annihilate them. We hope that you, king, will allow us to forge amicable relations as older and younger brother, achieving an endless amity that lasts for generations." He also sent one good

41 In the area of modern Fengcheng city, Liaoning Province.

stallion.

When the letter arrived, the senior officials were strongly opposed to forging friendly relations. Vice-censor-in-chief Kim Puch'ŏl then sent a memorial that argued as follows: "Since the Jin people have recently defeated the Great Liao, they dispatched an envoy to us requesting to become older–younger brother countries, with a view to establishing eternal relations of friendship. Our court is now rejecting this. [However,] your subject happened to observe the relations between Han and the Xiongnu, and between Tang and the Tujue. The former addressed them as 'your subject,' the latter gave a princess in marriage. In order to establish peaceful relations, there was nothing that was off the table. Now the Great Song and Liao alternate between relations of senior and junior uncle, or older and younger brother, and have maintained peaceful relations across generations. The Son of Heaven is peerless in the awe he inspires in All under Heaven. As for the act of bending over towards the various so-called barbarian countries and serving them, this is what is called the sage's use of skillful means to save the way, a strategy of preserving the state. Formerly during the time of King Sŏngjong a mistake was made in the management of the border, and immediately the Liao took advantage of this to raid. Truly this is something to be used as a warning for us. Your subject wishes that your highness will consider the long-term strategy of preserving the country and prevent anything that will cause regret." All of the officials ridiculed him and moreover expelled him. In the end there was no reply [to the letter from the Jin ruler].

Summer, fourth month. Six Han'er came from Liao to submit.

The censors and remonstrators submitted a memorial requesting that corvée labor for Anhwa-sa 安和寺 be stopped. The king followed this.

Fifth month. Retired Executive Chief of the Chancellery Im Ŭi died. In his youth he put all his efforts in studies and passed the civil service examination. When King Sŏnjong was still heir apparent, he learned about his reputation and recommended him to the king. After becoming king he promoted him several times, up to the office of senior transmitter. In the beginning of Sukchong's reign, because some courtiers harbored a grudge against him they slandered him several times. But Sukchong knew that he was simple and upright and that there was no ground to the slander, so he did not act on it.

Yi Charyang returned from Song. When he reached Bianjing 汴京,[42] the emperor went to Ruimo Hall 睿謀殿 and summoned the whole embassy and bestowed a banquet upon them. Then the emperor composed a poem, showed it to them, and ordered a matching poem to be presented. Yi Charyang immediately responded, and the emperor greatly praised and rewarded him. When it was time for them to return, the emperor secretly told him: "I heard that your country borders on that of the Jurchen. Later when you come again to our court bring with you a few of their people." Yi Charyang replied "The Jurchen have the faces of people but the minds of animals. Among the various barbarians they are the most covetous and evil. They should not be allowed to communicate with your august country." A favorite councilor of the emperor then said "Many precious and strange goods come from the Jurchen, and Koryŏ has been trading with them for a long time. They do not wish to share their profits with others, and that is why they are obstructing. Your majesty has showered Koryŏ with affection like a baby, and now they turn their backs on your virtue like this. However, you do not need to rely on Koryŏ. You can simply dispatch a single servant to summon them to court."

The presented scholars Kwŏn Chŏk, Cho Sŏk, and Kim Tan returned together with Yi Charyang. The emperor entrusted them with an edict that he had personally written down: "Considering that you serve the great with utmost loyalty and sincere filial devotion, you have passed this beautiful custom down through the generations, appreciating what is worthy of admiration. Crossing the sea to dispatch envoys and receive academic instruction from masters, approaching the imperial halls you were tested on various skills in the courtyard and granted official titles. Bringing glory upon your return, you are highly recommended [for office] to your home country." Earlier the emperor had personally examined Kwŏn Chŏk and the

42 The capital of the Northern Song dynasty, modern Kaifeng.

others, four people in all, in Jiying Hall and given them the passing grade of presented scholar. Kang Ch'wijŏng and Kyŏn Yuji had died in Song.

Sixth month. The king ordered the establishment of the Ch'ŏnjang-gak 天章閣 within the forbidden precinct to store the autographs bestowed by the Song emperor together with calligraphy and paintings by kings.

Three Han'er came to submit.

There was a banquet for the princes and the [councilors of the] Chancellery and Security Council at the Ch'ŏngyŏn-gak. They had the cassia-flavored wine, dragon-phoenix tea, and precious fruits in precious plates all bestowed by the Song emperor. The king bestowed a rhinoceros-horn encrusted belt and robes upon each and ordered Executive Chief of the Chancellery Kim Yŏn to compose a "Record for the Ch'ŏngyŏn-gak" and ordered the Pomun-gak Academician Hong Kwan to execute the calligraphy for the different stones.[43]

Kim Yŏn was appointed jointly as Executive Chief of the Royal Secretariat; Kim Chun was made Minister of Punishments; Kim Chihwa 金至和 was appointed Minister of Works; Kim Kwe 金軌 was put in charge of the Finance Commission; Im Yumun was made Junior Vice-director of the Department of Ministries, and intendant of the Palace Library; Ch'oe Hongjae was appointed Censor-in-chief.

Eighth month. The king traveled to the Southern Capital.

Notary of the Security Council Kim Hwangwŏn 金黃元 died. From a young age Kim had loved learning and after passing the civil service examination his writing was considered the best in the country. He was upright and uncompromising by nature and did not associate with the powerful. He shared a reputation with his colleague at the Hallim Academy, Yi Chae. At the time the Khitan envoy visited and Kim Hwangwŏn composed the eulogy for the palace banquet. It contained the lines: "The

---

43 The text of the inscription was copied by Xu Jing and included in his description of Koryŏ, the *Xuanhe fengshi Gaoli tujing*. However, according to Xu the banquet for which the inscription was created took place in the fourth month rather than the sixth. Sem Vermeersch, *A Chinese Traveler in Medieval Korea* (Honolulu: University of Hawai'i Press, 2016), 89.

phoenix descended from heaven holding the imperial rescript in his beak. The giant sea turtle came from across the sea, carrying Penglai on its back." The envoy marveled at this and requested to copy the whole text. However, the two people both loved the old style[44] and did not follow the fashion of the times. State Councilor Yi Chawi hated them and said "If this lot occupy the seats of literature for a long time, they will mislead later generations." He then petitioned to have them removed from office.

Later he was appointed Commissioner of Kyŏngsan District and practiced humane government. When King Sukchong opened Yŏnyŏng Hall[45] he summoned him to manage the books and documents. Whenever he had a question while reading a book he immediately asked him, addressing him as "senior" rather than using his name. When [the present] king was enthroned, he made him Drafting Advisor and sent him on a mission to Liao. On the road he saw that many people in the northern regions were suffering from extreme hunger, with people eating each other. He urgently returned via the postal stations to deliver a letter requesting that the granaries be opened so as to relieve the hunger. On his way back when the people saw him they said: "This is the minister who saved our lives!" Later when the Jurchen invaded Liao and completely subjugated the eastern fortresses, only Naewon-sŏng and P'oju held strong and were not taken. When their food ran out they used their treasures to trade grain at reduced prices with us, but the border officials forbade the people from trading. Kim Hwanwŏn then sent a memorial saying "Regarding the misfortune of others as one's own good fortune is against humanity; being angry at one's neighbor is not righteous. I request that grain be sold to the two fortresses and that permission be granted for trade." The king did not reply to this. However, his character was unrestrained and he

---

44 *Guwen* 古文: also translated as classical style, a movement that started in the late Tang and advocated a return to the simple, pared-down style of the classics and avoided ornamentation or parallelism. It also has political implications in that advocates of this style also tended to regard themselves as upright and straight-laced in administrative matters.

45 開延英殿: since this building predates Sukchong, it is not clear what "opening" here means. Several kings passed away in this building, yet it also seems to have been associated with their learning, as is evident in its later name, 集賢殿 (Hall of Worthies), and in the fact that there were academicians associated with the hall.

liked music and women. After his death Office Chief at the Ministry of Rites Kim Pusik requested that a posthumous title be bestowed upon him, but some in the seats of power were displeased with him and blocked this.

The king arrived in the Southern Capital. Some Khitan people who had naturalized and lived dispersed within the Southern Capital petitioned that they would like to welcome the royal carriage with Khitan song and dance as well as various plays. The king halted the carriage for a while to watch them.

The king went to Yŏnhŭng Hall to receive felicitations from the court. He composed a poem and showed this to the ministers.

A banquet was given for the princes and the [councilors of] the Chancellery and Security Council as well as attending officials in the temporary palace.

The king went to Sŭngga cave[46] and Changŭi-sa 藏義寺.

Ninth month. A banquet for the Double Ninth Festival was held in Yŏnhŭng Hall. The king was very happy and composed poems that he showed to those around him.

The king summoned the hermit from Ch'ŏngp'yŏng 淸平, Yi Chahyŏn 李資玄, to his temporary residence. Yi Chahyŏn was the grandson of the Royal Secretary Yi Chayŏn 李子淵. His appearance was imposing and he was very bright. After passing the civil service examination he served as assistant secretary at the Bureau of Music, but suddenly he rejected office and entered Mt. Ch'ŏngp'yŏng in Ch'unju[47] where he built Munsu-wŏn 文殊院[48] as his abode. He ate only vegetarian food and wore rough clothes; he loved Sŏn and delighted in the way, free and at ease he enjoyed himself. The king dispatched his palace attendant to bestow tea, incense, and brocade, and also frequently sent decrees summoning him back to the capital. However, Yi Chahyŏn told the emissary: "When this subject first left the gates of the capital, I vowed never again to set foot in such an

46 Sŭngga-gul 僧伽崛: A temple dedicated to the early Tang Indian monk Sengjia. See Nam Tongsin, "Pukhansan Sŭngga taesa sang kwa Sŭngga sinang," *Sŏulhak yŏn'gu* 14 (2000): 5-48.

47 Modern Ch'unch'ŏn, Kangwŏn Province.

48 Mañjuśrī cloister. For more on the background of this temple and Yi Chahyŏn's relation to it see the inscription for it composed by Kim Puch'ŏl. *Tongmun sŏn* 64.

opulent place. Therefore I do not dare to accept the decree." Then he sent a memorial to the throne refusing the summons, which contained the words "Raising birds as birds, then there is no need to worry over the sound of bells or drums; looking at the fish one knows the fish, please allow me to accord with nature." When the king read this memorial he knew that it would not be possible to make him come. Taking avail of his journey to the Southern Capital he sent Yi Chayŏn's younger brother, Vice-minister Yi Chadŏk, to instruct him to come to his temporary palace. He bestowed one poem that he had written himself. Yi Chahyŏn responded positively to the summons [and traveled to the Southern Capital]. The king told him "I have long longed for your [instruction] in the way and its power, so it is not proper to meet as ruler and subject." He then ordered him to ascend the hall for his prostrations, bestowed a seat and hot tea. They then talked in a relaxed manner. The king also ordered him to remain in Ch'ŏngnyang-sa 清凉寺 on Mt. Samgak, and to meet again to discourse on the essentials of nurturing one's nature. Yi Chahyŏn responded "Nothing is better than reducing desire." The king showed his special admiration and made lavish rewards. But as he insisted on returning to his mountain, the king then bestowed tea, incense, and dharma robes as tokens of his special favor.

Winter, tenth month. The king returned from the Southern Capital.

A Hundred Seat Assembly was held in Hoegyŏng Hall, and 10,000 monks were given a maigre feast on the palace courtyard, and 20,000 in the regions.

Eleventh month. The king summoned the councilors of the Chancellery and Security Council for a small banquet in Ch'ŏngyŏn-gak.

The king went to Ch'ŏngyŏn-gak and ordered Hallim Academician Pak Sŭngjung to lecture on the poem "Guan ju" from the *Book of Odes*.[49]

Executive Chief of the Chancellery Yi Chagyŏm finished construction of his new residence. The king dispatched an envoy to with lavish gifts.

The king went to Ch'ŏngyŏn-gak and ordered Executive of the Chancellery Kim Yŏn to lecture on the *Book of Rites*, Royal Recording Secretary Ho Chongdan to lecture on the chapter "Against Luxurious Ease" of the *Book of*

---

[49] Guan ju 關雎: "*Guan-guan* go the ospreys", a poem about the ideal consort for a prince.

Documents, and licentiates Kwŏn Chŏk, Cho Sŏk, and Kim Tan[50] to read and explain the texts. This continued till deep into the night.

Twelfth month. Executive Chief of the Chancellery O Sujŭng died.

On the *kyŏng'o* day [the 11th] there was an earthquake.

The king banished the Count of Hoean 淮安伯, Wang Ki 王沂, to Ch'ŏnan District. Wang Ki was the son of the Marquis of Chin Han, Wang Yu. Wang Ki frequently associated with licentiate Ch'oe Towŏn 崔道元 and presented scholar Paek Sayun 白思允 and Royal Transmitter Kwŏn Sado 權思道. Ch'oe Towŏn divined fate on the basis of stars, and Paek Sayun and the others also engaged in irresponsible activities. Wang Ki and Ch'oe Towŏn also organized illegitimate sacrifices[51] at North Mountain Temple 北山寺, and when this was discovered all those implicated were banished. Wang Ki was summoned back shortly after.

The king ordered Kim Yŏn to lecture on the chapter "The Great Plan" from the *Book of Documents*.

Kim Chun was appointed Junior Vice-director of the Department of Ministries; Yi Kwe was appointed Assistant Executive in Letters and Intendant of the Hallim Academy; Pak Kyŏng'in was made Vice-minister of Taxation and Intendant of the Security Council; Wang Chaji was made Vice-minister of War and Intendant of the Security Council; and Han Kyoyŏ was made Jointly Intendant of the Security Council, Hallim Academician and Transmitter of Edicts. The king also bestowed upon him the name An'in 安仁.

---

50 *Kŭpche* 及第: those who passed the *kwagŏ* civil service examination; they are likely identified as such and not as "presented scholars" (*chinsa*) since they had passed the examination in China and hence were not tested before the king after the test.

51 Ch'o 醮: although the term Ch'oje 醮祭 is defined in Korean dictionaries as "sacrifice to the stars," individually it simply means an ancestral sacrifice. *Mathews' Chinese-English Dictionary* (no. 727) adds "idolatrous thanksgiving service" as one possible meaning, but it is not clear whether this is a missionary perspective or whether Chinese officialdom regarded it as suspicious. Most likely the sacrifice was the prerogative of the court, and hence it was not so much the sacrifice itself that was a problem but who performed it.

Yejong thirteenth year [1118]

First year of the Chonghe era of Song, eighth year of the Tianqing era of Liao, second year of the Tianfu era of Jin

Spring, first month. The king went to Ch'ŏngyŏn-gak and ordered Academician Hong Kwan to lecture on the "Canon of Shun" [from the *Book of Documents*] and then bestowed a banquet.

Second month. The king ordered Edict Attendant[52] Kim Puil to lecture on the "Odes of Lu" from the *Book of Odes*.

Forty-one Jurchen arrived to present local products.

The king ordered Han An'in to lecture on the hexagram "peace" (*tai* 泰) from the *Book of Changes*.

Third month. Junior Vice-director of the Department of Ministries Yu Chae died. He was originally from Quanzhou in Song, and once arrived on a trading ship. He was frugal and simple, and did not engage in commercial activities. He was good in letters, and people of the time cherished him.

Director of the Chancellery Yi Wi retired. Yi Chagyŏm was made Minister of Personnel; Kim Yŏn was made Minister of War; and Yi Kwe was made Vice-minister of Taxation and Minster of Rites.

Summer, fourth month. The restoration of Anhwa-sa was completed. The king personally held a maigre feast for five days to celebrate the occasion. He gave presents commensurate with rank to the officials and clerks in charge of mustering the corvée labor and craftsmen. Initially the close ministers in charge of overseeing the project went for extreme luxury, and the effort and expenses were beyond counting. They also requested a calligraphed board from the Song emperor. When he heard this [request] the emperor personally wrote on the board for the Buddha Hall "Hall for the one skilled in humaneness."[53] He also ordered Cai Jing 蔡京 to write the calligraphy for the gate board "Anhwa temple pacifying the country" and bestowed both

52 Taeje[gwan] 待制[官] According to Hucker (6129) a literatus assigned to take notes during the ruler's meeting with officials.

53 Nŭng'in chi chŏn 能仁之殿: "Skilled in humaneness" was a Chinese epithet for the Buddha.

boards [on Koryŏ].

Fifth month, *kyemi*, the first day of the month. There was a solar eclipse.

Kim Pog'yun 金福允 and twenty-two others passed the composition test of the civil service examination.

Sixth month. The king went to Ch'ŏngyŏn-gak and ordered the Pomun-gak Academician Yi Yŏng to lecture on the "Charge of Yue" from the *Book of Documents*.

Autumn, seventh month. Song dispatched Audience Usher Cao Yi 曹誼. Prior to this, the heir apparent had sent an additional memorial requesting medical experts in major arteries,[54] ulcers and swellings etc. The emperor ordered Cao Yi to take with him seven people including the Hallim Physician Yang Zongli 楊宗立.

Eighth month. The king dispatched Chŏng Kŭg'yŏng 鄭克永 and Yi Chimi 李之美 to Song to give thanks for granting a hand-written decree to Kwŏn Chŏk and the others upon receiving their degree. The king composed and wrote the memorial himself.

Ninth month. The royal consort, the Yŏndŏk Princess née Yi, died. She was the daughter of Yi Chagyŏm. She had a soft disposition and was intelligent, and the king greatly cherished her. Since she came down with a disease the king was greatly worried and personally administered the medicine to her. When she died the king wailed several times in front of her body. He granted the posthumous title Queen Sundŏk 順德王后, and she was buried in Sunŭng 綏陵. The king personally sent her off outside Sinbong Gate.

The Royal Inspector for Local Government of Chŏlla-do, Ko Chinmyŏng 高進明, impeached the Commissioner of Namwŏn District 南原府 Chi Chun 池俊, the Administrative Assistants Ch'ae Kŭksŏng 蔡克成 and Mun An'gyŏng 文安慶, and others, for extorting the people. They were dismissed from office.

A Tripitaka Assembly was held in Hoegyŏng Hall and the king personally offered incense. His close officials Pak Sŭngjung and Hong Kwan were

---

54 Taebangmaek 大方脈: In medical usage, "taebang" is used for adult as opposed to pediatric medicine, but it is not certain if that is what is meant here.

laughing and chatting, and these sounds reached the king. The Censorate officials impeached them, requesting they be removed from office.

Intercalary [ninth] month. The State Councilors thrice petitioned the king, requesting that he resume normal dishes. The king complied.

The king went to Ch'ŏngyŏn-gak, and ordered Han An'in to lecture on Laozi's [*Daode jing*].

The heir apparent shed his mourning clothes.

Vice-director of the Department of Ministries Ch'oe Chŏng died.

Winter, tenth month. The king ordered Reviewing Policy Advisor Ch'oe Chasŏng 崔滋盛 and others to raise troops across all provinces.

The king went to the mourning hall of Queen Sundŏk. The remonstrance official sent a protest, saying "A few days previously for the first mourning [your majesty's] show of grief was excessive. During the funeral and the sacrifices you personally prostrated and offered wine, which in the eyes of ministers and people was secretly seen as beyond the ritual pale. Today again for a minor affair you bent your august body in front of the spirit tent; we fear that this will damage your great body." The king said "Affairs of the ancestors are not my personal whim. I once heard that when the Song emperor sent off Queen Jinghe 靖和皇后 he personally left [the city] through Duan Gate and outside made libations and prostrated himself. Thus I merely follow his example. All the more so since this is just an outing to the mourning hall, how could it be harmful to righteousness?"

Eleventh month. The king went to Ch'ŏngyŏn-gak and ordered Han An'in to lecture on the hexagram "return" (復) from the *Book of Changes*.

Twelfth month. Kim Sangje 金尙磾 was made intendant for the Office of Audience Ceremonies and Yi Yuin 李惟寅 was made Director of the Palace Treasury. Both these men were intent on guarding their integrity, and wherever they were posted they enjoyed high reputation and good results. However by keeping their distance from those who wielded authority, they had yet to reach a respectable position. Associate Administrator of the Security Council Han An'in had sent a letter to the throne requesting for their promotion so as to encourage other officials [like them]. Hence these appointments.

Yejong fourteenth year [1119]

First year of the Xuanhe era of Song, ninth year of the Tianqing era of Liao, third year of the Tianfu era of Jin

Spring, second month. Jurchen came to court.

The king went to the mourning hall for Queen Sundŏk.

The Jurchen ruler dispatched an envoy with presents, who presented the following letter: "I raised an army to attack Liao, and thanks to Heaven's assistance on several occasions we defeated the enemy troops. From the Supreme Capital in the north to the sea tribes in the south, the people are now all settled and at ease. Today I dispatch the *beijin*[55] *Shubei* 朮孛 to communicate my instructions and also to bestow one horse. Please accept it upon arrival."

The king went to Changwŏn Pavilion.

Third month. Kim Chihwa was made Vice-director of the Department of Ministries and Assistant Executive in Political Affairs; Ch'oe Chi was made Junior Vice-director of the Department of Ministries and Intendant of the Royal Library.

Summer, fourth month. The king's younger brother, Marquis of Thorough Counsel[56] Wang Kyo, died. He was clever and assiduous in his studies, and esteemed the wise and liked scholars.

Sixth month. Yi Chagyŏm was invested as Merit Subject of Equal Virtue, First Rank;[57] Wang Chaji was made Commissioner of the Security Council and Administrator of the Finance Commission; Han An'in was made Vice-minister of Punishment and Administrator of the Security Council; and Kim Ko 金沽 was made Censor-in-chief.

Autumn, seventh month. The king decreed that schools should be widely established to foster and train the students. Sixty positions for Confucianism

55 *Beijin* 孛堇: given as *bojin* 勃堇 in Hucker (no. 4723), a native Jurchen word for a clan leader.

56 *T'ongŭi hu* 通義侯: while most royal princes not in line for the throne were given titles of old charter polities or other regions, this title resembles that of the prestige title for officials of rank 6B, *t'ongŭirang* 通議郎 (Hucker no. 7488).

57 *Samjungdaegwan* 三重大匡: rank title for officials of rank 1.

were created and seventeen for military arts. Close ministers to the king were entrusted with managing affairs and selecting eminent Confucians as officials and scholars to lecture and debate the meaning of the Classics. At the beginning of the dynasty the Shrine for Confucius (Munsŏng-wang myo 文聖王廟) was established in the National Academy and administrators and lecturers were appointed. However by the time of King Sŏnjong [although] he wished to foster education he did not find the opportunity to do so. The king was very keen on classical learning and the spirit of letters was therefore slightly revived.

Eighth month. The king went to Ch'ŏngyŏn-gak and ordered Hallim Academician Pak Sŭngjung to lecture on the chapter "the Great Plan" [from the *Book of Documents*].

The king dispatched Master Scribe of the Royal Secretariat Cho Sun'gŏ 曹舜擧 with presents to Jin. However, as the letter contained the phrase "Moreover their origins lie in our country" the Jin ruler refused to accept them.

The king went to the mourning hall of Queen Sundŏk.

Executive Chief of the Chancellery Cho Chungjang died.

Khitan dispatched Xiao Gongting 蕭公聽 and Yelü Zunqing 耶律遵慶 with the following instruction: "Recently because the roads have been blocked it has been difficult [for you] to present tribute or congratulations. It has also been impossible [for us] to bestow rites of benefice for several years now." They also came to bestow robes.

Winter, eleventh month. The king went to Ch'ŏngyŏn-gak and ordered Pak Sŭngjung to lecture on the chapter the *Doctrine of the Mean*.

The king inspected archery at Ch'ŏngyŏn-gak.

The king inspected archery at Chunggwang Hall and gave prizes to those who hit the mark.

The Long Wall was increased in height by three feet. The Jin border officials raised an army to stop this, but this was ignored. We reported "Repairs are being carried out to the old walls." The Jin ruler instructed the border officials as follows: "You should not invade, but be on your guard against any eventuality. Strengthen the fortifications and be vigilant at all times."

Yejong fifteenth year [1120]

Second year of the Xuanhe era of Song, tenth year of the Tianqing era of Liao, fourth year of the Tianfu era of Jin

Spring, second month. The king went to the Southern Capital

Fourth month. The king returned from the Southern Capital.

Fifth month. Yi Chijŏ 李之氐 and thirty-seven others passed the composition test of the civil service examination. At the time the king was fond of music; the kisaeng Yŏngnong 玲瓏 and Arun 遏雲, because they were good at singing, on several occasions received presents from the king. The National Academy student Ko Hyoch'ung 高孝冲 lampooned this with a poem entitled "Enticed by two women." Drafting Advisor Chŏng Kŭg'yŏng told this to the king, who was displeased. When Ko Hyoch'ung took the examination the king ordered him to be expelled and after this he was put in jail. Pomun-gak Edict Attendant Ho Chongdan wrote a petition arguing for his release; he was then set free.

The king received a Buddha bone within the forbidden precinct. Before this, when Wang Chaji returned from his mission to Song the emperor bestowed a Buddha tooth and piece of the skull stored in a golden casket. After it had been placed in the Oejesŏg-wŏn 外帝釋院, it was now put in the Sanho Pavilion 山呼亭.

Sixth month. The king went to Ch'ŏngyŏn-gak and ordered Pak Sŭngjung to lecture on the chapter "the Great Plan" [from the *Book of Documents*].

Kim Chun was appointed Executive Chief of the Royal Secretariat; Yi Kwe was made Acting Minister of Works, Vice-director of the Department of Ministers, and Assistant Executive in Political Affairs; Im Yumun was appointed Junior Vice-director of the Department of Ministries, in charge of affairs at the Chancellery; Pak Kyŏng'in was made Administrator of the Security Council; Han An'in was made Vice-minister of Rites; Ch'oe

Hongjae was appointed Vice-minister of Punishment and Associate Administrator of the Security Council.

The king went to Ch'ŏngyŏn-gak and ordered Master of Sacrificial Wines Chŏng Kŭg'yŏng to lecture on the "Monthly Ordinances" from the *Book of Rites*.

The king personally sacrificed in Pogwŏn-gung 福源宮[58] and then went to Anhwa-sa to the portrait hall of Queen Sundŏk. He wept while making the libation.

The Song merchant Lin Qing 林淸 and others offered flowering trees.

The king went to Ch'ŏngyŏn-gak and ordered Kim Yŏn to lecture on the chapter "Tai Jia" 太甲 from the *Book of Documents*.

Autumn, seventh month. Liao dispatched Assistant Commissioner at the Court of Music Xiao Zunli 蕭遵禮 with the following decree: "You sir have established the territorial shrine on the eastern border and proclaimed yourself a protective screen of the northern court. Since the rise of the two bastard armies, one side of the road has been blocked. Despite your desire to establish the royal succession, yet it has not yet been possible to implement the investiture. In recent years we did all we could for the king, but the enemies for a long time frustrated this. Whenever I think about this it becomes more frustrating. Now we are waiting for the right moment to suddenly destroy the bandits. Recently a secret decree was dispatched to inform you of these thoughts, but there were many troubles along the way and it was difficult for people to go there together. Or [traveling via the sea] adverse currents made rowing difficult and the sealed container [with the edict] did not get delivered; some of the presents bestowed did manage to get through, barely enough to show our good intentions. But suddenly there was a letter of thanks, confirming all the more your sincerity. Furthermore these words stemming from correct feelings look forward to repaying the suzerain country. With these noble intentions further increased, this will necessarily

58 A Daoist temple; according to the Chinese emissary Xu Jing it was founded during the Zhenghe era (1111–1117), undoubtedly in connection with the Song emperor Huizong's strong support of Taoism. See Vermeersch, *A Chinese Traveler in Medieval Korea*, 134.

render the matter clear and transparent. Stuck with a common enemy, by thus following the great you can look forward to positive outcomes. I will await further news."

Song dispatched Gentleman of Trust[59] Xu Lijin 許立進 and Lieutenant Lin Darong 林大容 and others. When they were about to return the king wanted to meet Xu on top of the stairs. Royal Recording Editor Han Ch'ung, Left Reparationer Ch'oe Kŏrin 崔巨麟, and Attendant Censor Ch'oe Hongnyak 崔洪略 remonstrated, stating "Now the edict envoy is originally a merchant who in the past came to our country to buy and sell to people in the markets. He is of very low office, moreover on the day of delivering the edict he already greeted on top of the stairs. This is already too demeaning; he should greet from below the stairs." The king followed this.

Retired Executive Chief of the Royal Secretariat Kang Chŭng died. He was from an ordinary family with no influence. Although he did not have talent he was diligent and deferential in his work. During the three Jurchen campaigns he established merit in battle and finally reached high office.

Eighth month. It had not rained since summer. In this month the grains still had not ripened and infectious diseases were rampant.

The king went to Oejesŏg-wŏn and ordered the five sections [of the city of Kaesŏng] to read the *Prajñāpāramitā sūtra* for three days to pray for a delivery from the pandemic.

The king went to Sŏnjŏng Hall to personally adjudicate heavy crimes.

The king went to the portrait hall for Queen Sundŏk in Anhwa-sa and grieved there for a long time. Some among the entourage shed tears.

Senior Policy Monitor Hong Yag'i 洪若伊 presented a memorial on the state of government, discussing both achievements and failures. The king praised him and accepted [the advice].

On *ŭlyu* day [the 14th] the king went to the Western Capital.

On *muja* day [the 17th] day the South Pole Star was visible.

The king went to Hŭngbok-sa and Yŏngmyŏng-sa to watch the tide.

The king went to the Taedong River and took a boat to watch the fish.

---

59 *Chengxinlang* 承信郎 (Hucker no. 485), prestige title of rank 9b.

Ninth month. The king went to Yŏngmyŏng-sa to watch the tide.

A decree read: "Since I became king, I went on inspection tours to the Western Capital twice. Formerly, as soon as I arrived I had to turn back. This time I can take my time and linger without worry. Now I wish to pass on the favor so as to comfort the minds of the people. Those who since *ŭlyu* day in the eighth month erred and committed crimes, let the relevant authority remit the impeachment against them, and also remit those [sentenced to] 'redeeming with copper and levying tiles.'"[60]

The king gave a banquet for his officials in Changnak Hall. He personally composed a *ci* poem on the Southern Pole Star, and ordered the court musicians to sing it.

Retired Commissioner of the Security Council Kim Hanch'ung died. From a young age he was valiant; applying himself to study he passed the civil service examination. For a long time he served as commissioner for the Ansŏ Protectorate. He was mild in administration and favored simplicity, greatly easing the burden of clerks and ordinary people. When Yun Kwan first attacked the Jurchen, he acted as military commissioner. Together with Yun Kwan he planned on placating the Jurchen with humble words and lofty ritual; securing peace with them thus secured the border and made it peaceful. Later he again marched along with Yun Kwan; the Jurchen, complacent because of the peace deal, had not prepared for them; following an ambush they were defeated. His wife was the daughter of a servant girl of Munjong. Therefore, although he reached important office, he was not allowed to serve in the censorial agencies.

Winter, tenth month. On *mujin* day, the first day of the month, there was a solar eclipse.

Eleventh month. The king returned from the Western Capital.

Attendant Censors Chin Suk 陳叔 and No Wŏnsung 盧元崇 were demoted[61] and appointed Executives at the Slave Agency. Previously the Censorate

---

60 贖銅徵瓦: It is not clear what this refers to, but it is likely a kind of fine or labor (manufacturing tiles) to redeem one's crime.

61 *Chwach'ŏn* 左遷, literally "moved to the left," a term usually denoting demotion (Hucker no. 6955).

had petitioned: "Recently the customs are becoming more lavish by the day, and at both official and private banquets and meetings the vessels and dishes are opulent, without differentiation of higher and lower. We request that the old regulations be implemented again so that this is forbidden. As for those who break the regulations, in the case of worthy people it should be reported first and then adjudicated; in the case of base people, they should first be imprisoned and then reported." The king agreed with this. Thereupon following the usual procedure of the P'algwan Assembly, the fruit table of the Security Council exceeded regulations, and the Censorate officials apprehended and imprisoned the office manager and administrative aide [of the Security Council]. Commissioner of the Security Council Wang Chaji and Intendant of the Security Council Han An'in, who were already drunk, angrily cursed them and wanted them to release the clerks, but the Censorate officials ignored them. Wang and Han then petitioned the king saying "Your ignorant and unworthy subjects have been insulted by minor officials, please relieve them of their office." The king found it difficult to go against the will of his high officials, and thus demoted Chin and No. He then dispatched close officials to Wang and Han to give encouraging words and urge them on in their work.

The king went to Ch'ŏngyŏn-gak and ordered Kim Puil to lecture on the poem "Ban shui" 泮水 from the *Book of Odes*.

Twelfth month. As the mourning period for Queen Sundŏk was over, the king summoned the heir apparent, Executive Yi Chagyŏm, Administrator of Memorials Yi Charyang and others for drinks. The king was overjoyed and bestowed munificent gifts.

Pak Kyŏng'in was made Acting Minister of Works, Vice-director of the Department of Ministries, Assistant Executive in Political Affairs, and was then retired.

Yejong sixteenth year [1121]

Third year of the Xuanhe era of Song, first year of the Bao[da] era of Liao, fifth year of the Tianfu era of Jin

Spring, first month. The king decreed "In regulations on [relations between] man and woman, upholding the grand moral principles is particularly important. All great emperors and kings were assisted by their consorts in their endeavors. For family members to attain their correct place, the harmonious relations between partners should be like that between ospreys. Now I am about to take as spouses the oldest daughter of the Duke of Chin Han,[62] and the youngest daughter of the Grand Minister Ch'oe Yong 崔湧. The officials should determine their titles in accordance with ritual classics and report to me." The Ministry of Rites suggested that Lady Wang be designated Precious Consort (*kwibi* 貴妃) and Lady Ch'oe Virtuous Consort (*sukpi* 淑妃). The king agreed.

The heir apparent dressed in adult robes in the Such'un Palace. All the officials presented memorials of congratulation. Earlier, when the heir apparent was in the temporary palace, he expressed his wish to go through the capping ceremony.[63] Executive Kim Yŏn petitioned: "Capping is the first of the rites [of passage] and hence very important. Therefore performing the three stages [of the capping ceremony] on the eastern steps will enhance the prestige of the rite and duly express the meaning of reaching adulthood. As the precious firstborn son, holding the ceremony outside [the main palace] does not accord with the precedents set by earlier kings. The officials should be ordered to hold the ceremony as prescribed." The king agreed.

At the occasion of the Hamnyŏng Festival [the king's birthday], the king received felicitations in Kŏndŏk Hall and held a banquet for the officials.

Second month. The king demoted Drafting Advisor Han Ch'ung to Assistant Resident Governor of the Western Capital. Senior Policy Monitor

---

62 I.e. Wang Yu, a son of King Munjong through the latter's marriage with a daughter of Yi Chayŏn. See KRS 88.19a.

63 This refers to Wang Ku, later Injong, who was born in 1109, hence he would have been only 12 years old.

Im Wŏnjun 任元濬 was appointed Intendant-secretary at the Department of Royal Clan Affairs. What had happened was as follows: Associate Administrator of the Security Council Ch'oe Hongjae had followed Yun Kwan when he subjugated the Jurchen. Secretly having prayed for divine protection, when this was granted in fulfillment of his wish he had to complete a Buddhist Canon Hall at Kaeguk-sa. To achieve this he requested an army general to transport building material. Han Ch'ung and others accused him of construction on false pretenses. The king convinced them to stop this, but when Han Ch'ung and the others kept insisting that Ch'oe be dismissed, the king therefore made these appointments [to positions where they could not harass him].

Third month. The king went to Ch'angsin-sa 彰信寺. The king changed into inconspicuous clothes to travel incognito to Su-nŭng Tomb. When he was about to go the remonstrance official petitioned saying "From old the rulers never personally travelled to the tombs of queens and consorts. I consulted the ritual canons and there is also no mention of such a thing. The tomb has been covered in a thicket of plants. When the most respected person bows down before such a place, how could I not feel saddened? Your subject cannot overcome his feelings of dread. Prostrate, I express the hope that you will constrain yourself with ritual and yield to the hopes of the people." The king did not accept this.

Song dispatched Yao Xi 姚喜.

The king went to Ch'ŏngyŏn-gak and ordered Hallim Academician Pak Sŭngjung to lecture on the "Monthly Ordinances" from the *Book of Rites*, and Royal Recording Editor Kim Pusik to lecture on the "Charge to Yue" from the *Book of Documents*.

Summer, fourth month. The king went to Anhwa-sa and on the way back went to Yi Chagyŏm's mountain studio for drinks.

The king bestowed upon Yi Chagyŏm the title of Merit Subject Promoting Loyalty and Assisting Reason, Dynasty-founding Earl[64] of Sosŏng District.

64 Kaeguk-paek 開國伯: Third level merit subject, after Kaeguk-kong and Kaeguk-hu but above Kaeguk-cha and Kaeguk-nam.

He appointed his sons Yi Chimi and Yi Kongŭi 李公儀 to office.

Fifth month. All the officials prayed for rain in Hŭngguk-sa 興國寺 for five days.

Intercalary [fifth] month. A decree read: "The seasons have lost their right order, and the drought has become a catastrophe. Looking back, it is my lack of virtue that has caused this calamity, thus I pity the people who are blameless in this yet lost their lives. Prayers for rain did not bring any response, and I worry without end. My hope is that by bestowing favors a harmonious energy can be summoned. Apart from those sentenced to beheading and strangulation, all those who are imprisoned should be pardoned. If there should be officials or clerks who on account of public law extract riches through cruelty and oppression, or who extract interest by forcing rotten grains on the people, or levy land taxes from fallow land, or who levy corvée labor for non-urgent work, this should all be forbidden and [infractions] punished."

The king ordered Royal Recorder Im Chon 林存 to lecture on [the poem] "The Milky Way" from the *Book of Odes*.

Sixth month. The king went to Changnyŏng Hall and ordered Pak Sŭngjung to lecture on the "Monthly Ordinances" from the *Book of Rites*.

Pak Kyŏng'in, who had retired as Assistant Executive in Letters, died. From a young age he had studied hard and passed the civil service examination. Three times he served as remonstrance official. In his speech and in debates he always remained upright and principled, so that there was no room for obfuscation. At the time he was considered an important person.

Autumn, eighth month. The king went to Yŏng-nŭng and Sung-nŭng tombs.

The king went to Changwŏn Pavilion.

Winter, tenth month. A Hundred Seat Assembly was set up in Hoegyŏng Hall. The king ordered that vegetarian feast should be held for 30,000 monks in the capital and throughout the country.

Imja day [the 21st]. Venus appeared during the day and was observed and for more than a month passed through the sky.

Twelfth month. The king went to Ch'ŏngyŏn-gak and displayed the calligraphy, paintings, and other goods bestowed by the Song emperor to the state councilors and close officials.

The king went to Pogwŏn-gung and then to Kwisan-sa and Anhwa-sa. He then went to Okcham [Jade Peak] Pavilion 玉岑亭 and gave a banquet for his entourage.

Yejong seventeenth year [1122]

Fourth year of the Xuanhe era of Song, second year of the Baoda era of Liao, sixth year of the Tianfu era of Jin

Spring, first month. The king went to Ch'ŏngyŏn-gak and ordered Drafting Advisor Kim Pusik to lecture on the hexagram "Heaven" from the *Book of Changes*.

Second month. On *kyŏngin* day, the first day of the month, there was a solar eclipse.

Ch'oe Hongsa, who had retired as Executive Chief of the Chancellery, died. He was born in a poor and insignificant family, but gained fame thanks to his literary talent and behavior. He was upright of character and had few desires; at court he did not belong to any faction. At home he did not talk about official business, and his wife and children never saw him make fun or laugh. If someone sent him a gift, even it was just vegetables or fruit, he did not accept it. The king greatly cherished him. However, in carrying out his work he was very fastidious, and if people made even the slightest mistake he would not forget it. People at the time considered this a weakness.

Third month. Kim Chun was appointed Probationary Minister of Education, and Minister of Ritual; Im Yumun was appointed Probationary Minister of Works, Assistant Executive in Political Affairs, Minister of Punishment, and Jointly Junior Preceptor of the Heir Apparent; Wang Chaji was appointed Vice-minister of Personnel, Assistant Executive in Letters, and Minister of Taxation, and Jointly Junior Mentor of the Heir Apparent; Han An'in was appointed Assistant Executive in Political Affairs, Minister of

Works, and State Historiographer; Ch'oe Hongjae was made Commissioner for the Security Council, Jointly Advisor to the Heir Apparent, Administrator of the Finance Commission; Kim Yag'on 金若溫 was made Administrator of the Security Council and Jointly Advisor to the Heir Apparent; Yi Charyang was appointed Vice-commissioner of the Security Council and Jointly Adviser to the Heir Apparent.

The king went to the Gossamer Tower[65] and summoned fifty-six civil officials for an impromptu poetry composition,[66] and ordered to write a prose poem on the poem "Peonies." Registrar at the Household of the Heir Apparent An Porin 安寶麟 gained first prize. Each was given silk commensurate to rank. At the time, because Kang Iryong 康日用 was famous for his poetic ability, the king stood and watched over his shoulders as he wrote. When the candle was nearly extinguished, Kang Iryong had barely mustered one line, which went "The white-haired drunken old man watches behind the hall; the bright-eyed old Confucian leans against the railing." He put the manuscript in his sleeve and hid it in the palace drain. The king ordered a small eunuch to retrieve it. When he saw it he exclaimed in admiration "This is what the ancients called 'Even if an ugly woman covers her face in exquisite makeup, she will not match the half-madeup face of Xi Shi.'"[67] He comforted him and sent him on his way.

The king went to Sunch'ŏn Hostel to give a banquet for the state councilors in Hyangnim Pavilion 香林亭.[68] Suddenly he felt there was a slight swelling on his back, and urgently rode back to the palace, where he prayed to the deities of mountains and rivers.

Assistant Executive in Political Affairs Wang Chaji died. His great-great-

---

65 Saru 沙樓: this is perhaps one of the viewing towers that Xu Jing refers to; see Vermeersch, *A Chinese Traveler in Medieval Korea*, 77.

66 *Kakch'ok* 刻燭: literally a marked candle; the composition had to be finished by the time the candle burned down to a certain line, or burned up completely.

67 The admiration on the king's part is here probably sarcasm. Xi Shi 西施 is the name of a legendary Chinese beauty. It is not clear however what the point of this anecdote is.

68 Sunch'ŏn Hostel was where the Chinese Song embassy of 1123 was lodged. Both the hostel and the pavilion are described in Xu Jing's *Gaoli tujing*. See Vermeersch, *A Chinese Traveler in Medieval Korea*, 180–182.

great grandfather Pak Yu had established merit in assisting T'aejo and was therefore granted the dynastic surname. Wang Chaji had worked his way up from a position as lowly clerk. When his brother-in-law Wang Kungmo killed Yi Chaŭi, he was guarding the palace gates. For this merit he was made Director of the Bureau of Handicraft. In 1107 during the reign of Sukchong he became administrative assistant to the military commissioner and several times established his merit in the war against the Jurchen.

On the *ŭlyu* day [the 26th] 10,000 monks were fed across several temples; on the *muja* day [the 29th] the same was done.

Summer, fourth month. A decree read "Since this insignificant person undeservedly succeeded to the throne, a number of years have passed. However when faced with the tasks of government I did not know how to resolve them, and thus Yin and Yang lost their order, calamities of heaven and earth increased, and moreover my disease kept lingering without getting better. Vexed and fearful, I kept pushing on, and hope to offer rewards to the numinous to express gratitude in this world and the next. All the great mountains and rivers that have a shrine dedicated to them should receive higher titles. All those who have committed crimes, apart from those sentenced to decapitation and strangulation should be released. Those who have been sent to exile should have their distance commuted [to bring them closer to home]."

Executive Yi Chagyŏm and others went to Sunbŏk Hall and addressed the following prayer to Heaven: "Formerly, when King Wu of Zhou was ill, the Duke of Zhou with utmost sincerity requested Heaven that he should live, and his illness then was cured. Now your subjects are all foolish and occupy their position with no merit. We have no political skills that would put the people at ease, and have no virtue worth boasting to the spirits about. Full of lusting and depravity, our lack of morals made us like insects to the country, causing Heaven to send punishments that befell the ruler above. Considering that Heaven is perspicacious, it is proper that the disease should be sent down upon our bodies, and let the disease that has long troubled the king subside."

On *ŭlmi* day [the 7th], the king's disease became critical; sitting propped up he convened the state councilors, telling them "Due to my lack of virtue Heaven sent down this calamity and my disease failed to improve. Although the heir apparent is still young, he is mature in terms of his virtuous behavior. If you gentlemen assist him with a single mind then the ancestral enterprise will not collapse." The officials prostrated themselves and wailed, not knowing what to say. The king then summoned the heir apparent and told him "My disease is all encompassing, and there is no longer any chance of recovery. I now relinquish my heavy responsibilities and pass them on to you. Looking back on my actions of a lifetime, what I achieved was little and my failures plenty; beware not to follow in my footsteps. Just study the path of ancient sages and worthies, and uphold the injunctions of T'aejo. Don't be indolent in your duties and forever support the people." The heir apparent wept with lowered head and could not rise. The king then instructed Han An'in to fetch the seal of state and hand it to the heir apparent. He then passed away.

At the time the heir apparent was still quite young, and the king's younger brothers had ambitions beyond their station. Yi Chagyŏm led the heir apparent and enthroned him in the Chunggwang Hall. Mornings and evenings he made offerings in the funerary hall, wailing and stamping his feet in grief. The close officials were moved by his grief and could not stop him.

On *kab'in* day [the 26th] the king was buried in Yu-nŭng 裕陵, and he was given the posthumous title of Great King of Letters and Piety [Munhyo taewang 文孝大王], and the temple name Yejong 睿宗.

The historians write: "Yejong was endowed with natural wisdom and insight. Already in the heir apparent's palace he received worthies with propriety and acted with piety and brotherly affection. After ascending the throne he worked diligently from dawn to dusk, putting all his energy and soul in the work of governing. But he was particularly keen on expanding the borders, and due to some fortuitous [initial] victories at the border never stopped his quarrel with the foe. He greatly admired Chinese culture and greatly trusted Ho Chongdan's words of advice: implementing his deceitful words led to many problems. However he became aware of the difficulty of waging war, and giving up his resentment cultivated good relations, making the neighbors at the border comply and submit. He took pity on widowers and widows, and sustained the elderly. He opened schools to foster students. He also established the two institutions of Ch'ŏngyŏn-gak and Pomun-gak, and daily listened to lectures on the six classics and debated with his literary officials. He thus gave up on war to cultivate letters, wanting to reform the customs through ritual and music. Thus the words by Han An'in that 'this seventeen-year reign is worth passing on to the next generation' are apt indeed."

Fifth month. The king's mother Queen Sundŏk was given the posthumous title of Queen Dowager Literary Reverence [Mungyŏng t'aehu 文敬王太后].

Yi Chagyŏm was made Merit Subject Assisting in Planning and Pacifying the Earth Deities, Acting Grand Preceptor and Royal Secretary, Marquis of Sosŏng; Kim Kyŏngyong was made Merit Subject Equalizing Virtue and Assisting Sagacity, Duke of Nangnang; Yi Wi was made Merit Subject Straightening the Country, Duke of Kyeyang; Im Yumun and Kim Chun were made Executive Chief of the Chancellery; Han An'in was made Executive Chief of the Royal Secretariat; Ch'oe Hongjae and Kim Yag'on were made Assistant Executive in Political Affairs; Yi Charyang was made Commissioner of the Security Council; Kim Ko was made Administrator of the Security Council; and Mun Kongmi was made Vice-commissioner of the Security Council.

The king bestowed upon the officials and clerks who had taken care of the queen dowager's investiture one [additional] rank.

The king declared an amnesty.

Sixth month. The king received the bodhisattva precepts in Kŏndŏk Hall.

The Song Letter-bearing Envoy, Lieutenant Promoting Martiality[69] Yao Xi,

69 Jinwu xiaowei 進武校尉: I here interpret Jinwu as an honorific title rather than part of the office title.

arrived.

Autumn, seventh month. Yi Kwe, who had retired as Assistant Executive in Letters, died. He had advanced in officialdom thanks to his passing the civil service examination. He was good friends with Kim Hwangwŏn, and both shared fame for their skills in composition.

A *Diamond Sūtra* ritual was held in Kŏndŏk Hall for three weeks.

A decree read: "Royal Secretary Yi Chagyŏm is the queen dowager's father, and also my maternal grandfather. His office rank and protocol requirements are thus not in the same league as other officials. The Chancellery and Security Council, together with the drafters of royal edicts and proclamations, and various attendant officials should deliberate on this and report to me." Pomun-gak Academician Chŏng Kŭg'yŏng and Censor of Miscellaneous Affairs Ch'oe Yu 崔濡 gave their opinion: "According to the tradition, 'There are three kinds of people the Son of Heaven does not use as subjects.'[70] The parents of the queen are one of those categories. Now Yi Chagyŏm when he submits a letter or petition should not address himself as 'your subject,' and when there is a banquet for all officials, he should not together with all the other officials give congratulations in the courtyard but go directly to the king's tent to bow to the king, and when the king has bowed in return he should then take his seat in the hall." All agreed on this, except Pomun-gak Edict Attendant Kim Pusik, who argued "When Emperor Gaozu of Han first pacified the realm, he held an audience with his father, Taigong, once every five days. The Household Provisioner told Taigong:[71] 'There are no two suns in the sky, and there are also no two rulers on earth. Although the emperor is your son, he is also a sovereign. Although you, Taigong, are his father, you are also a subject. So how can a sovereign bow to a subject?' Gaozu approved of the household provisioner's words and

70 Although there is a similar passage in the "yimin liezhuan" of the *Hou Han shu*, I could not trace an identical one.

71 Taigong 太公 is the title given to the father of Liu Bang, the founder of the Han Dynasty later given the temple name Gaozu. Jialing 家令 is the name of an official of the royal household, translated by Hucker as "Household Provisioner" (no. 669), though here clearly someone in charge of propriety and education rather than provisions. This passage occurs in *Shiji*, annals of Gaozu.

issued an edict saying 'The closest possible relation among humans is that between father and son. Therefore if the father obtains All under Heaven he passes it on to the son. If the son obtains All under Heaven, he attributes it to the father through honorification. This is the utmost way of being human. Now the kings, marquises, ministers, and grand-masers already have granted me the honorific title of emperor yet Taigong does not yet have a title. Now I give the title of Supreme Emperor [Taishanghuang 太上皇] to Taigong.'

From this discussion it is clear that if the father of the Son of Heaven does not have an honorific title, then the sovereign cannot bow to him. Therefore regarding the father of Emperor Xian 獻帝 of Later Han's queen, Marquis Buqi Fuwan 不其侯伏完, Zheng Xuan 鄭玄 argued 'When Marquis Buqi comes to the capital and enters the palace, in terms of greetings he should follow the rules for subjects. If the queen is resting in another palace or goes to her parent's place to pay her respects, then the greeting of the child to the parents should be used.' Thus when the marquis went to court for congratulations, he followed the protocol of subjects, but when the queen is in [her] palace she follows the protocol of child greeting parents. Furthermore, regarding the greeting protocol of the mother of Emperor Mu of the Eastern Jin 東晉穆帝, Queen Dowager Zhe 褚太后, to her father, people argued a lot for and against without reaching an agreement. The Professor Xu Chan 徐禪 then invoked Zheng Xuan's arguments: 'In the court of the king correcting the propriety of ruler and subject, in private meetings [with the ruler] preserving the closeness of father and son, this the way of greatly according [with principle].' Furthermore, the father of the Wei Emperor, King Yan 燕王 [Cao] Yu 曹宇 presented a memorial where he called himself your subject.

Even though the relation between father and son is that of utmost closeness, propriety and treatment are still just as in the cases mentioned. And as for the maternal grandfather, according to the five morning grades of the *Yili*, the mourning grade for the parents of one's mother is known as "lesser effort" and lasts for just five months. This is very far removed from the respect and closeness expressed for one's own parents. How could this compare to the high respect for the ruler? It would be fitting to address oneself as your subject when submitting a memorial, and using the protocol of ruler and subject at court just as all the other officials. As for inside the palace, you can use the protocol of greeting among family members. If you do this, public righteousness and private feelings will be in perfect harmony."

The state councilors presented the two views to the king. The king sent his close officials Kang Huhyŏn 康侯顯 to ask Yi Chagyŏm's opinion, and Yi replied "Although your subject is without knowledge, seeing Kim Pusik's arguments it is truly the public consensus of All under Heaven. Without this person, the various lords would have made this old subject fall into unrighteousness. Prostrate, I wish to follow this advice; do not have doubts." The king then decreed his approval.

Eighth month. Na Kyŏngsun 羅景純 and thirty others passed the composition test of the civil service examination.

Ninth month. The king decreed that the birthday celebration should be changed from Anjŏng [Peaceful and Pure] Festival 安貞節 to Kyŏngnyong [Felicitous Dragon] Festival 慶龍節.

The king ordered the compilation of the veritable records for Yejong's reign. Before this Executive Han An'in had petitioned "Yejong was on the throne for seventeen years. His achievements should be recorded in the history books so that they can be handed down to posterity. I request that following the precedent of the Song dynasty veritable record compilation officials should be installed." The Pomun-gak Academician Pak Sŭngjung, Hallim Academician Chŏng Kŭg'yŏng, and Pomun-gak Edict Attendant Kim Pusik were appointed editor of history.

Winter, tenth month. A Hundred Seat Assembly was held in Hoegyŏng Hall and 30,000 monks were given a maigre feast in the capital and throughout the country.

Yi Chagyŏm was invested as Duke of Hanyang.

Eleventh month. The Eastern Jurchen chief Shixian came to present horses.

The king personally gave a banquet for men and women over the age of eighty, as well as righteous husbands, chaste wives, the terminally ill and disabled on the palace courtyard, and bestowed presents commensurate with rank. He especially granted the mother of Yi Chagyŏm, Lady of Chosŏn State, née Kim, gold, brocade and medicine of higher class.

Twelfth month. The Duke of Taebang, Wang Po 王俌, was exiled to Kyŏngsan District. This was the work of Yi Chagyŏm. Executive Chief of the Royal Secretariat Han An'in and Vice-commissioner of the Security Council Mun Kongmi were exiled. Before this, Han An'in and Mun Kongmi were all working at the Security Council together with Yi Chagyŏm's younger brother Yi Charyang and with Ch'oe Hongjae. Yi Charyang relied on his [family] influence, and Han An'in and Mun Kongmi relied on his favor. Although on the surface they were amicable, inside they were jealous, and moreover they did not get along with Ch'oe Hongjae. Furthermore Han An'in perceived that Yi Chagyŏm as the supreme state councilor was in charge of all major decisions, yet being indolent did not hold audiences and covered up or hid many affairs [from the king]. Externally honoring Yi Chagyŏm, he had him invested as Supreme Duke, and did not allow him to take charge of affairs. Secretly he wanted to grab his power, and made the Transmitter Han Chu report this [to the throne]. All the [Kyŏngwŏn] Yi clan knew about his plan and resented him. Because the Grand Physician Ch'oe Sajŏn 崔思全 had diagnosed the swelling on Yejong's back as minor and had not started early treatment, Han An'in and Mun Kongmi wanted to have him tried. The king sentenced him to two years of labor. Therefore Ch'oe Sajŏn also resented them. At that time Yi Chagyŏm appointed Ch'oe Yujŏk 崔惟迪 as Reviewing Policy Advisor, which led to heated debates. There was one intendant-secretary named Chang Ŭngch'u 張應樞 who liked to interfere and attach himself to the powerful. He heard that Ch'oe Yujŏk had gifted Yi Chagyŏm twenty slaves as bribe to obtain this position, and secretly told this to Han An'in. Han An'in made a big ruckus [about this] in the Department. Ch'oe Yujŏk complained about him to Yi Chagyŏm, who, enraged, requested the Censorate to investigate him. Han An'in felt ashamed and afraid, took leave and remained at home. Subsequently Han An'in together with Mun Kongmi, his cousin Chŏng Kŭg'yŏng, his brother-in-law the Intendant of the

Censorate Yi Yŏng and others several times met for consultation till deep in the night. Ch'oe Sajŏn obtained [information from] their midst, and wanting to relieve his grudge, together with the crafty Ch'ae Sŏk 蔡碩 slanderously told Yi Charyang and Ch'oe Hongjae "Han An'in and Mun Kongmi have formed a faction that secretly plots harm against Yi Chagyŏm." Yi Chagyŏm was very suspicious; in the end he fabricated their crimes and advised the king to exile Han An'in to Kammul Island 甘勿島 in Sŭngju 昇州,[72] and had him drowned on the way. He also exiled Mun Kongmi, Han Chu 韓柱, Yi Yŏng, and Chŏng Kŭg'yŏng far away. Their brothers and children, sons-in-law and brother-in-law were all deemed guilty by association and went into hiding or were exiled. Many of the extended clan were fired from office. Han An'in was diligent in study and good at composition, and when the king was enthroned, on account of his tutoring the king used this old debt to secretly wield power over the king and apportioned key positions to his brothers and relatives. Among the elites there were none who did not associate with him. Suddenly rising to power he challenged the powerful and ended up defeated.

72 Modern Sunch'ŏn, South Chŏlla Province.

9. Injong

Injong, Great King of Respect and Filial Piety

His given name was Hae 楷 and his courtesy name was Inp'yo 仁表; his old given name was Ku 構. He was the oldest son of Yejong and his mother was Queen Sundŏk, née Yi. He was born on *ŭlhae* day [the 4th] of the tenth month of the fourth year of King Yejong, cyclical *sach'uk* [1109]. He was humane and filial by nature, generous and benevolent. He loved learning and had many talents, respected his teachers and friends with propriety. He was on the throne for twenty-four years and lived to the age of thirty-eight.

Injong first year [1123]

Fifth year of the Xuanhe era of Song, third year of the Baoda era of Liao, first year of the Tianhui era of Taizong of Jin

Spring, first month. The Song envoy Xu Li arrived.

The king went to Oejesŏg-wŏn. After this he frequently went to temples.

Former Intendant of the Security Council Yi Yŏng died in his place of exile. His father Yi Chungsŏn 李仲宣 had been chosen for the capital army as the village head of the district where he was registered. Yi Yŏng from a young age studied with a teacher. When his father died, he wanted to succeed his perpetuity land and become a clerk.[1] When he submitted the title to the chief clerk of the government office[2] he bowed with clasped hands but did not prostrate. Enraged, the chief clerk cursed him. Yi Yŏng immediately grasped the title and destroyed it, saying "I can pass the civil service examination and serve the country, why should I pay my respects to the lot of you?" He then studied hard and passed the examination; during his career he served in the Office of Historiography and the remonstrance institutions. When Han An'in was killed, Yi Yŏng as his brother-in-law was found guilty by association and was exiled to Chin-do 珍島. Someone told him "I have heard the rumor that your wife and sons have been enslaved." Yi Yŏng replied: "When I reflect on my life, I have nothing to be ashamed of, and therefore can bear dying or waiting for its moment. However if my mother falls down to the status of base person or slave on my account, how can I bear living?" He then drank a whole peck of wine, and died of frustration and despair. His contemporaries regretted this loss. Yi Chagyŏm dispatched a mantic specialist to bury him by the side of the road. Cows and horses did not dare to tread on his grave. Some who were suffering from malaria went to pray there and got cured. Later after Yi Chagyŏṃ's defeat his son requested to rebury him, and when the grave was dug up his corpse had not changed. The king posthumously appointed him Notary for the Security Council, and ordered the Ministry of Personnel to abolish the record of his crime. Yi Yŏng had an extraordinary spirit and was upright. He did not bend to those with power, but was unfortunate in choosing friends. Also he was involved when Ch'ŏk Chun'gyŏng and others planned to destroy Yi Yŏrim,[3] and when Chi Nog'yŏn 池祿延 and others removed Pak Sŭngjung.[4]

Executive Chief of the Royal Secretariat Yi Charyang died. He established himself thanks to the influence of his family. He loved reading books and

---

1 *Sŏri* 胥吏: a kind of local functionary.

2 Chŏngjo chusa 政曹主事: Chŏngjo refers to institutions in charge of appointment, and as such may refer to the Ministry of Personnel or/and the Ministry of War.

3 See chapter 7, 8th month of 1112.

4 See chapter 8, 8th month of 1116. However, when Pak Sŭngjung was demoted for making fun of others, no mention is made of Chi Nog'yŏn. This is his first mention in the *Koryŏsa chŏryo*, though the *Koryŏsa* mentions him as early as 1105.

studied the arts of Sunzi and Wuzi; he enjoyed having this reputation.

Third month. Rumors were spreading everywhere that officials would snatch small children from people and throw them into rivers. Panic spread to the point that some went into hiding in the mountains. This was especially severe in Sŏhae Province.

Summer, fourth month. Pyŏn Sunbu 卞純夫 and twenty-nine others passed the composition test of the civil service examination.

Kim Yŏn was appointed Intendant of the Department of the Palace Library and Supervising Editor of National Historiography. Kim Yŏn was famous for his mastery of letters and for his integrity. Yejong greatly esteemed his talents and made him state councilor, showing his indebtedness and respect. The king [Injong] came to the throne at a young age and maternal relatives wielded influence, so Kim Yŏn feared harm and firmly insisted on retiring, which was refused. Now as he had fallen of his horse he insisted even more firmly on his being relieved, hence there was this edict.

Fifth month. Because of the drought, the king avoided the main hall of the palace. He gathered monks in the inner halls to lecture on Buddhist sutras and pray for rain.

Sixth month. Commissioner for the Local Navy Command of the Southeastern Seas Pak Kyŏngnin 朴景麟 erroneously reported that thirty Jurchen war ships had encroached the border. The king dispatched Administrative Assistant for the Military Commissioner to Raise Additional Troops Yang Chebo 楊齊寶 and others to restrain them. When they reached Kyŏngju they did not perceive any caitiffs and returned.

Song dispatched Executive at the Ministry of Rites Lu Yundi 路允迪 and Drafting Advisor Fu Moqing 傅墨卿 with the following edict: "From afar we heard that you succeeded to you country's throne and are diligently governing it. Considering that this is the beginning of your auspicious succession, and that you exert your all to govern according to expectations despite the sudden bereavement that thrust you into deep sorrow, we hurriedly ordered envoys to encourage you in your devotion in following in the footsteps of your illustrious forebears. Many gifts are attached to express our condolences and honor. You should accept this imperial spirit and eternally follow in the footsteps of vassals. Now the list of all gifts we bestow is attached separately." The king went to the mourning hall to accept the sacrificial vessels and the edict of condolence. Lu Yundi and the others then told the king: "When the emperor heard of the previous king's demise, and of your succession to the throne, he dispatched envoys to convey condolences. The edict of condolence as well as the ritual text were all personally written in the imperial hand. During the Yuanfeng era [1078-1085] sacrifice and condolence were merely routine affairs; now the grace and courtesy are exceptionally showered as favors upon father and son. During the Daguan period [1107-1110], edicts bestowed exceptionally removed the character 'provisional' (權) to show the courtesy due a true king. Now the present letter personally written by the emperor also shows exceptional favor. However, in the case of previous kings who received investiture from the Liao, it was a matter of ritual avoidance [of taboo characters]. Now that the Liao mandate has expired, you can request the mandate to our court."

The king replied: "From the time of our founding fathers, this wretched country has enjoyed Chinese culture. Moreover, my late father served the great with propriety, and fulfilled his role with loyalty. Although we are a foreign country, our heart-minds are always with the imperial court. Therefore, the Son of Heaven looks at us positively and frequently extended his favors. Today he moreover especially composed the ritual texts, and showed the special favor of removing the character "provisional" from your subject's office title. Even though my late father in the past enjoyed this courtesy, how could his insignificant son deserve this? That which is called investiture is the great rite through which the Son of Heaven rewards his liege lords. Now the mourning has not yet ended, thus hurriedly seeking a grand rite sits ill at ease with righteousness, this truly makes me ashamed and uncomfortable. I hope to dispatch envoys next year to repay this favor and present a small token of our gratitude. I am sure that you gentlemen will well convey my thoughts [to the emperor]."

Autumn, seventh month. Executive Chief of the Royal Secretariat Kim Ko died. He had handsome features and excelled in letters and learning.

On *kisa* day [the 18th] a comet appeared in the Big Dipper. A Calamities Removing Ritual was held in Kŏndŏk Hall for five days.

Eighth month. On *sinsa* day, the first day of the month, there was a solar eclipse.

Yi Chagyŏm was made Intendant for the resident governor of the Western Capital.

The king dispatched Ha Ch'ikpo 河則寶 to Liao. From Yongju 龍州[5] he took a ship to cross the sea but after failing to reach shore he returned.

Winter, tenth month. A Hundred Seat Assembly was held in Hoegyŏng Hall and thirty thousand monks were fed.

Twelfth month. An amnesty was declared. Sacrifices to mountains and rivers were made in order [of importance]. A banquet was given for the elderly, the gravely ill, and the fatally ill, and presents bestowed commensurate with rank.

Kim Chihwa was made Minister of War; Im Yumun and Ch'oe Hongjae were made Executive Chief of the Chancellery; Kim Yag'on was appointed Executive Chief of the Royal Secretariat; Ch'ŏk Chun'gyŏng was appointed Vice-minister of Personnel and Assistant Executive in Political Affairs; Pak Sŭngjung was made Commissioner of the Security Council; Kim Ingyu 金仁揆 was made Associate Administrator of the Security Council; Yi Chadŏk was made Vice-commissioner of the Security Council.

Injong second year [1124]

Sixth year of the Xuanhe era of Song, fourth year of the Baoda era of Liao, second year of the Tianhui era of Jin

Spring, first month. Grand Preceptor and Royal Secretary Yi Chagyŏm stepped down from his functions due to his mother's passing. His mother Lady Kim was greedy and forced market traders to sell their goods to her,

5 Modern Yongch'ŏn, North P'yŏngan Province.

sometimes not even paying them. She also released slaves to commit violent acts. When she died the market traders rejoiced.

Executive Chief of the Chancellery Kim Chun died. He was intelligent and had a sharp mind. He loved learning and was good at composition. He came first in the civil service examination, and when he worked as the Manager of Records in Chinju he established merit in government. When Yun Kwan fought the Jurchen he was Office Chief in the Ministry of Punishment and was thus made Administrative Assistant to the Left Army. When the army was defeated, Yun Kwan was angry, tied up soldiers and was about to execute them. In a loud voice Kim Chun said "Today's defeat is due to Military Commissioner Im Ŏn's lack of discipline. Neglecting this without even taking him to task yet executing soldiers, how does this chime with the principle 'do not fear the strong, do not despise the weak?'" Yun Kwan was startled, released their shackles and freed them.

Second month. Associate Administrator of the Security Council Ch'oe Hongjae was banished to Yokchi Island 褥地島 in Sŭngju. Ch'oe hailed from a family of generals and was good at archery and horsemanship. Several times he went on campaign and as he became successful he arrogated power and set out to throw his weight about and become rich. At the time Yi Chagyŏm was arrogant yet knew that he would not submit to others. He feared that he would hatch plans and therefore was always suspicious of Ch'oe Hongjae. At that time a military person named Kwŏn In 權因, knowing his thoughts, slandered Ch'oe as follows: "Together with Generals Chŏng Chŏngsuk 鄭旌淑 and Yi Sinŭi 李神義, Ch'oe Hongjae is fomenting a plan to harm your excellency." Yi Chagyŏm then heard out Ch'ŏk Chun'gyŏng's thoughts, who said "Ch'oe Hongjae is hard to fathom, we cannot guarantee that it is not true." Yi Chagyŏm then secretly instructed the king to have Ch'oe Hongjae exiled. Also exiled to distant locations were Chŏng Chŭngsuk and Yi Sinŭi, along with Ch'oe's sons Sang 翔, On 溫, and Tan 端, and the monk Tohyu 道休, together with Ch'oe On's father-in-law No Yŏnggŏ 盧令琚.

Third month. Junior Vice-director of the Department of Ministries Yi

Tŏg'u died. Yi Tŏg'u occupied himself with letters, and once compiled the *Veritable Records* of Sukchong's reign.

Intercalary [third] month. On *imjin* day [the 15th] there was a fierce wind and it was dark during the day.

Summer, fourth month. Hyejong's spirit tablet was moved to Sun-nŭng 順陵 [his tomb], and Yejong was enshrined in the Ancestral Shrine [in his stead]. People at the time disputed this, saying "Hyejong had merit for the people, he should be an immovable ruler. Moving him is against propriety."

Fifth month. Ko Hyoch'ung and thirty-six others passed the composition test of the civil service examination.

The king dispatched Commissioner of the Security Council Pak Sŭngjung with an edict for Royal Secretary Yi Chagyŏm which went "You, Duke, are someone in whom the previous king invested his trust, and for me you are also an esteemed relative. Your remit is great and responsibility heavy, your merit is lofty and virtue deep. You cannot be addressed in the same way as other officials are. Henceforth both letters and decrees that are bestowed upon you shall not address you by name nor with the title 'minister.' Even though this is exceptional it is still in accord with the old statutes. You should respectfully accept [this order] and should not refuse it. Also lay down the mourning clothes and return to court." Many gifts were bestowed, including robes, belts, saddles, gold, silver, and brocade. Yi Chagyŏm expressed his thanks and requested the end of mourning.

The Song merchant Liu Cheng 柳誠 and others, forty-nine people in all, arrived. Previously, Du Daoqi 杜道濟 and Zhu Yanzuo 祝延祚 from Mingzhou had arrived here by merchant ships and had not returned home. Mingzhou twice transmitted a letter searching for them. The country [i.e. Koryŏ] then sent a memorial requesting that they remain. Now Liu Cheng and his party came to transmit a letter stating that Mingzhou had received imperial instruction that they could remain as they wished.

Sixth month. Pak Sŭngjung sent a letter requesting that the edict bestowed upon the Royal Secretary together with his memorial of thanks be transmitted to the historians to be included in the histories. This was because he wanted to flatter Yi Chagyŏm.

The king went to the four tombs of Hyŏn-nŭng, Ch'ang-nŭng, Yu-nŭng, and Su-nŭng.[6]

Autumn, seventh month. The king personally sacrificed at the Ancestral Shrine. T'aejo['s shrine] faced east, with the [shrines for] Tŏkchong, Chŏngjong, Munjong, and Yejong as the *zhao* 昭 line, and Hyŏnjong, Sunjong, Sŏnjong, and Sukchong as the *mu* 穆 line.[7]

The king dispatched an envoy to invest Yi Chagyŏm as Merit Subject of Bright Propriety Supporting the Mandate, Leader of the Chancellery, Department of Ministries, Department of State Affairs, Minister of Personnel and of War, Intendant of the Resident Governor of the Western Capital, Duke of the Chosŏn State, with a stipend village of 8,000 households, 2,000 of which were effective. His residence was called Sungdŏk 崇德, and his palace Ŭich'in 懿親. His wife Lady Ch'oe was enfeoffed as Great Lady of Chinhan. His son Yi Chami was made Director of the Palace Library, Vice-commissioner of the Security Council; Yi Kongŭi was made Executive at the Ministry of Punishment; Yi Chiŏn 李之彦 was made Office Chief at the Ministry of Works, concurrently Censor of Miscellaneous Affairs; Yi Chibo 李之甫 was made Office Chief at the Ministry of Taxation, in charge of the Tea Office; Yi Chiyun 李之允 was made Intendant-secretary at the Department of Royal Clan Affairs; Yi Chiwŏn 李之元 was made Audience Usher; and his son the monk Ŭijang 義莊 was promoted to *sujwa* 首座 [prior] rank.

The king came out of the gate of Kŏndŏk Hall to personally deliver the edict. All officials gathered in the courtyard to offer congratulations. Next he went to Yi Chagyŏm's personal residence to offer congratulations. Sungdŏk was originally the name of the Western residence of the traitor Kim Ch'iyang 金致陽,[8] but this became known only later.

At this time there was also an edict giving posthumous enfeoffment to

---

6 The tombs of respectively T'aejo, Sejo, Yejong, and Queen Sundŏk.

7 The *zhao* line would have been to the left [of T'aejo] and the *mu* line to the right.

8 See part Ia, p. 187-189. Together with Queen Ch'ŏnch'u he was involved in a plot to usurp the dynasty, and was killed in 1009.

Yi Chagyŏm's father and grandfather. Pak Sŭngjung proposed that on the day of the enfeoffment on bamboo tablets presented at the tombs [of his ancestors] the music of the Kisaeng School be performed.[9] Executive at the Ministry of Rites Kim Pusik protested that though the Ancestral Shrine uses music to represent daily life, at various types of graves the rule was to wear mourning clothes and shed tears—how could music be used? Pak Sŭngjung furthermore wanted Yi Chagyŏm's birthday to be designated Insu Festival 仁壽節. Kim Pusik opined that designating a birthday as a festival (節) was a custom not seen in antiquity; only from the time of Emperor Xuanzong of Tang was his birthday for the first time designated "Festival of Thousand Autumns" (千秋節). It was unheard of for a subject to designate his birthday as a festival. Kim Yag'on said "Executive Kim's objection is valid, I have nothing to add to this."

The king dispatched Vice-commissioner of the Security Council Yi Chadŏk and Vice Censor-in-chief Kim Puch'ŏl to Song to give thanks for the favor and to present local products.

Yi Chadŏk laid down his mourning clothes and resumed his office duties at the Royal Secretariat. State councilors and civil and military officials above the grade for attending audience ceremonies lined up above the steps, while officials of grade 7 and below lined up below the steps to proffer congratulations. That day it rained heavily and there was thunder and lightning. On the roads and markets the water was ten feet deep, and lightning struck Yŏng'ŭn-gwan 迎恩館.

Eighth month. Yi Chagyŏm gave his third daughter in marriage to the king. He was afraid that other surnames would betroth daughters, thereby dividing the effect of power. Therefore he forcefully requested the king, who had no choice but to accept. This day there were sudden showers and great gusts of wind that uprooted trees.

The king went to Sinbong Tower to declare an amnesty. The proclamation read "From the moment I undeservedly inherited the throne or even while

9 Kyobang 教坊: In Koryŏ thought to be the name of a school for kisaeng; though in this context it may designate a general music bureau.

still acting as heir apparent, I could not treat the royal lineage members with filial piety or listen to scholar-officials or people with humanity and virtue. Without [the support of] Heaven disasters followed; time passed and mourning ended, but holding bow and sword I cried in sorrow; seeing the broth [my parents ate] and the wall [where my parents walked] my longing lasts forever.[10] I wanted to honor the elders of my mother's family so as to soothe the former queen's spirit. Moreover the Duke of Chosŏn assists with loyalty and sincerity, his merit is already lofty. Sending an envoy I already invested the duke and his lady and also employed his sons and sons-in-law. It is fitting that remaining favors are spread further; throughout the country all crimes with punishment lower than beheading and strangulation should be pardoned; this should be implemented. From afar the mountains and rivers will be honored, banquets will be granted to the elderly, the severely and terminally ill, widows and widowers, orphans and those who are alone, righteous husbands and chaste wives, and presents bestowed commensurate with rank. Those with office rank should in order be promoted." All the presents offered from the provinces and capital were all returned to the Sungdŏk Residence.

Ninth month. [From] *kabo* day [the 21st] Venus was seen in the sky for six days.

The king went to Hyŏnhwa-sa and gave a banquet for state councilors and close officials.

Winter, tenth month. For the Kyŏngnyong Festival the king gave a banquet for all officials in Kŏndŏk Hall. He bestowed one horse each upon all the officials who took part in audience meetings. Furthermore he gave a banquet for state councilors and close officials in Hamwŏn Hall 含元殿.

Twelfth month. Im Yumun was made Merit Subject Establishing Principle, Acting Grand Guardian, Probationary Grand Marshal, and Minister of Taxation; Kim Yag'on was made Acting Minister of Education, Probationary Minister of Works, Executive Chief of the Chancellery; Ch'ŏk Chun'gyŏng

10 Both "bow and sword" and "broth and wall" are likely references to classics which I could not trace.

was made Commander Unequaled in Honor, Acting Minister of Education, Probationary Minister of Works, and Executive Chief of the Royal Secretariat; Yi Su was made Acting Minister of Education, Probationary Minister of Works, and Assistant Executive in Political Affairs; Pak Sŭngjung was made Acting Minister of Education, Assistant Executive in Letters, Intendant of the Hallim Academy; Kim Ingyu was made Acting Minister of Education, Vice-minister of Personnel and Intendant of the Chancellery; Yi Chadŏk was made Vice-minister of Works and Administrator of the Security Council.

Injong third year [1125]

Seventh year of the Xuanhe era of Song, fifth year of the Baoda era of Liao, third year of the Tianhui era of Jin

Spring, first month. Yi Chagyŏm also betrothed his fourth daughter to the king.

Third month. The king decreed "Junior Colonel Yu Ch'ŏng 庾淸 from Ŭiju had been taken prisoner by the northern Liao. Now he managed to extract himself and return. We should let him go to the capital and restore his old function. The accompanying soldier Ch'ungjŏm 忠占 should be given the position of lieutenant in his original prefecture."

The king went to Sungbok-wŏn 崇福院 and granted it the title Hŭngsŏng-sa 興聖寺. He organized a vegetarian banquet and music to celebrate its completion. He also gave a banquet for the state councilors and the attending officials. The next day he declared a pardon.

Summer, fourth month. Ch'ŏk Chun'gyŏng released himself from his office and returned to his hometown Kokchu. When the king learned about this, he dispatched Executive Ch'oe Sik 崔湜 and Palace Steward Yi Hu 李侯; they caught up with him in Ubong district and convinced him to return. Soon after he was restored to office.

The king decreed "Kaemyŏng House 開明宅 is the residence of the Duke of Chosŏn's father and grandfather. I ordered officials to repair it. This has now been done, and the name has been altered to Chunghŭng [revival] House 重興宅." Yi Chagyŏm was permitted to take up residence there. The king dispatched Assistant Executive in Political Affairs Yi Su and others to bestow the proclamation and a set of robes, goldthread brocade, land and slaves, a saddle—lavish gifts. The king then went to the residence to organize a banquet, using the etiquette of householders. When the night was over he returned. He appointed Yi Chimi Probationary Vice-minister of Rites, Associate Administrator of the Security Council, and Yi Kongŭi as Director of the Office of Regalia. All sons, younger brothers, and in-laws were given official positions commensurate with rank.

The hermit from Ch'ŏngp'yŏng-san, Yi Chahyŏn, died. He grew up in a wealthy family, and thanks to his in-law connections obtained office. But he grew disgusted with the hustle and bustle of the world and loved tranquility. He rejected his office and entered the mountains to spend the rest of his life. However he was stingy by nature and amassed wealth. He levied products and gathered grain, greatly troubling the farmers of the area. When he fell ill the king sent a palace physician to treat him. He also bestowed tea and medicine.

The king went to Poje-sa to pray for rain.

Fifth month. The king dispatched Vice-director of the Court for Royal Entertainment Chin Suk 陳淑 and Chief Steward of the Bureau of Royal Clothing Ch'oe Hangnan 崔學鸞 to Jin. Jin did not accept the mission because the state letter was not in the form of a memorial (表), and also because it did not use the self-reference "your subject."

The king went to Myot'ong-sa to pray for rain.

Autumn, seventh month. Yi Yangsin 李陽伸 and thirty-six others passed the composition test of the civil service examination.

Eighth month. The king went to the Western Capital.

Ninth month. The Earl of Nangnang, Kim Kyŏngyong, died. He was a man of imposing features and stature. When young he idled away the time with music and women. Once when he was fighting with a man in the street a Song merchant saw it and said: "Looking at your face and bone structure, they are beautiful and uncommon, you should become rich and live long. Please take care of yourself." Kim Kyŏngyong was proud of this. Once he served as Administrative Assistant of Kwangju Shepherdship; although he was not cruel the people feared and respected him. When he became state councilor he relied on his power and influence to amass wealth and built a grand and beautiful residence. People at the time ridiculed this.

Winter, tenth month. Im Yumun, who had retired as Executive Chief of the Chancellery, died.

Eleventh month. The king returned from the Western Capital.

Twelfth month. Ch'ŏk Chun'gyŏng was made Executive Chief of the Chancellery; Yi Su was made Executive Chief of the Royal Secretariat; Pak Sŭngjung, Yi Chadŏk, and Kim Ingyu were together made Assistant Executive in Political Affairs; Hŏ Chae was made Intendant of the Chancellery; Yi Chimi was made Administrator of the Security Council; Chi Nog'yŏn, Kim Chin, and Kim Puil were jointly made Associate Administrators of the Security Council.

Injong fourth year [1126]

First year of the Jingkang era of Emperor Xinzong of Song, fourth year of the Tianhui era of Jin

Spring, second month. The king invested the Queen née Yi-ssi as Yŏndŏk Princess. This was none other than the third daughter of Yi Chagyŏm.

On *sinyu* day [the 25th], Usher to the Palace Attendants Kim Ch'an 金粲 and Recording Officer to the Palace Attendants An Porin 安甫鱗, together with the Associate Administrator of the Security Council Chi Nog'yŏn and others planned to kill Yi Chagyŏm and Ch'ŏk Chun'gyŏng but failed.

At first when Yejong passed away the king ascended the throne as a young lad. Yi Chagyŏm, wanting to solidify his power and affinity to the king, gave two daughters in marriage to the king. He used a hundred ruses to harm anyone who did not wish to submit to him. Putting his relatives in important positions, he established a faction loyal to him. He honored himself as Duke and established his own office with officials. The protocol he used was the same as that for an heir apparent, and he named his birthday the Insu Festival. Felicitations and notes of thanks in the capital and in the provinces were referred to as "memoranda."[11] His sons vied in establishing residences, which lined the streets one after the other; their opulence and splendor increased by the day. They openly accepted bribes, and gave free rein to their servants and slaves to seize people's carts and horses and loaded them with their goods. Ordinary people responded by destroying their own carts and selling their oxen and horses; the roads were thus in chaos.

Yi Chagyŏm then wanted to control military affairs, and summoned the king to his house to force him to invest him. Although on that day his plans did not come to fruition, the king resented him for it. Kim Ch'an and An Porin, who were always by the king's side assisting him, guessed his mind and thus started planning with Chi Nog'yŏn, making the request to remove Yi. The king found this important, and dispatched Kim Ch'an to Executive Yi Su and former Executive Kim Injon to gain advice about this plan. Both said: "His Highness was born and raised in the house of his mother's family, and this debt cannot be cut off. Moreover, their party has filled all court positions and cannot be lightly removed. Please wait for another time." The king did not listen. Kim Injon is none other than Kim Yŏn.

Chi Nog'yŏn and the others summoned Supreme Generals Ch'oe T'ak 崔卓 and O T'ak 吳卓, Grand General Kwŏn Su 權秀, General Ko Sŏk 高碩 and others, and conspired to apprehend them and exile them to a distant place. Ch'ŏk Chun'gyŏng was the father-in-law of Yi Chiwŏn, and together with his younger brother Ch'ŏk Chunsin 拓俊臣 threw their weight about [on account of this connection]. Ch'oe T'ak and the others begrudged the fact that Ch'ŏk Chunsin had risen from a lowly position to become the Vice-minister of war over their heads, and thus gave their permission to the plan. With the agreement in place, at the beginning of the night of that day, they led soldiers into the palace and first killed Ch'ŏk Chunsin, and Ch'ŏk

11 *Chŏn* 箋: a slip of paper or placard. Likely this refers to a specific level of communication again reserved for the heir apparent.

Chun'gyŏng's son, the Palace Attendant Ch'ŏk Sun 拓純, as well as the Usher Kim Chŏngbun 金鼎芬, Recording Officers Chŏn Kisang 田其上 and Ch'oe Yŏng 崔英, and others, and threw their bodies over the palace walls.

Banner Head of Palace Attendants Hak Mun[12] jumped over the wall and asked Senior Colonel Chi Ho 池顥 to alert Yi Chagyŏm. Yi Chagyŏm did not know what to do. Office Chief Wang Ŭi 王毅 then also crossed the wall and ran to inform Yi Chagyŏm in detail about what had happened. Yi Chagyŏm, Ch'ŏk Chun'gyŏng, Yi Chimi and the other sons looked at each other in fear. They summoned the councilors and officials to their residence. Yi Chagyŏm was so agitated he did not know what to do, and sent Yi Chimi to again consult, but nobody knew how to react. Ch'ŏk Chun'gyŏng then said: "The situation is urgent, we cannot just sit about and wait." Then together with Executive Ch'oe Sik, Usher Yi Hujin 李侯進, Recording Officer Yun Han 尹翰 and others, he led several tens of people, and reached the Chujak Gate 朱雀門[13] at night, but could not enter.

They then made Yun Han jump over the wall to unlock the gate. Opening it they entered and reaching the Sinbong Gate[14] made loud noises that shook the earth. Chi Nog'yŏn, Ch'oe T'ak and the others thought that a large army had gathered outside; they lost their nerve and did not dare to go out. Yi Chagyŏm ordered people to set fire to the houses of Ch'oe T'ak, O T'ak, Kwŏn Su, Ko Sŏk, and others, and to imprison their wives, children, and servants. Vice-director of the Department of Ministries Hong Kwan was sleeping in the Department and sighed: "The ruler is disgraced and subjects have died, how can I be at ease?"

Imsul day [the 26th]. At the crack of dawn he reached Sŏhwa Gate and knocked on the door asking to be let in. Chi Nog'yŏn let down a rope for him to climb up and brought him to the king.[15] When Ch'ŏk Chun'gyŏng saw the

12 *Naejik kidu* Hak Mun 內直旗頭學文: There are several issues here regarding the offices and what appears to be the name of a person, hence this is a tentative translation.

13 Located in the southeastern corner of the outer palace wall, it gave access to the palace city.

14 This is the gate giving access to the palace itself: it was due south of the main hall, Hoegyŏng Hall. In between the Chujak and Sinbong Gates was Sŭngp'yŏng Gate, which was part of the inner compound wall.

15 It is not clear who was brought in. From the context it would appear to be Ch'ŏk Chun'gyŏng,

bodies of Ch'ŏk Chunsin and the others, he feared the same fate. Together with Yi Chibo, Ch'oe Sik, Yi Hujin, Kim Chŏnghwang 金鼎黃, Cho Sun'gŏ 曹舜擧, Yun Han, Mun Chunggyŏng 文仲經 and others they summoned a number of soldiers and went to the arsenal to get armor and weapons. They proceeded to surround Sŭngp'yŏng Gate 昇平門. Yi Chagyŏm's son the monk Ŭijang led 300 monks from Hyŏnhwa-sa to the palace walls. Those inside the palace walls did not dare to go out; instead they took up bows and arrows and spread out to guard the gates.[16] The king went to Sinbong Gate and opened a yellow parasol. When the soldiers of Ch'ŏk Chun'gyŏng saw this from afar they all bowed together and joyfully shouted "Manse!" The king made someone ask them: "Why have you taken up arms and come here?" They answered: "We heard that ruffians had entered the palace and therefore there was a request to guard the dynasty." The king said: "That is not the case. And I am fine. You may take off your armor and disperse." Then silver and silk from the palace treasury were lowered down and bestowed upon the soldiers. The king ordered Attendant Censor Yi Chung 李仲 and Royal Recorder Ho Chongdan to instruct the soldiers to take off their armor and throw away their weapons. Ch'ŏk Chun'gyŏng angrily drew his sword and drove away Yi Chung and Ho Chongdan, and ordered the soldiers to put their armor back on and take up their weapons. He was shouting loudly when a stray arrow landed in front of the king. Ŭijang's followers started hacking at the pillars of Sinbong Gate with axes when someone from atop the gate shot a monk in the head, killing him instantly.

Yi Chagyŏm then instructed Audience Usher Ch'oe Hangnan and Recording Officer to the Capital Military Command So Ŏk 邵億 to go to the palace gate and petition the king as follows: "We request that those who caused amok in the palace come out. Otherwise we fear that the palace will be thrown in turmoil." Their words were very insolent, and the king remained silent.

---

but we know that the body of his brother and the other brothers had been thrown over the palace walls, so he would not have needed to enter to ascertain this.

16 Chasŏngmun 子城門: This appears to refer to the palace walls, perhaps an inner wall surrounding Hoegyŏng Hall.

There was a palace attendant called Pak Simjo 朴深造 who was the son of Pak Sŭngjung. He left the palace via the latrines, so with clothes soaked in feces he reached Yi Chagyŏm's house to report on the situation in the palace. Yi Chagyŏm presented him with clothes and cap and comforted him.

Ch'ŏk Chun'gyŏng dispatched So Ŏk to tell Yi Chagyŏm: "Today when the sun goes down I'm afraid that the bandits will take advantage of the night to launch a stealth attack. Before they can do so we should set fire to the palace gates to ferret them out. What do you think?" Yi Chagyŏm instructed Yi Chimi to consult with Executive Yi Su and others, who said: "The palace buildings are all adjacent to each other, so we are afraid the fire will spread and then it cannot be brought under control. This is definitely not to be done." Ch'ŏk Chun'gyŏng had not waited for the outcome of the consultations. He fetched sweet leaf wood[17] from the Royal Workshops and wooden sticks from the Directorate of Construction and Maintenance. He piled them in the gallery of Tonghwa Gate 東華門 and set them alight. The wind fanned the flames so that the fire roared and spread, reaching the inner quarters. The palace women were frightened and hid themselves. When the day drew to a close Ch'ŏk Chun'gyŏng and Yi Chibo donned armor and rode their horses at the head of more than 100 soldiers. When they reached the Ch'undŏk Gate 春德門, Palace Attendant Yi Suksin 李叔晨 who guarded the gate opened it and let them in. But as soon as they entered the Chwaaek Gate,[18] former Palace Guard Sub-colonel Yi Chak 李作 and General Song Haengch'ung 宋幸忠 chased them out with drawn swords. Ch'ŏk Chun'gyŏng quickly withdrew, and Yi Chak closed the gate with his hands. Ch'ŏk Chun'gyŏng then sent out people to guard all gates, and gave them the following order: "If there is anyone coming out of the palace, kill

17 *Hwanghoemok* 黃灰木: a tree used to make yellow dye for textile. Various species of the genus symplocos, generally called sweet leaf, but Yellow Ash Tree (노란재나무) according to Soon-Young Kim ("Chosŏn hugi wangsil poksik ŭi yŏmsaek munhwa," *Hanguk ŭiryu sanŏp hakhoeji* 15, no. 2 (2013): 192-201), who specifies it is a mordant rather than a dye, i.e. a substance that helps the dye fix to the fabric. Why he chose this particular wood to make a fire is not clear.

18 Chwaaek 左掖: This could refer to the gate of the Bureau of Royal Stewards (Aekchŏng-guk 掖庭局).

them." Intendant of the Security Council Kim Chin was in his night duty room. Seeing the fire approach he said: "I have always cherished simplicity and uprightness, not bending to power and pressure. That sets me apart from people like Yi Chagyŏm and Ch'ŏk Chun'gyŏng. If I leave the building I will be killed. I'd rather choose my own ending than be killed at the hands of those ruffians." Then he ordered his servants to close the doors, and when the fire came he burned to death.

During the night the king walked to Sanho Pavilion, and sighed: "How I regret not heeding Kim Injon's words!" His attendants had all fled, only a good ten people including close advisor Im Kyŏngch'ŏng 林景淸 remained. The king feared coming to grief and composed a letter in which he requested relinquishing the throne to Yi Chagyŏm. Yi feared the deliberations of the Chancellery and Security Council, and did not speak. Yi Su spoke loudly from his seat: "Although His Majesty sent this decree, how could Duke Yi dare to accept it!" Yi Chagyŏm's intention being thwarted, he wept and returned the king's letter saying: "A subject cannot harbor two minds. Only Your Highness can decide this." There was someone called Hong Ipkong 洪立功, a senior colonel under General Yu Han'gyŏng 劉漢卿. Yi Chagyŏm ordered Yu Han'gyŏng to enter the palace and made Hong Acting General, making him take soldiers and be ready to take orders from Ch'ŏk Chun'gyŏng. Ch'ŏk Chun'gyŏng ordered Hong Ipkong to take about sixty soldiers to carry firewood to the road south of the Department of Ministries. Hong secretly told the soldiers: "I, just as you all, are all subjects to the king. Now carrying firewood to set fire to the palace is not how a subject should act." He then put down what he was carrying, and entered through a hole in Sŏngyo Gate 宣敎門. From afar he saw [the king] and bowed. The king was startled, and asked who he was. Hong Ipkong approached and stated his name. The king was overjoyed and offered him wine and food. From then on he acted as the king's guard and never left his side.

Kyehae day [the 27th]. At the crack of dawn, the king wanted to leave because the conflagration was drawing closer. Just at that time Yi Chagyŏm sent Transmitter of Edicts Kim Hyang 金珦 with the request to move to the

South Palace. The king walked to Kyŏngnyŏng Hall, and ordered Palace Attendant Paek Sach'ŏng 白思淸 to take the portraits of the ancestors and put them in a dry well at Naejesŏg-wŏn. He then left through Sŏhwa Gate and went on horseback to Yŏndŏk Palace. O T'ak led the way in front. Ch'ŏk Chun'gyŏng ordered Junior Colonel Chang Sŏng 張成 to draw his sword and catch up to O T'ak, seize him, and behead him. He also commanded others to capture Ch'oe T'ak, Kwŏn Su, Ko Sŏk, Yu Han'gyŏng, Song Haengch'ung, Yi Chak, and An Porin; Grand Generals Yun Sŏng 尹成 and Han Kyŏng 韓景; Generals Pak Yŏng 朴英, Song In 宋仁, Sa Yujŏng 史惟挺, and O Chŏngsin 吳挺臣; Junior Colonel Yi Yu 李儒; Palace Attendant Ch'oe Cham 崔箴; and Assistant Office Chief Pak Wŏnsil 朴元實, among others, and to kill all of them. Hong Kwan because of his old age could not walk, and was the last to leave Sŏhwa Gate; Ch'ŏk Chun'gyŏng had him killed too. The remaining soldiers who were killed were too numerous to count.

Chief Steward of the Palace Attendants Wang Kwan 王觀, Grand General Yun Sŏn 尹先, Junior Colonel Chŏng Ch'ongjin 丁寵珍, and Sub-colonel Chang Sŏngho 張成好 were all waiting on the king in the South Palace. Yi Chagyŏm requested as many as three times that they be removed, and the king had no choice but to agree. He made someone request that they would not be killed, but Yi Chibo killed them all. Yi Chagyŏm and Ch'ŏk Chun'gyŏng then raised the topic of killing all those who had been on night duty during the days of turmoil, regardless of whether they were noble or mean, but Yi Su was adamantly against it, so they desisted. Generals Yi Nokch'ŏn 李祿千, Kim Tan 金旦, and Kim Ŏn 金彦 all fled and went into hiding so as to escape [the slaughter]. On that day the palace burnt down completely; only Sanho, Sangch'un, and Sanghwa Pavilions, and a few dozen bays of the galleries of Naejesŏg-wŏn remained intact. All the officials ran away helter skelter, auxiliary at the Office of Historiography Kim Suja 金守雌 alone carried the national history on his back to Sanho Pavilion, where he dug a trench to its north and buried it. Thanks to his effort it escaped the fire.

Yi Chibo tied up Chi Nog'yŏn in Sunch'ŏn Hostel and cruelly tortured him till he nearly died. He then made Yun Han exile him under escort to a distant place. When they reached Ch'ungju he fell ill and could not get up, but his life force remained strong. Yun Han then cut off his limbs, buried him by the side of the road, and returned. Kim Ch'an was exiled to a location far from the capital. His and Chi Nog'yŏn 's wives and sons were relegated to the status of slaves at local government offices. O T'ak's son O Chasŭng 吳子升 and Ko Sŏk's younger brother Pojun 高甫俊 ran away and hid on North Mountain, and Pak Yŏng was ordered to track them down. They climbed up a high rock and from there hurled abuse at Pak Yŏng, saying "Yi Chagyŏm and his lot have stolen the affection of the king to arrogate power, poisoning the lives of the people; they are worse than jackals or tigers. They are about to overthrow the dynastic shrines and you lot have served them by fawning and treachery; you are worse than a slave. We strove to uphold righteousness to repay the people, but the fact that we failed shall be our fate. How could righteous scholars die at the hands of slaves like you?" Shouting to Heaven they then jumped off the rock and died. Chi Nog'yŏn was the great-grandson of Chi Ch'aemun 智蔡文 and was praised for his ability. In *kapsin* year [1104] he took part in the war against the Jurchen and established his merit. As a person he was rough and acted as he pleased; although he was without learning, he thought himself wise. However, his planning was clumsy and this led to his downfall. Hong Kwan hailed from Tangsŏng District 唐城郡.[19] He studied hard and was good at writing. Kim Chin had established a reputation for good government as magistrate of Yŏnggwang 靈光[20] and shepherd of Ch'ŏngju. People at the time supported him.

Third month. Yi Chagyŏm invited the king to take up residence in the Western cloister of Chunghŭng Residence. The king did away with the guard and used a shortcut to reach the residence gate. Directors[21] Kim Ŭiwŏn 金義元 and Ch'oe Chasŏng 崔滋盛, as the office managers of Chunghŭng Residence, came out to welcome him. Junior Colonel Chi Sŏksung 池錫崇,

---

19 Modern Namyang-ŭp, Hwasŏng-si, Kyŏnggi Province.

20 Modern Yŏnggwang-gun, South Chŏlla Province.

21 Taegyŏng 大卿: used here in the sense of directors of offices or office managers.

Executive Captain Kwŏn Chŏnggyun 權正鈞, and Sub-lieutenant O Ham 吳含 had not left the king's side as he went from Sanho Pavilion to the South Palace. Now Chi Sŏksung and the others were supporting the king as he was about to enter through the north gate. Yi Chagyŏm and Ch'ŏk Chun'gyŏng wanted to kill them. They ordered Junior Colonel Yi Chŏksŏn 李積善 to drag them away. But Chi Sŏksung grasped the king's robes and pleaded to be saved. The king turned back to face Yi Chŏksŏn, cursing him and kicking his chest. But as Chi Sŏksung was still holding on to his robes, he ended tearing it, while the king's winged cap hit the door frame and broke. Yi Miji and Yi Chibo stood by the gate watching the king but did not come down the stairs. Only Ch'oe Sik came out to bow to the king and cursed Yi Chŏksŏn: "There was a royal edict, how dare you act like this!" Yi Chŏksŏn then let go of Chi. Chi Sŏksung and the others were still afraid and did not dare to leave. At that time there was a eunuch called Cho Yŏng who fawned on Yi Chagyŏm. The king called Ch'oe Sik and Cho Yŏng and asked them: "Chi Sŏksung and the other two love their ruler with utmost sincerity; they have no other loyalty. Please on my behalf request that they not be put to death." Ch'ŏk Chun'gyŏng agreed, and had them exiled to a distant place.

The king ascended the hall, and Yi Chagyŏm and his wife came out to bow to him. Striking the floor with his hands, Yi wailed out loudly and said "We have wished for the birth of a heir apparent ever since the august queen entered the palace. Now that such a sacred person was born, we prayed to Heaven for his long life. There was nothing we did not do, all the spirits of Heaven and Earth are witness to my utmost sincerity. Unexpectedly, however, you recently believed in treacherous subjects who wished to harm your own flesh and blood." The king blushed bashfully and did not reply. After the king moved into the West Cloister, he was completely surrounded by Yi Chagyŏm's party. Depressed and idle, he no longer sat in on state affairs. The officials were moved to nearby offices and simply filled their quotas. Yi Chagyŏm and Ch'ŏk Chun'gyŏng's power grew even stronger, and nobody dared to do anything about it.

The historians comment: "The twisting and turning of fate is all the workings of Heaven. As Yi Chagyŏm's evils reached their peak, his demise was only a matter of time. Chi Nog'yŏn and the others could not bear this and sought to remove this evil from the side of the ruler. But his planning was shallow and forces insufficient, so he ended up being killed and throwing the country into chaos. Formerly in the Tang Dynasty, Yi Xun 李訓 and Zheng Zhu 鄭注 wanted to do away with the eunuchs but failed, leading to the disastrous 'sweet dew incident.'[22] These cases are roughly similar. They are truly lamentable."

Ch'ŏk Chunsin was posthumously appointed Probationary Minister of Works, Vice-director of the Department of Ministries; Kim Chŏngbun and Ch'ŏk Sun were both named Assistant Office Chief at the Ministry of Taxation; and Chŏn Kisang and Ch'oe Yŏng both became Audience Usher, and lavish condolence gifts were handed out. This was all in accord with Yi Chagyŏm's wishes. From then on the maternal relatives of the king were even more corrupt, from Pak Sŭngjung and Hŏ Chae down. They fawned and grafted for favors, cruelly asserting their power; how frightening! The king secretly consulted with Court Physician and Vice-director of the Directorate of Weaponry Ch'oe Sajŏn. Ch'oe Sajŏn said: "The reason why Yi Chagyŏm can act with such impunity is because he can rely on Ch'ŏk Chun'gyŏng. If Your Majesty can obtain Ch'ŏk Chun'gyŏng's [loyalty], then military power will side with the court, and Yi Chagyŏm will be just an individual." The king said: "Ch'ŏk Chun'gyŏng is the very heart and entrails of the Duke of State, and moreover connected to him through marriage; Ch'ŏk Chunsin and Ch'ŏk Sun were moreover killed by military officials, hence I doubt it." Then a divination produced an auspicious sign, and because of that Ch'oe Sajŏn went to Ch'ŏk Chun'gyŏng's house. He instructed him about loyalty and righteousness, saying: "The spirits of T'aejo and the successive sagacious [kings] are in Heaven; the misfortune or fortune [they control] is something

22 Ganlu zhi bian 甘露之變: This refers to an incident in 835 when said officials wanted to help Emperor Wenzong remove the eunuchs from power but failed.

to fear. Now Yi Chagyŏm has especially relied on the power of palace underlings, and has no sense of trust or righteousness, he is not someone with whom to share the vicissitudes of life. You, Duke, ought to serve the country with a single mind to establish a merit that will last through the ages." In his heart Ch'ŏk Chun'gyŏng agreed with this.

The examinations were not held as a result of the many events the country went through.

The king bestowed a letter of instruction upon Ch'ŏk Chun'gyŏng, saying: "Upon reflection, my lack of insight sparked this disaster, which has also caused you much grief. This is all the fault of this insignificant person. Reflecting on my past mistakes I repent, and pointing to Heaven I confirm this deeply in my mind. I hope that together with my subjects and the people this virtue may be renewed. You, Sir, may help me to cultivate it even more. Regardless of what happened in the past, exert your mind in assisting me so that there are no more calamities in the future."

All officials were summoned to discuss whether to serve Great Jin as a vassal state. All agreed that this should not be done. Only Yi Chagyŏm and Ch'ŏk Chun'gyŏng said: "Jin in the past was a small country that served the Liao and us, but now they have risen explosively; they have annihilated Liao and have created political relations with Song. Their military is strong and is getting stronger by the day. Moreover we share a border with them. The situation is such that we have no choice but to serve them. Moreover, the small serving the great, this is the principle of previous kings. We should first send envoys to request relations." This was followed.[23]

On *kyesa* day [the 27th] a yellow mist enshrouded the four directions.

On *kabo* day [the 28th] the sun was the color of blood.

Yi Chimi was sent to the Ancestral Shrine to divine whether or not the Jin should be served.

All crimes below those sentenced to decapitation or strangulation were pardoned. The Yi-Ch'ŏk party claimed that this was to protect the dynasty.

---

23 Usually it is implied that the kind accepted this advice, but since the king was sidelined it is not clear whether he gave even pro forma approval.

Offices were granted commensurate with rank.

Administrator of the Security Council Kim Puil was dispatched to the private residence of Ch'ŏk Chun'gyŏng to take orders and deal with the situation, and also to bestow a saddle. Prior to this, a slave of Yi Chiŏn had cursed the house slave of Ch'ŏk Chun'gyŏng, saying: "Your master shot at the ruler and set fire to the palace, this is a crime worthy of the death penalty. You should be degraded to official slave; how dare you insult me!" When Ch'ŏk Chun'gyŏng heard this he was enraged and ran to Yi Chagyŏm's house. Taking off his [official] robes and cap he said "My crime is severe, I should go to court to defend myself." Having said this he left without looking back. Someone stopped him [to placate him], but he returned home to lay down. Yi Chagyŏm sent Yi Chimi and Yi Kongŭi to make peace but Ch'ŏk Chun'gyŏng cursed them saying "The turmoil of the past days is all the result of your actions. Why only blame me as being guilty of a mortal crime?" In the end he did not meet them, and declared that he was going back to grow old in his native village. When the king heard this, he made this order [to Kim Puil].

Summer, fourth month. The king went to Anhwa-sa, and Yi Chagyŏm accompanied him. All the officials bowed [to the king] in front of [his] horse. When Yi Chagyŏm saw this he still remained calm. When the king looked back on his old palace his tears fell.

Chŏng Ŭngmun 鄭應文 and Yi Hu were dispatched to Jin to declare vassalage and to present the following memorial: "The great person [of the emperor] has completed the great unification, overawing the four quarters. Other countries have entered your court traversing ten-thousand leagues, so how could we as an adjacent country have any excuse not to hurry and show special sincerity? Prostrate, we venture that with Heaven-ordained valor and brightness, your virtue is renewed daily. If you issue an order, the myriad people will all gladly follow; with enhanced authority and reputation, none of the neighboring enemies will dare to resist. Truly the high achievement of the ruler is secretly assisted by Heaven and Earth. Prostrate, we venture that as subjects from a small and insignificant country, with weak bodies and insufficient virtue yet aware of the exceptional merit [of Jin], for a long time our minds have been turned towards you, and though our presents are insufficient, still we rashly present them with loyalty and trust. Although ashamed of what we present, may you accept it with great benevolence."

Jin returned the following edict: "We consider that expediating the demise [of failing countries] and strengthening those that remain is the work of all emperors and kings. A small country serving the great is the plan for maintaining the Altars of Earth and Grain. Leaders and men of talent should embrace the change of a distant empire. Your country has passed on the throne for generations, and received due investiture. Your memorial is fully respectful, and your praiseworthy sincerity is accompanied by the courtesy of local products presented; with self-deprecating style you fully show your readiness to be enfeoffed. With neither the threat of war nor the favor of lavish gifts, you came of your own accord. How can this not be called excellent? Moreover the mind of ruler and father is what I shall hold on to steadfastly; do not lightly forget the righteousness of the vassal."

Ch'ŏk Chun'gyŏng was made Executive of the Chancellery and Minister of War; Yi Su was named Executive Chief of the Chancellery; Yi Chadŏk and Hŏ Chae were both appointed Assistant Executive in Political Affairs; Kim Puil became Assistant Executive in Letters; Yi Chimi was designated Intendant of the Security Council; Kim Hyang and Kim Ŭiwŏn were both appointed Associate Intendant of the Security Council; and Kim Pusik was promoted to Censor-in-chief and Vice-commissioner of the Security Council.

Twenty-five palace attendants were dismissed, because Yi Chagyŏm disliked them.

Fifth month. The king moved to the Yŏn'gyŏng Palace 延慶宮. Yi Chagyŏm took up residence to the south of the palace and had a hole cut through the northern wall so that he could freely enter the palace grounds. He seized weapons from the armory and stored them in his house. The king used to go alone to the north garden [of the palace] and weep to Heaven. At the time of the king's moving, Yi Chagyŏm, because he received a prophecy of "Eighteen children"[24] planned sedition. He put poison in cakes and presented them to the king. But the consort secretly told the king; when the cakes were thrown to a crow it died. He also sent poisoned medicine, making the consort present it to the king, but she feigned stumbling when presenting the bowl and the medicine was spilled. The consort was none other than Yi Chagyŏm's fourth daughter.

A rift had already developed between Ch'ŏk Chun'gyŏng and Yi Chagyŏm, and Ch'oe Sajŏn used this to convince him further. Ch'ŏk Chun'gyŏng then decided on a plan, and he attached a letter to the king stating that he wished to do his utmost. The king then made someone tell Ch'ŏk Chun'gyŏng the following: "Although you went beyond the pale and used excessive measures, you did not go as far as create an insurrection. If I had first taken the initiative, how would that accord with the principle of loving one's relatives? It is not yet too late if we patiently wait for a change and then respond to it." He always made an intermediary observe him. When Ch'ŏk Chun'gyŏng was preparing the appointment certificates for military officials in the Ministry of War, the king secretly transmitted a small hand-written note through the eunuch Cho Ŭi 趙毅. It read: "Today officers from Sungdŏk Residence came to the north of [my] hall holding weapons. If they enter the gate to the royal quarters and I come to grief, that would be the result of my lack of virtue. But what is tragic is that if the dynasty founded by T'aejo and transmitted through successive ancestors to ultimately reach my insignificant body would change to a different surname, it would not just be my personal fault, it would also be a disgrace for all the councilors and high officials. Please consider this carefully." Ch'ŏk Chun'gyŏng showed the king's handwriting to vice-minister Kim Hyang. Kim Hyang sank to his knees and shouted to Heaven while crying: "If this is the king's will, it is only right to serve him till death, how can you, Duke, be at ease?"

Ch'ŏk Chun'gyŏng together with Kim Hyang then led seven officers along with twenty clerks and servants out the north gate. In their hurry they had

---

24 Sipp'alcha 十八子: this contains all the elements of the surname Yi 李, hence can be taken as prophesying Yi as future ruler.

not taken any weapons, so they used stakes from a fence. They entered the palace via the bridge south of the Golden Bird Division. Cho Ŭi came to meet them, shouting that the situation was urgent. They hurried in and then closed Kwanghwa Gate. Yi Kongsu 李公壽 followed after them, and he ordered one side of the gate to be opened to let him in. Yi Kongsu is none other than Yi Su. At the time, Commandant of Military Inspectors Chŏng Yuhwang 鄭惟晃 led more than 100 people into the Directorate of Weaponry and distributed weapons and armor, and then went to Yŏn'gyŏng Palace. On the way they met vice-director Ryu Wŏnsik 柳元湜; his words were not compliant, and he was killed. Ch'ŏk Chun'gyŏng, donning armor and helmet, rushed into the palace. The king, coming out of the Ch'ŏnbok Hall gate 天福殿門, was waiting for him. Ch'ŏk Chun'gyŏng accompanied the king outside, when Yi Chagyŏm's party started shooting at him. He drew his sword and gave one shout, and nobody dared to make a move. The king entered the Directorate of Weaponry, where he was strictly guarded. Ch'ŏk Chun'gyŏng then made Transmitter of Edicts Kang Huhyŏn 康侯顯 summon Yi Chagyŏm. Yi Chagyŏm came wearing mourning clothes. Ch'ŏk Chun'gyŏng and Yi Kongsu after deliberation locked up Yi Chagyŏm, his wife, and children in the P'algwan Foundation. They executed his generals Kang Ho 康好, Ko Chinsu 高珍守, and others, who were all agents of Yi Chagyŏm. He then dispatched people to apprehend other members of Yi's party.

The king emerged from Kwanghwa Gate and had someone announce to the public: "A coup d'etat was attempted in the palace, but thanks to loyal ministers and righteous servants, justice was upheld and the evil eliminated." The crowd erupted in cheers of "Manse," and everyone clapped their hands and danced with joy, some even let their tears flow. Hearing the commotion, Yi Chimi led more than 100 people to Kwanghwa Gate but could not enter. He hesitated and paced to and fro [in front of the gate], and then with Yi Chadŏk and Kim Ingyu went to the Ministry of War, not knowing that Yi Chagyŏm had been detained. Towards evening, the military inspector[25]

---

25 *Sungŏm* 巡檢: presumably this refers to Commandant of Military Inspectors Chŏng

arrived at the Ministry of War and apprehended Yi Chimi, locking him up in the Bureau of Inspection.[26] Yi Chadŏk and the others were frightened and fled. The king returned to Yŏn'gyŏng Palace. The close officials entered first to clean up. The monk Ŭijang was hiding in the king's quarters and was apprehended and sent to the P'algwan Foundation. Yi Chagyŏm, his wife Lady Ch'oe and their son Yi Chiyun were exiled to Yŏnggwang; Yi Chimi was exiled to Hapchu, Yi Kongŭi to Chindo, Yi Chiŏn to Kŏje, Yi Chibo to Samch'ŏk 三陟,[27] Ŭijang to Kŭmju 金州,[28] and Yi Chiwŏn to Hamjong 咸從.[29] Palace Ushers Pak P'yo 朴彪 and Mun Chun 文仲, Head of Auxiliaries Pak Yŏng, Grand Astrologer Yang Rin 梁麟, Director of the Winter Office Yang Hae 梁獬, Palace Attendants Yi Suksin and Yi Pun 李芬, Grand General Kim Ho 金好, Generals Chi Ho and Chi Poksin 池福臣, Junior Colonel Ch'oe Sayŏm 崔思琰, Sub-colonel Wi Ho 位好, Executive Captain Song Yongjung 宋用中, together with thirty of their children and more than ninety official and private slaves were exiled separately to distant regions

Among them Pak P'yo was the most treacherous and fawning of Yi Chagyŏm. All the acts of extraction and accumulation for profit were his doing. Therefore those seeking profit or an emolument all vied with each other to bribe him, making him extremely rich. Those at court hated him in particular, so he was killed on the way [to exile] and his body submerged in water. Furthermore the person who shot an arrow [at the king] at Sinbong Gate and Kim Ch'ung 金冲, retainer of Yi Chiŏn, were put in cangues at the market place for three days and then exiled to distant islands. As for those loyal to Yi Chagyŏm, the Executives Yi Chadŏk and Kim Ingyu, Associate Administrator of the Security Council Kim Ŭiwŏn, Director of the Foreign Relations Office Yi Chawŏn 李資元, Deputy Director of the Office of Royal

Yuhwang, mentioned above.

26 Kŏmjŏmso 檢點所: unique attestation of this term, hence difficult to assess its function. Chŏmgŏmso 點檢所 would appear to be a more likely sequence.

27 Modern Samch'ŏk, Kangwŏn Province.

28 Modern Kimhae, South Kyŏngsang Province.

29 Modern Hamjong-myŏn, Kangsŏ-gun, South P'yŏngan Province.

Clan Affairs Pak Hyoryŏm 朴孝廉, Office Chief of Palace Attendants Wang Ŭi, and Usher Yi Chon 李存 were all demoted to magistrates.

The king issued a decree saying: "I inherited the throne of my ancestors at a young age, so my intention was to rely on my maternal relatives. All affairs, whether small or big, were entrusted to them, but they abused this to oppress the people for their own profit and harm the country. Even though I knew this, I could not stop it, thus disasters arose and I could not help it. Then Minister of War Ch'ŏk Chun'gyŏng displayed his righteousness and settled the revolt. This merit cannot be forgotten. It is therefore fitting that the relevant offices should debate the level of merit and his reward. Likewise, Vice-director of the Directorate of Weaponry Ch'oe Sajŏn was of the same mind in secretly assisting the throne; his reward and merit level should also be discussed."

Executive Pak Sŭngjung was exiled to Ulchin 蔚珍,[30] and his son Pak Simjo and three others were sent to Namye 南裔.[31] Together with Hŏ Chae and Ch'oe Sik, Pak Sŭngjung through his flattery and collusion with Yi Chagyŏm was up to all kind of things. He was behind the setting up of separate offices and installing officials, and using royal titles for the documents and birthdays for Yi Chagyŏm. Thus the remonstrance officials decided to remove him from office.

Ch'ŏk Chun'gyŏng was appointed Director of the Chancellery. On account of the fact that he had jumped the hierarchical sequence, he adamantly refused, and did not accept the appointment.

Sixth month. Ch'ŏk Chun'gyŏng was made Merit Subject Promoting Loyalty, Pacifying the Country, Assisting in Policy, Equalizing Virtue, and Protecting the Dynasty, Honorary Grand Preceptor, Acting Grand Guardian, Executive of the Chancellery and Jointly Chief of the Royal Secretariat-Chancellery, Minister of Taxation and Concurrently Commissioner to the Resident Governor of the Western Capital, Supreme Pillar of State. His wife née Hwang was named Lady of Chean District. The king also bestowed

---

30 Modern Ulchin, North Kyŏngsang Province.

31 This location could not be traced.

clothes, gold and silver implements, cloth and silk, saddles, ten slaves, and thirty *kyŏl* of land upon them. Yi Kongsu was made Merit Subject Promoting Loyalty and Guarding the Dynasty, Minister of Personnel. Kim Hyang was appointed Merit Subject Guarding the Dynasty, and Vice-minister of Taxation, Intendant of the Chancellery; Ch'oe Sajŏn was designated Vice-minister of War.

Hŏ Chae was dismissed and made Defense Commissioner of P'ungju 豊州;[32] his son Hŏ Sun 許純 was appointed Administrative Assistant to the Defense Commissioner of Kŭmju. Initially the remonstrance officials had argued that Hŏ Chae's crime was the same as Pak Sŭngjung, but Ch'ŏk Chun'gyŏng defended him. But now he was implicated[33] and people at the time greatly rejoiced in this.

Remonstrance officials repeatedly sent memorials arguing that since the two daughters of Yi Chagyŏm [given in marriage to the king] were also his aunts, they definitely could not be his consorts. The king then sent away the two women and took the daughter of Intendant-secretary at the Department of Royal Clan Affairs Im Wŏnae 任元敳 as his consort. Her mother née Yi was the daughter of Director of the Chancellery Yi Wi. On the eve of her birth, Yi Wi dreamt that a big yellow flag was planted on the middle gate of his residential compound, but the tail end of the flag fluttered around the ridge-end tile of Sŏn'gyŏng Hall 宣慶殿. When she was born Yi Wi showed her special affection, saying: "This girl will one day roam Sŏn'gyŏng Hall." When she came of age, she was betrothed to the son of Executive Kim Ingyu, Kim Chihyo 金之孝. On the eve of the marriage when Chihyo arrived at the front gate of her residence, she became violently sick, almost dying. Because of this he was sent away. The following day a diviner determined the disease saying: "You should not worry, this girl is precious beyond words. She will definitely become the mother of the dynasty." At the time Yi Chagyŏm had already given two daughters in marriage to the king, so when

32 Modern Songhwa-gun, Hwanghae Province.

33 It is not clear if he was implicated in any new incident or whether this refers to his association with Yi Chagyŏm.

he heard this he resented her. He immediately requested that Im Wŏnae be demoted to Commissioner of Kaesŏng District. After more than a year had passed, the deputy prefect had a dream where the ridge pole and crossbeam of the prefecture building split, creating a big gap through which a yellow dragon escaped. The next day the deputy prefect carried official court robes as he went to see Im Wŏnae, relating him his dream and congratulating him, explaining: "A wondrous event will definitely occur in your excellency's household, this you should know." Then the king had a dream in which he obtained five pints of sesame and three pints of yellow sunflower. He told this to Ch'ŏk Chun'gyŏng, who replied: "Sesame (*im* 荏) signifies the [surname] Im (任). This is an omen that you will marry a queen surnamed Im. The number five signifies that she will give birth to five sons. The color yellow (*hwang* 黃) means august (*hwang* 皇), which is the same as august king (*hwangwang* 皇王). Sunflower (*kyu* 葵) signifies to administer (*kyu* 揆), similar to administering through the way [of virtue] (*togyu* 道揆). As for the yellow sunflower (*hwanggyu* 黃葵), this is a sign that the august king will administer the country upholding the way. As for the number three, this is a sign that of the five sons three will govern the country." His words were indeed verified by what happened.

Twenty people, including Chŏng Yuhwang were granted office commensurate to rank for their merit in following the royal carriage and catching the rebels.

Autumn, seventh month. Song dispatched Audience Usher Hou Zhang 侯章, Gui Zhongfu 歸中孚 and others, sixty people in all, with the following edict: "I spent more than ten years in the Spring Palace [as heir apparent] and never dared to be lazy or idle. For a long time the Daoist Supreme Emperor reigned.[34] Troubled by the vicissitudes of politics he decided to step down in my favor. I firmly refused but could not get my way, and in the end it was my fate to ascend the precious [throne]. Contemplating the loftiness of the dynastic institution, and the heavy burden of the previous emperor's trust,

34 Daojun taishang Huangdi 道君太上皇帝: one of the titles Emperor Huizong (r. 1100-1126), who put much faith in Daoism, gave himself.

I worried day and night, fearful of not being able fulfill my duty. Then the Jin people disregarded the way and used the opportunity of Guo Yaoshi's treason to make Yanshan surrender.[35] Then they also started harassing the border, even reaching as far as the capital area.[36] I was then just at the start of my reign, and because of this crisis I did not have the chance to inform you, King. Considering that your kings for generations showed loyalty and piety and accepted investiture from us, and as an ancient border state of ours always received our favor, my ancestor Emperor Shenzong sent envoys to establish relations. The ritual intentions were complete, feelings were like those connected by flesh and blood, and the righteousness was that of ruler and subject. Then our Daoist Supreme Emperor bestowed presents beyond count, thus raising the level of treatment.

Considering that you are far removed from us on the other side of the Liao Sea yet favors and ritual propriety are still like this, what else could we wish for but to tackle the enemy together in times of crisis? Your country and that of Jin are merely a few hundred leagues removed from each other, so if you cannot sweep away their lair to repay China, then what is the point of successive courts extending special treatment? As for the Jin people, they were definitely once subjects to the king; they are a contemptible lot huddled in a corner of the sea. They turned against Heaven and betrayed the gods, first annihilating Liao and then insulting China. Their depravity and violence being such, if we let them have their way, what do you think will happen to you, King? A solitary division entered deeply [into our territory] but in principle they should be annihilated [soon]. Since they made King Su[37] a

---

35 Yanshan 燕山 refers to Yanjing, modern Beijing. Guo Yaoshi 郭藥師 was a Liao general who defended the city but in 1125 surrendered to the Jin and changed his loyalty.

36 This is a very euphemistic account of the Jin siege of the Song capital Kaifeng (then named Bianjing) in 1126. In the face of the Jin advance, Emperor Huizong abdicated for his son, later known as Qinzong (r. 1126-1127). It is Qinzong addressing the Koryŏ king in this letter. The following year Kaifeng was sacked by Jin and the two emperors and much of the court were taken by them as hostages.

37 Su wang 肅王: This likely refers to a brother of Qinzong, Zhao Gou, who was sent to negotiate during the first siege of Kaifeng, but taken hostage. He was later released after a ransom had been paid. Escaping the sack of Kaifeng in 1127, he fled south and eventually became the first emperor of Southern Song, Gaozong. However, his actual title as prince

hostage and then took him away, I ordered my army to merely pursue them until they left our borders. Soon I will raise the realm's armies to punish the puny and ugly [Jurchen]. King, you should lead your troops so that we act as inner and outer [to take them from two sides] and exact Heavenly punishment. If you gather those who have betrayed you, King, from far away and then present the prisoners to our court so as to repay a debt to China stretching many generations, this would be supreme loyalty. Settling the revolt and attacking the darkness, punishing depravity and violence so as to extend authority beyond the deserts, this is great righteousness. Extending the territory and overturning their lair to avenge the arrogant and disloyal caitiffs, this is great authority. With one strike obtaining all these three results, what is holding you back to do this, King? I will not begrudge high office and generous reward, so please do your best."

Back in the hostel, Hou Zhang furthermore composed a letter to the king, saying: "When we arrived here we carried the emperor's edict. The imperial ancestors have practiced the way of Yao and Shun, worked hard at the roots and cherished the transforming effects. Amical relations with this country [i.e., Koryŏ] go back almost two hundred years, and were always accompanied by ritual propriety. Our Daoist Supreme Emperor continued that tradition, with lofty favor and generous treatment. But recently treacherous people argued for triggering border clashes, giving the Jin people the chance to foment trouble and raise a nameless army to create chaos and randomly strike at points where we were unprepared. They threw the central plains in chaos and plundered at will. At that time there were millions of troops at the ready, but great ministers argued, 'If we don't attack them south of the Yellow River, we can strike them north of the Great River [Yangtze]. Only by letting them enter so deep into our territory will it be possible to completely annihilate them in one fell swoop.' Now at this time our current emperor had just been enthroned. He is full of filial and brotherly piety, and respectful [to subjects] and frugal. He eats only after night has fallen and sleeps late; work is entrusted to the wise and able, trustworthiness is

was Kang wang 康王, so this appears to be a mistake.

esteemed and righteousness cherished, so complete annihilation [of the Jin] was out of the question. Thereupon the Jin people expressed regret over their past actions and declared peace. When they requested free passage to return to their desert, the ruler consented to aid them. He gave gold and silk, and also provisions for the soldiers. But again they made insatiable requests, and then spied an opportunity [to attack] the passes and garrisons north of the river, angering both men and spirits. In these circumstances, we are forced to wait for the autumn cool to raise an army and smite them. At that time, how can your country just stand by and watch? If you send an army to the border we can together eliminate them. This would be the culmination of boundless friendship. If this plan succeeds [i.e. if you agree] a separate emissary will be sent to you."

The reply was as follows: "From the time of its founding fathers our country has continued to serve the supreme dynasty, and has never dared to be indolent in the sincerity of its respect and obedience. Emperor Shenzong, though far removed from us on the other side of the Liao Sea, sent envoys down to us to cultivate relation, just as there is nowhere the bright rays of the sun do not shine; the favor and propriety bestowed by him were particularly generous. The Daoist Supreme Emperor continued this policy, but added even more to our treatment. The gifts he bestowed were twice the norm, truly a favor that is difficult to repay even over a hundred life times. Even though Heaven and Earth do not demand repayment, we are impatient to repay even one ten-thousands immediately.

Today, prostrate, we received the edict transferred to us by the envoys as well as the letter. We took note of the immorality of the Jin people, the extent of their depravity and violence, the plan to raise an army of the All under Heaven to punish this small and ugly lot, and the order for this insignificant country to lead an army matching [that of Song] to exact Heaven's punishment from both sides. Reading this, from the start I could not suppress my tears. Looking back to the beginnings of the Jin people, they were indeed vassals to our country in the past, but frequently they raided and attacked us. So as to safeguard the peace at our border, we did not want to create any conflict. When they came we warned them and defended ourselves; when they retreated then we prepared and guarded [the frontier]. Thus the key strategy was one of containment. During the time of my grandfather Sukchong there was a chief called Yingge. With force he controlled the various evil forces, and with authority he submitted the different tribes. Looking down on us from Paeksan,[38] several times he invaded our country. Wuda 吳達 and Huinu 惠奴 then succeeded him in turn,[39] and increased their aggressive stance towards us. Recently one of our countrymen who had been taken captive by the Great Jin returned and told us, 'When the envoys from the supreme dynasty arrived in the barbarian land, the ritual extended was the same as for the surrendered envoys of Northern Liao.' Furthermore, according to statements from people living at the border, the Jin people caused the fall of the Khitan and then violated the border of the supreme dynasty. Your emperor having just acceded to the throne did not wish to annihilate them and accepted their peace request; if a great country such as China is like this, how much more is this the case for a small country—isolated, to whom could we turn? In the fourth month of this year, we sent envoys to establish amical relations. Several months have elapsed yet we have not yet received a reply. Thinking back, several disasters that afflicted this country destroyed storage houses, and all the defensive weapons we need are entirely lacking. We are only now deliberating the drafting of workmen for their reconstruction. Now the decree gives us detailed instruction, and in fact this is the time to wipe away the old disgrace and repay for your grace. However, given the decrepit state of our army, I am afraid that even if we force ourselves we are no match for the caitiffs, who have renewed their victories. Still we hope to train and drill the army and repair the weaponry. Waiting for the moment when the sovereign army sets for that border to press [the Jin], how would this unworthy country then dare not to exert all its power from the outside? If we can rely on your divine authority and help pacify the barbarians, this is my wish. Heaven will truly witness this. Having

---

38 Paeksan 白山: a mountain in Chŏngp'yŏng-gun, South Hamgyŏng Province.

39 As seen above (chapter 7, note 34), this should be Wuyashu and Aguda.

received the proclamation transmitted by the envoys, when there is a result to report we will do so."

When Hou Zhang returned the king entrusted him with a memorial, the contents of which was roughly as follows: "Considering that we are a small country that has received generous virtue across the generations, we always wished to exert our loyalty to repay the emperor. How would our mind be anything but loyal towards the emperor? Suddenly we received an edict and when I read it, it was difficult to suppress my tears. We should immediately raise an army in accordance with this decree; however, our country is originally not a strong one. Moreover, recently we experienced a number of disasters that completely destroyed our provisions, so now we have to restock the granaries and prepare weapons. Only after this has been done can we make a move. However, it is difficult to know by when this can be accomplished. Moreover, the power of the enemy is cruelly strong, we cannot easily touch the caitiffs. And the territory is inhospitable, it is not easy to pursue them over a long distance. However, the emperor's order is at our doorstep, there is no way but to assist the sovereign army to subdue the enemy even if it aids the divine authority only slightly."

Ninth month. The king dispatched Vice-commissioner of the Security Council Kim Pusik and Executive at the Ministry of Punishment Yi Chuyŏn 李周衍 to Song to offer felicitations on the emperor's accession.

The Jin Promulgation Envoys, Jointly Notary for the Security Council[40] Gao Baishu 高伯淑 and Chief Minister of the Court of State Ceremonial Wu Zhichong 烏至忠 and others arrived with an edict by the Jin sovereign. They said: "Koryŏ, when sending envoys and in all its relations with us should follow what they used to do for Liao. As for their seizing Baozhou and the border population on the other side of the border, all should be returned. If you follow to the letter [all our instructions] then the Baozhou territory will be granted to you." Baozhou 保州 is none other than P'oju 抱州.

On *kyŏngin* day [the 27th] Venus was seen crossing the sky during the day.

Winter, tenth month. On *pyŏngsin* day [the 4th], on the occasion of the

40 I here read 簽書樞密院事 for 僉書樞密院事.

Kyŏngnyong Festival the king hosted a banquet for all officials in Ch'ŏnbok Hall.

The king held a parting banquet for the Jin envoys in Taemyŏng Palace 大明宫, and entrusted them with a reply memorial thanking them and pledging to follow the old Liao system completely.

The king summoned back Kim Ch'an and appointed him Intendant-secretary at the Department of Royal Clan Affairs. The sons and sons-in-law of Hong Kwan, Kim Chin, and Chi Nog'yŏn were granted office rank. Kim Ch'an later changed his name to Kim An 金安.

The king traveled to the Southern Capital.

Eleventh month. The king gave a banquet at Yŏnhŭng Hall 延興殿 for the officials.

The king returned from the Southern Capital.

Intercalary [eleventh] month. The king proclaimed a pardon, and gave a banquet for those aged over eighty, widowers and widows, orphans and lonely elderly, filial sons and grandsons, virtuous wives and righteous husbands, and bestowed presents commensurate with rank.

The king decreed that Ch'ŏk Chungyŏng's portrait should be made for the Merit Subjects Hall.

Twelfth month. Yi Chagyŏm died in Yŏnggwang Prefecture.

The king dispatched Director of the Office of Regalia Kim Charyu 金子鏐 and Office Chief at the Ministry of Punishment Yu Tŏngmun 柳德文 to Jin to give thanks for the oral promulgation [of the imperial instructions]. The memorial went: "Gao Baishu arrived to secretly transmit the emperor's missive that the territory of Baozhou fortress is to be reattached to Koryŏ, and will not be reclaimed. We venture that the original Kuryŏ territory[41] was centered on yonder Liao Mountain;[42] the old location of Pyongyang was limited to the Amnok River, but underwent many changes.[43] During

41 Kuryŏ 句麗 i.e. what in modern historiography is referred to as Koguryŏ.

42 It is not certain which mountain this refers to; there was a place called Yosan 遼山 (modern Suan, North Hwanghae Province; about 50 km. southeast of Pyongyang), but it is more likely to refer to a mountain along the northern border of the peninsula.

43 I have tried to translate this passage as literally as possible, because it bristles with

the time of our founding fathers it was annexed by the Northern Dynasty which also went as far invading the territory of the Samhan. Although they talked about neighborly friendship they never returned our old territories. Now the Heavenly Mandate has been renewed and a sage ruler has taken the throne. Seeing that his troops practice righteousness, the fortress remained unoccupied. At the time when your subject's father was king, the border official of the Great Dynasty, Shayihe 沙乙何, came to transmit an imperial writ that said 'Baozhou is originally Koryŏ territory, thus it should be returned to Koryŏ.'[44] The previous king then repaired the fortress and moat, and filled it with households. At the time, although this insignificant country was not yet vassal to your supreme dynasty, the previous emperor wanted to show his special favor to his neighboring country and granted us the old territory with words of encouragement. His successor then encountered one of sagacious virtue succeeding to the Heavenly [Mandate], and becoming the receiver of virtuous words, he respectfully cultivated the role of subject. Considering that this narrow strip of land by the eastern seashore is originally a frontier vassal country, although we in the past were robbed by the Khitan, we already acknowledged the kindness of the previous generations, and now thanks to a special munificence have submitted this derelict fief. How would this have happened by chance! The enormity of the favor we encountered, the deep humanity and great righteousness—there are no words to describe this. With weak power and shallow talent, to repay this grace, all we can do is tend to the affairs of spring and autumn and ensure the regular flow of tribute. The whole country will happily perform this, and I will transmit this to my children and grandchildren as an eternal pledge. This we swear with undivided loyalty as the truth before Heaven on high."

Kim Injon was made Merit Subject Supporting Sagacity and Equalizing

difficulties concerning how the territory of Koguryŏ was conceived in Koryŏ.

44 Shayihe does not occur in any other source; perhaps it refers to the Jin general Sahe 撒喝. See the entry for the eighth month of 1116, when this general attacked Baozhou, then still in Liao hands. It was only in the third month of the following year that Liao transferred the fortress to Koryŏ. Note that the *Koryŏsa* version of this memorial has Great Liao 大遼 rather than Great Dynasty 大朝, so perhaps the *Koryŏsa chŏryo* compilers also felt that this might refer to the Jin general rather than a Liao official.

Virtue, Acting Grand Preceptor, Director of the Chancellery, Supervising Editor of National History, Supreme Pilar of State, Minister of Rites.

Injong fifth year [1127]

First year of the Jianyan era of Emperor Gaozong of Song, fifth year of the Tianhui era of Jin

Spring, first month. Jin dispatched Gao Sui 高隨 to congratulate the king on his birthday.

Second month. The king traveled to the Western Capital.

The king visited T'aejo's portrait shrine.

Third month. Kim Charyu and Yu Tŏngmun returned from Jin carrying the emperor's edict, which read: "Even before people were sent to you to induce you [to submit], you first expressed the wish to submit. Since this happened after our mutual exchanges had already started, we will work ever harder and with more pleasure. To praise this mind of respecting the [Son of] Heaven, I committed to the favor of bestowing land. Recently the tribute presented was accompanied only by a letter of thanks. Having perused it, although it may be sincere in its admiration, there are still excuses regarding the households, and there is no separate memorial letter that reports on it. However much I believe that you will complete all the things [you promise] and be loyal throughout the generations, if in my instructions the words are not firm, what would you rely on as proof for the land you obtained?"

The remonstrance officials said: "Kim Charyu failed to control his underlings when in Jin, and they fought with and hurt the Jin people. The [Jin court] rebuked him and had the Chief Administration Office[45] request that they be punished with bastonade [when back in Koryŏ]. We request that they be tried for demeaning the mandate." They were then dismissed from

45 Dubushu 都部署: According to Hucker (no. 7268) a common abbreviation for agencies staffed by eunuchs and in charge of arranging the emperor's temporary accommodations. Perhaps in this case they were in charge of the accommodations for the Koryŏ envoys. Note that in the Korean context I translate this term as Local Navy Command.

office.

The mantic monk from the Western Capital, Myoch'ŏng 妙淸, and the Astrological Officer Paek Suhan 白壽翰 convinced the king to hold an initiation ritual[46] in Sang'an Hall. Their rituals were fraudulent and cannot be known.

The king, his consort, and two princesses travelled to Hŭngbok-sa. Then together with state councilors and close officials they took the covered boat on the Taedong River. Stopping midstream, they had a banquet and music.

The king ordered Assistant Executive in Letters Kim Puil to lecture on the "Great Plan" of the *Book of Documents*. He also ordered Transmitter of Edicts Chŏng Hang 鄭沆 to lecture on "The Charge of Yue" and "Officers of Zhou" from the *Book of Documents*.

Executive Ch'ŏk Chun'gyŏng was exiled to Amt'a Island, and Senior Assistant Director at the Department of Ministries Ch'oe Sik to Ch'o Island.[47] Furthermore Vice-commissioner for Sangju Shepherdship Yi Hujin, Commissioner for Kuju So Ŏk, Office Chief Chŏng Yuhwang, Administrative Assistant for the Western Timber Reserve[48] Yun Han and others were exiled to distant places. Ch'ŏk Chun'gyŏng, having eliminated Yi Chagyŏm, relied on this merit to act at will. Senior Policy Monitor Chŏng Chisang knew that the king resented him, and thus sent the following memorial to the throne: "In the second month of *pyŏngo* year [1126], when Ch'ŏk Chun'gyŏng, Ch'oe Sik and others invaded the palace, Your Majesty ascended Sinbong Gate and instructed the soldiers to remove their armor. All were shouting for joy, only Ch'ŏk Chun'gyŏng did not obey the command, threatening the soldiers so that they would advance, so that an arrow even flew past the yellow tiles [of the gate roof]. Also he led troops to dash into [Chwa]aek Gate and set fire to the palace. The next day when the king travelled to the South Palace, he

46 Kwanjŏng toryang 灌頂道場: abhiṣeka bodhimanda: normally designates an esoteric initiation ritual in which water is sprinkled on the head of the person to be initiated.

47 The location of these islands is unknown, but their names sound ominous: Amt'a 嵒墮 means "rocks falling" and Ch'o 草 simply "grass," both implying very inhospitable places.

48 Sŏjaejang 西材場: A Koryŏ office instituted under Munjong, which managed either the timber or perhaps even the forests producing timber.

apprehended and killed all those attending to the king. From old, even among unruly ministers there was rarely a case such as this. What he did in the fifth month was just one moment's merit, but his actions in the second month are a crime that happens only once in ten-thousand generations. Even though Your Majesty has a mind that does not bear to inflict suffering on others, how could a one-off act of merit outweigh a once-in-ten-thousand-generations crime?" Because of this the king gave the order [of exile].

The king ordered Chŏng Chisang to lecture on the chapter "Against Luxurious Ease" of the *Book of Documents*. He also summoned attendant officials and twenty-five Confucian scholars from the Western Capital to compose poems. He bestowed drinks and food.

The king, together with his consort and the two princesses, took the dragon boat on the Taedong River. Floating along they enjoyed food and music. The king summoned the state councilors and attendant officials and encouraged them to join the banquet.

A decree read: "I bear the heavy mandate of Heaven and Earth, and succeeded to the foundations laid by my ancestors; it has been six years already since I have been charged with the Samhan. My knowledge is not sufficient for strategy, and my intelligence does not grasp anything. Disasters have come one after the other, so that there was nary a year of peace. Last year in the second month unruly ministers and rebels saw their chance to rise up but their plot was discovered, and I had no choice but to try them according to the law. Since then I have identified my faults and reproached myself for the many lapses in my virtue. Now, thanks to the recommendation of the astrologer, I traveled to the Western Capital to reflect deeply on my past mistakes. In the hope that these instructions may trigger a renewal, I promulgate them throughout the country, both center and provinces, so that all may learn about them. First, offer to the earth spirits at the Square Pond,[49] and welcome the *ki* in the four suburbs; second, dispatch commissioners

---

49 *Pangt'aek* 方澤: According to the section on the Fen 汾 River in the *Commentary on the Water Classic* (*Shuijing zhu* 水經注) this refers to a square pond in the middle of which is a square mound

across the prefectures of the country to secretly inspect the virtuous and harmful behavior of prefects and county magistrates, and reward or censure accordingly;[50] third, make sure that the system of carts and dress is verified and agreed on; fourth, do away with unnecessary offices and non-urgent tasks; fifth; encourage farmers in their toil to till the fields so that the people can be fed; sixth, have the accompanying officials each select one person; if that person is not capable the recommender should be punished; seventh, make sure that the official granaries are well stocked so that they can provide relief to the people; eighth, apart from the land rent and taxes that the people are due, nothing else should be appropriated; ninth, soldiers should be supported with compassion, and outside the periods of military drills they should not be forced to do labor; tenth, the people should be supported and their land secured so that they do not resort to vagrancy; eleventh, the Disaster Relief Stores and the Court of Great Charity should remain well stocked to aid the injured and sick; twelfth, grains stocked in official granaries should not be forced onto poor people to extract interest, and people should not be forced to grind rotten grain in their mills; thirteenth, when selecting scholars they should again write poems, prose poems, and essays; fourteenth, establish schools in all prefectures to promote learning and morality; fifteenth, mountains and ponds should be for the shared benefit of the people, and should not be encroached upon."

Summer, fourth month. On *kyŏngo* day [the 11th] the king's son, Wang Hyŏn 王晛,[51] was born.

Mun Kongmi was appointed Vice-minister of Personnel; Han Anjung 韓安中, Junior Assistant Director of the Department of Ministries; Han Ch'ung Executive at the Ministry of Rites; Mun Kongyu 文公裕, Audience Usher; Yi Sinŭi, Supreme General of the Thousand Bull Division; Chŏng Kŭg'yŏng, Commissioner to the Resident Governor of the Eastern Capital; Im Chon, Vice-commissioner of the Chinju shepherdship; and Ch'oe Kŏrin,

---

50 This point and some others are absent from the *Koryŏsa* version of this edict, which includes only ten of the fifteen points. KRS 15.23a-b (same date). However, the missing points are found as separate edicts in relevant sections of the monographs.

51 Later King Ŭijong (r. 1146–1170).

Vice-commissioner of the Sangju Shepherdship. Mun Kongmi and the others had all been exiled by Yi Chagyŏm. They were now called back and restored to office.

Fifth month. Associate Administrator of the Security Council Ch'oe Yujŏk was exiled to Kyŏngju and Executive at the Ministry of Punishment Ch'ae Sŏk to Chindo County.

The king went to Yŏngbong Tower 靈鳳樓 and ordered the Divine Cavalry of the two capitals to play polo. He bestowed presents commensurate to rank.

When Kim Pusik and the others arrived in Mingzhou of Song it so happened that Jin troops entered Bian.[52] The roads were blocked and they could not enter [the capital], thus they returned. Earlier there was a report from the border that said: "The Jin people have invaded Song but were defeated, and the Northern Song army took advantage of this victory to penetrate deep into Jin territory." Chŏng Chisang and Kim An petitioned: "We cannot miss this opportunity; please dispatch troops to link up with the Song army and achieve great merit, so that Your Majesty's merit will be recorded in the Chinese histories and passed on for thousands of generations."

The king then asked Kim Injon's opinion, who replied: "Rumors that have been passed on are usually found out to have no substance. You should not heed such rumors. Raising an army for a campaign will anger a strong enemy. Moreover Kim Pusik is due to return, so please wait for him to verify the truth of these rumors." Just then Kim Pusik returned and the report from the border was proven to be false.

Vice-director of the Department of Ministries Hong Kwan was posthumously appointed Merit Subject Promoting Sincerity and Protecting the Country, Acting Grand Marshal, Chief of the Chancellery and Jointly Executive of the Royal Secretariat, Minister of Rites and Supreme Pillar of State. His posthumous title was Ch'ungp'yŏng 忠平. Intendant of the Security Council Kim Chin was given the posthumous title Yŏlchik 烈直.

Sixth month. Wang Chwajae 王佐材 and thirty-two others passed the

52 Bianjing 汴京: The capital of Northern Song, corresponding to modern Kaifeng.

composition test of the civil service examination.

Kim Injon was appointed Minister of Personnel; Yi Kongsu, Minister of War; Kim Puil, Vice-minister of Taxation and Minister of Rites; Kim Hyang, Acting Grand Marshal, Honorary Minister of Works; Kim Pusik, Administrator of the Security Council; Ch'oe Chasŏng, Jointly Intendant of the Security Council; and Ch'oe Sajŏn, Vice-minister of Personnel and Associate Administrator of the Department of Ministries.

Autumn, seventh month. The king returned from the Western Capital and bestowed favors commensurate to rank.

The Song Military Instructor from Mingzhou, Vice Commissioner Zhang Xian 張誢, arrived.

In the Western Capital and the Northwest Province there was a locust infestation.

Eighth month. Yi Wi was appointed Royal Secretary.

Ninth month. The king dispatched Supervisor of Education Yi Chung to Jin to offer congratulations on the Tianqing Festival.

Hallim Academician Chŏng Kŭg'yŏng died. He was intelligent and sharp-minded, diligent at learning and good at composition.

The Jin Congratulatory Envoy,[53] Surveillance Commissioner for the Jurisdiction of Yongzhou, Yelü Juqin 耶律居瑾,[54] and the Military Training Commissioner[55] for Qinzhou 秦州,[56] Zhang Huai 張淮, came bearing the following edict: "To remove a strong enemy from his throne with the help of Heaven, this is an extra-ordinary affair. Since the liege lords act as my fence, in order to promulgate principle, this fact should be announced as it is to them. Originally Bian [the capital of] Song requested the return of Youzhou 幽州 and Yanzhou 燕州, and secretly made overtures across the sea, seeking

---

53 *Sŏngyŏngsa* 宣慶使: the first and only occurrence of this term, perhaps referring to the fact that it is the first (?) official Jin mission—although not yet one of investiture.

54 Note that this is the same type of official, even bearing the same surname, as during the period of Liao investiture.

55 *Tallyŏnsa* (Ch. *tuanlianshi*) 團鍊使 (standard spelling would be 團練使): according to Hucker (no. 7387) a regular military post at the prefecture level in Song but in Liao a member of the Southern Administration in the central government.

56 Modern Tianshui city, Gansu.

to seal friendship with its neighbor. Our previous emperor stooped down to take pity on this earnest request, and immediately gave permission. Yet they never showed due respect to this firm pact, and overturned it by accepting refugees, thus setting themselves up as enemies. Then [Zhao] Huan 趙桓[57] succeeded, but he repeated the words and actions of [Zhao] Ji 趙佶.[58] Despite having shown restraint and magnanimity for a long time, in the end they did not show any remorse for their transgressions, inviting the ire of men and gods; Heaven nor Earth could accept this. With merely one attack our generals managed to overturn their nest, and their ancestral halls and shrines were bereft of protection. Father and son were taken prisoner.[59] Now considering the extent of the accumulated grievances, it came to pass that there was a change of surnames,[60] as the divine seat could not be left vacant. The bestowal of a new investiture was discussed; as the people cherished him for his utmost humanity, together they promoted the former councilor. In the third month of this year already we instructed the military command to dispatch people to deliver the Zhao rulers, father and son, together with more than 470 clansmen, to the palace [of the Jin?]. Furthermore, with due ceremony we invested the great councilor of the defunct Song Dynasty, Zhang Bangchang 張邦昌, as emperor of the Great Chu 大楚 state, with its capital in Jinling 錦陵.[61] Aha, having apprehended the fully proven originator of all the evil, we give notice of its completion and the establishment of this merit for all, something that merits felicitation. We bestow upon your excellency robes and belt, rhinoceros horn, gold, silver, various kinds of silk,

57 Personal name of Emperor Qinzong 欽宗 (r. 1126-1127,

58 Personal name of Emperor Huizong (r. 1100-1126).

59 This appears to refer to Huizong and Qinzong, the abdicated emperor and his replacement, who was tasked with solving the Jin problem.

60 I.e. of royal surnames, hence a change of dynasties.

61 I.e. the modern Nanjing. It was the intention to create a buffer state that would help appease the population and help the Jin, who were overwhelmed by the sudden victory over the Northern Song, administer northern China. However, in the same year Zhang recognized the legitimacy of the Southern Song, submitted, and was executed. See Herbert Franke, "The Chin Dynasty," in Franke and Dennis Twitchett, eds. *The Cambridge History of China, vol. 6: Alien Regimes and Border States, 907–1368* (Cambridge: Cambridge University Press, 1994), 229–230.

and other presents, please accept them."

Winter, tenth month. The king ordered relevant offices to strike off the record all the lands and slaves that the Yis had grabbed from people, and restitute them to their original owners.

A Hundred Seat Assembly was held in Ch'ŏnsŏng Hall 天成殿. The king ordered [officials] throughout the country to give vegetarian feasts to 30,000 monks.

Eleventh month. The king dispatched Sŏk Chun 石峻 to Jin to give thanks for the birthday wishes, and Yi Zhen 李瑱 to offer felicitations for the new year.

Twelfth month. Director of the Chancellery Kim Injon died. He was the son of Executive Kim Sanggi. He was intelligent and passed the civil service examination at a young age. For a long time he served as palace attendant, managing reports to the throne. Kim Injon was made reception attendant when the Liao envoy, Academician Meng Ch'u, came. When Meng Ch'u saw him, it was like meeting an old acquaintance, he especially took of his golden belt and gave it to him. When Yejong was still in the eastern Palace, when reading the *Analects*, Kim Injon was the reading academician; he compiled a new interpretation and lectured on it. From his youth he was diligent in studying, and in old age he never let go of books. Many of the royal proclamations came from his hand. When Yi Chagyŏm controlled affairs he took leave and retreated to his house. After the defeat of Yi, he was elevated to first councilor, following the bequeathed instructions of Yejong. The edict of appointment was insistent and sincere, and he had no choice but to take charge. His posthumous title was Munsŏng 文成 [letters accomplished].

Yi Kongsu was appointed Minister of Personnel and State Historiographer; Kim Puil was named Director of the Chancellery and Jointly Executive of the Royal Secretariat-Chancellery; Kim Hyang and Ch'oe Chasŏng were made Assistant Executive in Political Affairs; and Mun Kongmi was appointed Associate Administrator of the Security Council.

Injong sixth year [1128]

Second year of the Jianyan era of Song, sixth year of the Tianhui era of Jin

First month. Jin sent Xiao Huaiyu 蕭懷玉 to give congratulations on the king's birthday.

The king summoned back the wife of Yi Chagyŏm, Lady Ch'oe.

There was a fire in Indŏk Palace 人德宮.

Second month. There was a fire in the palace buildings of the Southern Capital.

Yi Kongsu was appointed Director of the Chancellery; Kim Puil was appointed Probationary Minister of Education and Vice-minister of War; Kim Hyang was made Jointly Executive of the Royal Secretariat-Chancellery; Yi Suk was designated Acting Minister of Education, Probationary Minister of Works, Vice-director of the Department of Ministries, Minister of Rites; and Ch'oe Chasŏng was named Minister of Works.

There was famine in Chŏngju, and a decree ordered that granaries be opened to provide relief.

Ch'oe Sajŏn was made Merit Subject Promoting Loyalty and Guarding the Earth Shrine, Probationary Minister of Works, Vice-director of the Department of Ministries.

A decree read "encouraging agriculture and sericulture, ensuring that there is enough to wear and to eat, these are the most urgent tasks of sage kings. Recently many magistrates have amassed [grains] for profit, and few are those who are diligent and upright in assisting the people. The granaries and storage houses are empty, and the ordinary people are destitute. This is further aggravated by forced corvée labor, so that the people have nowhere to turn to. Many rise up and gather to form bandit groups. This is totally against the principle of making the country prosperous and the people at ease. Give the order that prefectures should stop unnecessary projects and interrupt non-urgent business."

Summer, fourth month. A decree read: "Recently heavenly patterns show anomalies and the seasons are out of order. Relevant authorities should reconsider prison sentences and pardon sentences lower than the death penalty. Sacrifices should be made to the mountains and rivers inside our country. A feast should be prepared for the aged as well as those with serious or fatal illness, chaste [wives] and righteous [husbands], filial [sons] and docile [grandsons], widows and widowers, and those orphaned or living alone, and presents given commensurate with rank."

The Duke of Taebang, Wang Po, died in Kyŏngsan District. After Yi Chagyŏm died the king wanted to summon him back, but before the order was given he died.

On *kapsul* day [the 21st] Venus was observed traversing the sky.

A decree read: "The banished Ch'ŏk Chun'gyŏng, although sentenced for the crime of the second month of *pyŏng'o* year [1126], his merit for the fifth month of the same year is still not minute. As for Ch'oe Yujŏk, he was implicated through the crimes of his son, but in fact did not do anything. As for Pak Sŭngjung, even though he is guilty, with his writing talents he served successive kings and achieved wide renown. They should all be allowed to move from their place of exile to their home villages." Ch'ŏk Chun'gyŏng moved to Kokchu and Pak Sŭngjung to Muan county 務安縣,[62] where he subsequently died.

Yi Wŏnch'ŏl 李元哲 and twenty-eight others passed the composition test of the civil service examination.

Fifth month. Prayers for rain were held at the Ancestral Shrine, the Earth and Grain Deities Altar, and mountains and rivers.

Sixth month. Ch'oe Hongjae was made Executive Chief of the Chancellery. Earlier, when Yi Chagyŏm banished Han An'in, Ch'oe colluded with Yi. As a result the remonstrance officials impeached him, and hence he was the last to be recalled.

Song dispatched Vice-minister of Punishment Yang Yingcheng 楊應誠, Defense Commissioner for Qizhou Han Yan 韓衍, and others. Initially when Yang Yingcheng arrived at Pyŏngnan Pavilion 碧瀾亭, he delivered a letter to the escort commissioner, which read "Your esteemed country is diligent and generous in ritual observance, so unless we appraise you beforehand

---

62 Modern Muan-gun, South Chŏlla Province.

there would surely be both useless and burdensome efforts on your part. Since our two sages are in distant parts,[63] we as subjects cannot bear to listen to music, so apart from the days of the reception of the imperial edict and the presentation of the memorial, you should not use music. Also forgo the sending of robes, belts, and flower wine."

The king received the edict in Such'ang Palace 壽昌宮. The edict read "The country's fortunes diminished in the middle, and rebellions arose outside of its borders. When I had just succeeded to the throne I immediately had to make contingencies for the pacification [of the external threat]. Now the country of the Sam Han of old, has in fact across the generations aligned itself with our country. You took the trouble of sending a state-letter envoy to offer tribute, but due to the long-standing troubles, the response embassy was delayed. Yet even considering these many factors, we should not change our normal feelings. Having received a letter from Great Jin, we especially dispatched this embassy across the sea and borders. Despite all the hardship and confusion, to mitigate disasters and save the people, one should extend help. A few insignificant gifts are entrusted [with the envoys], falling far behind what is usual, but please accept them."

Yang Yingcheng and the others then also presented a petition[64] that read: "In the past when the Zhou royal house was plagued by disasters, someone told [Duke] Wen of Jin: 'If you want to obtain the hearts of the liege lords, nothing is better than working diligently for the king. The liege lords will then trust him and moreover this is great righteousness.' As Duke Wen of Jin thus settled the royal house, he became hegemon [over the other states].[65] This is recorded in books and canons, leaving an undying bright legacy. Now we would venture to say that your esteemed country has established its

---

63 This refers to Huizong and Qinzong, who had been taken by the Jurchen.

64 Ch'aja 箚字: usually 箚子, a kind of petition or letter to a superior; perhaps an individual letter by the envoy, or else a letter indicating protestation or rebuke. According to *Koryŏsa*, Yang gave a verbal account (語錄), or "transcribed conversation."

65 Duke Wen of Jin 晉文公 (r. 636-628 BC). He showed his loyalty to Zhou by reinstating King Xiang of Zhou in 635 BC after he had been driven out by his brother. One of the so-called "five hegemons" (*wuba* 五霸). See Durrant, Lee, and Schaberg, *Zuo Tradition*, 389–91, 2086.

reputation as the greatest land east of the sea, showing its loyalty throughout the generations. Since the beginning of the exchange of envoys, our dynasty has treated your esteemed country with lavish grace and ritual, which from the beginning never flagged. But now we have encountered times of hardship, with our country afflicted by many troubles. Unexpectedly the northern barbarians employed a ruse and forced the two sage kings on a long march. Those above and those below are all extremely worried and cannot put our minds to rest. Again we venture to say that your esteemed country upholds ritual and cherishes righteous, and moreover for many years has enjoyed the accumulated favors of our court, something no other country comes close to. Now in this crisis the time has come to work diligently for the king[66] by showing righteousness and redressing what is wrong. Now our emperor has just ascended the precious throne and dispatches envoys to show his concern to your king, and also to trouble you with crossing over and sending [an embassy] to meet and request [the return of] the two emperors.

On the day of receiving the edict, the situation has already been stated face to face, and next again through an official letter that troubled you with the sincere and earnest request; so I am sure that you will take due care in considering it. Your esteemed country is of the opinion that the road to Jin is dangerous and traveling there is impossible. Yet in the time of your ancestors the Jin people used to be attached to the tribute embassies [to China] of your esteemed country. At the time the roads were naturally connected, there was no report of them being inaccessible. Your esteemed country furthermore fears that the Jin people will use this [road] to send envoys. However after destroying the Khitan, the Jin people all sent envoys through the Hedong and Shanbei routes, so it is not necessary for them to arrive via this route.[67] If your esteemed country fears that the Jin people might use this as a pretext [for escalation], Yang Yingcheng and his party merely consist

66 I.e. the suzerain, the Song emperor; in parallel with Duke Wen of Jin's working diligently for his overlord.

67 Hedong 河東 and Shanbei 山北: It is not clear which route Yang has in mind, but given the geography of the peninsula this might signify a route via the eastern seaboard, rather than the habitual road north on the western side of the peninsula.

of 110 unarmed guards; with the state letter and presents we will go first to negotiate peace, so this will not lead to armed struggle. Your esteemed country will then cross the sea and dispatch envoys to the border, whence you report to the Jin and ask for permission [to proceed]. If, for example they demand that the number of people be reduced, this will all be carried out so no trouble shall arise from this. Should your envoys via the route taken by your esteemed country manage to meet and request [the return][68] of the two emperors, then 200 years of loyal service will not have been in vain, and it will be a good repayment for the grace shown by successive emperors. The country [i.e., Song?] will repay the merit double compared to the past, and your reputation among neighboring countries will soar. Trusting and following such lofty righteousness will have a limitless enjoyment, and the important ministers of your country will display the loyalty of cooperation and upholding, the reward will be passed on for generations without end; this is not simply a one-time selfish advantage for the envoys. Now having revealed all that is on our minds, we hope that Your Majesty will confer with your ministers and consider extending your help. Do not let this violent revolt by barbarians make you lose a long-standing pact with China. We hope for a speedy resolution so that we do not have to tarry for a long time."

The king replied with a letter: "From the time of my forefathers, this country has served the great with sincerity. Therefore, from the time of Emperor Shenzong to that of the Supreme Daoist Emperor we have been considered to belong to the same family; how could we facilely speak of the exquisite favor and lavish rituals [they bestowed upon us]? Now we consider that Heaven and Earth cannot demand us to repay the favor, yet stimulate our mind in mysterious ways, so that we are adamant to repay even one small fraction [of this favor]. Prostrate, I have heard that the two emperors were taken far away and that the whole country is worried and angry. Even though I could not convey my words of comfort in a timely manner, as an

68 The text has 迎請二聖; I have translated literally since it is not entirely clear if the Chinese envoys actually expected that a Koryŏ embassy would be able to take the emperors back with them or that they might simply meet them and at least make the effort of supplicating their return.

official and as a subject, how could my mind be at peace? Moreover, as the emperor is filial and brotherly, as a matter of course the various lords are loyal and righteous. Moving Heaven and Earth and imploring the spirits, Heaven and Earth and the spirits will together render assistance. How could we let the two emperors suffer for long in the desert? Every time we pray for their speedy return to the capital and palace in fulfillment of the hopes of All under Heaven. When the emperor [i.e. Gaozong, 1127-1162] first ascended the throne, one of the first things he did was dispatch close officials to transmit an edict, requesting this insignificant country to cross the sea and go there [i.e. Jin] to request meeting the two emperors. Furthermore on the day of transmitting the edict the chief and deputy envoy instructed everything in detail during a face to face meeting, and then also made sincere pleas in further official letters. How would I dare not respect this order?

However, in the beginning the Jurchen lived scattered across different tribes, and had not selected a leader. Hence they used to subordinate themselves to our country, sometimes joining our envoys to present tribute to your esteemed country. After this they gradually became stronger and frequently caused trouble at the border. Recently they toppled the Great Liao dynasty, and even attacked your esteemed country. Thenceforth their military might grow even stronger, and they forced this insignificant country to declare itself subject. When it came to settling the ritual protocol, everything was to be exactly as for the old relation with Liao, and we had no choice but to follow this. However, not only is it their custom to love war, they are also jealous of our joy in following your esteemed country. Recently they have started building fortifications along the border and garrisoning troops with the clear intention of invading our country. If they hear that we let the [Song] envoys use our roads to enter [their] country, they will most assuredly grow suspicious and cause problems. Moreover, they will surely use a return mission to your country as an excuse to use our roads for a mission to your country. How can we then refuse? Then once they find out the convenience of the sea roads, the security of our country will be imperiled. Also, the Huainan and Zhejiang circuits along the coast would become liable objects for their plundering. If it were not for these things, how would we dare ignore the emperor's command? This is in truth a very serious matter, we would not dare to embellish it. We hope that the chief and deputy envoy will sincerely consider our feelings, and report our intentions even partially to the emperor."

Autumn, seventh month. Assistant Executive in Political Affairs Yi Suk was dismissed. His wife née Kim and his half-brother [Kim] Ingyu quarreled over property without finding resolution. His son Yi On'gyŏng 李溫卿 wrote an anonymous letter with false charges against Kim Ingyu; he wanted to post it to the Censorate at night but was apprehended by the patrolling guards. The father was thus found guilty by association of the son's crime.

Eighth month. The Song envoy Yang Yingcheng and his party returned. The king entrusted them with a memorial of gratitude saying: "The imperial family has encountered many vicissitudes, and the carriages [of the abducted emperors] have been taken on a distant tour. What is even more frightening is that we do not know anything about their whereabouts, so unfortunately there is no way for us to rush to them, and calling at their abode is impossible. To share the misfortune and to help from disaster is the way to show loyalty and release the grudge carried by your sovereign. With scant power and insufficient resources, it is difficult for us to be of any effective help to your sovereign. His Majesty will surely understand the extent of our concern and shame. Your subject has undeservedly succeeded to the throne, and as a result the population has been hit with disasters; natural calamities and bad harvests have left people and animals depleted. Within we have been beset by treacherous officials who wanted to usurp the throne, and on the outside we are troubled by a powerful enemy that is still looking for a chance [to attack]. We have barely managed to quell the calamities and made peace with the neighboring state. Although it cannot be called meritorious, we are relieved that there are no major problems. It is not that we do not know that even exerting our modest forces to the utmost in response to this command is the least we can do to repay the favor of successive emperors, but the circumstances are not favorable and it is difficult for us to adapt to this situation. However, we hope that Your Highness will deign to understand the sincerity of our feelings, and will show clemency to your subject in consideration of the difficult situation we find ourselves in. It is truly not because of evasiveness or arrogance. May your benevolent virtue forever be extended [to us], and may you soon recover [the lost territory and emperors] and become whole again .... [69] Pointing to the bright sun we swear this in our minds, and hope that the Emperor and Heaven will shine on us brightly."

At the time Yang Yingcheng and his party kept going to and from [the palace], so the king again replied: "Your esteemed country in the past sent us an order to convince the Jurchen to come to the [Song] court. We then could not help but observe that the Jurchen should not be allowed to spy on China's wealth, and hence did not dare to follow this order. Your court thought otherwise, and then tried to entice them in various ways, bestowing lavish gifts of gold and silk. They thus realized China's empty words, and once their thievish minds were awakened, they rushed far and deep [into the territory of China], pillaging the capital. Our country has been in close contact with the Jin country through the shared border, and knows all too well the phoniness of their feelings. Now if your embassy goes there through our country, we guess that conflicts will arise and the calamity will prevent you from returning. If your embassy goes to them via us, they will certainly return the courtesy [in the form of a return embassy] through us. Moreover they are very good at naval warfare on the great ocean on their eastern seaboard, so they will use the return courtesy mission to inspect and will find out the lay of Huainan and Zhejiang Provinces. If they equip their battle ships and traverse the sea to strike unexpectedly, I am afraid that in the north you will suffer from land battles and in the south from naval battles; so both head and tails will be troubled by enemy attacks. Then the situation will definitely be severe. If it comes to this, even if you come to regret the decision, how can you be saved? This is the reason why our country is not able to honor the edict, so Heaven and Earth be our witness, we do not dare

---

[69] This is only part of the letter that Injong wrote to the emperor. For the full version see KRS 15.32b-34a (Injong 6, 8th month, *kyŏng'o* day).

to embellish our words. No matter how long you hold on to this, in the end we cannot change our position."

Again a day was chosen [for the return journey] and a request was made to accept the return memorial. Yang Yingcheng and the others replied: "The ruler and ministers of your country must be convinced that there will be harm and thus do not accord [with our edict]. You merely wish the envoys to return, this means in the end there will be no permission [to travel to Jin?]." Then they refused to accept the attached memorial, and also refused the habitual banquet and presents and left.

The king dispatched Executive of the Ministry of Rites Yun Ŏni 尹彦頤 to Song to present a memorial: "Recently we learned that the two emperors had to flee the capital. The whole of our country was aggrieved. Now we could not rush there to enquire after their health, merely holding on to our position and displaying the sincerity of a subject. Also, we failed to first raise a righteous army and save the country from its troubles. Now prostrate facing your majesty, who has emerged from the military command post to succeed to the throne of your forefathers, we hope that you together with subjects and the people will be able to welcome the two emperors. When the edict came young and old shed tears, the manifestation of Your Majesty's virtue has been deeply inscribed in people's hearts, both near and far, and your utmost sincerity has moved the spirits. How would there not be a response! The time for the return of the two Sons of Heaven is none other than now!

Yet the dynastic house of your subject is still in disarray in the aftermath of several disturbances. We are ashamed not to have observed celebratory rituals, and instead were humbled by the fact that it was China that first dispatched envoys. Even though the edict was stern and weighty, because of the circumstances it was difficult to honor. Now the Jin state borders us along the Amnok River, and riding the tide of their onslaught on China, they are now threatening to harm their neighbor. They frequently send spies to search for any pretext. If they learn that we lend passage to the embassy then they will certainly respond by provoking an incident. Either they will raise a force to intimidate and rebuke us, or they will use a return embassy as pretext and request to use our roads. These roads are strategically placed, but how can we then refuse them? They are numerous and we are small in numbers, so it is difficult to fight them. If the lips are gone the teeth are cold; how could this not end in disaster! Yet this is not the vexation of a single day; there will definitely be cause for regret later. There are many difficulties to deal with; it is certainly not on account of laziness in our attending to affairs. Prostrate, we hope that you will understand that our minds are full of respectful devotion, so please take pity on the fact that your subject is threatened by invasion. Accordingly, please display a magnanimity of mountains and forests, and restrain an anger like thunder. Fortunately this insignificant country is still intact, so your esteemed country is not without a protective fence. Although we cannot pledge to follow into the footsteps of [Duke Huan] of Qi and [Duke Wen] of Jin, who led the feudatories to respect Zhou, as in the "Tribute of Yu" we do not wish to relinquish Qingzhou and Xuzhou, we take care of this territory."[70]

A royal proclamation[71] said: "I became king at a young age, and my maternal relatives abused power for their own fortune, harming many. They killed Han An'in and exiled Mun Kongmi, Ch'oe Hongjae, and others, more than fifty people in all. The court was emptied [of loyal ministers], and I became isolated and alone. From then onwards many factions were formed, and their harm is beyond measure. Then in the second month of *pyŏng'o* year [1126] close officials and one or two great ministers requested permission to remove them from power. I did not dare refuse this request, but this sparked a violent reaction from their part, setting ablaze palace buildings, government buildings, and storage facilities till nothing was left. I left for Yŏndŏk Palace, and all those who had served or protected me were either executed or exiled. Their evil fires shone bright, and left untold destruction in their wake. Ch'oe Sajŏn then secretly convinced Ch'ŏk Chun'gyŏng to join forces and they

70 Yu gong 禹貢: The "Tribute of Yu" is a chapter in the *Book of Documents*. Yu the Great divided the territory and set the boundaries; though the text mentions Xuzhou, Qingzhou is not mentioned.

71 *Sŏnji* 宣旨: this term is not often used in the *Koryŏsa chŏryo*; it may have the meaning of being addressed to the whole country rather than to officials.

devised a plan to purge the evil rebels and restore peace to the Ancestral Shrine and the Altar to the Gods of Earth and Grain. Their merit cannot be forgotten, so it is fitting that officials should write [their names] next to the upper merit subjects of the back wall of the Samhan [shrine]."[72]

The king travelled to the Western Capital. The monk Myoch'ŏng and the Local Acting Vice-director Paek Suhan, calling themselves experts in the Yin-Yang arts, had deluded the masses with spurious and unorthodox theories. Chŏng Chisang, also someone from the Western Capital, deeply believed these words and said that the basic karma of the capital had been depleted; moreover, the palace buildings had all been reduced to ashes, while the Western Capital had royal energy: the king should therefore move there and make it the capital. He then planned with the close official Kim An, saying: "If we support the ruler in moving to the Western Capital and turning it into the supreme capital, we should become Merit Subjects Reviving the Dynasty;[73] this will not only enrich us in this life, it will also be a limitless blessing for our descendants." Thus they egged each other on. The close officials Hong Isŏ 洪彝敍 and Yi Chungbu 李仲孚, and the high minister Mun Kongin 文公仁 and Im Kyŏngch'ŏng tagged along. They then memorialized the throne as follows: "Myoch'ŏng is a holy person, and Paek Suhan is second to him. If you take their advice on all affairs of the country and then implement what they advise without fail, then government will be accomplished and all affairs will be achieved, and the country will be safe." They then went around all officials to obtain their signatures. Only Executive Kim Pusik, Assistant Executive in Political Affairs Im Wŏnae, and Transmitter of Edicts Yi Chijŏ refused to sign. After the letter was presented, although the king harbored doubts, since everybody around hum strongly argued for it, he had no choice but to trust them. Then Myoch'ŏng and the others advised the throne "Your subjects have observed the location of Imwŏn Station 林原驛 in the Western Capital and conclude that it is what Yin-Yang specialists call a great flower shape. If you establish the

72 Samhan hubyŏk sanggongsin 三韓後壁上功臣.

73 Chunghŭng kongsin 中興功臣.

palace there and move into it, you will unify the All under Heaven; Jin will surrender and come to offer tribute, and thirty-six countries will become your consorts." Hence the royal progress.

Ninth month. The king dispatched Yi Yu 李愈 to Jin to offer congratulations on the Tianqing Festival.

The king ordered the state councilors who had traveled with him to establish together with Myoch'ŏng and Pak Suhan the new palace at Imwŏn Station.

Im Kyŏngch'ŏng was made Vice-commissioner of the Security Council.

Winter, tenth month. Royal Commissioner of Pacification for the Southeastern Sea Chŏng Ŭngmun reported: "In the three counties of Myŏngjin 溟珍, Songbyŏn 松邊, and Aju 鵝洲,[74] the pirate Chwasŏng 佐成 and others, 820 people altogether, came to submit and register themselves. In Samgi County 三岐縣[75] of Hapchu we already established two places for them to settle called Kwihu and Ch'wian,[76] and in Ŭiryŏng County 宜寧縣[77] of Chinju we established a settlement called Hwasun 和順 to house them." All the officials gave felicitations.

The king returned from the Western Capital.

The king dispatched Vice-minister of Personnel Ch'oe Yu 崔濡 and Vice-director of the Office of Regalia Song Kŭn 宋覲 to Jin to express gratitude for the message of congratulations and to present local products.

Eleventh month. The king dispatched Yu Wŏnsŏ 俞元胥 to Jin to give thanks for the birthday wishes, and Kim T'aek 金澤 to give new year congratulations.

Imwŏn Station was moved to make way for the new palace. The king ordered Palace Attendant, Office Chief Kim An to supervise the corvée labor. At the time the cold weather had started, and the people were dissatisfied and grumbled.

---

74 These were all located on Kŏje-do, South Kyŏngsang Province.

75 Now Samga-myŏn in Hapch'ŏn, South Kyŏngsang Province.

76 Kwihu-jang 歸厚場, Ch'wian-jang 就安場: the suffix "chang" refers to a special administrative unit.

77 Modern Ŭiryŏng-gun, South Kyŏngsang Province.

Twelfth month. Yun Ŏni returned from Song with an edict saying: "I recently sent an embassy to speedily reach a distant land; since my father and brother have been transported to a distant place, I miss them like the river and mountain looking at each other. Since you did not lend right of way, my worry for their safety has become even more acute. For the sake of old favors as a liege country, I was hoping for passage through your territory. Then suddenly a memorial arrived with your remonstrance; it was formulated with utmost sincerity, and after contemplating it for a few days, I inwardly sighed. Looking back, I realize that filial and fraternal thoughts, no matter how much I want them to be put into practice, yet we cannot ignore considerations of what might happen in the future, and hence we should do our utmost in [considering] human feelings. Having taken note of your respectful diligence, please do not forget to safeguard the border country."

Ch'oe Sajŏn was made Assistant Executive in Political Affairs, and Han Ch'ung was appointed Vice Commissioner of the Security Council.

Jin dispatched Surveillance Commissioner for the Jurisdiction of Jinzhou Si Gude 司古德 and Vice-director of the Office of Imperial Regalia Han Fang 韓昉 with an edict, the context of which can be summarized as follows: "The Song Supreme Emperor Zhao Ji and the minor emperor Zhao Huan have, we considered, betrayed grace and lost trust. Therefore we have subjugated and taken them prisoner. Recently we summoned them to court and personally exposed their wrongdoings. However, crimes can be forgiven, and stupidity can be pitied, so in the end we did not terminate them. Yet we could not bear that their names were not correct and their words not obedient. Thus they were given new titles. Zhao Ji was demoted to Duke of Muddled Virtue, and Zhao Huan to Duke of Doubly Muddled Virtue. We considered that this changed situation ought to be reported." They also bestowed robes, silk, silver utensils, and other presents.

Si Gude and the others then personally delivered an oral report, which was roughly as follows: "We received the following letter from the Security Council, 'according to the imperial proclamation regarding Baozhou's territory [that was sent to you], an earlier edict promised that there was no intention of reclaiming [Baozhou], and told your country that it could uphold the old system and maintain the royal house. Hence the court did not begrudge the land and specially cut it off and bestowed it. After that, a few years elapsed, but your country still did not submit a pledge, and clung to the aforementioned prefectures and fortresses. How can this accord with principle? Moreover the households that were threatened to come there or fled [there] were rather numerous, so saying that they have almost all died is hard to understand. If your country is indeed sincere in serving the great, then you should immediately submit the pledge to our court. Then we can in return send a pledge edict and at the same time give other instructions and draw the border, we will be lenient in all affairs to establish a long-lasting relationship.'"

The king replied: "Listening to this instruction, I cannot suppress my feelings of gratitude and shame. Afterwards I will send a memorial to report [on the outcome of our deliberations]."

Injong seventh year [1129]

Third year of the Jianyan era of Song, seventh year of the Tianhui era of Jin

Spring, first month. Jin dispatched Surveillance Commissioner for the Jurisdiction of Ningzhou Yang Gongxiao 楊公孝 to offer congratulations on the king's birthday.

Vice-commissioner of the Security Council Han Ch'ung died. He was strong of character and outspoken, devoted to learning and able in composition. In political affairs he was honest and loyal, and wherever he went he became famous and established merit.

The new palace in the Western Capital was completed.

Second month. The king travelled to the Western Capital and moved into the new palace. At the time there were some who memorialized the throne, urging the king to call himself emperor and use his own era name;

some requested to forge an alliance with the Qi state[78] and jointly attack Jin and annihilate it. Those in the know disapproved of this. The followers of Myoch'ŏng made all kinds of glib promises, but in the end the king did not listen to them.

Third month. The king moved into Kŏllyong Hall 乾龍殿 of the new palace and received the congratulations of his officials. Myoch'ŏng, Paek Suhan, Chŏng Chisang and the others said that as soon as the king sat in the hall, they heard the sound of music in the sky. How could this not be an auspicious sign about the new palace? Then they drafted a congratulatory memorial and requested the state councilors to sign it. The state councilors replied: "We may be old, but we are not deaf. There never was any music in the sky. You can deceive men, but Heaven shall not be deceived." Thus they did not comply. Chŏng Chisang angrily told them: "This is an extraordinary omen. This should be recorded in the historical drafts to show to later generation. It is truly regrettable that you great ministers are like this." In the end no memorial was submitted.

The king gave a banquet for the officials.

Because the people of the Western Capital were exhausted due to the construction of the palace, the granaries were opened to provide relief, and taxes for the year were exempted.

The king returned from the Western capital and declared an amnesty. He also bestowed food and wine upon the aged, filial sons and grandsons, chaste wives and righteous husbands, widows and widowers, orphans and lonely, and those afflicted by serious or terminal disease in the prefectures and counties they passed through, and also bestowed presents commensurate to rank, and remitted taxes for the year. The attending officials and the civil and military officials of the Western Capital, and the officials and clerks who had managed the construction of the new palace, were all promoted by one rank, and below even servants and slaves were shown favor.

---

78 Qi 齊: This probably refers to the state of Great Qi, a puppet state created by the Jin in late 1129 to act as a buffer between Jin and Southern Song. It only lasted till 1137. Since it was allied with Jurchen, the proposal for Koryŏ to forge an alliance with Great Qi shows the ignorance of the Myoch'ŏng faction. See Franke, "The Chin Dynasty," 230–232.

The king attended the sacrifices to past sages at the Royal Academy, and presented two silver basins and thirty bolts of fine silk. He then went to Tonhwa Hall 敦化殿 and ordered Superintendent of the Academy Kim Puch'ŏl to lecture on the chapter "Against Luxurious Ease" in the *Book of Documents*. He also made Royal Recording Secretary Yun Ŏni and the academy students ask questions. The king bestowed food and wine upon the state councilors, close officials, academy officials, and students. All the academy officials and students presented their felicitations to the king.

Summer, fourth month. The king received a bone of the Buddha at Taean-sa 大安寺 and enshrined it in Indŏk Palace.

Fifth month. Royal Recording Secretary Yun Ŏni, Junior Reparationer Chŏng Chisang, and Senior Policy Monitor Kwŏn Chŏk presented a memorial[79] on the successes and failures of contemporary policies. The king received it with pleasure.

Lady Im was invested as queen.

A decree read: "The way of former kings consisted of establishing correct punishment and clearly dividing the official positions; as for the way of wearing caps and the dress code, high and low were distinguished, and noble and base did not mingle. Therefore the noble did not harass [those below] and the base did not dare to transgress. Hence people's hearts and minds were settled! The virtues of yore decayed, and the law has deteriorated with the times. There are no gradations in dress and people do not have a sense of measure and frugality. When T'aejo founded the country, he was modest, frugal, and virtuous, only thinking about the long-term project [of the dynasty]. He implemented the laws of China, and strictly forbade the barbarian Khitan customs. Now from the court above to the people below, everybody competes in ostentatiousness, and follows the barbarian Khitan customs. That this tide cannot be turned back is truly lamentable. Now I hope to lead the way in reforming these debased customs. In things such as carriages and clothing, the luxurious should be discarded and the essence upheld. Ah, you dukes, ministers, and lords, may you respect and implement

79 Note that it is a *so* 疎 rather than *p'yo* 表

my intentions!"

Sixth month. The Royal Secretariat-Chancellery petitioned: "A man named Yu Chŏng 劉挺 from Ch'ungju killed his father. The magistrate of the shepherdship as well as the local clerks failed to edify the people. They should all be tried and the prefecture should be demoted to the level of district." The king asked his officials for advice, and they said: "According to the *Rites*, during the time of Duke of Ding of Zhulou 邾婁定公, there was someone who killed his father. He was killed and his house was destroyed and turned into a pond.[80] This is all it says, as for demoting a prefecture to a district, there is no precedent in the ancient laws." The king followed this advice [and did not demote Ch'ungju to a district].

Autumn, seventh month. *Chŏngch'uk* day, first day of the month. Venus was visible during the day traversing the sky for fifteen days altogether before disappearing.

Eighth month. The king went to the library and ordered Transmitter of Edicts Chŏng Hang to read the *Collection of the Loyal and Righteous from the Song Dynasty* (*Songchao zhongyi ji* 宋朝忠義集). Before this, the king wanted to use some time off from political affairs for lectures and study with academicians. They used the house of Director of the Chancellery So T'aebo next to Such'ang Palace as a library, gathering various writings there and then ordering Superintendent of the Academy Kim Puch'ŏl, Assistant Office Chief at the Ministry of Rites Im Wan 林完, and various other Confucian officials to take turns staffing it.

Because of the continuing rains, prayers for clear skies were held a mountains and rivers [shrines] and Buddhist temples.

Intercalary [eighth] month. The king dispatched Ch'oe Kwan 崔灌 to Jin to give felicitations on the occasion of the Tianqing Festival.

Ninth month. On *pyŏng'o* day, the first day of the month, there was a solar eclipse.

A Hundred Seat Assembly was held at Pŏbwang-sa for three days, and orders were given to feed 30,000 monks in the capital and throughout the

---

80 *Li ji*, "Tan Gong xia," 201.

country.

Winter, tenth month. Commissioners were separately dispatched to two border circuits of the northeast to encourage the officials and clerks at all the fortresses, inquire about the people's state of health, and inspect military equipment.

Eleventh month. The king dispatched Ho Inyŏng 胡仁穎 to Jin to offer new year's congratulations and No Yŏnggŏ and Hong Yag'i to present a pledge memorial, saying: "When your embassy came, bending down low for the stern instructions delivered, we could not help trembling and lost our composure when we heard the command. We could not help but observe that according to the *Rites of Zhou*, the manager of covenants[81] oversees the stipulations of covenants and treaties. When the vassal countries do not cooperate, or the people disobey the orders, he curses their lack of fidelity, nothing more. When it came to the waning years of the Spring and Autumn period, the various countries in their mutual exchanges were full of envy and doubt, so it was not possible to rely on trust, hence only the covenant pledge was emphasized. Therefore poets ridiculed the frequent covenants, and the master favored attending to the orders [of the supreme ruler].[82] Respectfully we submit that the supreme virtue of Your Highness the Emperor outshines that of previous emperors, and your great trustworthiness illumines All under Heaven, brightly opening the path to unification of the four directions. The great countries were trembling in fear, while the small countries were embraced by its grace. Now considering that this small polity of ours, wedged in a small corner of the earth, still happened to learn that a true man had arisen, and was the first among all countries to travel to the court to give felicitations, hence managed to evade the punishment like that of Fangfeng[83] and rather obtained a reward like Yifu.[84] Various small

---

81 *Simeng* 司盟: see *Zhou li*, "Qiuguan sikou," 79.

82 This appears to be based on the *Xunzi*, "Da lüe," 77.

83 Fangfeng 防風: mythical person who assisted Yu the Great in controlling the waters. At a vital meeting he was however three days late, and was executed by Yu. See e.g. *Kongzi jiayu*, "bian wu."

84 Zhu Yifu 邾儀父: Yifu is the courtesy name of Zhu Angong 邾安公 (d. 678 BCE). See *Zuozhuan*, first year of Duke Yin, 16th year of Duke Zhuang. See Durrant, Lee, and

mistakes you benignly overlooked, instead treating us with rare ritual, and bestowing upon us this marginal land; you also instructed us on how to offer tribute. As your esteemed court did not give any indication to the contrary, how would this vassal country have any divided loyalties? With stern edicts continuously arriving, how would we dare not accept them? Respectfully, it is fitting to pledge the righteousness of the ruler-subject relation, and through the generation fulfill the role of screen. Our loyal and trustworthy mind is like the bright sun. If we change our mind, may the gods kill us."

On *kyŏngsin* day [the 16th] day there was a thick fog, so that it was dark during the day.

The king recalled the Duke of Taewŏn, Wang Hyo, who had once been driven away by Yi Chagyŏm.

The king dispatched Mun Kongyu to Jin to offer thanks for the congratulations on the king's birthday.

Twelfth month. A grand inspection [of the troops] was held in the eastern suburbs.

The Duke of Taewŏn, Wang Hyo, was made Concurrent Director of the Department of Ministries, Supreme Pillar of State; Ch'oe Chasŏng was named Assistant Executive in Political Affairs; Mun Kongin was designated Intendant of the Department of the Chancellery; Im Kyŏngch'ŏng was installed as Associate Administrator of the Security Council; and Yi Chunyang 李俊陽 was appointed Vice-commissioner of the Security Council.

Injong eighth year [1130]

Fourth year of the Jianyan era of Song, eighth year of the Tianhui era of Jin

Spring, first month. Jin dispatched Liu Bian 劉汴 to congratulate the king on his birthday.

Schaberg, *Zuo Tradition*, 6–7, 177. Zhu was a small domain in the state of Lu, which had a covenant with the lord of Lu; this is probably what is being referred to here.

Summer, fourth month. Song dispatched Lieutenant Promoting Martiality Wang Zhengzhong 王政忠 with the following edict: "As we know, you succeeded to a long line of kings that have cherished equalizing culture and norms [with China], and now have sent us an embassy to express the wish to present tribute. Perceiving your devout loyalty, free of any other designs, this is something that can be presented to the spirits without shame. Hearing about this wish to attach yourself through diplomatic relations made us sigh in admiration of your good plans. Looking back on the last years, there were truly many disasters, with the strong enemy shaking everyone in the Central Plains. They already penetrated deep into our land, but having raised an army this is far from over. We have moved the defensive forces temporarily to the area of the Lakes and Rivers, but if an embassy comes under these circumstances, we are afraid that the officials will not be alerted. Awaiting the end of the border alarm, you should inquire for the right time to resume relations. Just as the hostel for the envoys to Jin was removed to make way for the carriages,[85] we hope that there will be no regrets. We do not wish to close the gates and refuse the envoys as the Han did.[86] Please understand our mind of longing and the sincerity of our thoughts."

On the *chŏnghae* day [the 16th] day king made sacrifices in the Ancestral Shrine.

Administrator of the Security Council Yi Chuyŏn, Vice Censor-in-chief Im Wŏnjun 任元濬, Censor of Miscellaneous Affairs Hwangbo Yang 皇甫讓, Attendant Censor Ko Tangyu 高唐愈, Palace Censor Mun Kongwŏn 文公元 and others presented a memorial that discussed corruptions of the day. The king adopted two or three things from it.

Pak Tongju 朴東柱 and thirty-one others passed the composition test of the civil service examination.

---

85 This refers to an incident where Zichan, on a mission for the Duke of Zheng, protested the shabby reception by demolishing the wall of his hostel to make place for his carriage. See *Zuozhuan*, 31st year of Lord Xiang (542 BC). Durrant, Lee, and Schaberg, *Zuo Tradition*, 1279.

86 This probably refers to the Han emperor Wu's refusing of Xiongnu envoys, but I could not trace a precise reference in the *Han shu*.

The hermit from East Mountain, Kwak Yŏ, died. When young he studied diligently, and mastered letters, Daoism, Buddhism, Medicine, Yin-yang thought, archery, horse riding, playing the zither, *paduk*,… there was nothing he did not master. After passing the examinations he advanced through several offices, reaching that of Assistant Office Chief at the Ministry of Rites, from whence he retired to Kŭmju. When Yejong became king, he summoned him for the sake of old friendship and always kept him close, frequently talking and laughing with him informally, or matching verse couplets. In order for him to be able to spend a long time in the palace and since [otherwise] he might want to escape and roam freely, the king gave him a separate residence outside Sŏhwa Gate. But as Kwak Yŏ firmly requested to retire, he granted him a house on Yaktu Mountain 若頭山 in the east of the capital, which he called East Mountain Studio 東山齋. One day the king travelled incognito to the mountain studio but Kwak Yŏ just happened to be in the city that day. The king dallied for a long time, and then wrote a poem on the walls before leaving. When the king came to the mountain studio the next time, he held Kwak's hand and made him compose the reply verse on the spot. This is the degree of favoritism Kwak received from the king. When he died the king dispatched close officials to make sacrifices and ordered Chŏng Chisang to make a "Record of the Mountain Studio" and establish a stele [on which the text would be inscribed]. Kwak Yŏ never married, but when he was prefect of Hongju 洪州[87] he had an affair with a female entertainer. When his tenure was nearly over, he made her drink a potion and falsely say that the immortal had left. He secretly took her with him to the capital, but when her features faded he sent her back. Furthermore when he was in the mountain studio he was often accompanied by female slaves or concubines, making him the object of ridicule at the time.

Sixth month. Executive Kim Puil thrice requested retirement on account of illness. He was instead appointed Acting Grand Marshall, Intendant of the Department of the Palace Library, Pillar of State. Kim Pusik was made Administrator of the Finance Commission.

---

87 Modern Hongsŏng-gun, South Ch'ungch'ŏng Province.

The National Academy petitioned: "In recent years the quality of the classics examination takers has regressed, forcing us to select fewer than thirty candidates for the academy. Besides education, concurrently we should send out instructors, one of the level of rank 3 to 6, and one of the level of rank 7 or lower, to encourage learning." The king followed this.

Autumn, seventh month. All the students of the National Academy went to the palace to deliver the following letter: "Your subjects surreptitiously learned that the Censorate had petitioned that the National Academy was nurturing too many scholars, leading to waste in provisions; they requested a reduction in the number of scholars, letting only some remain, i.e. those accomplished in conduct and the academic program, and to expel the rest. Your subjects find this regretful for the country above us. Cherishing learning and fostering talent are the fundamentals of ordering the country. From the Three Ancient Kingdoms of China down to the present, the government of former kings necessarily made this their foremost task, because they knew what was basic. Formerly our Confucius, despite not gaining office, roamed around in the four directions, fostering 3,000 disciples. Duke Wen 文公 [Han Yu 韓愈, 768–824] of the Tang once served as magistrate of Chaozhou 潮州, a minor prefecture. Yet he said 'this prefecture's learning has been derelict for a long time, I have never heard of anyone of accomplished learning presented to the court, this is our prefecture's disgrace.' He then ordered the *xiucai*[88] *Zhao De* 趙德 to manage the prefectural academy and gather students, providing their food through his own salary. How much more for our country, which has enjoyed the riches of the Samhan for a long time, and has plenty of people. If the schools foster talent, then the customs and culture will be at once transformed, and the Way achieved. Now the number of students at the nation's academy barely reaches 200. If there are officials who consider this an expense and wish to do away with it, how can this accord with our ruler's intention of esteeming the Way and cherishing Confucianism? Moreover Buddhist temples and Daoist monasteries are all

---

88 *Xiucai*: refined talent, a term for someone who passed the first degree of the Chinese civil service examination.

around in the center and the provinces, and who knows how many thousands, nay tens of thousands of people dodge the corvée labor and idle there with full bellies! The officials never even considered this yet want to get rid of the way of helping the world. This is neither speech conducive to the public good, nor the supreme reasoning. We request that Your Majesty rejects and does not use [this memorial to reduce the number of students]." The king acquiesced.

The king brought the Buddha bone into Chunghwa Hall.

The historians comment: "When Xianzong of Tang received a bone of the Buddha in the palace, Han Yu vehemently remonstrated, arguing that the more diligently emperors served the Buddha, the shorter their reigns would be. Now as for serving the Buddha, this is done to seek blessings and long life. Those who advocate it appear loyal, while those attempting to block it appear disloyal. In the end this led to the disaster of Chen Hongzhi's 陳弘志 depravations,[89] and the tribulations of the Tang dynasty really started from this. However, in this case Han Yu's attempt at blocking was actually an act of extreme loyalty, while those encouraging the emperor to receive [the relic] were extremely disloyal. These are the mistakes of previous generations, so later generations should guard against following in their tracks. Despite the king's wisdom he still did not heed this warning, welcomed the putrid bone and enshrined it within the hallowed palace halls. What was he thinking? After this the evil monk Myoch'ŏng caused successive calamities due to his revolt in the Western Capital. It was only thanks to the combined efforts of loyal ministers and righteous soldiers that the revolt was eventually quelled. As for serving the Buddha to procure blessings, where in effect are these blessings? That the Tang managed to get over the calamity of Chen Hongzhi was due to diligence, integrity, and benevolence, owing to the fact that the emperor employed wise people who pitied the people. Where did Buddha

89 Chen Hongzhi 陳弘志 (d. 835) was a powerful eunuch at the court of Emperor Xianzong (r. 805-820), and was widely rumored to be behind the emperor's death in 820. The worship of the Buddha bone in the palace against which Han Yu remonstrated took place in 819. After penning his famous essay against the Buddha Bone, he was exiled to Chaozhou.

help in this?"

The king demoted Attendant Censor Ko Tangyu to Assistant Office Chief at the Ministry of Works. Earlier when Yi Chagyŏm was in charge, he took avail of the advice of the mountain monk Sŏnsŏ 善謂 to repair Honggyŏng-wŏn 弘慶院.[90] The monk rector Chabu 資富 and the administrator for Suju, Pong'u 奉佑, were in charge of these works. They drafted local men, which greatly harmed the prefecture and its counties. After Yi Chagyŏm was defeated, Chabu was implicated and exiled to an island. Only Pong'u, thanks to his connections to eunuchs, luckily managed to be restored to his position. Ko Tangyu stubbornly insisted that this was not right and thrice sent memorials urging for his dismissal. For this he was demoted.

Eighth month. The king dispatched Ch'oe Chae 崔梓 to Jin to offer congratulations on the Tianqing Festival.

The king traveled to the Western Capital.

Ninth month. The king ordered the organization of the Kat'ap'agu deity[91] ritual at Honggyŏng-wŏn and the Prajñā ritual at the Military Selection Bureau, each lasting two times seven days. This was in accordance with Myoch'ŏng's words.

The pagoda of Chunghŭng-sa 重興寺 in the Western Capital caught fire. Someone asked Myoch'ŏng: "The reason you, Master, requested the king to travel to the Western Capital is to suppress calamities. Then how come there is this great calamity?" Myoch'ŏng was flustered and could not reply. He lowered his head for a long time, then shook his fist and raised his head saying: "If the king would have been in the supreme capital [i.e. Kaesŏng]

---

90 This temple and its guesthouse were established by Hyŏnjong in 1026. A stele written by Ch'oe Ch'ung still remains in Ch'ŏnwŏn, South Ch'ungch'ŏng Province, on the place where the temple stood; it is known as the *Pongsŏn Hŏnggyŏng-sa kalgibi* 奉先弘慶寺碣記碑.

91 Kat'ap'agu 呵吒波拘: this is likely either a newly made term or a seriously garbled form of an Indian deity. While the first two characters have the meaning of "to rebuke, scold," the last two can form part of the transliterated form of Vakkula, a disciple of the Buddha known for his strict observance of discipline, thanks to which he never suffered from disease and lived very long.

then the calamity would have been bigger than this. Now that he has travelled here the calamity occurred on the outside, and His Majesty is safe." Those who believed in Myoch'ŏng said: "So it is, how can we not trust this!"

Winter, tenth month. The king returned from the Western Capital and declared an amnesty. He reduced this year's taxes of the prefectures and counties he had passed through, and gave a banquet for the elderly, filial sons and grandsons, chaste wives and righteous husbands, widows and widowers, orphans and the single, and the severely and terminally ill, and bestowed presents commensurate with rank. He also ordered Ch'ŏk Chun'gyŏng's wife and sons to gather in one place.

An invincible ritual was held at the Military Selection Bureau for three times seven days, again following the words of Myoch'ŏng.

The king gave a banquet for the state councilors in his official residence, and asked about and discussed government affairs till late at night.

Eleventh month. The king dispatched Vice-commissioner for Audience Ceremonies Yi Chŏ 李䛖 to Jin to give thanks for the birthday wishes to the king, and Intendant-secretary at the Department of Royal Clan Affairs Ch'oe Yunsuk 崔允淑 to give new year felicitations.

Policy Critic An Chiksung and others sent a memorial discussion contemporary politics.

Twelfth month. The king decreed to his attendant officials that each should select one talented person without office.

Officials of the third rank and upwards, remonstrance officials, and attendant officials were gathered at the Department of Ministries to record the crimes of Yi Chagyŏm and Ch'ŏk Chun'gyŏng and their sons and grandsons, and these were then stored at various relevant offices.

The king dispatched First Office Chief at the Department of Ministries Kim Tan to Jin to request that the search for the populations assigned to Poju be suspended.

Mun Kongin was made Assistant Executive in Political Affairs; Kim Pusik was named Executive in Letters; Im Kyŏngch'ŏng was appointed Intendant of the Security Council; Yi Chunyang was designated Associate Intendant of the Security Council; and Im Wŏnae was appointed Vice-commissioner of the Security Council.

Injong ninth year [1131]

First year of the Shaoxing era of Song, ninth year of the Tianhui era of Jin

Spring, first month. Jin dispatched Li Julie 李鋸烈 to give felicitations on the king's birthday.

Censor of Miscellaneous Affairs Chŏng Chŏm 鄭漸 and others sent a memorial discussing the successes and failures of contemporary politics.

Second month. The king bestowed a large residence upon retired executive Ch'oe Sajŏn and an edict of praise.

The Duke of Chean, Wang Sŏ 王偦, died. When Yi Chagyŏm seized power, he was suspicious of the royal family, and petitioned to have the Duke of Taebang and the Duke of Taewŏn removed from their positions. Wang Sŏ then requested to have his security guards taken away, shut himself in, never received guests, and indulged in alcohol. Thus hiding himself from society, he escaped harm.

Third month. The king ordered the civil officials who partake in the daily audiences, as well as officials of the Hallim Academy, Office of Historiography, National Academy, Pomun-gak, Directorate Generate of National Affairs, Capital Military Command, Directorate-General of State Visitor Reception and Departure, Recording Officers of the Field Army, and Staff at the Reserve Corps, together with military officials of rank 4 and higher, to each present a letter on the stakes in military and government affairs.

Senior Policy Advisor Chŏng Chunhu 鄭俊侯 and Intendant of the Censorate Yi Chuyŏn and others presented a memorial on current affairs.

The king ruled that no trees ought to be cut [outside the season] and no young animals or eggs killed, that abandoned corpses should be gathered and buried, and that the Eastern and Western Courts of Great Charity and the

Disaster Relief Shop should be repaired so as to save the people from illness.

It was forbidden for the students [of the State Academy] to study Daoist books.

Summer, fourth month. Vice-director of the Palace Attendants Kim An petitioned: "I obtained a holy writ according to which Paek Suhan petitioned that the trinity of Heaven, Man, and Earth is right as should be, and his report is to be transmitted to the attending officials." The report was copied into three versions, one for the Department of the Royal Secretariat-Chancellery, one for the Censorate, and one for the other relevant offices. The drafters of royal edicts required each to discuss this. It was reported: "Paek Hansu calls himself the disciple of Myoch'ŏng and deceives the people with strange and unorthodox theories. People like Paek Hansu, Chŏng Chisang and even Mun Kongin call themselves saints. This talk about the trinity is of the same kind."

The Song Chief Merchant Zhuo Ying 卓榮 came to report: "From Zhejiang to the Hebei region, everything is now almost at peace. The emperor is temporarily residing in Yuezhou and has changed the era name from fifth year of Jianyan to the first year of Shaoxing." The king told the state councilors: "Formerly Hou Zhang and Gui Zhongfu came to request aid, but we could not comply. Then Yang Yingcheng wanted to us to give right of passage to Jin, but again we did not comply. Methinks that since the time of my ancestors, we have established good relations and been rewarded with munificence and grace, yet twice we refused their command. How is this acceptable in terms of trust and righteousness?" Ch'oe Hongjae and the others all agreed that an envoy should be dispatched to report; this was deemed convenient.

Within the Imwŏn Palace in the Western Capital, everywhere the footprints of birds could be found, from the sand on the steps in the courtyard to the dust hidden in deep corners. People took this as a sign that the buildings would soon become derelict and a gathering place for wild animals.

Fifth month. The king ordered that during the first audience of the first month of each season the officials should be made to read the calendar.[92]

The Department of Royal Secretariat-Chancellery petitioned: "Now for the repair of the palace it was ordered that the state councilors of the Chancellery and Security Council were to supervise the construction work. This is what is called 'nine shepherds for ten sheep.' The number of supervisors should be reduced." The king agreed. He then made Executive Ch'oe Hongjae, Assistant Executive in Political Affairs Mun Kongin, and Intendant of the Security Council Im Kyŏngch'ŏng supervise the labor.

The craftwork of patterned silk embroidery was halted for ten years across the country.

The king ordered all officials to copy T'aejo's "Warning to the officials" to instruct their sons and grandsons.

It was forbidden for commoners to wear gauze and silk trousers, or to ride horse in the capital. Slaves were forbidden to wear leather belts.

On *ŭlch'uk* day [the 30th] Venus was visible during the day, and its course continued to be visible during the day for 100 days.

Sixth month. The Commission for Deliberations on Divination[93] reported: "Recently lay and monks have mingled together in groups they call ten-thousand Buddha fragrant followers.[94] Some chant or read sutras and make all kinds of spurious claims; in some temples the monks sell alcohol and scallions [or other pungent plants normally forbidden to monks]; some carry arms and commit evil, dancing and playing around. It is clear that they violated customs and degraded moral norms. We request that the Censorate and the Golden Bird Division inspect and clamp down on this." The king agreed.

As there was drought and hunger in Yŏmju 塩州,[95] grain from the

---

92 *Siryŏng* 時令: according to the dictionary, this refers to the twenty-four solar terms, important especially for agriculture. Probably what is intended is the *wŏllyŏng* 月令 or scheduled events, rituals, and other important court dates.

93 Ŭmyang hoeŭi so 陰陽會議所: this is the only occurrence of this term,

94 Manbul hyangdo 萬佛香徒: the *hyangdo* is a well-known organization in Koryŏ, a kind of local group of devotees whose existence is often attested through monuments commemorating the ritual burial of incense in the hope of Maitreya's advent.

95 Modern Yŏn'an, Hwanghae Province.

Yongmun granary was moved there for relief.

The king decreed: "According to the *[Zuo] Tradition*, 'in order to make the country flourish, regard the people as your children; for the country to perish, regard the people as wild sesame.' Hence the rulers of old had a compassionate mind towards the people, and practiced a compassionate government. Last winter trees were felled in the three provinces to build the palace, and many died during the corvée labor. It is fitting that official grain be provided to comfort the bereaved wives and children."

Assistant Executive in Political Affairs Yi Suk died.

Autumn, seventh month. The Great Granary was opened to provide relief for the poor.

Fifty-six people awaiting the death penalty had their sentences reduced after investigation, and were exiled to inhabited islands after a beating.

On account of his age Director of the Chancellery Yi Kongsu thrice requested to retire. The king gave permission.

Eighth month. The king summoned the state councilors of the Chancellery and Security Council to his official residence to discuss state and military affairs.

The astronomical officials reported: "Recently shamanism has become all the rage, and their licentious rituals increase by the day. Please order the officials to chase away all the shamans." A decree approved this. All the shamans were greatly worried by this and gave more than 100 silver bottles in bribes to the powerful elite. These elites[96] reported: "Ghosts have no shape, so we cannot know whether they are real or false. I'm afraid we cannot know this." The king agreed, and applied the ban loosely.

The king dispatched Palace Attendant Yi Chungbu to construct a wall for Imwŏn Palace in the Western Capital and to establish Eight Sages Shrine[97]

96 Kwŏngwi 權貴: Given the awkwardness of the sentence, it is possible that an official by the name of Kwŏn Kwi is meant here.

97 P'alsŏng-dang 八聖堂: as becomes clear from the names of the deities, these were not established deities but rather a strange blend that was evidently concocted by Myoch'ŏng. I have given possible translations, but the idiosyncratic nature, mixing Buddhist beings with native mountains and other elements, makes this far from straightforward. It appears that the first part of each title can be interpreted as a local manifestation (*sujŏk* 垂迹) of an

in the palace. The first [of the sages] was called State-protecting White-head Peak Venus Immortal [with the] True Virtue [of] Mañjuśrī Bodhisattva; the second Dragon-encircling Peak Six-perfections Venerable [with the] True Virtue [of] Śākya Buddha; the third Moon-city Peak Heavenly Immortal [with the] True Virtue [of] Sarasvatī;[98] the fourth Koryŏ Pyongyang Immortal [with the] True Virtue [of] Dīpaṃkara;[99] the fifth Koryŏ Mongmyŏk Immortal [with the] Virtue [of] Vipaśyin;[100] the sixth Pine-peak Thunder-lord Hermit [with the] True Virtue [of] Vajrapāśa[101] Bodhisattva; seventh Cauldron-city Peak Spirit [with the] True Virtue [of] Lakṣadeva;[102] eighth Head-peak Heavenly Woman [with the] True Virtue of Upāsikā Acalā.[103] All their portraits were drawn following Myoch'ŏng's weird explanations. Kim An, Yi Chungbu, Chŏng Chisang and others thought that these ways of sages would benefit the country and extend the dynasty.

The king dispatched as Envoy in Charge of Ritual the Audience Usher Yu T'oe 庾僓 to the Eastern Capital of Jin. But as the Jin emperor was on his way to the Eastern Capital, he did not achieve his mission [to meet the emperor] and returned.

The king dispatched Office Chief at the Ministry of War Wang Su 王洙 to Jin to give congratulations on the Tianqing Festival.

Ninth month. The king made Yi Kongsu Merit Subject Promoting Loyalty, Guarding the Altar and Equal in Virtue, Acting Grand Preceptor,

---

original Buddhist entity (*ponji* 本地), which is given in the second part. There seems to be a strong influence of esoteric Buddhism, yet no clearly discernible logic.

98 I here interpret Taebyŏnch'ŏn 大辨天 as 大辯天, a translation of Sarasvatī. In Indian mythology the wife or female energy of Brahmā, goddess of eloquence, learning and music; one of the seven gods of luck. See Digital Dictionary of Buddhism: http://buddhism-dict.net/ddb/index.html [hereafter DDB].

99 Yŏndŭngbul 燃燈佛: one of the Buddha's of the past, the twenty-fourth predecessor of Śākyamuni. Note that Koryŏ is here spelled Kuryŏ 駒麗.

100 Pip'asi 毗婆尸: Vipaśyin, the first of the seven Buddhas of the past.

101 Kŭmgangsaek 金剛索: *vajrapāśa* refers to the diamond lasso, an attribute of Acala and other deities of the esoteric pantheon [DDB].

102 Nŭkch'ach'ŏn 勒叉天: *lakṣa* means red, or red dye [DDB]. I could not find which deity this might refer to.

103 Pudong up'ai 不動優婆夷: one of the fifty-three spiritual guides of the boy Sudhana in the *Avataṃsaka sūtra*. [DDB]

Probationary Grand Mentor, and Director of the Chancellery; Ch'oe Sajŏn was designated Probationary Grand Marshal, and Executive Chief of the Chancellery; Kim Hyang was named Merit Subject Guarding the Altar, Acting Grand Marshal, Probationary Minister of Works, Chief of the Chancellery and Jointly Executive Chief of the Royal Secretariat; at the same time all were retired. Ch'oe Hongjae was made Minister of Personnel; Ch'oe Chasŏng was appointed Chief of the Royal Secretariat and Jointly Executive Chief of the Royal Secretariat-Chancellery; Mun Kongin was appointed Executive Chief of the Royal Secretariat; Kim Pusik was made Assistant Executive in Political Affairs; and Ch'oe Yu and Im Wŏnae were designated Associate Administrators of the Security Council.

Intendant of the Chancellery An Chiksung, Junior Policy Critic Yi Chung, Drafting Advisor Im Chon, Senior Reparationer Ch'oe Ham 崔諴 and others protested: "The Secretary to the Envoy in Charge of Ritual to the Eastern Capital, Ch'oe Pongsim 崔逢深, is originally a military official, hence acting as secretary is not within his remit. Also, he habitually makes crazy remarks and has the intention of slighting the Jin. Hence we are afraid that he will cause trouble, and submit that he should not be dispatched." They prostrated themselves in front of the Office for Audience Ceremonies, and insisted for three days yet the king did not allow their petition. Ch'oe Pongsim was allied to Chŏng Chisang, and esteemed Myoch'ŏng as a master. Once he told the king "If you wish to pacify the Samhan, without the three sages of the Western Capital, nothing can be done together." This refers to Myoch'ŏng, Paek Suhan, and Chŏng Chisang. Also he once loudly stated "If the country grants me one thousand stout soldiers, I can enter Jin and take their ruler prisoner and offer him to you." Such were his crazy and deluded statements.

Kim An and others requested to hold a sacrificial rite at Eight Sages [Shrine] in Imwŏn Palace. Chŏng Chisang drafted the text [for the rite]: "Fast without hurrying, arriving without going, this is called the numinous obtaining of the one; this is none other than being yet non-being, being real yet empty: this is what is called the original Buddha. Now the Heavenly Mandate controls the myriad beings, and the virtue of the earth ruling the four quarters. Finally in the middle of Pyongyang we divined this shape of the Great Flower, and constructed a palace in accord with Yin and Yang. In its midst we enshrined the eight immortals, starting with Whitehead[104] as the first. With a bright shining light such as this, it is as if the wonderful response is apparent before our eyes, how mysterious! Even though the supreme true appearance cannot be represented, the quiescence is the true virtue, this is nothing but the Tathāgata [i.e. Buddha]. Having ordered the painting of their likeness with due ornaments, knocking on the shrine gates we pray that you accept these offerings." Such were their absurdly worded deceits.

Winter, tenth month. The king travelled to Pŏbwang-sa and organized the Hundred Seats Assembly for three days. He ordered that 30,000 monks across the country should be given a maigre feast.

On *kyŏngjin* day [the 17th] a royal prince, Wang Ho 王晧, was born.

Eleventh month. The king dispatched Office Chief at the Ministry of Rites Ko Tangyu to Jin to give thanks for the birthday felicitations, and Chief Steward at the Bureau of Royal Clothing Yi Chungyŏn to give new year felicitations.

Twelfth month. The king again dispatched as Envoy in Charge of Ritual Yu T'oe to the Eastern Capital of Jin.

Ch'oe Hongjae was granted the title of Merit Subject Assisting in Principle, and made Acting Grand Mentor.

104 Paektu 白頭: Now identified with Mt. Paektu, but it may have designated other peaks and was also associated with the planet Venus (T'aebaek 太白).

10. Injong (II)

Injong tenth year [1132]

Second year of the Shaoxing era of Song, Tenth year of the Tianhui era of Jin

Spring, first month. Jin dispatched the Surveillance Commissioner for the Jurisdiction of Yongzhou, Gao Chengshan 高成山, to congratulate the king on his birthday.

Construction on the palace [in the Western Capital] was started by laying the foundations. Myoch'ŏng required three or four state councilors, including the Executive Ch'oe Hongjae, as well as managers of corvée and clerks all to line up in official dress. A ritual was conducted, with four generals wearing armor and [holding] swords standing in the four directions; 120 soldiers with lances, 300 with torches, and twenty with candles forming a circle; and with Myoch'ŏng occupying the middle, holding four threads of white hemp 360 feet long, pulled from four directions. He himself said: "This is the Supreme One Jade Curtain Pace Ritual.[1] Sŏn Master Tosŏn 道詵禪師 transmitted it to Kang Chŏnghwa 康靖和, and Kang Chŏnghwa transmitted it to me. Being advanced in age I made sure to transmit it to Paek Suhan. This is not something that the masses would understand."

Second month. The king dispatched Assistant Office Chief at the Ministry

1 T'aeil okchangpo pŏp 太一玉帳步法: A literal translation of an otherwise unknown rite.

of Rites Ch'oe Yuch'ŏng 崔惟淸 and Audience Usher Sim Ki 沈起 to Song to present the following memorial: "Respectfully, as is known, we could not rush to ask about the welfare of the two abducted emperors, [as is the duty] of our office, and we also could not personally congratulate Your Highness on your succession at the imperial palace. In *musin* year [1128] the state letter envoy Yang Yingcheng wished to be given right of passage to enter Jin. Although the order was of extreme importance, due to circumstances it was extremely difficult to accept. Shortly after we dispatched an embassy to show our respect and sincerity. Then in *kyŏngsul* year [1130] Wang Zhengzhong came to transmit an edict telling us to wait until the border situation was stable and you would inform us of the time to send envoys. Your subject took your instructions very seriously and did not dare to send envoys to the imperial court. Yet moved by your munificence and sincerity, we earnestly wish to extend our allegiance to you. Hence with a mind as small as crickets or ants we endeavor to announce [our intentions] for the inspection of Heaven. In esteeming the Zhou house we regret not being able to match the merit of the Jin Count;[2] in subordinating to the Han court, we hope not to lose Chosŏn's service of old."

When the king traveled to the Western Capital, Myoch'ŏng, Paek Suhan and others submitted the following report: "The territorial force of the Supreme Capital is depleted, and hence Heaven has rained down disasters and the palace has burned down. [But] by traveling to the Western Capital frequently you will enjoy an endless continuity of the dynasty." The king consulted with his astronomical officials, who all said that this was not the case. Chŏng Chisang, Kim An, and various great officials then said: "What Myoch'ŏng has said are the methods of a sage. One cannot ignore his words." The king then made Myoch'ŏng "Field of Merit Accompanying the Royal Chariot" and added Paek Suhan to this staff of palace officials. When they passed the National Academy, several students came out to meet the

---

2 Chin paek 晉伯: Duke Wen of Jin (Jin Wen gong 晉文公), r. 636-628 BCE. One of the five thearchs (wuba 五霸); his merit to the Zhou is not clear.

king on the road. The student of the Yangjŏng Studio,[3] Ch'oe Kwangwŏn 崔光遠, presented a memorial that discussed contemporary affairs.

When the royal cortege reached the road to Kŭmam Station 金岩驛, they were hit by a violent rainstorm, which suddenly made everything dark. The king's guards stumbled and fell and the king, holding on to the reins of his horse, got lost. Sometimes he fell into the mud, and at other times he hit trees or rocks. The king's attendants lost track of the king, and some among the palace ladies were wailing loudly. Towards evening the rain turned to snow and it became very cold. More than a few of the people, horses, and camels died. Myoch'ŏng said: "I already knew that on this day there would be rain and wind, and I commanded that the Master of Rain and the Count of Wind 'not let the wind blow and rain fall when the royal carriage enters the road' and received their consent. However, the fact that you reneged on your words is deeply resentful [to the gods]." So outrageous were his lies.

Third month. The king gave a banquet for the officials in Kŏnyong Hall.

Yi Chejŏng 李齊挺, an elderly statesman and retired Acting Grand Preceptor of the Western Capital, and others, fifty people in all, presented a memorial requesting that the king adopt new honorary titles as well as an era name. They were following the intentions of Myoch'ŏng and Chŏng Chisang. Chŏng Chisang and the others hence explained to the king "The Taedong River has an auspicious vigor. This is the saliva spit out by the divine dragon; this is a once in a thousand years event. We request that the king above accords with Heaven's mind and below follow the people's expectations, and suppress the Jin state." The king consulted with Yi Chijŏ, who said: "Jin is a powerful country and is not to be taken lightly as an enemy. Moreover, the important officials of the Chancellery and Security Council are guarding the capital, so you cannot listen to the biased opinion of one or two individuals to make such an important decision." The king agreed.

The king went to Kirin-gak,[4] and ordered Supervisor of Education [at the

3 Yangjŏng-jae 養正齋: one of the seven studios established in the 8th month of 1109 [q.v.].

4 Kirin-gak 麒麟閣: The Unicorn pavilion.

National Academy] Yun Ŏni to lecture on the hexagram "Kŏn" [Heaven] from the *Book of Changes*. He also ordered Chŏng Hang to lecture on the chapter "Doctrine of the Mean" from the *Book of Rites*. The king also ordered to set a poetry topic and ordered Professor of the Taehak College Kwak Tongsun 郭東珣 and seventeen others to compose matching poems.

The Envoy in Charge of Ritual from the Eastern Capital of Jin, Wu Yanzhen 烏彦貞, arrived.

The king inspected cavalry and infantry outside Tanbong Gate 丹鳳門.

Summer, fourth month. Probationary Grand Marshal and Intendant of the Palace Library Kim Puil died. His ancestors belonged to the royal family of Silla. When young he studied diligently and passed the civil service examination. When King Yejong established the Pomun-gak, every day he attended lectures or discussions with Confucian scholars on classics or histories. Kim Puil valiantly debated and always found compromise with others, so that nobody regarded him as an adversary; his reputation was very high among his contemporaries. His composition style was both ornate and rich, and for all the edicts and commands of the country he was invariably asked to polish the style. Once he composed the "Closing Ode for the P'algwan Assembly" and when Yejong read it, he was so pleased that he decreed that it should always be used and never replaced. When the Song musician Kui Zhongli 夔中立 came to submit, he was made an official musician. Later he returned [to Song] and intoned the words [of the Ode] to the emperor. When Yi Charyang entered Song [as an envoy] the emperor asked him who had composed the "Closing Ode for the P'algwan Assembly" and praised the beauty of its lyrics.

Since the three brothers Kim Puil, Kim Pusik, and Kim Puch'ŏl all excelled in letters and served the king, Yejong invested their mother as Grand Lady, and ordered his officials to grant her forty *sŏk* of grain from the official stores. However, the mother reasoned that since she was already sustained by her sons' salaries, she already owed an immeasurable debt towards the country, so how could she accept such a shamefully lavish emolument? In the end she did not accept it. After Injong was enthroned, powerful ministers controlled the country. Once the king had killed or exiled them, he made Kim Puil state councilor. Kim Puil suffered from a stroke which weakened him, so he repeatedly sent memorials requesting retirement. The king found it hard to go against his wishes, so he gave him permission. As a person Kim Puil was generous to others, yet frugal for himself. He did not enjoy slighting or criticizing people; also he did not engage in profitable enterprises. His posthumous title was Mungan 文簡.

The king twice made Chŏng Hang, Yun Ŏni, and Chŏng Chisang lecture on the classics. He bestowed upon each of them one horn-encrusted ornate belt. Chŏng Chisang wanted the king to reside in the Western Capital permanently, so he hinted at the remonstrance officials that they should request halting repairs to the palace in the supreme capital. Chŏng Hang twice sent a memorial requesting the ongoing repair of the old palace so that the king could return to the supreme capital. His words were sincere and direct, and the king approved of this.

The king took a dragon boat on the Taedong River. As it was the month in which Yejong's death was commemorated, the musicians did not perform music. Chŏng Chisang petitioned: "The Rites mention commemorative days, but not commemorative months. If there are commemorative months there then should also be commemorative years! Please perform the music in accordance with the expectations of the people of the city." The king complied with this.

Intercalary [fourth] month. The king returned from the Western Capital and declared an amnesty.

Ch'oe Kwangwŏn and twenty-four others passed the composition test of the civil service examination. Executive Ch'oe Chasŏng served as examiner and Executive at the Ministry of Personnel Im Chon served as joint examiner. Im Chon set as the topic for the prose poem composition: "The Sage can form a single family with the whole under-Heaven (聖人耐以天下爲一家)." Officials of the Chancellery protested: "Using the character 'nae 耐' as an old form of the character 'nŭng 能' [in the sentence] means that the word 'nae' is the rhyme, which does not work. Please order someone else to redo the examination." This was not allowed. Hence the king ordered Ch'oe Chasŏng and others to set another topic. The additionally ordered topic was: "The Heavenly Way does not idle and can therefore last long (天道不閑而能久)." The Chancellery and Censorate again protested "According to the *Book of Rites* it is 'The Heavenly Way is not closed off and can therefore last long (天道不閉而能久).' The Korean edition of the 'family instructions' [of Confucius] has 'does not idle' (不閑) rather than 'is not closed off' (不閉). This is a mistake. Now the Examination Office has not verified the correct edition of the classics and has thus relied on an erroneous copy. Please dismiss Ch'oe Chasŏng and the others from office and invalidate this year's selection." The king ordered simply that the classics emendation and essay [papers] be retained and twenty-five people selected from them.

Myoch'ŏng, Paek Suhan and others secretly made a great cake with a void in the middle. They made a hole and filled it with cooked oil, and then sank it in the Taedong River. The oil floated to the surface creating a five-colored film. Paek Suhan and the others said: "The divine dragon has spit its saliva, creating this five-colored film. This is an extremely auspicious sign. Please have all officials submit memorials of congratulation." The king dispatched Executive Mun Kongin, Assistant Executive in Political Affairs Yi Chunyang and others to inspect this. At the time there was someone specializing in the oiling of saddle mud guards who said: "When cooked oil floats on the water it has this strange effect." Then they made people good at swimming explore the river and they obtained [the cake] and thus knew it was a deceit.

Fifth month. Censor-in-chief Im Wŏnjun and others requested that this year's roster of successful examinees be rendered void and that the examination be held from scratch. The king did not acknowledge this, and Im Wŏnjun and the others then retired, and the Censorate was empty for seven days as they awaited punishment. Furthermore the National Academy student Chŏng Ŏnbaek 井彦伯 and others, fifty people in all, sent a letter requesting that the examination be redone. The king ordered Supervisor of Education Yi Chijŏ to placate the students, saying: "Slandering the court is a crime that should always be punished; however this time you will be exceptionally pardoned. You should exert yourself and improve your skills and wait for the next examination."

Ch'oe Yuch'ŏng and others returned from Song. The reply decree read: "We observe that even when located in the southern country [i.e. Southern Song] there is a road leading to the eastern border state [i.e. Koryŏ]. Your respectful intention of resuming tribute is praiseworthy. As for your request to partake of our country's culture, again this has been turned over to the councilors in charge. Traveling with the aim of causing an effect is a sign of diligence and sincerity, yet gathering all the liege lords at Tushan 塗山 [as Yu the Great had done] is unfortunately something my virtue does not live up to. The place where the imperial carriage is traveling to should by nature also be the court where the state envoys arrive. Considering that in autumn the border horses are fat[5] and we can hence not let our guard down, the spring tides should carry [the envoys'] boat smoothly and without trouble."

Sixth month. Ch'oe Chasŏng and Im Chon were dismissed from office.

Autumn, seventh month. Ch'oe Chasŏng was reinstated as Chief of the Royal Secretariat and additionally Executive [of the same office].

There was hunger in the capital, and the corpses lined the streets.

Eighth month. There was a great flood, which carried away many homes.

Associate Intendant of the Security Council Im Wŏnae sent the following letter to the throne: "Myoch'ŏng, Paek Suhan and others are given free rein for their treacherous plans; they deceive the people's minds with strange stories. A few high officials as well as some close attendants to the king also deeply believe his words. Above they confound the ruler's ears. I am deeply concerned that there will be an unfathomable disaster. I request that Myoch'ŏng and his ilk be executed on the market place to cut off the evil shoots." The king did not respond.

Senior Policy Monitor Pak Chŏngyu 朴挺蕤 prostrated himself at the Office for Audience Ceremonies with a petition on [current] affairs for three days. The king did not respond.

On *imja* day [the 25th] a comet appeared.

---

5 Mabi 馬肥: I.e. well fed and ready to be used for the cavalry.

Winter, eleventh month. Executive Chief of the Royal Secretariat Mun Kongin and Palace Attendant and Assistant Office Chief at the Ministry of Rites Yi Chungbu took the king's robes to the Western Capital for use in implementing of a dharma rite. At the time Myoch'ŏng had said "The king should be residing in the Taehwa Palace 大華闕 for a long time, but if he does not do so, then dispatch a close official to prepare the ritual to install the royal throne, and place the king's robes there with utmost reverence as if it were the king himself. Then the blessings will be the same as if the were there personally." This he called "implementing a dharma rite."

The king ruled: "Despite my lack of virtue I succeeded to the dynastic throne just as it showed signs of entering a decline, with successive revolts and changes. Therefore I exerted myself day and night in the hope of achieving a revival. There is an [old] injunction that says 'If you wish to accumulate several myriad years, you first need to obtain a *kapcha* day[6] on the winter solstice. When the sun, moon and five planets all gather in the north[7] it is called the first primordial,[8] the beginning of the calendar.' This year the winter solstice falls on the sixth of the eleventh month. The middle of the night corresponds to *kapcha* and the first of the three primordials. Now is the time to reform the old and establish the new. Thus I ordered the officials to find the bequeathed injunctions of old sages and establish Taehwa Palace in the Western Capital. Hark! You great dukes and ministers, and all the officials should together engage in the policy of reform so as to create a foundation that will last eternally."

The king ruled: "I gained the throne when still young, and was not ready to deal with the many family disasters. Even though I wished to conduct good government, I had no respite, and completely lacked the virtue to see me through. Unsurprisingly, in all I endeavored I could not handle Heaven's mind [bestowed upon me]. Therefore such strange events as mountains crumbling or

---

6 *Kapcha* 甲子: the first term of the sexagenary cycle.

7 Cha[bang] 子[方]: the northern quadrant in a 24-section division.

8 Sangwŏn 上元: first of the three primordials (samwŏn 三元), key dates in the Daoist calendar in particular. The *sangwŏn* is normally considered the first full moon of the new year (i.e. the 15th of the first lunar month).

springs suddenly emerging occurred again and again. Trembling and scared, it was as if I had fallen into a deep pond. Yet relying on the assistance of wizened loyal and righteous ministers I managed to correct my past mistakes and renew government. Looking back, due to my lack of competence, whether they were small or large affairs, the cases where I did damage to the country were many. But what I regret the most is the affairs of *pyŏng'o* year [1126]. Then the power of my maternal family surged, and they committed all kinds of egregious actions, even plotting sedition: they were secretly plotting for the throne. The foundations laid by my ancestors were very nearly lost. Therefore I had no choice but to listen to the advice of the officials and mete out punishment according to the law. Aah! Killing one's relatives in the name of righteousness, this is something that also occurred in antiquity. Yet loving the benefice of one's relatives is a natural affair. Whenever I think my mind is so pained that it is as if my bones are cut. Furthermore, as to the so-called associates of the [Yi Chagyŏm] party, even though they did ally themselves with the powerful, how would they all have planned together the revolt? Therefore I issued a number of lenient orders, yet officials did not comprehend my mind and launched ceaseless memorials. This truly disserves to be punished for failing to act as dutiful subjects; it went as far as instigating people's minds [to do bad] and harmed the atmosphere of harmony. Apart from those who were banished and those whose misdeeds were judged and whose names are written down in the historical records, all those records of the judicial processes that are kept in relevant government offices should be burnt in the outer courtyard so as to wash away the crimes and mistakes of the past and open the way for self-renewal.

As for Ch'ŏk Chungyŏng, his crime was extremely heavy, yet his merit is also well documented. The law should distinguish between merit and crime. The office land should be restored to his sons. Apart from Ch'ae Sŏk and Yi Hujin, wives and children should not be proven guilty by association. This is the right of the sons or wives of criminals not to be implicated automatically. According to the *Book of Documents*, "If an order is issued it should simply be executed, not countered.' Since *pyŏng'o* year I have issued some four edicts that officials refused to implement. If the subject does not execute the sovereign's order, the national order will slowly become imbalanced. I am deeply concerned about this. Henceforth if there is anyone who dares to raise this question again, he will be tried for insubordination."

Twelfth month. Kim Pusik was made Probationary Minister of Works, Chief of the Royal Secretariat, and jointly Executive Chief of the Royal Secretariat-Chancellery. Yi Chunyang was appointed Vice-director of the Department of Ministries; Yi Ch'ongnin 李寵麟 was made Assistant Executive in Political Affairs; and Ch'oe Yu was appointed Intendant of the Security Council.

Injong eleventh year [1133]

Third year of the Shaoxing era of Song, Eleventh year of the Tianhui era of Jin

Spring, first month. Jin dispatched Gao Chenke 高陳可 to congratulate the king on his birthday.

Second month. The king invested his oldest son Wang Ch'ŏl 王徹 as heir apparent. Later he changed his name to Wang Hyŏn 王晛.[9]

The king dispatched Han Yuch'ung 韓惟忠 and Yi Chijŏ to Song to give thanks for the grace bestowed. When they reached Hongju they encountered a wind that could not be overcome and so they returned.

Third month. Because of the investiture of the heir apparent the king issued an amnesty.

Summer, fourth month. Executive Chief of the Royal Secretariat Ch'oe Chasŏng retired. Mun Kongin was appointed Minister of War; Ch'oe Yu and Im Wŏnae were appointed Assistant Executive in Political Affairs; Im Kyŏngch'ŏng was made Junior Vice-director of the Department of Ministries; Im Wŏnjun was appointed Joint Intendant of the Security Council; Ch'oe Yuch'ŏng was designated Vice-commissioner of the Security Council.

The king ruled: "The incessant sunshine has caused lots of damage, so

9 This is the future King Ŭijong (r. 1146–1170).

that the drought has now turned into a disaster. I fear that the administrative orders are burdensome and the punishments too cruel. Perhaps those who have been incarcerated can no longer bear their suffering. The capital officials, together with the resident governors of the two border circuits, the military commissioners, and the royal inspectors of local government should personally inspect the prisons, and should show leniency to those imprisoned for heavy crimes and set free those imprisoned for minor crimes."

Fifth month. A decree read: "Owing to my lack of virtue I encountered many disasters; the palace burnt down and the granaries are empty. In administering government my skills are insufficient, and the institutions have all gone awry. People's hearts are getting coarser and viler by the day, and the livelihood of the people is getting more precarious as each day passes. Day and night I live in fear and have no chance to find any rest. Now remonstrance officials are telling me 'In the mountains and fields of the capital area locusts are eating the pine trees. The people of old used to say "When the subjects have a stable salary and position, this will lead to greed, and the disaster of insects eating the roots. When virtue is fickle, this will lead to trouble, and the [disaster of] insects eating leaves. If those without virtue are not driven away, the insects will eat the main trunk. When the right agricultural season is not observed, the insects will eat the stem. When evil is covered up, disasters will arise and the insects will eat people's minds." Formerly Emperor Wu of Jin 晉武帝 favored Jia Chong 賈充 and Yang Jun 楊駿 and gave them positions; hence locusts arose, which are the consequences of not getting rid of those without virtue. In the beginning years of the Datong era of Liang (535–545), locusts ate the leaves of pine trees and cypresses. According to Jing Fang, "Eating a salary without providing benefit [to the people], Heaven's sagely transformation displays this through insects. Insects have no benefit to the people and only eat everything."[10] This corresponds to simply enjoying a state salary without

[10] Jing Fang 京房 (77–37 BCE) was a scholar from the Western Han who specialized in the *Book of Changes*. This passage is attributed to his *Yi fei hou* 易飛候 by the *Sui shu* (fasc. 23, treatises 18, five elements 2), which quotes the exact same passage.

giving anything in return. We request that you promote the wise and demote the unworthy. Please be decisive and have no doubts.' This is merely a case of the officials attributing good to the ruler and mistakes to oneself: it is merely a confession of being in the wrong. As for my pursuit of principle [in government], even though it is desperate and my virtue is in truth not sufficient, the fact that government is corrupt and the people destitute is [due to the fact that] the crafty are promoted and the loyal and diligent driven out. This is the disaster that Heaven above has brought down on us. Now the state councilors and assorted dignitaries quote from old texts and list many instances of correct, brilliant even, reasoning—how would I not happily follow these? It is not that I do not know about all the greedy, profit-seeking, violent, and weak among the central and local officials; however, punishing without first trying to identify is not something that I can bear to do. The relevant officials should earnestly instruct and edify so that they may reform themselves. If they continue in their evil ways for a long time without attempting to change, then regardless of whether they are relatives or strangers, high or low, they should be tried according to the law. If there are those who remain pure and are exceptional in their dedication to their work, they should be rewarded and given a new position."

Because of the drought the markets were moved.

The king went to Sungmun Hall 崇文殿 and ordered Executive Kim Pusik to lecture on the *Book of Changes* and the *Book of Documents*. He then had Hallim Academician and Recipient of Edicts Kim Puŭi 金富儀, Administrator of Memorials Hong Isŏ 洪彛敍, Transmitter of Edicts Chŏng Hang, Royal Recording Editor Chŏng Chisang, Supervisor of Education Yun Ŏni, and others ask questions on difficult passages. Kim Puŭi is none other than Kim Puch'ŏl.

The king ordered Kim Puŭi to lecture on the chapter "The Great Plan" [of the *Book of Documents*], and Yun Ŏni to lecture on the "Doctrine of the Mean."

Sixth month. The king ruled: "Recently the way of the world has slowly deteriorated, and the customs have become frivolous. There is no filial piety or friendship; some cast away the orphans or young, their wives or concubines; some have fun while mourning their parents, or entrust the corpses of their parents provisionally to temples; there are even those who do not bury them for several years. The local officials should be ordered to inspect and punish those cases. When people are too poor to conduct proper funerals, the officials should provide burial expenses."

The remonstrance official Ch'oe Yuch'ŏng and others sent a memorial to the throne that accused Executive Chief of the Royal Secretariat Ch'oe Hongjae of "being greedy and cruel, violating the law at will. He is a great harm to the country. Recently, the country has been plagued by drought and locusts for a long time. This is due to the fact that the greedy and evil are in office, fleecing the country and making the people ill. He should be demoted and punished in response to Heaven's warning." He was then demoted to Probationary Minister of Works, Junior Vice-director of the Department of Ministries. Yi Chunyang replaced him.

Autumn, seventh month. The king went to Surak-dang 壽樂堂 and ordered Kim Pusik to lecture on the hexagram "kŏn" 乾 [Heaven] from the *Book of Changes*, and then also on the hexagram "t'ae" 泰 [Peace].

Eighth month. Kim Ubŏn 金于蕃 and twenty-four others passed the composition test of the civil service examination.

Ninth month. The king dispatched Deputy Director of the Foreign Relations Office Chŏng T'aek 鄭澤 to Jin to give felicitations on the Tianqing Festival.

Retired Director of the Chancellery Yi Wi died. He was the son of Director Yi Chŏnggong. The son succeeded the father as Minister of Personnel.[11] His daughter married Im Wŏnae and gave birth to a royal consort. His house was prosperous yet he was stingy and hoarded goods.

Winter, tenth month. A Hundred Seat Assembly was held. The king ordered central and local officials to prepare meals for 30,000 monks.

---

11 Ch'ongjae 冢宰: one of the six ministers of Zhou; this became a term for the minister of personnel (吏部判事), although according to Hucker this occurred only in the Ming; in Koryŏ it may have signified another high office, or may be synonymous with state councilor (Hucker 1632)

The king personally gave a banquet for old people aged 80 and over, filial sons and grandsons, chaste widows and righteous husbands, widows and widowers, orphans and the solitary, as well as those with serious or fatal disease or disability, and bestowed presents commensurate with rank.

Eleventh month. The king dispatched Office Chief Kim Yŏngsŏk 金永錫 to Jin to give thanks for the birthday wishes and Sin Hwaji 愼和之 to offer new year's felicitations.

Intendant of the Chancellery Yi Chung, Attendant Censor Mun Kongyu, and others sent a memorial saying "Myoch'ŏng and Paek Suhan are both devious people. Their words are bizarre and untrustworthy. Close officials Kim An, Chŏng Chisang, and Yi Chungbu, as well as the eunuch Yu Kae 庾開 are working in cahoots with them. On several occasions they have arranged official positions for each other, and have called [Myoch'ŏng and Paek Suhan] holy people. There are even prominent officials who follow and trust them. Therefore Your Highness does not think it doubtful. Upright people and straight officials all resent them as enemies. We request that you immediately reject them and remove them." Their words were very serious and direct. The king did not respond. Thereupon Yi Chung and the others retreated from work until punishment was delivered.

Twelfth month. From *pyŏngsul* day [the 6th] there was fog that lasted five days. The trees were covered with ice.

The king summoned the censoring and remonstrance officials to resume their duties.

Kim Pusik was appointed Minister of War, and Im Wŏnjun Administrator of the Security Council.

Injong twelfth year [1134]

Fourth year of the Shaoxing era of Song, twelfth year of the Tianhui era of Jin

Spring, first month. Jin dispatched Grand Master of Remonstrance Zhang Hao to congratulate the king on his birthday.

On *muin* day [the 28th] a white rainbow intersected the sun.

Myoch'ŏng was made triple great overseer, intendant of the Water Clock Court,[12] and bestowed the purple [robes].

Second month. The king traveled to the Western Capital.

The royal carriage reached the Taedong River and the king boarded the dragon boat. He gave a banquet for the officials when a strong wind suddenly arose from the north, shaking up tents and utensils. The weather grew very cold, and the king swiftly got up, changed clothes, and took his carriage into the palace.

Third month. The king moved to Taehwa Palace, but when the palanquin was about to set off a violent wind kicked up dust so that neither men nor horses could advance.

On *kyŏngsin* day [the 10th] it snowed.

The king returned from the Western Capital.

The *Classic of Filial Piety* and the *Analects* were distributed among small children in the streets.

Summer, fourth month. Im Wŏnae was appointed Executive Chief of the Royal Secretariat.

On *musul* day [the 19th] there was rime.

On *kapchin* day [the 25th] there was a violent thunderstorm, and Registrar at the Bureau of Construction and Maintenance Ch'oe Hyosuk 崔孝淑 was struck; also, more than forty trees were struck by lightning.

Fifth month. There was a drought.

Hŏ Hongjae 許洪材 and twenty-eight others passed the composition test of the civil service examination.

A decree read: "Recently there have been many abnormalities in the weather, and the drought is very serious. Day and night I worry and do not know what to do. Hence I consider that all you officials of the third grade and above should send a letter stating the abuses of government and the

12 Samjung taet'ong, chi Nugak-wŏn 三重大統, 知漏刻院: these are all ad-hoc titles, and the sole occurrence of them. The *Koryŏsa* entry identifies him as Chŏngsim 淨心, which is apparently a name Myoch'ŏng later took. KRS 16.28a-b.

hardship of the people without hiding anything."

Supervisor of Education Im Wan sent a memorial, the contents of which is roughly as follows: "Your subject once stated, 'Giving advice is not difficult, but listening to it is; listening to advice is not difficult, but acting on it is particularly difficult.' Hence it is said 'In serving his lord, if the subject's words are sincere and straight, then he is not employed and his life is in danger; if they are not sincere and straight, then it is insufficient to clarify the Way.' Formerly during the time of Emperor Wen of Han, it can be said that the All under Heaven was in peace, yet Jia Yi 賈誼 (200–168 BCE) was still said to have ailed in anguish and cried, heaving a long sigh.[13] Recently, natural phenomena are irregular, so Your Majesty, in awe of the Heavenly Mandate wants to listen to straight advice, issuing an edict seeking such words. This is a blessing for myriad generations!

Your subject once read Dong Zhongshu's 董仲舒 (179–104 BCE) essay, which says, 'When a country is about to lose the Way, Heaven will first display disasters and strange phenomena to castigate and warn. If [the people] do not reflect [on their mistakes], Heaven again sends strange signs to warn and frighten them. If they still do not know how to change themselves, this will produce harm and defeat. From this we can see that the Heavenly mind loves the human ruler and wishes to stop the chaos he is suffering from. By criticizing a world that has completely lost the Way, Heaven shows its complete support [for the king] and pacifies the world.'[14] The way for the ruler to respond to Heaven's censure above, how could it be anything but forcing himself to truthfully respond? The 'Biographies' [of the *Han shu*] says: 'Responding to Heaven is done by truthfulness, not by artfulness.'[15] What is called truthfulness is virtue; what is called artfulness is such things like the current Buddhist or Daoist rituals. If the ruler of men cultivates virtue to respond to Heaven, without expecting blessings they will arrive of themselves. If he does not cultivate virtue and handles affairs

13 On this see his biography in *Han shu*, chapter 48.

14 This can be found in Dong Zhongshu's biography in the *Han shu*, chapter 56.

15 *Han shu*, chapter 45, biographies of Kuai, Wu, Jiang, and Xifu (蒯伍江息夫傳).

with empty artfulness, then not only will there be no benefit, it will be even an insult to Heaven. The *Book [of Documents*] says, 'Heaven does not have private feelings, it merely helps does who are virtuous.'[16] It also says, 'It is not the millet nor the blood [used in sacrifices] that is fragrant, bright virtue is the only thing fragrant.'[17] That which is called 'virtue,' how could it be obtained any other way but by the ruler's applying of his heart-mind and then practicing it in daily affairs. Heaven is far removed from men, and cannot be persuaded by words: it repays the good with blessings and the evil with disaster, just like a shadow [follows its object] or an echo [follows a sound].

During the past few years, disasters have occurred frequently and hunger has been rampant. Recently a white rainbow pierced the sun, and in the month of prime Yang [fourth month] lightning struck. Such particular anomalies are Heaven's warnings, they suffice to show how Heaven's mind cherishes the ruler, wholeheartedly wishing to support him, keep him safe and complete him. Your Majesty, how can you merely serve by maigre feasts or sacrifices, and not bend your body [towards Heaven] and cultivate and practice [virtue] in response to Heaven's warning? This way is not different from the bequeathed injunctions by T'aejo; it is contained precisely in Munjong's old statutes.

As the bequeathed customs and remaining virtue of Munjong's reign are not so distant from the present, sometimes when I hear about it from an elder, unwittingly tears flow, wetting my sleeves. Thus I observe that Munjong personally practiced frugality and uprightness, and promoted those of wisdom and talent to high offices, not employing those who were not right; that he did not transfer power or authority to those close to him. Even if it were a very close relative, those without merit he would not reward without reason. If one among those close to and beloved by him would be found guilty, that person would face punishment. As for eunuchs or attendants, he would choose those who were diligent and careful, not more than a few tens of them would be assigned to cleaning. As for palace attendants, he would

16 See the "Book of Zhou," "Charge to Zhong of Cai" in the *Shang shu*.

17 See the "Book of Zhou," "Jun chen" in the *Shang shu*.

select those who worked hard and had ability, not more than twenty of them. All those assigned to office did their utmost; useless offices were abolished and the work simplified. Costs were saved and the country was prosperous, and hence the granaries were full and people had enough. It was called a time of great peace, and he was truly a sage ruler of our dynasty.

Recently, everything has been turned upside down. The number of functions is twice what it used to be, and arrogance and opulence grow from day to day; any sense of shame has disappeared. Those wielding power harm and extort the people; to add insult to injury, the people are burdened by heavy taxes and labor duties, and the people harbor deep resentment. If Jia Yi were to see this situation, how could he stop at deeply sighing, shedding tears, and wailing? Prostrate, I beseech Your Majesty to execute good government with utmost sincerity, and to suppress the crafty and cheating people that surround you; to cut off the bizarre theories of Yin and Yang, and instead to carefully live each day so as to obtain blessings that last for a myriad generations without end. Your subject has observed Myoch'ŏng, and thinks that he is simply using deceit to cheat his ruler above him. He is no different from Lin Lingsu of Song.[18] Lin Lingsu deceived the emperor with unorthodox Daoist teachings, thus speeding up the disaster and chaos. This is something that Your Majesty has personally heard of. Since Your Majesty cherishes and believes Myoch'ŏng, those officials surrounding you, even up to great officials, elevate and promote each other, treating him as a saint. The roots [of this evil] are deep, and its branches strong, so it is very difficult to uproot. Since the start of levying corvée labor [for the construction] of Taehwa [Palace], it has already been seven or eight years, and disasters have accumulated. Heaven definitely does this to warn and enlighten Your Majesty through this. Your Majesty, how could you begrudge one villainous official and go against Heaven's will? I wish that you would execute him in response

---

18 Lin Lingsu 林靈素 (1076-1120) was a Daoist master who exerted great influence on Emperor Huizong. See Paul R. Katz, "Lin Lingsu," in Fabrizio Pregadio ed., *The Encyclopedia of Taoism* (London: Routledge, 2008), 657-659. According to his biography (*Koryŏsa* 98), Im Wan hailed from Song. Though it is not specified when he came to Koryŏ, it seems that he may have personally observed Lin Lingsu.

to Heaven's warning and to comfort the people."

The king prayed for rain at the Ancestral Shrine, the Altar for the Earth and Grain Deities, and the [shrines for] mountain and river [spirits]. He also visited the portrait hall for T'aejo, and informed him while shedding tears: "Your subject truly is without virtue. I cannot comply with the laws and government of previous kings, and hence my reign is insufficient to illuminate Heaven and Earth, to harmonize Yin and Yang. For this reason Heaven has rained down disasters. In the third month there was snow, and in the fourth month, frost. Add to this thunder and lightning, which hit more than forty people and objects. It has not rained for months, and the earth is barren; the corpses of those who died of starvation are lined up for a thousand leagues. The blame truly lies with your subject, not with the people. All I hope for now is to cleanse the mind, repent my wrongdoings, and take the ancestor's injunctions as model. The *Odes* say, 'How would the parents and ancestors bear to see me like this?' Prostrate, I hope that you will look upon your relative with sagacious benevolence, and gather an auspicious numen to invigorate the myriad spirits and let an abundant rain fall. Let me, your small child, together with the officials and the people together receive this blessing; let us eternally rely on the spirits." On this day a pardon was declared.

On *muin* day [the 29th] there was an earthquake and it rained blood in Kwangju.

Sixth month. On *kimyo* day [the 1st] there was an earthquake in the Eastern Capital.

On *sinsa* day [the 3rd] the king went to the Surak-tang in Taemyŏng Palace and ordered Hallim Academician Kim Puŭi to lecture on the "Monthly Ordinances" [of the Book of Rites].

Venus was visible traversing the sky during the day.

On *kapsin* day [the 6th] lightning struck Kŏllyong Hall of Taehwa Palace in the Western Capital.

The king went to Yŏngt'ong-sa and prayed for rain.

The king went to the Surak-tang and ordered Hallim Academician Chŏng

Hang to lecture on the "Seventh month" from the *Book of Odes*.

In Ch'ŏngp'ung County 靑楓縣[19] the water in a big pond turned into blood and flowed into the Han River.

Autumn, seventh month. The king ordered Auxiliary Academician of the Pomun-gak Yun Ŏni to lecture on the "Monthly Ordinances."

The sea channels below Anhŭng Pavilion 安興亭[20] are characterized by several currents clashing; moreover there are many dangerous cliffs everywhere so that ships keep perishing. Someone then proposed to carve a channel on the boundary with Sodae County 蘇大縣,[21] through which the ships could then pass. The king ordered Palace Attendant Chŏng Sŭmmyŏng 鄭襲明 to raise several thousand men in neighboring districts to carve the channel. In the end it could not be achieved.

Eighth month. The king went to Myŏngin Hall and ordered Hallim Academician Kim Puŭi to lecture on the "Charge to Yue" from the *Book of Documents*.

The king dispatched Acting Executive at the Ministry of Rites Pak Kyŏngsan 朴景山 to Jin to give congratulations on the Tianqing Festival.

Ninth month. The king went to Changwŏn Pavilion. At the time Myoch'ŏng's party strongly requested the king go on an inspection of the Western [Capital]. This would greatly aid them in their plans for an insurrection. The king ordered the Chancellery and Security Council to debate this. Kim Pusik argued: "Now a summer lightning struck Kŏllyong Hall, which is not an auspicious sign. And is not the fact that you averted danger in this place [by not being there] further evidence? Now the autumn harvest has not yet been completed, so if the royal cortege leaves, it will

---

19 Modern Ch'ŏngp'ung-myŏn, Chech'ŏn-gun, North Ch'ungch'ŏng Province.

20 This was located on Ma-do, situated at the end of a promontory jutting out west of the T'aean promontory. There is still a harbor called Anhŭng facing Ma-do, and numerous Koryŏ ship wrecks have been excavated near here over the past few decades, showing how dangerous this place was. Several attempts were made to cut a channel through the land bridge between the T'aean promontory and the mainland, but none succeeded. See Vermeersch, *A Chinese Traveler*, 228, 327 n. 848 for the location of this pavilion.

21 This is the only occurrence of this place in either the *Koryŏsa* or *Koryŏsa chŏryo*; it is not known to which locality it might refer.

surely trample on the grains, which is not the way to cherish the people and love all things." Then together with remonstrance officials he sent a strongly worded memorial. The king said: "What was said is exceedingly right, so I would not dare travel to the Western Capital." Then he took the advice of the astronomical official and traveled to Changwŏn Pavilion instead.

Winter, tenth month. On *muja* day [the 13th] a white rainbow pierced the sun.

The king issued a decree exhorting all officials to do their best at their jobs.

Eleventh month. The king dispatched Assistant Office Chief Kim Yŏnggwan 金永寬 to Jin to give thanks for the birthday wishes and Assistant Office Chief at the Ministry of Taxation Yi Sik 李軾 to give new year's felicitations.

From the tenth month to this month Venus was visible traversing the sky during the day.

Twelfth month. Junior Policy Monitor Hwang Chuch'ŏm 黃周瞻, second-guessing the intentions of Myoch'ŏng and Chŏng Chisang, requested that the king declare himself emperor and start using era titles. The king did not respond.

Injong thirteenth year [1135]

Fifth year of the Shaoxing era of Song, twelfth year of the Tianhui era of Jin

Spring, first month. On *ŭlsa* day, the first day of the month, there was a solar eclipse, but due to the cloud coverage it could not be seen.

On *musin* day [the 4th], Myoch'ŏng, Ryu Ch'am 柳旵, the local Executive [for the Western Capital] Cho Kwang 趙匡, and others started an insurrection in the Western Capital. They forged a royal order to imprison the resident governor and his staff, and also sent out a fake Transmitter of Edicts, Kim Sin 金信, to apprehend the Military Commissioner for the Northwestern Sector, Yi Chung, as well as the officers of all fortress armies. All those from the Supreme Capital residing in the Western Capital, regardless of their status, were also all rounded up. They dispatched soldiers to block the Chŏl Pass 岊嶺 road, and also sent out people to various fortresses to threaten and cajole the soldiers. They called their country Taewi 大爲, and the first era name Ch'ŏn'gae 天開, established a bureaucracy, and called their army the Heaven-sent Loyal Righteous [Army] 天遣忠義. Myoch'ŏng, Cho Kwang, and others gathered in Kwanp'ung Hall 觀風殿 and gave orders to the army. They wanted to divide them across several roads and aim directly for the supreme capital. Paek Suhan's son Paek Ch'ŏng 白淸 left the Western Capital for Kaesŏng. A friend of Paek Suhan called him over with a letter saying that the Western Capital had already revolted, so he should extract himself [from Kaesŏng] and come [to the Western Capital]. Paek Suhan reported this letter to the king, who summoned Mun Kongin and showed it to him. Mun Kongin said "I have my doubts about this; it is difficult to ascertain whether this is true, so let's keep this secret for the time being." On *sinhae* day [the 7th] the soldiers Ch'oe Ŏn 崔彦, Han Sŏn 韓善, and others came from Hwangju and reported that "people from the Western Capital had led troops to Tongsŏn Station 洞仙驛, seized Manager of Records Ko Pojŏng 高甫正, and also took the horses from the station and sent them back to the Western Capital. They forbade people from going to or coming from the main capital, so we hid during the day and traveled at night along sideroads."

The king summoned the state councilors to discuss this. He ordered Executive Kim Pusik, Assistant Executive in Political Affairs Im Wŏnae, and Transmitter of Edicts at the Security Council Kim Chŏngsun 金正純 to take up office in the Ministry of War to direct the war strategy to subjugate the rebels. Thereupon he also issued an edict that appointed Kim Pusik and Im Wŏnae as supreme leaders of the Central Army; Kim Chŏngsun, Chŏng Chŏngsuk, No Yŏnggŏ, Im Yŏng 林英, Yun Ŏni, Yi Chŏn 李瑱, Ko Tangyu, and Yu Yŏng 劉英 as their assistants. Minister of Personnel Kim Puŭi was made general of the Left Army, and Kim Tan, Yi Yu 李愈, Yi Yugae 李有開, and Yun Ŏnmin 尹彦旼 as their assistants. Intendant of the Censorate Yi Chuyŏn was made general of the Right Army, with Chin Suk, Yang Uch'ung 梁祐忠, Chin Kyŏngbo 陳景甫, and Wang Su as their assistants.

On *imja* day [the 8th], it was falsely said that the army of the Western Capital had reached Kŭmgyo Station, so the people living in the western suburbs were frightened and all took their families inside the city walls. The king ordered his Palace Attendants Ryu Kyŏngsim 柳景深, Cho Chinyak 曹晉若, and Hwang Munsang 黃文裳 to go and talk to the [rebels of the] Western Capital. The rebels opened the gates and led them to Kwanp'ung Hall. Ryu Ch'am, Cho Kwang, and Myoch'ŏng came at the head of the civil and military officials, all wearing military attire. When Ryu Kyŏngsim and the others reached the gate of the hall, Ryu Ch'am and the others came down from the courtyard and greeted them, asking about the sovereign's health and providing them with food and drink before sending them back with the following words: "Normally we should present a memorial to inform the throne, but due to this sudden visit there was no time to prepare one. Please take this to report." They then handed over a letter which said: "We wish that the ruler would move to this capital. Otherwise there will be a great calamity." Their words were very insolent.

When the king learned that the rebels had faked a decree to raise troops from the two border circuits, he urgently dispatched Chin Suk, Yi Chuyŏn, Chin Kyŏngbo, and Wang Su to divide 2000 soldiers of the Right Army among them and instruct all fortresses in the Eastern Circuit [of the situation] and apprehend the envoys sent by the rebels. He ordered Kim Puŭi to lead the Left Army and move first for the Western Capital.

Jin dispatched Surveillance Commissioner for the Jurisdiction of Guizhou 桂州[22] Gao Chun 高春 and others to congratulate the king on his birthday.

On *kyech'uk* day [the 9th], because Hong Isŏ and Yi Chungbu were regarded as belonging to the Western Capital rebels, they were entrusted with a letter of instruction to be delivered [to the rebels]. Hong Isŏ moved very slowly, taking all of four days to reach Saengyang Station 生陽驛. Afraid, he did not dare to go any further, so he made a station clerk deliver the letter

22 There does not appear to have been a prefecture with these characters in Jin territory; the only Jinzhou attested with these characters corresponds to modern Guilin, Guangxi Province, in southern China.

instead.

The rebels dispatched Acting Supervisor of the Household of the Heir Apparent Ch'oe Kyŏng 崔京 to deliver a memorial, the contents of which was roughly as follows: "Your Majesty, believing the utmost words on Yin-Yang, and examining the secret arts of prognostication, constructed Taehwa Palace, modeling it after the imperial city of the Heaven of Balance.[23] Your subjects identify with Lou Jing's advice,[24] and look forward to a move of the capital such as that executed by Pan Geng.[25] How could you think that your subjects do not know the sovereign's mind and criticize for only thinking of a nice place to live as motive for moving the capital again, and for allegedly obstructing merit and harming affairs? The mind of the people is something to be in awe of, and the masses' wrath hard to stem. If the royal carriage moves here, however, the military action can be ceased." When the memorial arrived, because it was a case of the subject summoning the sovereign, all deemed it right that the messenger should be executed. The king however wanted to stop military escalation and bestowed wine and food upon Ch'oe Kyŏng, as well as presents, and decreed that he should be appointed local Assistant Office Chief at the Ministry of Taxation. Comforting him, he sent him back [to the Western Capital].

On *kabin* day [the 10th], the king summoned the great officials of the Chancellery and the Security Council for consultation; on this day the army was going to march on [to the Western Capital]. Kim Pusik and the other generals convened at the palace to await orders. Kim An and others wanted to win time in connection with their seditious plans, and petitioned: "If you first call a meeting with the Jin envoy to receive the edict and after that dispatch the generals, it will still not be too late." Some reported that Kim An and the others had secretly amassed weapons and had privately coordinated their words to secretly plan something unfathomable. Kim Pusik discussed this

---

23 Kyunch'ŏn 鈞天: middle of the nine heavens, keeping the other eight (at the compass points) in balance.

24 Lou Jing 婁敬: A soldier of the early Western Han who advised Emperor Gaozu to move the capital to Luoyang.

25 Pan Geng 盤庚: name of a Shang era king who moved the capital to Yin.

with all the councilors saying: “The insurrection of the Western Capital has been planned together by the likes of Chŏng Chisang, Kim An, Paek Suhan, and others. If we do not remove these people, the Western Capital will never be pacified.” All councilors completely agreed with him. Then he summoned Chŏng Chisang and the other two to the palace, but secretly instructed Kim Chŏngsun to take three strong men with him and execute them outside the gates of the palace. [After the deed was done] he then reported this to the throne. Some said that as Kim Pusik shared a reputation for letters with Chŏng Chisang, in the course of time he bore a lot of complaints, and then used the plot as an excuse to kill him.

The king ordered Im Wŏnae to stay behind and defend the capital, and then bestowed the battle axe upon Kim Pusik. Before sending him off he said: “I entrust to you everything that happens outside of these gates. However, even the rebels of the Western Capital are still my people, so eliminate their leaders, but take care not to kill much.”

On *ŭlmyo* day [the 11th] the following people belonging to Myoch’ŏng’s party were exiled to a distant island: Ch’oe Pongsim 崔逢深, Ŭm Chungin 陰仲寅, Yi Sunmu 李純茂, and O Wŏnsa 吳元師.

The Central Army reached Kŭmgyo Station when it started to snow heavily. Men and horses were freezing and hungry, and the soldiers’ hearts sank. Kim Pusik then comforted them and provided relief food to the army so that their feelings were settled. A patrolling cavalryman caught a spy for the Western Capital called Chŏn Wŏnjik 田元稷. Kim Pusik released him from his shackles, comforted him and sent him back saying: “You go back and tell the people in your fortress that a great army has already set forth. Those who repent and become compliant [with the established order], I will guarantee their life.”

That day a general from the Western Capital called Ilmaeng 一孟 arrived, giving detailed information about the rebels’ situation. The king rewarded him with an office and gave him a house.

On *pyŏngjin* day [the 12th] Hong Isŏ and Yi Chungbu returned from the Western Capital. Kim Pusik arrested Hong Isŏ because he had used a station clerk to transmit the edict, and incarcerated him in P'yŏngju. He exiled Yi Chungbu to Paengnyŏng Garrison.

Rebels from the Western Capital came to Sŏngju 成州[26] and with a false royal order grabbed and shackled the Defense officials. They then dispersed to people's houses to get food and drinks. The prefecture's people realized they were fake, and struck and killed five or six of them, and took prisoner more than twenty. This was all rapidly reported to the king, who issued a decree praising them, and bestowed silver cases with medicine upon the officials, and silk products on the clerks and officers commensurate with rank. Furthermore the village headman from Yŏnju 漣州,[27] Kang Anse 康安世, and Senior Colonel Kim Ingam 金仁鑑 captured a fake Vice Military Commissioner called Yi Chagi 李子奇, General Yi Yŏng 李英, and more than 600 soldiers. The king issued a letter of instruction to praise them and bestowed brocade and colored silk. When the various castles heard about this they caught or killed more than 1200 rebels from the Western Capital.

On *chŏngsa* day [the 13th] the Central Army reached Posan Station 寶山驛. For three days the soldiers practiced. [Kim Pusik] then gathered all the assisting generals to discuss the strategy. They said "In military operations speed is crucial; we should advance twice as fast and capture the enemy when they are not prepared, so that we may capture those puny little crooks in a matter of days. If we tarry in every place we pass through we will lose the initiative. Moreover, this would allow the enemy the time to come up with a better strategy, so it is not to our advantage." Kim Pusik said: "That is not the case. The Western Capital has been planning this rebellion for five or six years, so their plans must cover everything. We must first make sure that both attack and defense are sufficient and only then make a move. Today if we want to take avail of their unpreparedness, isn't it too late already? Moreover, we now take the enemy too lightly and our weapons are insufficiently ready. Our soldiers might fall into an enemy ambush that has been secretly laid, this is the first kind of danger we face. We are camping

---

26 Modern Sŏngch'ŏn, South P'yŏngan Province.

27 Modern Yŏnch'ŏn, Kyŏnggi Province.

below the stout ramparts; the weather is cold and the earth frozen, and we have not made any defensive fence yet, so there is a chance that the enemy will suddenly seize this opportunity; this is the second kind of danger we are in. Also, I have heard that the rebels have forged royal commands to raise troops from the two border circuits, but several fortresses have not decided a side yet, making it difficult to distinguish true from false. If treacherous people however do respond [favorably to the rebels' fake summons] and inside and outside link up, the roads will be blocked, and the situation would become truly dire. Now the best thing to do is to lead the army through side roads to circumvent the rebels along their backs and seize the military provisions from several fortresses so as to feed the main army. Making [the fortresses] declare their loyalty, we can then make them cut off contact with the rebels in the Western Capital. After that we can boost our numbers and give the troops a rest; thus displaying the country's full force, we can then send an ultimatum to the rebels, whilst slowly approaching them with the main army. This is a failsafe plan."

On *ŭlch'uk* day [the 21st] the Central Army moved its troops from P'yŏngju to Kwansan Station 管山驛. The Left and Right Army all followed one after the other. The Central Army then moved via a shortcut along Saam Station 射嵒驛 and the Sinsŏng pugok 新城部曲 to Sŏngju, where the troops rested for a day. Ultimatums were sent to all fortresses informing them of the intention of punishing the rebels.

On this day the king issued a decree saying: "When still young I was given the reins of government. Not having the talent of discerning the right people, I gave too much credit to one-sided theories by persons of trust, which led to the disaster at the Western Capital. Looking down [to earth] and up [to Heaven] I reflected deeply and could not suppress my feelings of painful remorse. Then you, loyal subjects of the Censorate and Chancellery, and other people of principle at court and beyond, discussed the strategy of pacifying the Western Capital, the failures of government, and my own mistakes. I have nothing to say for myself." The king then ordered palace attendants Audience Usher Chŏng Sŭmmyŏng, Vice Commissioner of the Disaster Relief Store Hŏ Sun 許純, and Director of the Office of Miscellaneous Textiles Wang Sik 王軾 to go to the islands in the sea southwest of the Western Capital and raise a navy of 4,600 people and 140 battle ships. They were to enter the river south of Sunhwa County 順化縣[28] and block the enemy ships.

Kim Pusik sent the military clerk No Inhae 盧仁諧 to call on the Western Capital to convince them again and at the same time to observe the actual situation within the city. Then he led the army to Yŏnju. When they reached Anbuk District,[29] they joined up with Chin Suk, Yi Chuyŏn and the rest [of the Right Army]. Earlier he had dispatched Recording Officer Kim Chaho 金子浩 and others with a royal missive to travel to various fortresses and garrisons in the two border circuits via side roads to inform them of the rebellion at the Western Capital. Although their minds had not yet been made up, when the main army arrived, the fortresses, trembling with fear, welcomed the official army one after the other.

Kim Pusik again sent officials or clerks to the Western Capital to reason with them up to six or seven times. Cho Kwang and the others realized they could not resist, and they wanted to surrender, yet since they realized the gravity of their crimes they hesitated and could not come to a decision. Then the Administrative Assistant of P'yŏngju, Kim Sunbu 金淳夫, entered the city carrying a royal decree. The rebels then cut off the heads of Myoch'ŏng, Ryu Ch'am, and Ryu Ch'am's son Ryu Ho 柳浩. They then made local Director of the Palace Treasury Yun Ch'ŏm 尹瞻, Vice Director Cho Ch'angŏn 趙昌言, Grand General Kwak Ŭngso 郭應素, Junior Colonel Sŏ Chŏng 徐挺 and others go with Kim Sunbu to be tried for their crimes at court.

They also sent a letter to the Central Army saying: "We would like to comfort the troops with mutton and wine, so please decide a date and time."

---

28 Modern Sun'an, South P'yŏngan Province. Since this is twenty km. north of Pyongyang it is not clear which river is being referred to.

29 Modern Anju, North P'yŏngan Province. However, being more than 50 km. north from Pyongyang, this is a very considerable distance from Yŏnju (modern Yŏnch'ŏn, Kyŏnggi Province).

Thereupon Kim Pusik sent Recording Officer Paek Nokchin 白祿珍 to report [to the throne], and also transmitted a letter to the Chancellery and Security Council saying: "The rebels of the Western Capital want to surrender. You should treat Yun Ch'ŏm and the others generously so as to open the path to self-rectification." The State Councilors Mun Kongin, Ch'oe Yu, and Han Yuch'ung told Paek Nokchin: "Your supreme leader did not go straight to the Western Capital, but took a long detour to Anbuk. It is we who urged the king to send someone with an order to surrender, so it is not the merit of your supreme leader. What did you come here for?" Kim Sunbu personally tied up Yun Ch'ŏm and the others and delivered them to the suburbs. The Chancellery and Security Council then dispatched a law official who put them in cangues and iron shackles, bringing them to court and requesting them to be imprisoned. The Censorial officials also requested the highest punishment, but the king would not allow this. He ordered for them to be released from their shackles and brought to him. He gave them wine and food and comforted them. Shortly after [however] they were thrown into prison. The heads of Myoch'ŏng and the other two were put on display on the market place. The king bestowed a decree praising Kim Pusik and granting him silver medicine cases in reward for his merit.

When Cho Kwang and the others heard that Yun Ch'ŏm and the others had been imprisoned, they understood that they would not be able to escape [the same fate], and thus resumed the rebellion. The king dispatched Palace Censor Kim Pu 金阜 and Palace Attendant Hwang Munsang together with Yun Ch'ŏm to promulgate an edict to the Western Capital. Kim Pu and the others, however, rather than saying soothing words and showing a graceful attitude, tried to scare them with shows of authority. The rebels were both resentful and angry.

Second month. The rebels retaliated with violence and killed Kim Pu and Hwang Munsang, together with their attendants. Yun Ch'ŏm, carrying the portrait of T'aejo, tried to escape but he was caught and killed. The rebels defended the city even more strongly.

Kim Pusik sent the Recording Officer Yi Tŏkkyŏng 李德卿 to talk with the rebels, but he too was killed.

On *imo* day [the 8th], there was a halo around the sun and a white rainbow piercing it.

Kim Pusik and his generals swore before the gods of heaven and earth, as well as to the gods of mountains and rivers, stating respectfully: "The evildoers have gathered in the Western Capital to foment rebellion. Your subjects respectfully received the royal summons to lead the army and punish them. We humbly observe that a supreme army conquers through strategy, but a good formation may make a fight unnecessary. If we move into the city with the full force of our army, then innocent civilians will be randomly killed by our swords. This is not the original intention of safeguarding the people and punishing the guilty. We used the plan of resting the army and instead use reason to make the rebellious pliant, and turn misfortune into fortune, and eventually kill the leaders, reaching the palace to mete out punishment. Though it looked good, it turned out not to work. Thus we observe that repeatedly they did not trust the edict, and did not follow them even after repeated attempts. Envoys met with disaster just after arriving, such degree of wrongdoing is difficult to accept. Spirits of Heaven and Earth, we hope that you will secretly keep the people safe and increase the vigor of the Three Armies. May the perpetrators of evil offer up their heads to pacify the dynasty, and may the arms be laid to rest."

Kim Pusik considered that the Western capital was backed up to a mountain ridge in the north and surrounded by water on the other three sides, while its ramparts were high and dangerous, so they would be difficult to take. It would be better to build camps to keep them under pressure. Moreover, as the Taedong River is a crucial means of transport, it should first be controlled. He divided the army into five and advanced to below the ramparts. The Central Army was camped in Ch'ŏndŏk-pu 川德部, the Left Army in Hŭngbok-sa, the Right Army west of Chunghŭng-sa, the Front Army east of Chunghŭng-sa, and the Rear Army at the Taedong River. Also, fearing that some of those people living outside the city walls who had run away to hide in mountains or valleys would band together and help the rebels, he divided military clerks and sent them out to comfort and convince them. All those who had fled thus left [their hiding places and returned]. Those who volunteered to carry military provisions and help the army lined up without end; all were given food and clothing and were settled comfortably.

Retired Executive Chief of the Royal Secretariat Kim Hyang died. Originally he belonged to the class of local functionaries (*sŏri* 胥吏), and although he had no learning, he was pure and respectful and good at handling affairs. His daughter married Yi Chagyŏm's son Yi Chibo, yet he did not attach himself to Yi Chagyŏm despite these affinal relations. Rather, he assisted Ch'ŏk Chun'gyŏng in apprehending Yi Chagyŏm, yet never bragged about this. The king used to praise him saying: "Having merit yet not pursuing this fact, this is how one can recognize true wisdom."

Retired Executive Chief of the Chancellery Ch'oe Hongjae died. He was the son of a general. Full of vigor, he loved riding fast horses. He was drafted by Yun Kwan to attack the Jurchen, in which he achieved merit. Also, together with Kim Injon he recovered P'oju. Later he became part of Yi Chagyŏm's party and his power and influence grew by the day, to the point that Yi Chagyŏm became jealous. So he hid in a remote place. When Yi Chagyŏm was defeated he was appointed as Executive [Chief]. He himself said: "Since I had to hide my family's assets were completely exhausted." Then he received goods [i.e. bribes] and sold offices, and was impeached by remonstrance officials.

Jin dispatched Acting Junior Policy Advisor Wang Zheng 王政 to announce that the emperor had died.[30]

Intercalary [second] month. The Western Capital rebels constructed a wall that measured 1730 bays along the river from Sŏnyo Gate 宣耀門 to Tagyŏng Tower 多景樓.

The king dispatched Vice-director Kim Tan and Attendant Censor Yi Simin 李時敏 to Jin to express condolences.

The king dispatched Supreme General Yi Nokch'ŏn 李祿千, Grand General Kim T'aesu 金台壽, Recording Officers Chŏng Chun 鄭俊 and Yun

30 This refers to Emperor Taizong (r. 1123-1135), personal name Wuqimai.

Yuhan 尹惟翰, and Drill Master Wi T'ongwŏn 魏通元 from the Western Sea route to lead fifty navy vessels to assist in the subjugation of the Western Capital. When Yi Nokch'ŏn reached Ch'ŏl Island 鐵島 he wanted to take a shortcut to the Western Capital, but the sun was setting and the tide was retreating so the Administrative Assistant for the Navy Ships Chŏng Sŭmmyŏng said "The waterway is narrow and shallow, you should wait for the tide to come in." But Yi Nokch'ŏn did not listen to him and advanced. Halfway through the water became shallow and the ships ran aground. The rebels loaded more than ten small boats with firewood soaked in oil and set them alight, releasing them to follow the tide. Before that they had hidden hundreds of archers in bushes along the road, and prepared them to launch an attack as soon as the fire was set. When the fire boats hit their targets, the army vessels caught fire, and at that moment the archers all together let fly their arrows. Yi Nokch'ŏn was desperate and did not know what to do. The ships and weapons were all burned, and the soldiers fell into the water and nearly all died. Kim T'aesu and Chŏng Chun also died. Yi Nokch'ŏn reached the shore by stepping over the corpses, and barely made it out alive. Because of this the rebels started to slight the government army.

A decree read: "Taking the blame for one's own mistakes in order to reinvigorate [the country], this is how the historian of Lu[31] praised the virtue of Yu the Great. Not holding back in correcting one's past mistakes, this is what the *Book of Documents* says about King Tang's[32] intelligence. Today I retrieve these ancient displays of the cultivation of virtue to accomplish such beauty. With my deficient intellectual and physical capabilities I succeed to the splendor of previous generations. Growing up in the palace, I remained in the dark about the various tasks needed to run the country. Working diligently day and night, even though I enhanced my capacity to embrace [the minds of others], still I failed to foresee the need to control treacherous officials in time. Thus Yi Chagyŏm started doing as he pleased, leading to the disturbance of *pyŏng'o* year [1126], when the king had to

---

31 I.e. the author(s) of the *Spring and Autumn Annals*.

32 Chengtang 成湯: King Tang, the founder of the Shang Dynasty.

move to another place as the palace was burned. Above this is an insult to the project entrusted to me by the ancestors: every time I failed at extending and building on the dynastic project. Then it so happened that a specialist in Yin-Yang emerged from the Western Capital; moreover he was recommended by those around me, and treated like a great sage. I am truly not bright, and was then deluded by his theories, thus newly constructing Taehwa Palace with the aim of renewing the ancestral project. Without thinking twice about the efforts I frequently visited the Western Capital on inspection tours, yet the auspicious responses were few, and the disasters and anomalies gradually increased. In the end there were no clear omens, and this absence led to people's criticisms; ultimately nothing was accomplished. Finally, I took the warnings to heart and followed them, but they remained willfully ignorant and grew more resentful by the day. They requisitioned soldiers and horses, and incarcerated officials. They declared the era name Ch'ŏn'gae, and used words such as 'loyal' and 'righteous' for their army. Publicly they raised an army and had the intention of assaulting the supreme capital. The revolt became unpredictable, and their force could not be contained. From old the crime of sedition [has existed], yet who would have suspected the Western Capital? Among Lü [Fu]'s 3000 crimes,[33] none exceeds that of removing the ruler. Among the twenty virtues of Shun, the most fundamental is that when employing people one should start by removing the evil.

First, I executed the internal plotters, and then dispatched the military leaders. However, it was agreed not to strike immediately but to wait until they submitted voluntarily. Yet unexpectedly they firmly ignored the royal summons, strengthened the fortifications and firmly resisted. The soldiers had no choice but to wait outside, biding their time and unable to go home. Since the march continued, the provisions had to follow along the roads ceaselessly. The people stopped toiling [in agriculture], and near and far everything was in turmoil. Moreover, now I worry that this will interfere with agriculture for a long time, as it may be many months to victory. This is

---

33 Lü Fu hou 呂甫侯: a minister of King Mu of Zhou who made a code of punishments known as the *Lüxing* 呂刑.

where the story ends, no one knows what will happen next.

Like treading on frost or solid ice, missing the original instruction [of the forefathers] has led to much physical and mental pain, but the blame resides with me. What I hope for is that the court ministers, and the soldiers fighting for the king, will do their utmost and join forces to annihilate this evil bunch. Above this will comfort this insignificant person's mind, and next it will alleviate the anger of the Samhan; then together we can complement what is as yet out of reach, and have hope for the future. Forever I mention self-improvement, to make sure there are no repeated mistakes. All the past regretful things I blame on myself." The decree was promulgated in the capital and across the country so that all could hear it.

Kim Pusik considered that since the rear army was weak and lacked soldiers, at night he secretly sent 1000 infantry and cavalry to augment them. At the crack of dawn the rebels crossed the Mat'an 馬灘 and Chap'o 紫浦 [Rivers] and struck straight at the rear army, burning the camp in their sudden raid. The monk Kwansŏn 冠宣, who had responded to a draft for the army, brandishing a big axe struck first at the rebels, killing more than ten people. The official army took avail of this momentum to crush the enemy, killing more than 300. The enemy trampled over each other on their way to the river, where they drowned. Many weapons, armor, and ships were retrieved. This meant a major setback for the rebels. At the time the army had been camping in the open for several months, and spring was about to turn into summer. [Kim Pusik] feared that with the rainy season and floods, the rebels would launch raids. He therefore proposed constructing fortifications to keep them in check, but not fight. Troops from prefectures and garrisons would rest and do agricultural work in turns. Thus they could hold this situation for a long time and wait for a chance.

Others all argued: "The Western Capital has few soldiers, so if the whole country raises an army, they can be conquered in a matter of days. If it is not resolved after several months, it would lead to stagnation and delay. Moreover, constructing a fortress to strengthen yourself, isn't this an admission of weakness?"

Kim Pusik replied: "There are plenty of troops and food in the city, and their minds are strong. If we attack it will be difficult to conquer them, so it is better to achieve this through a good plan. Why should we rashly attack and kill many people?" Then he made the plan to have the prefectures from the northern border region, together with the soldiers from the southwestern provinces and those near [the capital], be divided into five armies, each constructing a fortress. Furthermore in Sunhwa County and at Wangsŏng River 王城江 he had small fortresses constructed, which were finished in a few days. Weapons and grain were stocked, the gates were closed and the soldiers rested. Although skirmishes with the enemy sometimes took place, there was no great victory or defeat. Sometimes provinces were separately ordered to attack the fortress [of the Western Capital], but the walls were high and the moats deep. Even though arrows and stones hit and killed or injured many, the official army also suffered [many] injuries.

The king dispatched his close officials Ch'oe P'ohang 崔褒抗, Assistant Office Chief Cho Sŏk 趙碩, and others, to deliver an edict to summon and instruct. Kim Pusik [in response] dispatched Recording Officers Cho Sŏyŏng 趙諝榮, Kim Chaho, and Kang U 康羽, together with the monk P'umsŏn 品先 and others, to use various stratagems to convince the court; [in the end] the king allowed that [those who submitted] would not be killed.

Every time a rebel spy or someone gathering firewood was caught, they were all given clothes and food before being sent back. Cho Kwang and the others were fully aware of the gravity of their crime, yet had no intention of submitting, so they were hoping for an external threat that would make the king's army desist from [their siege]. At the time it so happened that the Jin envoy was arriving, and the rebels wanted to intercept and harm him in order to create a rift. The government army knew of this and waited and observed carefully and ostensibly for his arrival; hence the rebels did not dare to execute [their plan]. Also, the rebels feared that their party would submit to the authorities, so they forged a document by the Central Army and showed this to the crowd, saying: "All those captured by the government armies or those that submit, regardless of whether they are old or young, are killed." The rebels tended to believe this. But then they heard that those who submitted were treated generously, and hence the rebel party gradually turned towards submitting.

Then a court official made the following argument: "From old, military tactics depend on observing the balance of power. How can you compete for a single victory or defeat? Although our country has friendly relations with the northern dynasty, their intentions are difficult to gauge. Now we have raised an army of several tens of thousands yet after several years nothing has been decided. If the neighboring enemy uses this rift and makes a move, together with the rebellion this will lead to an unfathomable problem. How would we then deal with it? I request that important officials be dispatched who, not concerned about dying or injury, are able to smash the rebels in a day. If there are those who try to evade the chaos of battle, they should be tried by military law." The king showed this to Kim Pusik, who replied: "One cannot be but concerned about an emergency at the northern border and the rebellion; it is truly as what was argued [by the court official]. However, as for marking a day to attack the rebels, disregarding whether one lives or not, why not measure the present advantage or disadvantage this will bring? Your subject observes that the Western Capital is blessed with natural defenses, and is not easy to conquer. Moreover, many crack troops are within the city, and it is well defended. Every strong soldier who attempts to climb the walls only reaches the base; none has yet managed to get over the walls' parapet. Neither cloud ladders nor battering carts are of any use. Even children and women toss bricks and hurl tiles; they are a particularly strong enemy. Even if the five armies join up and attack the walls with all their might, after a few days even the best generals and bravest soldiers will all be eliminated by arrows or stones. The rebels know that our force is insufficient, so even if we attack with all our might, we won't even be able to reach their sword tips, then how would there be any chance for an alternative plan? Now we have united an army of several tens of thousands for several years without reaching a conclusion. Your old subject bears the responsibility for this. However, with the rebellion, we cannot but be heedful for the need to guard the border, hence I want to conquer them with a perfect plan, without hurting soldiers and without jeopardizing the country's sovereignty. In war it is impossible to guarantee a speedy victory. Today I will annihilate the evil rebels, who turned their backs on the spirits of the dynasty and the earth and grain gods, and also on the authority of the king. Please entrust the smiting of the rebels to your old subject. If you allow me to manage affairs as I see fit, I will definitely conquer the rebels to repay Your Majesty." The king agreed, and thus finally set aside the other arguments and entrusted everything to him.

Third month. The king dispatched Vice-minister of Taxation Kim Ingyu and Office Chief at the Ministry of Rites Wang Ch'angyun 王昌胤 to Jin to congratulate [the new emperor] on his accession.

The five armies together attacked the walls of the Western Capital, but could not break through.

Summer, fourth month. The king appointed Chŏng Chŏngsuk as Vice-director of the Department of Ministries.

The king made sacrifices at the Ancestral Shrine.

Sixth month. Song dispatched Gentleman for Meritorious Achievement Wu Dunli 吳敦禮 with the following message: "Recently we learned about the revolt in the Western Capital. Should catching [the rebels] prove difficult, we are willing to send 100,000 soldiers to assist."

Autumn, eighth month. The king went to Ch'ŏnsŏng Hall and ordered Hallim Academician Chŏng Hang to lecture on the *Tang Mirror*.[34]

Ninth month. Wu Dunli returned. The king entrusted him with a report saying: "As for the rebels of the Western Capital, their leaders have already been killed. The remaining rebels have gathered on a steep [hill] which they have fortified. We want to swiftly attack and destroy them, but considering this may cause a lot of casualties, we have surrounded the city and are waiting for it to fall. Their strength is waning by the day, so it should be possible to destroy them sometime soon. However, we venture that as this

34 *Tang jian* 唐鑑: a work composed by Fan Zuyu 範祖禹 of Song, and covering the essentials of the history of all Tang emperors.

is a small affair in a border region across the sea, it should not trouble the emperor's mind. Hence we did not dare report on it. Now you especially dispatched an envoy to inquire whether or not we want military assistance. Even though we are moved that the Great Dynasty has taken of the small one, in terms of principle it is not easy to accept. Moreover, the dangers across 10,000 leagues of oceans are hard to fathom. For the Heavenly [i.e., the Song] army to descend to the east, we fear that it would not be easy at all. We therefore request that you rescind the instruction you sent us."

The king dispatched Mun Sŭngmi 文承美 and No Hyŏnyong 盧顯庸 to Song.

Winter, tenth month. The king dispatched Office Chief at the Ministry of Taxation Kang Bogyŏ 康福輿 to Jin to give thanks for the birthday felicitations.

The king went to Pŏbwang-sa and organized a Hundred Seat Assembly; he then ordered that 30,000 monks ought to be given vegetarian food across the country.

When food in the Western Capital started running out, the old and weak were driven out, but some soldiers also sneaked out to submit. Kim Pusik knew that there was an opportunity here, so he ordered his generals to start raising a mountain of earth. First a palisade was erected on a mountain near Yangmyŏng Port 楊命浦, and the Front Army's camp was moved here to hold it. A total of 23,300 soldiers from the prefectures and counties, as well as 550 monks were commandeered to construct an earthen mound. General Ŭibo 義甫 and three others were separately ordered to take 4200 elite soldiers as well as 3,900 battle-hardened soldiers from the Northern Border Region and its Prefectures and Garrisons to form a roving army that would prevent raids [by the rebels].

Eleventh month. Im Kyŏngch'ŏng was made Probationary Minister of Works, Vice-director of the Department of Ministers, Commissioner of the Security Council, and then was ordered to retire. At the time Senior Policy Advisor Yi Chung and Drafting Advisor of the Royal Secretariat Yi Chijŏ sent a memorial saying: "The tiger and the one-horned bull have escaped their pen; the tortoise shell and the jade lie broken in their box;[35] whose fault is this? The rebels of the Western Capital have been planning for a long time. One or two high officials have not only not prevented this, on the contrary they believed in these plans and boosted them. This ultimately led to the disaster we are dealing with. We request that you make a clear decision to remove those of their party." They were talking about the likes of Mun Kongin and Im Kyŏngch'ŏng. Im Kyŏngch'ŏng was retired because of this.

The five armies gathered at the front army's encampment. The earthen mound they raised straddled Yangmyŏng Port and approached the southwestern corner of the rebels' wall. Day and night the work continued, greatly alarming the rebels. Daily they charged out with elite troops to give battle. They also installed an arbalest and stone-thrower at the corner of the wall, resisting with all their might. Depending on the situation, the government forces either defended or attacked the walls so as to divide the rebel forces. Also, a visitor[36] called Cho Ŏnhŏn 趙彦獻 designed a stone thrower that was placed on top of the earthen mound. It was very big and could hurl stones that weighed several hundred *kŭn*. The stones destroyed the battlement buildings; later fire balls were hurled, setting the buildings on fire. The rebels no longer dared to approach. The earthen mound was 80 feet high and more than 700 feet long, with a width of 180 feet. It stood at several tens of feet from the rebel walls. Still the five armies could not break through the walls, and Recording Officer Pak Kwangyu 朴光儒 was killed.

The king dispatched Assistant Office Chief Kwak Tongsun to Jin to give new year's felicitations, and Office Chief Mun Kongwŏn 文公元 to give felicitations on the Wanshou Festival 萬壽節.

At night the rebels divided their army into three groups and charged out, attacking the camp of the front army. Kim Pusik ordered the monk Sangsung 尙崇 to carry an axe and strike back. He killed more than ten rebels, and the other soldiers ran away. General U Pangjae 于邦宰 and four others led

35 While the general thrust of these metaphors appears clear, it is not certain whether they have a precise referent.

36 Kyoin 僑人: though probably referring to a foreign visitor, it is not clear whether this is the case here.

soldiers to pursue and strike them. The rebels threw away their armor and went back into the city.

Twelfth month. On *pyŏngjin* day [the 18th] Venus was visible during the day while it traversed the sky.

Ch'oe Yu was made Probationary Minister of Works, and Executive Chief of the Royal Secretariat; Kim Kŭkkŏm 金克儉 was made Vice-director of the Department of Ministries; Im Wŏnjun was appointed Commissioner of the Security Council; Kim Puŭi was named Administrator of the Security Council; and Yi Chung was designated Associate Administrator of the Security Council.

Injong fourteenth year [1136]

Sixth year of the Shaoxing era of Song, Fourteenth year of the Tianhui era of Jin

Spring, first month. Jin dispatched Surveillance Commissioner for the Jurisdiction of Taizhou, Xiao Shou 蕭綬, to congratulate the king on his birthday.

Second month. Jin dispatched an envoy to announce the demise of the Grand Emperor Grand Dowager's funeral. The whole country wore mourning for three days.

Because our side had built an earthen mound to put pressure on them, Cho Kwang and the others wanted to build a second wall inside the main wall. When Kim Pusik heard this he said: "Even though the rebels may build [another] wall, what good will it do them?" Yun Ŏni and Chi Sŏksung said: "Two years have already passed since the great army rode out. Many days have already gone by idly. Although the course of the rebellion is difficult to predict, it would be better to employ a stealth army to suddenly attack the second wall. This can succeed." Kim Pusik did not listen, but Yun Ŏni kept insisting. Thereupon he divided elite troops along three paths. Chin Kyŏngbo and others led 3,000 soldiers along the central road; Chi Sŏksung and other generals led 2,000 soldiers along the left road; Yi Yu and other generals led 2000 soldiers along the right road. General Kongjik 公直 travelled the Sŏkp'o 石浦 road with his army, and General Yangmaeng 良孟 followed the Tangp'o 唐浦 road with his troops. The reason the armies took different routes to attack the walls was to divide the enemy's forces. After the divisions were determined, the soldiers were lavishly rewarded, and Kim Pusik returned to the Central Army camp. At the strike of the fourth watch,[37] wearing light armor he galloped to the Front Army, and roused all the generals for the great attack.

On *chŏngsa* day [the 19th] at the crack of dawn, Chin Kyŏngbo's army entered Yangmyŏng Gate 楊命門, removed the rebels' palisade, and proceeded to attack Yŏnjŏng Gate 延正門. Chi Sŏksung's army crossed the wall and entered to attack Hamwŏn Gate 含元門. Yi Yu's army also crossed the wall and attacked Hŭngnye Gate 興禮門. Kim Pusik, leading the local official army,[38] attacked Kwangdŏk Gate 廣德門. The rebels, noticing that our earthen mound was not yet completed and that it was no longer defended by the various armies, suddenly arrived. [Our troops] were in panic and did not know what to do. Kim Pusik and Kim Chŏngsun oversaw the battle. Generals and soldiers all fought fiercely, and all the armies were spurred on by drum rolls and shouts. Fire was launched, and the walls and houses were burning. The rebel army collapsed completely, and the government army rode to victory, indulging in the cutting off of heads and ears.[39] Kim Pusik then ordered: "Those who capture rebels alive will be rewarded; those who kill those that submit or loot will themselves be killed." The soldiers then all sheathed their swords in their advance. When night fell it started to rain, and all troops were called to retreat from the city. Those that were caught alive were sent to Sunhwa County and given food and drink.

That night the city was in complete disarray. Cho Kwang did not know what to do and his whole family burned themselves and died. Office Chiefs Yu Wihu 維偉侯, P'aeng Suk 彭淑, Kim Hyŏn'gŭn 金賢瑾 all cut their

---

37 Sagyŏng 四更: usually between 1 and 3 AM.

38 Abyŏng 衙兵: denotes the army of a local administration.

39 *Koek* 馘: literally the cutting off of the ear or part of the head; usually as proof of the number of enemies slain.

throats and died. Chŏng Sŏn 鄭璇, Yu Hanhu 維漢侯, Chŏng Kŭksŭng 鄭克升, Ch'oe Kongp'il 崔公泌, Cho Sŏn 趙瑄, and Kim T'aeksŭng 金澤升 all cut their own throats. The rebels grabbed their leader Ch'oe Yŏng and others and left the city to submit. Kim Pusik accepted this, and handed them over to clerks. He comforted and instructed soldiers and citizens, old and young, women and girls. He ordered them to enter the city and safeguard their houses; he also distributed soldiers across the gates to guard them. He then had Censor of Miscellaneous Affairs Yi Insil 李仁實, Attendant Censor Yi Sik, and Censor Ch'oe Chayŏng 崔子永 enter the city and seal the storehouses and granaries. He also ordered Kim Chŏngsun together with Yun Ŏni and Kim Chŏnghwang 金鼎黃 to take 3,000 soldiers, enter the city, and garrison at Kwanp'ung Hall to take command of the city. Looting in the city was forbidden. Office Chief Sin Chich'ung 申至冲 was made Commissioner for Gathering Weapons 收拾兵仗使;[40] Intendant-secretary [at the Department of Royal Clan Affairs] Yi Hu 李侯 was made Commissioner for Pacifying and Settling the Populace 百姓和諭安居使; Assistant Office Chief Pak Chŏngmyŏng 朴正明 was made Commissioner for Inspecting the Storehouses 倉庫監檢使; Audience Usher Yi Yangnul 李若訥 was designated Commissioner for Repairing the Guest Houses 客館修營使; Recording Officers Ch'oe Yuch'ing 崔褎偁 and Paek Sach'ŏng were respectively appointed Commissioners for Patrolling the Left and Right [sectors of the city] 城內左右巡檢使.

On *sinyu* day [the 23rd] Kim Pusik entered the city to comfort and put at ease the residents. He dispatched someone to make sacrifices at the Shrine for the City God and other spirit shrines, and sent Administrative Assistant to the Military Commissioner No Su 魯洙 to present a memorial of offering victory. Receiving a royal order, they beheaded the rebel leaders Ch'oe Yŏng, Grand General Huang Rin 黃麟, General Tŏksŏn 德宣, Administrative Assistant Yun Chuhyŏng 尹周衡, Registrars Kim Chi 金智 and Cho Ŭibu 趙義夫, and *changsa* Na Son'ŏn 羅孫彦, and publicly displayed their heads

---

40 This and the next functions appear to have been made ad-hoc to deal with the situation; they are not part of the regular bureaucracy.

for three days. Local Vice-minister of Taxation Song Sŏnyu 宋先有 faked illness when the war started and stayed indoors; Supervising Recorder O Sŏn'gak 吳先覺 faked madness and thus did not join the rebels; while Assistant Secretary at the Great Granary Chŏng Ch'ong 鄭聰 because of his filial conduct had received a special memorial gate; [these people hence escaped punishment]. Professor of Medicine Kim Kongjŏng 金公鼎 knew that Cho Kwang planned to assassinate the assistant general No Yŏnggŏ dispatched by Kim Pusik and secretly alerted him so that he could avoid this fate. Vice-director Wi Kŭnyŏng 韋瑾英 could not turn his back on the rebels because of his old mother, but together with Han Yugwan 韓儒琯, An Tŏkch'ing 安德偁, and Kim Yŏngnyŏn 金永年 pretended to have a funeral, and as pallbearers they wanted to leave the city gates. However, they were exposed, and Wi Kŭnyŏng and Han Yugwan were subjected to torture, but they preferred death to revealing the others. Hence An Tŏkch'ing and Kim Yŏngnyŏn escaped harm. From Kim Kongjŏng down all people, together with Yun Ch'ŏm's family and associates, the old and young, and the sick, were all pardoned. All the other civil and military officials were rounded up and sent to the capital for punishment. Those who had resisted the most were branded with the characters "Traitor Rebels of the Western Capital" and banished to islands. Next, [those who had resisted less fiercely] were branded with the characters "Western Capital" and sent to *hyang* and *pugok* across the country. The rest were distributed across the various greater prefectures, prefectures, districts, and counties. Their wives and children had the choice of where to reside according to their preference, and were allowed to remain as commoners.[41] The wives and children of seven people, including Cho Kwang and Ch'oe Yŏng, as well as Chŏng Sŏn, Kim Sin and his younger brother Kim Ch'i 金致, Chŏng Chisang, Yi Chagi, Paek Suhan, Cho Kan 趙簡, Myoch'ŏng, Ryu Ch'am and his son Ryu Ho, Chŏng Tŏkhwan 鄭德桓 and others, were all stripped of their rights and sent as slaves to the various fortresses on the northeastern border. A remonstrance official impeached Mun Kongin for recommending and employing Myoch'ŏng and others, thus

41 Yangin 良人: I.e. the majority population, between the elite officials and the unfree.

harming the country and spreading poison among the people. He was then demoted to Probationary Grand Marshal, Intendant of the National Academy.

The historians comment: Mun Kongin as state councilor first recommended this treacherous person, thus harming the country. Also, he did not follow Kim Pusik's words and mistreated Yun Ch'ŏm, thereby finally making the rebels who were ready to submit resume the rebellion. His crime is great indeed. With a demotion as punishment he came off very lightly.

The king went to Changwŏn Pavilion.

The king dispatched Director of the Office of Royal Clan Affairs Yun Ŏnsik 尹彦植 and Senior Reparationer Ch'oe Yunŭi 崔允儀 to Jin to express condolences.

Third month. The king dispatched Senior Transmitter Yi Chijŏ and Vice-director of the Office of Royal Clan Affairs Im Ŭi with an edict to praise and instruct the generals who had subjugated the Western Capital. They bestowed upon Kim Pusik robes, saddle, golden belt, golden drinking vessels, incense, and medicine; upon Kim Chŏngsun a golden belt; upon the military commissioners of the four [other] armies, and the vice-administrative assistants and lower, silver, fine silk, silk, to each commensurate with rank. As for the old, sick, young, and infirm in the Western Capital and around it who could not sustain themselves, they were provided with relief grain according to need. They were also to inspect the temples and shrines in the city and around it that were destroyed, and repair or rebuild them as needed.

Kim Pusik was made Merit Subject Conveying Loyalty, Suppressing the Rebellion, and Pacifying the Country, Acting Grand Guardian, Probationary Grand Marshal, Director of the Chancellery, and Minister of Personnel.

Chin Suk was made Associate Administrator of the Security Council.

Summer, fourth month. Kim Pusik returned in triumph. The king went to Kyŏngnyŏng Hall to announce the pacification of the Western Capital rebels. He bestowed upon Kim Pusik a big residence. He reduced the number of officials in the Western Capital. Also, he divided the four Kyŏnggi routes[42] and [newly] created the six counties of Kangdong 江東, Kangsŏ 江西, Chunghwa 中和, Sunhwa 順化, Samdŭng 三登, and Samhwa 三和.[43]

Fifth month. The Military Commissioner for the Central Army petitioned: "Vice Commissioner of the Security Council Han Yuch'ung disregarded the nation's security by obstructing the movement of troops, and the Pomun-gak Auxiliary Academician Yun Ŏni was deeply involved with Chŏng Chisang; these crimes cannot be pardoned." Thereupon Han Yuch'ung was demoted to Commissioner of the Ch'ungju Shepherdship, and Yun Ŏni to Defense Commissioner of Yangju.

With the pacification of the Western Capital, the king issued an edict of pardon. He also stated in an edict "Formerly Lord Zhuang of Zheng installed Lady Jiang in the city of Ying, swearing 'until the Yellow Springs, we shall not meet again.'[44] Later he regretted this, and resumed the relation of mother and son as before. Now my maternal grandfather surnamed Yi,[45] even though he died, the meaning of 'loving one's family' in the end cannot be forgotten. He shall be posthumously appointed Acting Grand Preceptor, Duke of Hanyang. His spouse Lady Ch'oe shall be invested as Lady of Pyŏnhan."

Another edict said: "When the stables burned, Confucius asked 'were any people hurt?', he did not ask about the horses. This means that a sage cherishes people and rates animals as less important. Now the law officials are prosecuting the killing of a cow according to the same standards as the crime of killing people, branding their face and banishing them to islands. This is not the original intention of the law statutes; henceforth crimes should be judged according to the original category of the crime."

---

42 分京畿四道: the meaning is not clear; probably it refers to four routes rather than provinces. It might also mean that the six new counties were carved out of Kyŏnggi and four surrounding provinces.

43 All these were located around the Western Capital, Pyongyang, and were the result of new administrative divisions, likely meant to reduce the administrative power of the Western Capital.

44 Lady Jiang, the mother of Lord Zhuang (r. 743–701 BCE), had plotted rebellion with his younger brother.

45 I.e. Yi Chagyŏm.

Sixth month. On *chŏngyu* day, the first day of the month, the Ch'ŏngju plain flooded, carrying away 180 houses.

On *kimi* day [the 23rd], Venus was observed traversing the sky during the day.

Autumn, eighth month. The king went to Changwŏn Pavilion.

Ninth month. The king dispatched Kim Ch'igyu 金稚規 and Yu Taegŏ 劉待擧 to Mingzhou in Song. A letter [they carried] said: "Recently the merchant Chen Shu 陳舒 came with a letter saying that China wanted to send envoys to Koryŏ to discuss serving [the great]. We consider that the Samhan since the time of Han and Tang through the generations has served the Middle Plains. Moreover it has been 200 years since our ancestor quietly attached himself, and due to this we received the favorable treatment of successive generations of Chinese emperors. How would we not want to act as border-guarding subject with a single mind? However, we share a border with the Jin state, so we had no choice but to request peace. If they would find out that you dispatched envoys and that we have friendly relations with [Song] China, they will surely suspect that we are secretly planning something, and grow envious and angry. They may use this as a pretext to send their army, and that case the fate of this small country will be in the balance. If you lose our country as a defensive shield, that will mean that the coast around the Huai [River] and Zhe [Provinces] will border on Jin, which will not be to your advantage. Furthermore, if you forge a path to us by raising an army, then they will also use this [to get to you], and in that case all the counties along your seaboard will have to be on guard permanently. Prostrate, we hope that you will carefully consider your options, and do not make this small country incur the wrath of Jin. Then you will also not suffer the fate of 'the lips gone, the teeth will be cold,' and will be happy."

Mingzhou reported back: "Our court treats all countries with deep favors and righteousness. After the disaster of the Jingkang era, it has become somewhat more difficult to send embassies. Recently we dispatched Wu Dunli and Chen Shu to your king to restate our old friendship. Moreover, since we learned that you have been close neighbors to Jin from the beginning, and that you exchange trusted emissaries, it would only be natural that you could obtain news of the two emperors' situations. As for raising an army and using your roads to launch an attack, these are all the improvised words of Wu Dunli and the others, these are not the instructions of the court. Please consider this carefully, and you will see there is no reason to start doubting."

Winter, tenth month. The king dispatched Vice-director of the Palace Treasury Sin Chich'ung to Jin to give thanks for the birthday felicitations.

Thieves robbed the sacrificial vessels for the Wŏn-nŭng 元陵 Tomb,[46] and killed three tomb guardians.

Intendant of the Security Council Kim Puŭi died. When the king was still heir apparent, Kim Puŭi was chosen as the resident official for the prince's palace, and was especially relied on and trusted for his literary skills. When the prince was enthroned, he appointed Kim Puŭi as Hallim Academician. The king once asked him about border affairs, and Kim replied: "Shenzong of Song once discussed border affairs with Wen Yanbo 文彦博 (1006–1097) and Wang Anshi 王安石 (1021–1086). Wen Yanbo said, 'One should first rule oneself, it is not proper to treat lightly what is near and stress out about what is far.' Wang Anshi said, 'Wen Yanbo's words are completely correct. If you can rule yourself, with an area of 70 leagues you can be king of All under Heaven. Now with an area of 10,000 leagues under Heaven, and yet being afraid of people, this comes from not being able to rule oneself.' Now the country of Samhan, how would it be a mere 70 leagues! Yet if you still cannot escape the fear of others, this problem comes from not first ruling yourself, and nothing else. Also, I heard that the barbarians are good at deciding a battle in an instant on the steppe, where the clashing of swords and exchange of arrows settles victory. This is what China is not good at. Setting up strong arbalests on walls, firmly guarded by strong companies that can wait till the enemies' strength is sapped, this is what China is good at, and what the barbarians are not good at. One should prioritize one's strengths, and observe the perversions [of the enemy]. This is truly the

46 The tomb of Hyŏnjong's mother, Queen Hyosuk. See Part Ia, 222 (fifth month of 1012).

urgent task of this time. You should make high walls and deep moats for the capital as well as the prefectures and garrisons, and equip them with strong arbalests, poisonous arrows, thunder stones, and fire arrows. Dispatch commissioners to inspect the clerks in charge, and reward or punish them as necessary, and that is all."

When Myoch'ŏng requested the construction of a new palace in the Western Capital, Kim Puŭi strongly protested against it. When Myoch'ŏng rebelled, and an army was sent out to quell the rebellion, Kim Puŭi offered a ten-point plan for pacifying the Western Capital. In outline it argued that since the walls of the Western Capital were formidable and his supplies plentiful, it could not be taken in one fell swoop, rather one should bide time and wait till they slacken before using a stratagem to snatch victory. The king praised him and accepted the plan. When the Western Capital was pacified just as the plan had stipulated, the king especially granted him a golden belt.

He had a calm demeanor and was relaxed in dealing with people. He did not concern himself with his family's possessions, and did not engage in power games. He excelled in poetry and prose, and was popular among the people.

Eleventh month. The king dispatched Vice-director Yi Yugae to Jin for new year's felicitations, and Executive at the Ministry of Rites Yi Insil to give felicitations on the Wanshou Festival.

Administrator of Memorials at the Security Council Chŏng Hang died. He was intelligent by nature and loved learning. After passing the examination he became Manager of Records in Sangju. Because of his youth the people did not take him seriously, but when he showed his decisiveness in handling issues, everyone was won over. For a long time he served as palace attendant, handling all the correspondence to the king with trustworthiness. Later when he served as royal inspector for the provinces of Yanggwang and Ch'ungch'ŏng, Yi Chagyŏm's power awed everyone, so people competed in bringing him gifts to win favors. Chŏng Hang alone was not like this. After Yi's defeat the king appointed him Transmitter of Edicts. He recommended the king read books, and after that the king's daily progress in letters was thanks to Chŏng Hang. When his illness became serious, he was promoted to Administrator of the Security Council, but the day after the edict was issued he died. The king was deeply saddened, and when he heard that his family did not have even a *sŏk* of grains in storage, he said: "For thirty years a close official, for eleven years a transmitter of edicts, and yet so poor! How wonderful." He then gave very lavish condolence gifts and personally composed his posthumous title, Mun'an 文安.

Twelfth month. Kim Kŭkkŏm, Yi Chadŏk, and Im Wŏnjun were all made Assistant Executive in Political Affairs, and Chin Suk was appointed Intendant of the Security Council.

Injong fifteenth year [1137]

Seventh year of the Shaoxing era of Song, fifteenth year of the Tianhui era of Jin

Spring, first month. Jin dispatched Drafting Advisor of the Royal Secretariat Wu Ji 吳激 to congratulate the king on his birthday.

Third month. The king went to Changwŏn Pavilion.

Im Wŏnae was made Merit Subject Equalizing Virtue, Acting Grand Guardian, Provisional Minister of Education, Intendant of the Department of the Palace Library.

On *ŭlhae* day [the 13th] there was an earthquake in the Western Capital.

Yi Sin 李信 and twenty-seven others passed the composition test of the civil service examination.

Im Wŏnjun was appointed Executive Chief of the Royal Secretariat, and Kang Huhyŏn 康侯顯 Intendant of the Chancellery.

Summer, fourth month. Kim Ch'igyu and Yu Taegŏ returned from Song. The emperor's edict said: "Due to the disruption and chaos of war, young and old have been uprooted. Not forgetting the friendship of old, [you] pitied our people who have long lived in temporary housing. Thanks to the ship borrowed they have already returned to their fields and houses, and each obtained what they cherished. Considering that the vagrant people are still many, there will be more bothersome favors to take pity on them."[47]

Fifth month. Because of the drought the markets were moved.

Autumn, seventh month. Retired Director of the Chancellery Yi Kongsu died. When Yi Kongsu was administrative assistant in the Western Capital, Yejong came to the Western Capital. Yi Kongsu accompanied him without disturbing the people. The king praised him and when he returned [to the capital] he ordered him to follow the royal carriage. He refused, saying: "Of old it is said that on the day the royal carriage returns, only the manager of affairs at the resident governor's office can accompany the king. How could you because of a favor upset the old rules?" The king complied. For fourteen years he selected soldiers at the Ministry of War, becoming famous for his work there. As a person he was generous and broad-minded, worked diligently, and was frugal. But he was stingy and liked Buddhism.

Ninth month. The king moved to Changwŏn Pavilion and returned to the palace only in the tenth month.

Intercalary [ninth] month. A Hundred Seat Assembly was organized in Sŏngyŏng Hall for three days. The king ordered officials throughout the country to prepare maigre feasts for 30,000 monks.

Eleventh month. The king dispatched Assistant Office Chief at the Ministry of War Ryu Ang 柳昻 to Jin to give thanks for the birthday felicitations, Assistant Office Chief at the Ministry of War No Su to present felicitations on the new year, and Office Chief at the Ministry of Rites Yi Ryang 李亮 to give felicitations on the Wanshou Festival.

On *chŏngsa* day [the 29th] Venus was visible during the day traversing the sky.

Twelfth month. Intendant of the National Academy Mun Kongin died. His original name was Mun Kongmi. He was elegant and handsome, with soft and quiet demeanor. Director of the Chancellery Ch'oe Sach'u gave one daughter in marriage to Mun. Although their family circumstances were poor, after having an aristocratic family as in-laws, the Muns started to act

47 The edict sounds as if the emperor is thanking the Koreans for helping him return some of his people, but I am not certain if this is the correct translation.

as grandees. Mun Kongin was once sent to Liao as an envoy, and gave the official in charge of guests a precious gift from his private funds. After this, every time our envoys visited Liao, they always raised Mun's example to demand gifts without restraint. Thus this became a big nuisance [because of his actions].

Injong sixteenth year [1138]

Eighth year of the Shaoxing era of Song, first year of the Tianjuan era of Jin

Spring, first month. Jin dispatched Surveillance Commissioner for the Jurisdiction of Yongzhou, Du Yi 杜誼, to congratulate the king on his birthday.

Second month. The king sent Audience Usher Ch'oe Myŏn 崔沔 to the Eastern Capital of Jin.

A decree read: "The foremost virtue of emperors and kings is modesty. Therefore Laozi said: "Kings and dukes refer to themselves as 'the solitary one,' 'this insignificant person,' or 'carriages without a nave.'"[48] Emperor Guangwu of Han decreed that when writing to the throne, one could not use the word 'holy.' Now subjects in esteeming the ruler want to embellish and use titles that are too grandiose. This is completely against reason. Henceforth in all memorials to the throne as well as in official documents one should not use the words 'divine,' 'holy,' 'emperor,' or 'king.'"

Third month. Yi Taeyu 李大有 and twenty-eight others passed the composition test of the civil service examination.

Summer, fifth month. The king declared a pardon, and ordered all officials throughout the country to promote the bright and encourage the dull, and to aid those who were ill.

All the names of palace buildings and gates were changed, and the king personally wrote the name boards.

---

48 See *Daodejing* 39. As for *bugu* 不轂, I follow James Legge's translation as "carriages without a nave."

Autumn, seventh month. Intendant of the Censorate Ch'oe Kwan, Censor of Miscellaneous Affairs Pak Chŏngyu, Attendant Censors In Ŭi 印毅, Ch'oe Sulchung 崔述中, An Suk 安淑, and others, prostrated themselves in front of the Office of Audience Affairs for three days. They wanted to impeach Commissioner of the Security Council Chin Suk. During the campaign against the Western Capital, he had received slaves and a precious belt [as bribes]. The king did not respond. Thereupon they all bolted the doors and did not come out. The king summoned Ch'oe Kwan and the others and convinced them to attend to affairs. Only Pak Chŏngyu and Ch'oe Sulchung stood firm and did not go back to work. In the end [Chin Suk] was dismissed from office.

Eighth month. Yi Chung was made Assistant Executive in Political Affairs, Ch'oe Chin 崔溱 Intendant of the Security Council, and Kim Chŏngsun and Yi Chijŏ Vice-commissioners of the Security Council.

Executive Chief of the Royal Secretariat Yi Chadŏk died. Yi Chadŏk was respectful, filial, and a good friend. He loved learning and also enjoyed the worship of Buddha.

The king went to the portrait halls of Hyŏnjong and Munjong.

Winter, tenth month. On *imsul* day [the 9th] the king moved to Kukch'ŏng-sa. On *kapcha*[49] day [the 11th] he returned to the new palace. Before this, because the original palace had burned down, the king ordered officials to repair it. On this day all officials offered their congratulations, and wine was served in the king's official residence. The princes, State Councilors, and attending officials all served the king. The party lasted all night.

Eleventh month. The Intendant for Ritual and Guest Affairs of the Eastern Capital of Jin, Xia Mu 夏睦, came in response to Koryŏ's earlier mission.

The king dispatched Assistant Office Chief of the Ministry of Punishment Kim Sillyŏn 金臣璉 to Jin to give thanks for the birthday felicitations, and Assistant Office Chief at the Office of Merit Evaluation Yu Pang'u 劉邦友 to give felicitations on the Wanshou Festival.

---

49 Here it is important to note that the *kapcha* day marks the start of a new sexagenary cycle; hence this day was chosen to enter the new palace.

The king went to Chiphyŏn Hall[50] and ordered Kim Pusik to lecture on the hexagrams "Taming Force of the Great" (大畜) and "the Return" (復). He also made all the academicians ask questions on difficult parts and afterwards bestowed a banquet which lasted all night.

Twelfth month. Ch'oe Yu was appointed Executive Chief of the Chancellery; Yi Chung was made Vice-director of the Department of Ministries; Yi Chijŏ was appointed Censor-in-chief, and Associate Intendant of the Security Council; Kim Chŏngsun was designated Associate Intendant of the Security Council.

Injong seventeenth year [1139]

Ninth year of the Shaoxing era of Song, second year of the Tianjuan era of Jin

Spring, first month. Jin dispatched Surveillance Commissioner for the Jurisdiction of Gaozhou, Yelü Ning 耶律寧, to congratulate the king on his birthday.

Second month. The king declared a general amnesty. He ruled: "I received the final command of the last king, and thus succeeded to the great dynastic enterprise. But my virtue being slight and the task heavy, I could not rule effectively. This caused the emergence of powerful ministers who behaved with impunity, ending in the destruction of the palace. I am deeply ashamed of this. Today fortunately, thanks to the assistance of Heaven and Earth and the cooperation of ministers and people, the reconstruction was finalized. Last year in the tenth month I moved into the new palace. There is no joy greater than this, and this great benefice should be shared together with the people."

The king gave a banquet for all officials in Taegwan Hall and granted them one horse apiece.

---

50 Chiphyŏnjŏn 集賢殿: The Hall of Gathering Worthies; this is the new name of the hall previously called Yŏnyŏngjŏn 延英殿. It is one of the new names for buildings introduced earlier that year. It is not clear whether it had any of the functions already of its more illustrious Chosŏn successor, but it was meant to house scholars. See *Koryŏsa* 76.29b.

Third month. Retired Executive Chief of the Chancellery Ch'oe Sajŏn died. He first progressed under the medical course, but after advising Ch'ŏk Chun'gyŏng to remove Yi Chagyŏm, thanks to this merit he was suddenly promoted to state councilor. In his later years, since he had risen from poverty to high station, and because of the ruler's affection, he firmly insisted on retiring. He had two sons, one called Ch'oe Pyŏn 崔弁 and the other Ch'oe Yŏl 崔烈. To each he gifted a gold cup. After he died, a concubine stole one. Ch'oe Pyŏn was very angry and wanted to whip her, but Ch'oe Yŏl said: "This is someone that our late father cherished, so we should wager all our family assets to pity her. Moreover, as for this thing, the one I, your younger brother, received is still here, so please older brother, take mine." When the king heard this he praised him saying: "This can be called at once filial and benevolent." Then he personally wrote down and bestowed upon him the name Hyoin 孝仁.

The king summoned Kim Pusik, Ch'oe Chin and others for drinks, and ordered Kim to read Sima Guang's "Bequeathed memorial" 遺表 and "Instructions on simplicity" 訓儉. The king admired the beauty of his writing, and after a while said: "Sima Guang was such a loyal and righteous person, yet his contemporaries labeled him a traitor, how is this possible?" Kim Pusik responded: "It is possible because he did not see eye to eye with Wang Anshi's party. In fact he did not commit any crime." The king added: "The demise of [Northern] Song is certainly not unrelated to this."

Summer, fifth month. The king went to Kyŏngnyŏng Hall.

Sixth month. Ch'oe Kŭp 崔伋 and nineteen others passed the composition test of the civil service examination.

Autumn, eighth month. The expelled queen Lady Yi died. She was the daughter of Yi Chagyŏm. Although she was expelled due to Yi Chagyŏm, the king showed great affection and munificence [in the funerary arrangements].

Ninth month. The king dispatched [Audience] Usher Ch'oe Sayŏng 崔思永 to the Eastern Capital of Jin.

Winter, tenth month. A Hundred Seats Assembly was held in Sŏngyŏng Hall for three days, and 30,000 monks were fed.

Eleventh month. Senior Policy Advisor Kang Yŏngjun 康英俊 and others submitted a memorial discussing more than ten ongoing issues, among which the king only accepted the one revoking the exile of former Administrator of the Security Council Ch'oe Yujŏk and the monk Ŭijang and having sent them back to their original prefectures.

The king dispatched Assistant Office Chief at the Ministry of Punishment Chin Kwan 陳灌 to Jin to give thanks for the birthday felicitations for the king.

The king personally held a banquet for the elderly, filial sons and grandsons, chaste wives and righteous husbands, as well as the seriously ill.

The king dispatched Chief Steward at the Bureau of Royal Clothing Ch'oe Siyun 崔時允 to Jin to present new year's felicitations, and Assistant Office Chief at the Ministry of Taxation Wang Chŏngp'yo 王正彪 to give felicitations on the Wanshou Festival.

Kim Yag'on was appointed Probationary Grand Tutor, Merit Subject Promoting Loyalty and Upholding the Correct, and Director of the Chancellery, and was then ordered to retire.

Retired Assistant Executive in Political Affairs Kim Kŭkkŏm died. Although he had no scholastic ability, he worked tirelessly for the common good, and held several posts in the center and in the provinces, where he invariably earned praise for efficiency and clarity. But when he reached a high position he was merely sincere and self-effacing to hold down his position, nothing more.

Twelfth month. Ch'oe Chin was made Assistant Executive in Political Affairs; Yi Chijŏ was appointed Administrator of the Security Council; and Wang Ch'ung 王冲 was made Vice-commissioner of the Security Council.

Injong eighteenth year [1140]

Tenth year of the Shaoxing era of Song, third year of the Tianjuan era of Jin

Spring, first month. Jin dispatched Surveillance Commissioner for the Jurisdiction of Taizhou, Wanyan Bing 完顏昺, to congratulate the king on his birthday.

Second month. Retired Director of the Chancellery Kim Yag'on died. His old name was Kim Ŭimun 金義文. His character was respectful and frugal, and he was upright. He studied hard, and served successively in posts in the capital and the provinces. Wherever he went he put the people at ease. When Yi Chagyŏm grabbed power, all those craving profit fought to associate with him. Although Kim Yag'on was a cousin to Yi Chagyŏm, he was not close to him. Although due to his high position he had luxury and influence, he never used his riches or position to treat others haughtily.

Third month. On *kapsin* day [the 9th] it snowed heavily, and again on *chŏnghae* day [the 12th].

Summer, fourth month. Im Wŏnae was made Minister of War, and Yi Chung was made Executive Chief of the Royal Secretariat.

A decree determined the dress code for sacrificial rites.

The king personally sacrificed at the Ancestral Shrine and gave higher posthumous titles to the nine shrines and twelve royal tombs. His decree explained "My virtue is insufficient, and in my time I encountered many troubles. The Western [Capital] bandits rebelled, but fortunately I could rely on the virtue of my ancestors to turn the tables and pacify them. Now I personally come to sacrifice and present better titles, hoping that you will spread your munificent grace throughout the country. Those below the highest crime [which deserve the death penalty] shall be pardoned."

Fifth month. The Intendant for Ritual and Guest Affairs of the Eastern Capital of Jin, Wang Gao 王杲, came in response to Koryŏ's earlier mission.

P'aeng Hŭimil 彭希密 and twenty-five others passed the composition test of the civil service examination.

Intercalary sixth month. The king prayed for rain at the Pŏbun-sa 法雲寺, and then again prayed at the Oejesŏg-wŏn.

The State Councilors Kim Pusik, Im Wŏnae, Yi Chung, and Ch'oe Chin, and the five remonstrance officials,[51] including Ch'oe Chae and Chŏng Sŭmmyŏng,

---

51 *Sŏngnang* 省郎, also *nangsa* 郎舍: officials across various institutions with the ability to remonstrate.

presented a letter in ten points on contemporary wrongs. For three days they prostrated themselves in front of the Office of Audience Ceremonies, but the king did not respond to any of their demands. Until their demands for dismissal [of certain officials] were met they refused to come to work.

Autumn, seventh month. Based on what the remonstrance officials had said, the king dismissed the administrator of memorials [at the Security Council] and reduced the number of palace attendants and special commissioners at various offices, and also at the Court of Palace Attendants and the Special Storehouse. Then he summoned Ch'oe Chae and the others and ordered them to resume work. Only Chŏng Sŭmmyŏng refused to return, because he thought that not all the points raised had been followed. Junior Policy Advisor Ch'oe Kwan was the only one who did not join the memorial, and continued working as usual. He was criticized for this at the time.

Eighth month. Executive Chief of the Chancellery Ch'oe Yu died. When young he was very smart and good at composing texts. As he was incorruptible and impartial, he was employed in all the important positions. In old age he struggled with illness and could barely walk. Still he did not request retirement. People at the time ridiculed him for this.

Winter, tenth month. The king bestowed gold and silver, a saddled horse, rice, cloth, and musical instruments upon Kim Pusik as reward for his merit in pacifying the rebels of the Western Capital.

The king dispatched Assistant Office Chief at the Ministry of Punishment Pak Sunch'ung 朴純冲 to Jin to give thanks for birthday felicitations to the king.

Eleventh month. The king dispatched Assistant Office Chief at the Ministry of Punishment Hwang Chuch'ŏm to Jin to give felicitations on the new year, and Executive at the Ministry of Rites Ch'oe Ham to give felicitations for the Wanshou Festival.

Injong nineteenth year [1141]

Eleventh year of the Shaoxing era of Song, first year of the Huangtong era of Jin

Spring, first month. The heir apparent was capped.

Jin dispatched Associate Intendant of the Court Ceremonial Institute Zhao Xingxiang 趙興祥 to congratulate the king on his birthday.

Vice-censor-in-chief Ch'oe Yuch'ŏng and others submitted a petition that discussed[52] various cases [of misdemeanor]. The king did not acknowledge it.

Jin reported that the emperor had received a new title and established a new era name.

Summer, fourth month. The king dispatched Executive at the Ministry of Rites Kwŏn Chŏk 權迪 and Junior Reparationer Kim Yŏngyak 金永若 to Jin to give felicitations on the emperor's new title. When they reached the border however they were told that on account of interfering with the agricultural season they would not be allowed to enter, hence they returned.

Autumn, seventh month. Granary Inspection Commissioner for Myŏngju province Yi Yangsil 李陽實 dispatched someone to Ullŭng-do to gather strangely shaped fruits and shrubs to present them [to the throne].

Ninth month. The king again dispatched Kwŏn Chŏk and Kim Yŏngyak to Jin.

Winter, tenth month. A Hundred Seat Assembly was held in the palace for three days, and 30,000 monks were fed.

Eleventh month. The king dispatched Yi Chimu 李之茂 to Jin to give thanks for the birthday wishes to the king, Pak T'aejin 朴台進 to give felicitations on the new year, and Ryu Pŏm 柳帆 to give felicitations on the Wanshou festival.

Twelfth month. Im Wŏnae and Yi Chung were appointed Executive Chief of the Chancellery; Ch'oe Chin was made Executive Chief of the Royal Secretariat; Kim Ingyu was made Vice-director of the Department of Ministries and Assistant Executive in Political Affairs; Yi Chijŏ was named

52 *Non* 論 should here probably be interpreted as *nonhaek* 論劾, to impeach: I.e. a memorial requesting the impeachment or punishment of various officials.

Assistant Executive in Letters; and Kim Chŏngsun and Wang Ch'ung were appointed Intendant of the Security Council.

Injong twentieth year [1142]

Twelfth year of the Shaoxing era of Song, second year of the Huangtong era of Jin

Spring, first month. Jin dispatched the Defense Commissioner for the Jurisdiction of Zhaozhou, Wuling Xixia 烏陵錫瑕, to congratulate the king on his birthday.

Remonstrance officials impeached Vice-director of the Palace Library and Edict Attendant at the Pomun-gak Kim Chŏng for visiting [Intendant of] the Security Council Kim Chŏngsun's house, indulging him with wine, and cursing the supervisor of education, and Royal Recording Editor Chŏng Sŭmmyŏng for requesting permission to stay temporarily in Kim Pusik's detached house. As they had thereby disgraced their office of remonstrance officials, it was requested that they be punished. As a result Kim Chŏng was stripped of his title of edict attendant at the Pomun-gak, and Chŏng Sŭmmyŏng was stripped of his title of royal recording officer. The remonstrance officials persisted that Kim Chŏng's crimes were grave yet his punishment light, and requested that he be dismissed from office altogether. The king complied.

Second month. During the Lantern [Festival] the Jin envoy requested to view the festivities; the guesthouse attendant Kim Tan requested permission for this, which was granted.

The king dispatched Kim Kŏgong 金巨公 to the Eastern Capital of Jin.

Third month. Director of the Chancellery Kim Pusik thrice requested retirement, and this was granted. He was additionally granted the title of Merit Subject Equalizing Virtue and Assisting Transformation.

Ko Chu 高儔 and twenty-nine others passed the composition test of the civil service examination

Summer, fourth month. Im Wŏnae was appointed Minister of Personnel.

Fifth month. Assistant Executive in Political Affairs Kim Ingyu died. His daughter married Yi Chagyŏm's son Yi Chiŏn, and hence when Yi Chagyŏm was defeated he was guilty by association and demoted to prefect of Ch'unju. Soon after however he was recalled and restored to his position. As a person he was generous, and not given to either praising or criticizing people. Yet he was also indecisive, and merely did enough to hold on to his position and salary. Although he was originally from a wealthy family, when Yi Chagyŏm held sway he never relied on that to behave arrogantly towards people. This is where he is praiseworthy.

Jin dispatched Director of the Palace Treasury Wanyan Zongli 完顏宗禮 and Auxiliary Hanlin Academician Tian Gu 田瑴 to invest the king as Unequalled in Honor,[53] Pillar of State, King of Koryŏ. They also bestowed crown and robes, an ivory palanquin, saddled horse, and other presents. They also promoted him to Commander Unequalled in Honor,[54] Supreme Pilar of State. Of old the edict of investiture had to be received in the southern suburbs, but now the emissaries had received instruction from the palace to promulgate the edict within the royal palace for the first time.

Autumn, eighth month. When the king was travelling to Changwŏn Pavilion, a woman carrying twin boys approached him on the road, and he bestowed twenty bolts of cloth upon them.

Winter, tenth month. The king travelled to Changwŏn Pavilion and inspected archery. Those who hit the target were bestowed presents commensurate with rank.

The king dispatched Associate Administrator of the Security Council Ch'oe Kwan and Senior Policy Critic Ch'oe Yuch'ŏng to Jin to give thanks for the investiture.

The king personally held sacrifices at the Ancestral Shrine and declared an amnesty.

---

53 *Ŭidong samsa* 儀同三司: a prestige title in China, but as Hucker notes (no. 3024), its reference is not clear. More commonly used was the title *Kaebu ŭidong samsa* 開府儀同三司, "Commander Unequalled in Honor" (Hucker no. 3105) which had been conferred on Koryŏ kings from the beginning of the dynasty.

54 See the previous note.

The king dispatched Ch'oe Yuch'ing to Jin to give thanks for the birthday felicitations.

Eleventh month. The Commandant of Flying Cavalry of the Eastern Capital of Jin, Pucha Zhongan 蒲察忠安 came in response to our mission.

The king dispatched commissioners to the eight provinces to inspect the performance of officials and clerks in the prefectures and counties.

The king dispatched Yi Yŏngjang 李永章 to Jin to present local products, Yi Yangsŭng 李陽升 to present new year felicitations, and An Chŏngsu 安正脩 to present felicitations on the Wanshou festival.

Twelfth month. Yi Chijŏ was appointed Probationary Minister of Works, Vice-director of the Department of Ministries; Kim Chŏngsun was named Probationary Minister of Works, Administrator of the Chancellery; and Han Yuch'ung was made Vice-director of the Department of Ministries, Commissioner of the Security Council.

Injong twenty-first year [1143]

Thirteenth year of the Shaoxing era of Song, third year of the Huangtong era of Jin

Spring, first month. On *ŭlch'uk* day, the first day of the month, there was a solar eclipse.

Jin dispatched the Defense Commissioner for the Jurisdiction of Mingzhou, Xiao Sizhen 蕭嗣貞, to congratulate the king on his birthday.

Third month. On *pyŏngsin* day [the 9th] it snowed heavily and there were people who froze to death.

Summer, intercalary fourth month. The heir apparent was betrothed to the daughter of Minister of Education [Wang] On 王溫.

Fifth month. Yŏndŏk Palace caught fire.

Autumn, ninth month. Pae Kyŏngsŏng 裵景誠 was appointed Minister of Personnel. When he was serving as transmitter of edicts, he had taken a courtesan as spouse. The remonstrance officials said: "With a spouse doing this kind of activity, he is not fit for a position at the heart of government."

So he was appointed instead Intendant of the Censorate, but the remonstrance officials again said: "Entrusting him with the task of investigating other officials is particularly inappropriate." Since they held fast to this criticism, in the end there was this appointment.

Winter, eleventh month. A Hundred Seat Assembly was held at Sŏngyŏng Hall for three days, and 30,000 monks were fed.

The king dispatched Assistant Office Chief at the Ministry of War Im Chung 林仲 to Jin to give thanks for the birthday felicitations, Yi Tŏksu 李德壽 to present local products, Chief Steward at the Bureau of Royal Diet Yun Ŏnmin to give felicitations for the new year, and Yu P'il 庾弼 to give felicitations for the Wanshou Festival.

Twelfth month. On *kyemi* day [the 1st] the Grand Astrologer reported there would be a solar eclipse, but it did not materialize.

Retired Executive Chief of the Royal Secretariat Ch'oe Chasŏng died. He was strong-minded and astute, and there was not office he did not pass through. Yet during the disturbance of *pyŏng'o* year he took charge of affairs at Yi Chagyŏm's private residence. People hence belittled him.

Yi Chijŏ and Kim Chŏngsun were made Assistant Executive in Political Affairs.

Injong twenty-second year [1144]

Fourteenth year of the Shaoxing era of Song, fourth year of the Huangtong era of Jin

Spring, first month. Jin dispatched Director of the Palace Treasury Xiao Li 蕭隸 to present birthday felicitations to the king.

The king personally sacrificed at the Round Altar.[55]

The king personally drew the first furrow in the fields. The king made five

55 Wŏngu 圜丘: Although its exact function cannot be determined, this appears to be an altar for sacrifices to Heaven. Note that although I translate 祀 as sacrifice, that is but one of the terms used: previously eg. 享 was used for the king's sacrifices at the Ancestral Shrine. The different terms likely denote different hierarchic levels rather than inherently different practices.

pushes [of the plow], the princes three, the dukes seven, various ministers and vice-ministers nine. After returning to the palace the king declared an amnesty, and the officials offered memorials of congratulation.

Second month. Retired Vice-minister of Taxation Hŏ Chae died. He started as a lowly clerk,[56] but because of his integrity established a reputation. During the construction of the nine fortresses, he guarded Kilchu as recording officer for the Central Army. When the Jurchen attacked, he closed the gates and guarded the fortress tightly for several months. When it nearly fell he constructed a second wall to deter them, and the Jurchen retreated. For his merit he was appointed investigating censor. But since he had not studied and had no skills, he attached himself to Yi [Chagyŏm] and Ch'ŏk [Chun'gyŏng], becoming councilor. When the two were defeated, remonstrance officials strongly argued for his guilt, and he was demoted to prefect of P'ungju. When his term there was over he was appointed Vice-minister of War and retired. The Censorate disputed this, but at the time it so happened that the royal inspector for the Sŏhae Province reported that he had established merit in governing P'ungju and should not be discarded. Hence he was appointed Vice-minister of Taxation and retired.

The king gave a banquet for his officials in Taegwan Hall and presented them with one horse apiece.

A decree read: "Even though Ch'ŏk Chun'gyŏng violated his role as subject, at the same time he had the merit of protecting the shrine [of the earth and grain deities; hence the dynasty]. He should be appointed Acting Vice-minister of Taxation." Several weeks later, he developed a tumor on his back and died in Kokchu. His ancestors were clerks in Kokchu. Since they were poor he could not study and fell in with unreliable types, roaming around. He wanted to become clerk but failed. When Sukchong was still Duke of Kyerim he went to his palace and became a retainer. Eventually he became administrative aide for the Security Council. After he established his merit in the construction of the Nine Fortresses he came to prominence.

A decree exempted those among the people who were filial or fraternal,

---

56 *Top'illi* 刀筆吏: literally a "knife and pencil clerk," after the utensils used by lowly clerks.

and those diligent in farming [from taxation].

Summer, fifth month. Kim Tonjung 金敦中 and twenty-five others passed the composition test of the civil service examination. Kim Tonjung was the son of Kim Pusik. Initially he was adjudicated in second place, but the king, wishing to placate his father, raised him to first place. Hence he was attached to the Office of Palace Attendants. Although he was young of age, he was vigorous and sharp. Later, during the ghost exorcising ritual on the last day of the year,[57] with his candle he burned the beard of Royal Carriage Guard Chŏng Chungbu 鄭仲夫. Chŏng Chungbu smacked and cursed him for this. Angrily, Kim Pusik told the king to tie him up for punishment, but the king thought that Chŏng Chungbu was extraordinary, and allowed him to escape. From this, Chŏng Chungbu resented Kim Tonjung. Chŏng was originally from Haeju. He had big eyes and a broad forehead, a pale complexion, and beautiful full beard, and was more than seven feet tall. Initially when his prefecture submitted the military records, he was tied up and sent to the capital.[58] When State Councilor Ch'oe Hongjae saw him he thought him extraordinary, and assigned him to the Restraining Crane Palace Army. He became close to the king and served him personally.

Autumn, seventh month. On *kyŏngsin* day [the 11th] the royal prince Wang T'ak 王晫 was born.

Because the banner head Na Sin 羅信 harmed what he had given life to[59] with a sword, [he was executed and his body] exposed in the marketplace.

Winter, tenth month. A Hundred Seat Assembly was held in Sŏngyŏng Hall for three days, and 30,000 monks were fed.

The king gave a banquet for elderly men and women, as well as filial sons and grandsons, righteous husbands and chaste wives, widows and widowers, orphaned and single, and those with a serious disease or handicap, and bestowed presents commensurate with rank. The king personally went to see

---

57 Chesŏk narye 除夕儺禮

58 The military records (*kunjŏk* 軍籍) seems to refer to the census records for those to be drafted into the military. It is not clear whether it was customary to dispatch the draftees tied up, or whether Chŏng had committed a misdemeanor.

59 Sosaeng 所生: i.e. his own child.

a filial son and asked him about his deeds; deeply moved the king shed tears.

Eleventh month. The king dispatched First Office Chief Pak Ŭisin 朴義臣 to Jin to give thanks for the birthday felicitations, and Vice-director of the Office of Regalia Ko Yŏngbu 高瑩夫 to present felicitations on the new year.

Twelfth month. The king heard that the Jin sovereign had traveled to the Eastern Capital, so he dispatched Director of the Palace Library Kwak Tongsun to inquire after his health, Vice-director of the of the Directorate of Royal Workshops Kim Kwibu 金龜符 to present local products, and Executive at the Ministry of Taxation Ch'oe Chayŏng to give felicitations on the Wanshou Festival.

Kim Chŏngsun was appointed Vice-director of the Department of Ministries; Han Yuch'ung was made Assistant Executive in Political Affairs; Wang Ch'ung was named Commissioner of the Security Council; and Pak Chŏngyu was designated Vice-commissioner of the Security Council.

Injong twenty-third year [1145]

Fifteenth year of the Shaoxing era of Song, fifth year of the Huangtong era of Jin

Spring, first month. Jin dispatched Auxiliary Hanlin Academician Zhao Jiong 趙泂 to congratulate the king on his birthday.

Second month. Vice-commissioner of the Security Council Pak Chŏngyu died. Pak was broad-minded by nature, so when he was working for censorial offices he did his work roughly and was not inclined to harshness. His father Pak Yŏnghu 朴永侯 instructed him in the way of loyalty and filial piety, and Pak Chŏngyu did his best to follow that. However, he appropriated the land, house, and slaves of his maternal uncle's concubine, leaving the mother and son cold and hungry. At the time he was criticized for his cold-heartedness.

Third month. The king dispatched Secretarial Receptionist at the Office of Audience Ceremonies Sŏ Kong 徐恭 to the Eastern Capital of Jin.

Ch'oe Chae was appointed Associate Administrator of the Security Council.

Summer, fourth month. The king bestowed 600 *sŏk* of grain upon the sons and daughters of Yi Chagyŏm.

A comet was seen in the northwestern quarter for fifteen days. It was more than ten feet long.

Fifth month. Assistant Executive in Letters, Assistant Executive in Political Affairs Yi Chijŏ died. He was the son of Yi Kongsu. He came first in the civil service examination. When he was appointed junior policy monitor, since he went against the consensus in his positions, at the time the state councilors changed his appointment to intendant-secretary at the Department of Royal Clan Affairs,[60] and he was sent out as royal inspector to the Sŏhae Province. At the time Yi Chagyŏm ruled the country, those craving profit fought to attach themselves to Yi. Only Yi Chijŏ, despite being of the same clan, did not associate with Yi Chagyŏm. When Yi Chagyŏm's envoys crisscrossed the country to extract wealth and bribes, Yi Chijŏ strictly forbade this. Yi Chagyŏm hated him for this, and had him appointed commissioner of P'yŏngju. When Yi Chagyŏm was defeated, he was recalled and after successive promotions became royal recording editor. Yi Chijŏ had a distinguished and cultivated appearance; he had a strong will and was broad-minded. In terms of his composition and political skills, he was outstanding among his generation. However, he was stingy in his management of assets; when his father died, he did not distribute anything to his younger siblings. His slaves behaved with impudence, going as far as stealing and robbing, and he was unable to control them. For this he was ridiculed at the time. His posthumous epithet was Munjŏng 文正.

Cho Munjin 趙文振 and thirty-one others passed the composition test of the civil service examination.

Sixth month. On *ŭlhae* day, the first day of the month, there was a solar eclipse.

On *kapsin* day [the 10th] here was flooding in the two prefectures of Munju and Yongju in the Eastern Border Circuit. Mountains collapsed and water

60 Although this was the same rank (junior 6 從六品), this office likely did not entitle him to remonstrate.

surged, destroying walls and gates; many households perished as well.

Jin dispatched Director of the Palace Treasury Wanyan Sihai 完顏思海 as ad-hoc envoy.

Autumn, seventh month. The seven prefectures of Ch'angju, Sakchu, Kwiju, Ŭiju, Chŏngju, Yongju, and Ch'ŏlchu in the Northern Border Circuit, together with Haeju in the Sŏhae Province were affected by locusts. The grand astrologer petitioned: "Now locusts and other insects have emerged across the four directions, this means that there are many evil people in the country, and no loyal officials at court: they merely fill their position and eat their salary like insects. One should select people of the way and place them in various important positions so as to mitigate the disaster."

Eighth month. Han Yuch'ung was made Minister of Rites, State Historiographer, and Junior Guardian to the Heir Apparent; Wang Ch'ung was made Assistant Executive in Political Affairs, Minister of Works, Junior Guardian to the Heir Apparent; Ch'oe Kwan was appointed Commissioner of the Security Council, Administrator of the Finance Commission; Yi Insil was made Associate Intendant of the Security Council, Advisor to the Heir Apparent.

Associate Executive in Political Affairs Kim Chŏngsun died. He came from a poor family, put was full of vigor and derring-do. He was good at archery and horse riding, and used to tell people: "A man should achieve merit at the border so as to establish his reputation. How could I sit dejectedly and lifelessly in small alleys!" Around that time the country was attacking the Jurchen, so he requested to join the army, and gained merit. When he was posted as prefect of Hwaju and Suju, although he was not familiar with clerical affairs, and did not concern himself with the details of accounts and letters, he did grasp the essence and avoided mistakes. He also joined Kim Pusik when he pacified the Western Capital and thence entered government. Due to his contraction of a serious disease, he was made Merit Subject Pursuing Loyalty and Settling Revolt, Probationary Grand Guardian, Chief of the Chancellery and Associate Executive of the Royal Secretariat. Kim Chŏngsun was valiant and fearless by nature, and also inspired of character.

Yet he had no learning and loved wealth, enjoying opulence, something that was considered his shortcoming at the time.

Winter, tenth month. A Humane Kings Assembly was held in Sŏngyŏng Hall for three days, and 30,000 monks were fed.

Eleventh month. Junior Policy Advisor Pae Kyŏngsŏng, [Senior] Policy Critic Ch'oe Ham and others, six people in all, sent a petition on several issues, but the king did not respond. The remonstrance officials then all requested to stop work and the department was empty for two days.

Lieutenant of Trust,[61] Commandant of Flying Cavalry of the Eastern Capital of Jin Wang Haogu 王好古 came in response to our earlier mission.

Intercalary [eleventh] month. The king dispatched Acting Director of the Office of Regalia Chŏng Ŏnsim 井彦深 to Jin to give thanks for the birthday felicitations to the king; Acting Executive at the Ministry of Taxation An Chagyu 安綽裕 to give thanks for the ad-hoc envoy; Acting Deputy Director of the Office of Royal Clan Affairs Yi Chijŏng 李之正 to give felicitations for the new year; Acting Deputy Director of the Foreign Relations Office Yi Inwi 李仁威 to present local products; and Acting Executive at the Ministry of Rites Ye Akchŏn 芮樂全 to give felicitations on the Wanshou Festival.

Twelfth month. On *chŏngsa* day [the 17th], the beginning of spring,[62] at night there was a sound like thunder from the sky. The grand astrologer prophesied: "A sound like wailing from the sky on the beginning of spring means that the king is worried and afraid."

Director of the Chancellery Kim Pusik presented the "History of the Three Kingdoms of Silla, Koguryŏ, and Paekche" that he had compiled to the throne.[63] The king dispatched Palace Attendant Ch'oe Sanbo 崔山甫 to his house to reward him, and granted a generous amount of flower wine.

Im Wŏnae was made Probationary Grand Guardian, Intendant of the Resident Governor of the Western Capital; Ch'oe Chin was appointed Executive Chief of the Chancellery; Han Yuch'ung was designated Executive

---

61 *Chengxin jiaowei* 承信校尉: probably a prestige or merit rank.

62 Ipch'un 立春: one of the 24 solar terms in the traditional calendar.

63 This is the famous *Samguk sagi*, Historical Records of the Three Kingdoms.

Chief of the Royal Secretariat, Junior Guardian to the Heir Apparent; Wang Ch'ung and Ch'oe Kwan were named [respectively] Vice-director and Junior Vice-director of the Department of Ministries.

Injong twenty-fourth year [1146]

Sixteenth year of the Shaoxing era of Song, sixth year of the Huangtong era of Jin

Spring, first month. Jin dispatched the Defense Commissioner for the Jurisdiction of Weizhou, Wanyan Sheng 完顔昇, to congratulate the king on his birthday.

The king ordered the heir apparent to induce the Executive at the Ministry of Rites Chŏng Sŭmmyŏng to lecture on "Counsels of the Great Yu," from the *Book of Documents*.

The king gave a banquet for the Jin envoy in Taegwan Hall. After it he felt indisposed.

The king declared an amnesty.

The king's illness worsened. An oracle said: "Yi Chagyŏm is the cause." The king dispatched Han Chak 韓綽 to move Yi Chagyŏm's wife and sons back to Inju. All the officials went to pray in Poje-sa. They also prayed at Siwang-sa 十王寺 and the Ancestral Shrine and the Altar [of the Earth and Grain Deities].

Second month. Executive Im Wŏnae together with all the officials gathered in Sŏngyŏng Hall to pray to the Supreme Emperor in August Heaven 皇天上帝: "Heaven is far and mysterious, hence it is difficult to interpret. People are small and base, still they can express their faith sincerely. With utmost despair, like dogs and horses, we look up, at the risk of soiling the divine mirror. Formerly when King Wu was on the throne he became ill and as it could not be cured, the Duke of Zhou wrote a pledge to take the disease on his body instead. Although the present is different from antiquity, loyalty and righteousness remain the same. Thus your subjects shed tears of blood to write these words, calling on Heaven with the request for [the king's] life.

Entrusting all our minds to the blue yonder, we wish that our king's disease be transferred to our bodies. If his life span is increased, so that we may rely again on the dynastic house, how would we dare not to take the path of renewal? Leaving behind all the mistakes of the past, following the king we will promote good and stop evil, bring benefit to the people and remove their afflictions. We shall not engage in greedy activities and shall not flatter or deceive, and strive to maintain purity without change throughout our lives. If we break this covenant, may we be killed by the divine force."

Ch'ŏk Chun'gyŏng was posthumously restored to the office of Executive Chief of the Chancellery, and his sons and grandsons were summoned back to the capital and given office. The reason for this is that a shaman had said that Ch'ŏk Chun'gyŏng was the cause of this calamity.

The king declared an amnesty.

The king dispatched Palace Attendant Pong Sŏl 奉說 to Kimje Prefecture to remove the dam retaining Pyŏkkol Pond 碧骨池. This was according to the instructions of a shaman.

On *kapcha* day [the 25th] the king's disease worsened. He handed the throne to the heir apparent Wang Hyŏn, and decreed: "Despite my lack of virtue I succeeded to the dynastic line. Just like venturing into the deep while steering a rotten [ship], I did not know what to do. Heaven sent down a calamity in the form of an incurable disease; above I dread the mind of Heaven, and below I put to shame the people's aspirations. Day and night I worked myself into a frenzy thinking about how to avert this punishment; yet the affairs of government cannot be left idle for long, and the divine vessel of the throne cannot be vacant even for an instant. The heir apparent Wang Hyŏn, as the eldest son residing in the prince's palace, with the brightness of the sun, and the virtue inherent in him, he is fit both above [for Heaven] and below [for the people]. For this reason, I follow the model of previous kings in formalizing the love [of parent to child], and accord with three generations of giving [the throne] to the son, entrusting him with this weighty office. As ruler of the Samhan, you should consult the old statutes and establish many achievements. Henceforth all the military and political affairs are to be decided by my successor."

On *chŏngmyo* day [the 28th] a bequeathed edict read: "It has been twenty-five years since I was burdened with the mandate bestowed by August Heaven, and succeeded the legacy of previous kings to rule the Samhan. Now my worries have peaked, yet with the disease lasting already several weeks, it is only getting worse, not better, and now entered a critical stage. Alas! The way of the sages cognizes being and non-being, and the words of Buddha and Laozi are singular across life and death. This is an inevitable process, a principle that is unavoidable. The one who goes follows the principle of transformation and does not remain, those who stay behind suppress their grief and perfect filial piety: This is the universal way of All under Heaven. Alas! You, Heir Apparent Hyŏn, endowed with the beauty of loyalty and filial piety, precociously assisted by Heaven, replete with virtuous projects, carrying the people's expectations, you should accede to the throne. For the mourning clothes, substitute months with days, and for the scale of the tumulus, follow the model of frugality. Follow in the footsteps of previous sages and worthies, and do not put to shame the bright virtue of your forebears. Work together with all officials with a single mind, assist each other in virtue and learn from those above in administering the country, protect and lead the dynastic house well." The king then died in Pohwa Hall 保和殿. The same day the heir apparent ascended the throne in Taegwan Hall. He gave the posthumous title Konghyo 恭孝 and temple name Injong on his father.

The historian Kim Pusik comments: "From a young age Injong had many talents and skills; he understood harmonies and was good at painting and calligraphy. He loved reading books and the volumes never left his hands; sometimes he read through the night. After he became king, he heard that the classics licentiate Sin Suk 申淑 was very poor so he called him to the palace and made him palace attendant and received [lectures in] the *Spring and Autumn Annals*, as well as classics and biographies. He was frugal by nature. Once when he was ill the state councilors entered the royal residence and visited his sickbed. The royal bed did not have any yellow silk rims, and his dress did not have any silk or brocade decorations. In his early years as king there were many eunuchs and attendants in the palace. Every time one was dismissed for a misdemeanor he was not replaced, so that in his later years there were only a few people attending him. He attended court audiences up to twice a day. If there was one who dallied in reporting, he always made your subject chase after him. He pacified the people only through virtue and grace, he never wanted to raise an army to resolve issues.

When the Jin rose violently, the officials after deliberation recommended becoming subject to them. The king received the Northern envoys with due ceremony, thus among the Northerners there was none who did not love and respect him. When the official drafting the edicts sometimes used the term 'barbarian' when referring to the Northern Dynasty, the king rebuked him, saying: 'How can we serve them like a great country yet arrogantly use such terms?' Eventually a satisfactory treaty could be concluded, and there were no more worries on the border.

Unfortunately Yi Chagyŏm acted wantonly and caused a palace revolt, in which the king was greatly humiliated. However, as it was his maternal grandfather, he endured and simply kept himself alive. When it comes to Ch'ŏk Chun'gyŏng, he ignored his transgressions and recorded his merit, and in the end preserved his life, showing the extent of his magnanimity. Thus when the king died, the whole country was in mourning. Even the Northerners sighed in grief when they heard the news. Hence it is really appropriate to use the character 'In' 仁 [humanity] for his temple name. The only regrettable thing is his infatuation with Myoch'ŏng's plans to move the capital, which led to the revolt of the rebels of the Western Capital, which took years to quell. This is a blemish on his virtue."

The historian Kim Sinbu 金莘夫[64] wrote: "In the latter years of Yejong's reign, the in-laws were rather favored, feeding their covetous and self-

64 This is his only appearance in official historiography. However, his name appears as author of a few epitaphs from the 1150s, e.g. that of Im Kwang 林光 (1152).

indulgent behavior. Injong became king at a tender age, State Councilor Han An'in and others, failing to think far ahead, tried to secretly wrest power from them but this merely fanned Yi Chagyŏm's anger, and they were either killed or exiled. This made the evil lot even more brazen, and their poison spread across the Samhan. They even fired arrows at the king and burned the palace and Ancestral Shrine. They threatened the life of the king, established private residence [to conduct government], and killed the king's officials. The dynastic project almost fell to the ground, let this be a warning! Furthermore he was deluded by Myoch'ŏng and Paek Suhan's theories of Yin and Yang, leading to the rebellion of the Western Capital. How is this possible? It is because though his nature was benevolent and loving, he was also indecisive. Hence the punishments for those involved in the rebellion of pyŏng'o year [1126] were not right, and the rebellious population was not punished equally. Furthermore, he deeply believed in Buddhism, causing great harm to the people, is not this regrettable! As for his not liking to wine and dine, reducing the number of eunuchs and attendants, living frugally and modestly, treating his neighbors with honesty—even rulers of antiquity would not outdo him in this."

Third month. On *kapsin* day [the 15th] Injong was buried in Chang-nŭng 長陵.

[Ŭijong's] mother Lady Im was honored as Queen Dowager.

Summer, fourth month. The [new] king's[65] birthday was designated the Hach'ŏng Festival 河淸節 and the king received the felicitations of all the officials.

All the officials from his time in the heir apparent's palace were rewarded.

Im Wŏnae was made Director of the Chancellery, Marquis of Chŏng'an.

The king went to the Ŭibong tower and declared a general amnesty.

Fifth month. The king bestowed upon the eunuch and palace attendant, Palace Servitor Chŏng Ham 鄭諴, a big house. He was the husband of the king's wet nurse.

---

65 I.e., Ŭijong (r. 1146–1170).

Ninth month. Executive Yi Chunyang died. Originally he was a clerk from Chŏnju, who worked himself up through integrity.

Executive Han Yuch'ung died. He was frugal, diligent, and upright. He was highly regarded in his time.

Winter, tenth month. Jin dispatched the Defense Commissioner of Qingzhou, Wuyan Zunli 烏延遵禮 Vice-director of the Palace Treasury Wu Juren 烏居仁 to conduct sacrifices for Injong; Associate Intendant for the Fiscal Commission of the Central Capital Circuit Xiao Qian 蕭謙 to offer condolences; and Notary for the Huining district Cao Yan 曹兗 to tell the king to stop wearing mourning dress.

The king personally organized a Hundred Seat Assembly in Sŏngyŏng Hall, and then went to the ball court to feed monks for three days.

Eleventh month. The king dispatched Cho Kain 趙可仁 to Jin to offer felicitations on the new year.

A P'algwan Assembly was held. In the royal tent the king successively received felicitations [from the officials]. He ordered the removal of female musicians from the building.

The king dispatched Yi Yangsil to Jin to give thanks for the favors bestowed, and Kim Yangjin 金陽晉 to present local products.

Executive Wang Ch'ung requested retirement. The kind decreed "Wang Ch'ung is integer, frugal, and impartial; he is still in good health, so we bestow upon him staff and table, and order him to continue serving."

The king dispatched Yang Wŏnjun 梁元俊 to Jin to give felicitations on the Wanshou Festival.

The Censorate petitioned: "Vice-commissioner for the Amnok Local Navy Command Yun Suŏn 尹粹彦 together with eleven ships carrying 290 soldiers drowned. This happened because the military commissioner failed in his command. He should be punished." The king agreed.

Twelfth month. A decree read: "Next year's Lantern Festival should be held on the full moon of the first month." As the second month is a month of mourning for Injong it was changed. After this it became a permanent practice [to hold it in the first month].

Map: Koryŏ ca. 1100

Legend:

● main capital ◎ three secondary capitals ◇ protectorate

◈ shepherdship ○ greater prefecture

provinces and circuits in capitals +++ great wall

Tables

Table 1. Department of Royal Secretariat – Chancellery 中書門下省: staff; one office per person, except were another figure is given (after Munjong's reign) (See Pak Yongun, "Chung'ang ŭi chŏngch'i chojik," *Han'guksa* 13, 31)

Junior 1	門下侍中 director of the Chancellery	中書令 royal secretary
Senior 2	門下侍郎平章事 executive chief of the Chancellery 門下平章事 executive of the Chancellery	中書侍郎平章事 executive chief of the Royal Secretariat 中書平章事 executive of the Royal Secretariat
Junior 2	參知政事 assistant executive in political affairs 政堂文學 assistant executive in letters 知門下省事 administrator	
Senior 3	左常侍 (=左散騎常侍) senior policy advisor	右常侍 (=右散騎常侍) junior policy advisor
Junior 3	直門下 intendant of the Chancellery	
Senior 4	左諫議大夫(=司議大夫) senior policy critic	右諫議大夫 junior policy critic
Junior 4	給事中 reviewing policy advisor	中書舍人 drafting advisor of the Roy. Sec.
Junior 5	起居注 royal recording editor 起居郎 royal recording secretary	起居舍人 royal recorder
Senior 6	左補闕 (after 1115: 左司諫) senior reparationer	右補闕 junior reparationer
Junior 6	左拾遺 (after 1115: 左正言 Senior policy monitor	右拾遺 (after 1115: 右正言) junior policy monitor
Junior 7	門下錄事 chief registrar of the chancellery	中書注書 chief scribe of the Roy. Sec.
	主事 (6) master scribe (chief clerk) 令史(6) scribe first class 書令史 (6) scribe second class 注寶 (3) keeper of seals 待詔 (2) decree attendant 書藝 (2) calligrapher 試書藝 (2) probationary calligrapher 記官 (20) recorder second class 書手 (26) copyist first class 直省 (8) department custodian 電吏 (180) message bearer 門僕 (10) page	

Table 2. Department of Ministries (尙書省) (after Munjong's reign)
(See Pak Yongun, "Chung'ang ŭi chŏngch'i chojik," *Han'guksa* 13, 42)

	都省 Department of ministries	6部 Six ministries	屬司 Subordinate offices
Junior 1	尙書令 director of the Department of Ministries	判…事 (one for each ministry) minister	
Senior 2	左僕射vice-director 右僕射 junior vice-director		
Junior 2	知省事 general administrat or		
Senior 3		尙書vice minister	
Junior 3	左丞 senior assistant director 右丞 junior assistant director	知部事 administrator	
Senior 4		侍郎 executive	
Junior 4			
Senior 5	左司郞中 first office chief 右司郞中 Second office chief	郞中 office chief	郞中 office chief
Senior 6	左司員外郞 first assistant office chief 右司員外郞 second assistant office chief	員外郞 assistant office chief	員外郞 assistant office chief
Junior 6			
Junior 7			

Table 3. Security Council 中樞院 (from 1095 樞密院)

Rank	office
Junior 2	判院事 (1) superintendent 院使 (2) commissioner 知院事 (1) administrator 同知院使 (1) associate administrator
Senior 3	副使 (2) vice-commissioner 簽書院事 (1) notary 直學士 (1) auxiliary academician
Senior 3	知奏事 (1) administrator of memorials 左右承宣 (1 each) senior / junior transmitter [of edicts] 左右副承宣 (1 each) senior / junior deputy transmitter [of edicts]
Senior 7	堂後官 (2) secretarial clerk
Administrative staff	別駕 (10) administrative aide 主事 (10) master scribe 試別駕 (2) probationary administrative aide 令史 (2) scribe first class 記官 (8) recorder second class 通引 (4) runner

Weights and Measures

Establishing the modern equivalents of Koryŏ-era weights and measures is very difficult, first of all because there are few material remains that allow us to ascertain what standards were used, and second because those standards fluctuated over time. Moreover, many units existed in different categories: for example, there existed different types of *ch'ŏk* (foot) depending on their area of use.[1] I have relied primarily on the research by Yi Chongbong[2] to compile the below table, whilst also referring to works on Chinese weights and measures, mainly to determine Western equivalent terms.[3] For each unit, the Sino-Korean pronunciation is given, followed by the character, the Korean vernacular equivalent (as far as I was able to establish these), which type of unit it is, a Western translation (often established during the Treaty Port era), its relation to other key units, and finally an approximate equivalent in the metric system (only for the key units).

ch'ŏk 尺, K. *cha*	length; "foot," a standard foot was about 31.5 cm. in early Koryŏ[4]
hap 合, K. *hop*	volume; "cup," ten cups make one *sŭng*
kok 斛 K. *hwi*	volume; "bushel," equal to half a *sŏk* or 7.5 *tu*
kŭn 斤	weight; "pound" (also "catty"), equal to 16 *yang*; 640 grams in early Koryŏ[5]
kyŏl 結	area; defined as "33 square *po*" in early Koryŏ, or about 3,840 m^2 (almost one acre);[6] from

1 Yi Chongbong, *Han'guk chungse toryanghyŏngje yŏn'gu* (Seoul: Hyean, 2001), 305.
2 Besides the work mentioned in the previous note, see also Yi Chongbong, *Han'guk toryanghyŏng sa* (Seoul: Somyŏng ch'ulp'an, 2016).
3 See Endymion Wilkinson, *Chinese History: A Manual*. Rev. and enl. ed. (Cambridge, MA: Harvard University Press, 2000), 554–556; http://www.chinaknowledge.de/History/Terms/duliangheng.html
4 Yi Chunbong, *Han'guk toryanghyŏng sa*, 119.
5 Ibid., 161.
6 Yi Chongbong, *Han'guk chungse toryanghyŏngje*, 238.

	Munjong's reign onward, land was graded in different categories, hence there were different *kyŏl* measures as well
kyŏng 頃	area; equal to 100 *mu* 畝 (240 *po* 步 "paces" by 1 pace)[7]
li (ri) 里	length; about 500 m.
mu 畝	area; equivalent to 240 *po* 步 "paces" by 1 pace
p'il 匹	length; bolt of cloth. In Silla, one bolt of silk is said to have measured 7 *po* (13 m.)[8]
po 步	length; "pace," six feet[9]
sŏk 石/碩, K. *sŏm*	as a unit of weight, "picul;" equal to 120 *kŭn*, or 76.8 kg.;[10] as a unit of volume "bushel," equal to 15 *tu*,[11] about 51 liters
sŏm 苫	volume; straw sack of rice; also sometimes in the sense of *sŏk* "bushel"
sŭng 升, K. *toe*	volume; "pint," ten cups (*he*); 0.340 liters in early Koryŏ,[12] 0.585 liters in Song[13]
tu 斗, K, *mal*	volume; "peck," equal to ten *sŭng*
yang 兩, K, *nyang*	weight; "tael" ("ounce"), 1/16th of a *kŭn*

7 http://www.chinaknowledge.de/History/Terms/duliangheng.html

8 *Han'guk minjok munhwa taebaekkwasajŏn*. http://encykorea.aks.ac.kr

9 Yi Chongbong, *Han'guk chungse toryanghyŏngje*, 305.

10 Following http://www.chinaknowledge.de/History/Terms/duliangheng.html; there is no clear evidence that it was also a unit of weight in Koryŏ.

11 Note that this is the official system; in common practice the more standard equivalent of 1 *sŏk* = 20 *tu* was used. Yi Chunbong, *Han'guk toryanghyŏng sa*, 131.

12 Yi Chunbong, *Han'guk toryanghyŏng sa*, 138.

13 Ibid., 133.

Glossary

Aekchŏng-guk 掖庭局 Bureau of Royal Stewards
anch'alsa 按察使 royal inspector
anmusa 按撫使 royal commissioner of pacification
allyŏmsa 按廉使 royal inspector of local government

Bingma dubushu 兵馬都部署 (Ch., Liao) Military Chief Administration Office

ch'a 借 acting; signifies that the appointee's regular office status was lower than the one he was temporarily assigned to
chaebo 宰輔. See *chaesin*
chaech'u 宰樞. See *chaesin*
chaesang 宰相. See *chaesin*
chaesin 宰臣 state councilor; councilor of state. Also *chaech'u* 宰樞, *chaesang* 宰相, *chaebo* 宰輔, *posin* 輔臣
ch'aja 箚子 letter to the throne
ch'amsang 參上 officials of rank 3 to 6
ch'amha 參下 officials of rank 7 and below. Also *ch'amoe* 參外
Changjak-kam (Changjak-wŏn) 將作監 (將作院) Directorate (Bureau) of Construction and Maintenance; *changjak-kam* director of this institute; *changjak sogam* 將作少監 vice-director
changsa 長史 officials of rank 6b in each of the Six Armies (Yukwi 六衛)
changsŏgi 掌書記 supervising recorder
Chapchik sŏ 雜織署 Office of Miscellaneous Textiles
chaptan 雜端 censor of miscellaneous affairs. Also *ŏsa chaptan* 御史雜端
chasa 剌史 prefect
chejŏnsa 祭奠使 sacrificial offerings envoy
Chewi-p'o 濟危鋪 Disaster Relief Store
chi 知 … *sa* 事 minister; concurrent appointment of an official to one of the

six ministries; or: manager, administrator of another institute

chibyŏngmasa 知兵馬事 administrator to the military commissioner

chich'ŏpsa 持牒使 letter-bearing envoy

chigonggŏ 知貢擧 examination administrator

chijego 知制誥 drafter of royal edicts and proclamations. In Koryŏ divided into *nae* 內 and *oe* 外, which are comprehensively designated *yangje* 兩制

chik- 直 as prefix: auxiliary- , intendant

chik Munhasŏng 直門下省 intendant of the Chancellery

ch'ikchesa 勅祭使 imperial sacrificial envoy

chikchang 直長 head of auxiliaries

chikhaksa 直學士 auxiliary academician; "someone … assigned to an agency without having nominal status in the agency… In time many such titles became regularized, with specified rank status" (Hucker no. 933)

chikkak 直閣 auxiliary to the hall

chiksagwan 直史館 auxiliary at the Office of Historiography

chinbong-sa 進奉使 letter-presenting envoy

chinsa 進士 presented scholar

chipsa 執事 office manager; in China: ~侍: office manager, eunuch official rank 6 in the Directorate of Palace Domestic Service (Hucker no. 1056)

chiryesa 持禮使 envoy in charge of ritual

chŏltosa 節度使 military governor

ch'ŏmsa 詹事 supervisor of the household of the heir apparent

Ch'ŏmsa-bu 詹事府 Household Administration of the Heir Apparent

ch'ŏmsŏ 簽書 abbreviated reference to the Notary of the Administrative Assistant in some military commissions (Hucker no. 918); also notary in the Security Council (see tables)

chŏnch'oe 殿最 evaluation by royal inspector of local magistrates, which took place twice a year; they were classified in the evaluation report as excellent (*ch'oe*) or fail (*chŏn*).

chŏngjŏn 丁田 fields allocated to adult males

chongluqing 崇祿卿 (Ch., Liao) director of the Court of Imperial Entertainments; normally Guangluqing, but Chonglu-si was an alternate designation for the Guanglu-si (Court of Imperial Entertainments, changed to avoid a name taboo [Hucker 1666])

Chongmyo 宗廟. See T'aemyo

Chŏngno-gun 精弩軍 (also 精努軍) Elite Arbalest Corps

Chŏngp'o togam 征袍都監 Directorate for Military Uniforms

Chŏnjung 殿中 Office of Royal Clan Affairs; Palace Administration (Liao, Song)

chŏnjung naegŭpsa 殿中內給事 intendant-secretary at the Department of Royal Clan Affairs

chŏnjung siŏsa 殿中侍御史 palace censor

chŏnjung sogam 展中小監 deputy director of the Office of Royal Clan Affairs

Ch'ŏnu-wi 千牛衛 Thousand Bull Division

chowisa 弔慰使 mourning envoy

-chu 州 greater prefecture

chubu 主簿 registrar

chumok 州牧 governor [of a first-tier prefecture]

Ch'unbang 春坊 palace of the Heir Apparent

chungnangjang 中郎將 senior colonel

chungsŭng 中丞 abbreviated reference to the *ŏsa chungsŭng* 御史中丞, vice censor-in-chief, palace aide to the censor-in-chief

chwach'ŏn 左遷 "shifting to the left," i.e., to demote

chwaeju 祭酒 master of sacrificial wines: official at Kukchagam or other academies

Chwa-u Chumu 左右酒務 First and Second Liquor Commission [in the capital]

Chwau-wi 左右衛 Left-Right Divisions

cishi (Ch.) 刺史: lit. censor, but usually prefect. Also: regional inspector (Han-Sui); regional chief (N-S Div-Song)

dafujian 大府監: should be Taifujian 太府監 (Ch.) supervisor of the Directorate of the Imperial Treasury (Hucker no. 6161) *dali shaoqing* 大理少卿 (Ch.) vice-minister of the Court of Judicial Review (Hucker 5986)

digonglang 迪功郎 (Ch.) Gentleman for Meritorious Achievement; prestige title for civil officials of rank 9b in Song (Hucker no. 6374)

feijiwei 飛騎尉 (Ch.) Commandant of Flying Cavalry; merit title (Hucker no. 1927)

guanchashi 觀察使 (Ch.) surveillance commissioner

Haengyŏng pyŏng 行營兵 Expedition Corps; Field Army

haengyŏng pyŏngmasa 行營兵馬使 military commissioner for the Expedition Corps

haksa 學士 academician

Hammun 閤門 Office for Audience Ceremonies

hammun chihu 閤門祗候 see *kangmun chihu*

hammun injinsa 閤門引進使 Reception Official at the Office for Audience Ceremonies

hammunsa 閤門使 commissioner for Audience Ceremonies

hammun sain 閤門舍人 presenting official at the Office for Audience Ceremonies

hammun sŭngji 閤門承旨 see *kangmun sŭngji*

hammun t'ongsasain 閤門通事舍人 secretarial receptionist at the Office for Audience Ceremonies

Hangma-gun 降魔軍 Dragon-subduing Army

hoeryesa 回禮使 returning the courtesy envoy

hoengsŏnsa 橫宣使 ad-hoc envoy

hoesajiryesa 回謝持禮使 embassy to return the courtesy

hondang 魂堂 funerary parlor; spirit shrine

hongluqing 鴻臚卿 (Ch.) chief minister of the Court of State Ceremonial (Hucker no. 2905)

hŏngwan 憲官 censorial official; common generic or collective references to the censors (Hucker no. 2509)

hu 侯 marquis

hwach'ŏn pyŏlgam 貨泉別監 special commissioner for Market Inspection

hyang 鄕 township; settlement for lower status groups

hyangni 鄕吏 local functionary, clerk

-hyŏn 縣 county

hyŏllyŏng 縣令 [county] magistrate

ilgwan 日官 astrologer

injinsa 引進使 commissioner of royal reception (usually at the Office for Audience Ceremonies)

jiaolianshi 教練使 (Ch.) military instructor

jianyi dafu 諫議大夫 (Ch.) Grand Master of Remonstrance (Hucker no. 831)

kaebuŭi tongsamsa 開府儀同三司 Commander Unequalled in Honor (Hucker no. 3105); prestige title of rank 1

kamch'al ŏsa 監察御史 investigating censor

kamch'angsa 監倉使 granary inspection commissioner

kammu 監務 deputy magistrate (usually of a county)

kamsuguksa 監修國史 supervising editor of national history

kangmun chihu 閣門祗候 audience usher

kangmun sŭngji 閣門承旨 memorial reception staff

kiboksa 起復使 interrupting the mourning envoy

kidu 旗頭 banner head

Kogong-sa 考功司 Office of Merit Evaluation

kojusa 告奏使 memorial envoy

kŏmgyo 檢校 prefix to a title: "acting," i.e. someone holding a certain position is assigned temporarily/irregularly to another position; sometimes also in the sense of "honorary," i.e., not holding any real responsibility

kong 公 duke

konggŏ 貢擧 local examination; tribute examination: selection of local

talents to send to the civil service examination
Konghak-kun 拱鶴軍 Restraining Crane Army
kongmokkwan 孔目官 clerk for all purposes
Kongwŏn 貢院 Examination Office
Kuje togam 救濟都監 Directorate to Save People
kujŏng 毬庭 polo court
Kukchagam 國子監 National Academy
kukcha saŏp 國子司業 supervisor of education
Kukhak 國學 National Academy (same as Kukchagam)
kukkong 國公 Duke of State
Kŭmo-wi 金吾衛 Golden Bird Division
-kun 郡 prefecture
kunhu 軍候 someone responsible for discipline; drill master
Kungi-kam 軍器監 Directorate of Weaponry
kunhuwŏn 軍候員 staff at the Reserve Corps
kŭnsin 近臣 attendant councilor; member of the royal coterie
kŭpsa 給事 official of rank 9a in the office of palace attendants
kwanban[sa] 館伴[使] hostel escort [commissioner]
kwanch'alsa 觀察使 royal inspector; see also *guanchashi* (same term but with a different function in the Chinese context)
-kye 界 border circuit
Kyobang 敎坊 kisaeng school
kyogam 校勘 proofreader
Kyŏngnyŏng-jŏn 慶靈殿 Hall of Spectacular Numina; shrine containing the portraits of former kings
kyoryŏnsa. See *jiaolianshi*
kyosŏrang 校書郎 editor-collator
kyowi 校尉 lieutenant
kyŏllyong 牽龍 royal carriage guard
kyŏm 兼 conjoint, concurrent
Kyŏnggung-gun 梗弓軍 Strong Bow Corps

-mok 牧 shepherdship
moksa 牧使 shepherdship commissioner
moksu 牧守 magistrate of a shepherdship
milchinsa 密進使 confidential envoy
-myŏn 面 circuit (used only for the northern border region)

naesi chihu 內侍祇候 usher to the palace attendants
naesi noksa 內侍錄事 recording officer to the palace attendants
naesi sogyŏng 內侍少卿 vice-director of the palace attendants
naesi 內侍 palace attendant
naeŭi 內醫 court physician
nakkibok sa 落起復使 end-of-mourning envoy
nangjang 郎將 junior colonel
nangsa 郎舍 generic name for the remonstrance officials of the Chancellery, Censorate, etc. See also *sŏngnang*
-no 路 circuit
nobu 鹵簿 cortege, procession of officials holding insignia
noksa 錄事 recording officer [Shultz 39]
noksa chamgunsa 錄事參軍事 administrative supervisor (Hucker no. 3860)
Nugak-wŏn 漏刻院 Water Clock Court; Clepsydria Office (Cf. Hucker no. 3835: 漏刻所, Water Clock Office)
nusŏn 樓船 tower boat; boat with one or more covered floors above its deck

oegwan 外官 outer officials; officials posted to local administrative units
ŏsa 御史 censor, censorial
ŏsa chaptan 御史雜端 censor of miscellaneous affairs. Also *chaptan* 雜端
ŏsa chungsŭng 御史中丞 vice censor-in-chief, palace aide to the censor-in-chief
Ŏsadae 御史臺 Censorate
ŏsadaebu 御史大夫 censor-in-chief
Ŏsŏwŏn 御書院 Royal Library (cf. Hucker no. 8189: abbreviation of Hanlin yushuyuan 翰林御書院, Imperial Academy of Calligraphy)

paek 伯 earl

paeyung puwi 陪戎副尉 vice-lieutenant aide-de-camp; military rank title, 9th rank

Palhwa-gun 發火軍 Firing Corps

p'an 判…*sa* 事 administrator; supervisor (temporary assignment of an official to another bureau)

pang'ŏsa 防禦使 defense commissioner

Pangt'aek 方澤 square pond

p'angwan 判官 administrative assistant

p'an samsasa 判三司事 Superintendent of the Finance Commission

Pisŏ-sŏng 秘書省 Department of the Palace Library

pisŏ kyosŏrang 秘書校書郎 editor in the Palace Library

pong'ŏ 奉御 chief steward; palace steward

posin 輔臣 see *chaesin*

-pu 府 district; can also refer to a section of a city

pugok 部曲 borough; locales where non-free or semi-free people were settled; in China the term originally referred to serfs: "private retainer … a reference to one category of indentured peasants close to the status of serfs or slaves working the agrarian lands of great families who formed the social elite." (Hucker no. 4776)

punsa- 分司 local; referring to Kaesŏng institutes that were replicated in the Western capital

-pusa ~府使 commissioner of a district

pyŏlchang 別將 sub-colonel

pyŏlga 別駕 administrative aide

pyŏlgam 別監 special commissioner

Pyŏlmuban 別武班 Special Army Corps

pyŏngmagŏmhal 兵馬鈐轄 controller of the seal for the military commissioner

pyŏngma noksa 兵馬錄事 recording officer for the military commissioner

pyŏngma pusa 兵馬副使 vice-military commissioner

pyŏngmasa 兵馬使 military commissioner

pyŏngsŏn 兵船 navy ships
pyŏngsŏn p'angwan 兵船判官 administrative assistant for the navy ships
p'yŏnjŏn 便殿 official residence (of the king)
p'yŏnsugwan 編修官 editor of history

sa 史 assistant
Sach'ŏn-dae 司天臺 Bureau of Astronomy
sach'ŏn pokchŏng 司天卜正 master of divination at the Bureau of Astronomy
sach'ŏn sogam 司天少監 Vice-director of the Bureau of Astronomy
sado 司徒 minister of education (ceremonial title)
sagong 司空 minister of works (ceremonial title); after 1122: refers to the vice-minister of the Ministry of Works (工部尙書)
Sagwan 史館 – 春秋館 Office of Historiography
Sajae-sa 司宰寺 Court of Royal Entertainment
Sajae sogyŏng 司宰少卿 vice-director of the Court of Royal Entertainment
Sajik 社稷 Earth and Grain Gods
Sajik-tan 社稷壇 Shrine to the Earth and Grain Gods
Sam-sa 三司 Finance Commission
sangch'am 常參 officials who regularly meet the king for policy discussions and briefing
sanggung 尙宮 matron
sangjanggun 上將軍 supreme general
Sangsik-kuk 尙食局 Bureau of Royal Diet
Sangŭi-guk 尙衣局 Bureau of Royal Clothing
sangwan 散官 prestige titles
Sangyak-kuk 尙藥局 Bureau of Medicine
Sangsŭng-guk 尙乘局 Bureau of Royal Carriages
sanwŏn 散員 executive captain
sarok 司錄 manager of records
si- 試 (prefixed to an office title) probationary
sigang haksa 侍講學士 royal lecturer

sigŭp 食邑 stipend village
siŏsa 侍御史 attendant censor
Sinbo-gun 神步軍 Divine Infantry Corps
Singi-gun 神騎軍 Divine Cavalry Corps
Singmok togam 式目都監 Directorate-general of National Affairs
sisin 侍臣: officials serving the king; variously translated as close officials, officials serving the king
sobo 少保 junior guardian
sobu 少傅 junior mentor
Sobu-gam 小府監 Directorate of Royal Workshops
sogyŏng 少卿 vice-director
sŏdu kongbong-gwan 西頭供奉官: palace servitor
Sŏjaejang 西材場 Western Timber Reserve
sŏjanggwan 書狀官 embassy secretary
sŏngdae 省臺 officials of the Chancellery and Censorate
sŏngju 星主 star-leader; ruler of T'amna (Cheju-do)
sŏngnang 省郎 generic name for the remonstrance officials of the Chancellery, Censorate, etc. See also *nangsa*
Sŏn'gun-ch'ŏng 選軍廳 Military Selection Bureau
sŏnyusa 宣諭使 promulgation envoy
sŏri 胥吏 local functionary, clerk. See also *hyangni*
sosa 少師 junior preceptor (to the heir apparent)
sŏsa 胥史 clerk
soyun 少尹 deputy director
-su 戍: military camp; guard station
su- 守 (prefixed to an office title) probationary
suguksa 修國史 state historiographer
sugyowŏn 讎校員 editor, collator
sŭng 丞 assistant secretary
sŭngji 承旨 recipient of edicts
sun'gŏmsa 巡檢使 chief military inspector
sun'gŏm toryŏng 巡檢都領 commandant of military inspectors

swi 倅 deputy; e.g., *puswi* 府倅 deputy district magistrate, deputy prefect

Tabang 茶房 Tea Office: manages tea and medical herbs
Taeak-sŏ 大樂署 Bureau of Music
Taebi-wŏn 大悲院 Court of Great Charity (east and west)
t'aebo 太保 grand guardian
t'aebokkyŏng 太僕卿 chamberlain for the royal stud
t'aebok sogyŏng 太僕少卿 vice-chamberlain for the royal stud
t'aebu 太傅 grand mentor
taebugyŏng 大府卿 director of the Palace Treasury
Taedodok-pu 大都督府 Superior Area Command
taehak paksa 大學博士 professor of the Taehak College
t'aehu 太后 queen dowager. Also *wangt'aehu*
t'aeja 太子 heir apparent
t'aeja pin'gaek 太子賓客 advisor to the heir apparent
T'aeja-bu 太子府 Office of the Heir Apparent
taejanggun 大將軍 grand general
taejejik 待制直 auxiliary awaiting edicts
taejegwan 待制官 edict attendant
taejŏng 隊正 sub-lieutenant
T'aemyo 太廟 Ancestral Shrine
t'aesa 太史 grand astrologer
t'aesa 太師 grand preceptor
T'aesaguk 太史局 Bureau of Astrology
taesang sogyŏng 大常少卿 vice-chamberlain for ceremonials
t'aesaryŏng 太史令 see *t'aesa* 太史
taesasŏng 大司成 superintendent (of an academy)
t'aesasŭng 太史丞 aide to the grand astrologer
Tae-Sŏng 臺省 Censorate and Royal Secretariat; remonstrance officials of the Censorate and the Department of Royal Secretary- Chancellery
t'aesu 太守 magistrate, prefect
t'aeŭi 太醫 grand physician

t'aewi 太尉 grand marshal
Taeyŏng-go 大盈庫 Repository of Clothing Materials
tanghugwan 堂後官 secretarial clerk
-to 道 province
Tobusŏ 都部署 Local Navy Command
Tobyŏngmasa 都兵馬使 Capital Military Command
togang 都綱 chief merchant (representative of foreign traders in Kaesŏng)
Togwan 都官 Slave Agency
Togyo-sŏ 都校署 Bureau of Handicraft ~令 director of~
Tohobu 都護府 protectorate
tohobusa 都護府使 regional military commander
tong- 同 as prefix: joint; associate: in the sense that more than one person is appointed to the same office
tonggwanjŏng 冬官正 director of the Winter Office (Hucker no. 7438: "one of five seasonal offices of calendrical specialists")
-tongjŏng 同正 (suffix): "equivalent to," a term occurring only in the Koryŏ bureaucracy for an appointment with no actual duties expected of someone with this office
t'ongp'an 通判 executive; office title at the Tohobu
t'ongsa sain 通事舍人 secretarial receptionist
toryŏng 都領 commandant (of specialized corps)
tot'ong 都統 commander-in-chief
Tosŏng 都省 = Sangsŏ tosŏng 尙書都省 Department of Ministries
tosun kŏmsa 都巡檢使 chief military inspector
Tot'ang-gun 跳蕩軍 (also 跳盪軍) Assault Raider Corps

ŭp 邑 town office (*ŭpsa* 邑司)

Wiwi-sa 衛尉寺 Office of Regalia

wangbi 王妃 queen, royal consort
wangt'aehu 王太后 dowager queen

wimunsa 慰問使 condolence envoy
wiwisŭng 衛尉丞 Assistant at the Office of Regalia

Xuanhui yuan 宣徽院 (Ch., Liao-Jin) Court Ceremonial Institute (Hucker no. 2664)

Yangbu 兩府 Chancellery and Security Council
Yangon-sŏ 良醞署 Bureau of Beverage Supervision
yangonsŏryŏng 良醞署令 director of the Bureau of Beverage Supervision
Yebin-si 禮賓寺 Foreign Relations Office
yebin sogyŏng 禮賓小卿 Deputy Director of the Foreign Relations Office
Yebinsŭng 禮賓丞 Assistant Director of the Foreign Relations Office
Yesa 禮司 Ministry of Rites (= Yejo, Yebu etc.)
yŏmch'al 廉察 to secretly inspect
Yŏngsong togam 迎送都監 Directorate-General of State Visitor Reception and Departure
yusu 留守 resident governor
Yuk-wi 六衛 Six Armies

zhongshu sheren 中書舍人 (Ch.) drafter in the Secretariat (Hucker no. 1618)
Zhuanyunsi 轉運司 (Ch.) Transport Commission (Tang); Finance Commission (Song) (Hucker no. 1492)

Index

U

W

Y

Z